"Professor Das' work is a much needed contribution to help both academics and practitioners obtain a wider picture of China in the context of the development of the whole of Asia, particularly the more dynamic economies of Asia. Previously, we have had to depend on either annual updates or country-specific studies. In such a dynamic environment China and the Asian Economies provides a concrete set of perspectives to see the bigger picture."

Professor Murray M. Dalziel, *Director, University of Liverpool Management School, UK.*

"This is a marvelously insightful book, telling the story of Asia's modern emergence as the engine of global economic growth. Professor Das describes the economic rise of the Newly Industrializing Economies, the dynamic Asia, and the flow-on to China as these countries come to dominate the world economic scene. We are moved smoothly through the success of the real economies, and guided to understand the challenges for them from the operations of financial markets where matters are more fragile. Professor Das' splendid book brings the reader up to the minute with its analysis and lays solid foundations for our understanding of the future for China and the Asian Economies."

Christopher M. Adam, *Professor of Finance and Associate Dean, Australian School of Business, The University of New South Wales, Australia.*

"This book is essential reading for anyone interested in the future of Asian economies, their interdependence, their impact on world business and China's role in particular now it has a new leadership team likely to deepen its reforms. Das's book on this important theme vis-a-vis 21st century Asia is not only informative and incisive but also highly readable. It deserves to be widely read by both academics and students, as well as policy-makers."

Malcolm Warner, *Professor and Fellow Emeritus, Wolfson College and Judge Business School, University of Cambridge, Co-Editor, Asia Pacific Business Review.*

"The global economy is on the cusp of a mega transformation, and the dynamic economies of Asia are its epicenter. They have become the driving force of the global economy. Professor Dilip Das, demonstrates that a China-centric economic structure has already evolved in the region, but that it is still in the process of maturation. He has empirically studied the de facto and de jure interactive dynamics of the region, and discussed the symbiotic growth pattern that has developed. In this very readable work, he demonstrates the positive interactive influences that have favorably affected industrialization, modernization and growth among the dynamic Asian economies. The result is an eminently readable book which brings together the ongoing contemporary academic and policy debates. It will make a great weekend read in front of a crackling fire, but the insights gained will outlast the decade."

Dr. John E. Endicott, *Vice Chancellor and President Woosong University, SolBridge International School of Business, The Republic of Korea.*

CHINA AND THE ASIAN ECONOMIES

The global economy is currently going through a period of transformation that has seen Asia emerge as the most rapidly growing, industrializing and modernizing region in the world economy. Whilst the rest of the world struggled during the financial crisis of 2007–09, Asia played the role of a linchpin for global economic recovery. This book analyzes the growth of key Asian economies in the latter half of the twentieth century, followed a little later by China. Notwithstanding the diversity in the region, rapid growth was instrumental in integrating the Asian economies initially in a market-led manner. Dilip K. Das focuses on the interactive dynamics and the process of integration in the region, exploring the synergy created as well as the resulting symbiotic growth among the Asian economies and China.

Written in a clear, comprehensive and critical manner by a world class expert in the field, this book brings together the contemporary academic and policy debates on the issues under examination. As such it is an essential read for students and scholars of economics, international political economy and Asian Studies as well as MBA students.

Dilip K. Das is the Director of the Institute of Asian Business (IAB) at SolBridge International School of Business, Woosong University, Republic of Korea. He is also a Professor of International Economics and International Finance.

CHINA AND THE ASIAN ECONOMIES

Interactive dynamics, synergy and symbiotic growth

Dilip K. Das

Routledge
Taylor & Francis Group

LONDON AND NEW YORK

First published 2014
by Routledge
2 Park Square, Milton Park, Abingdon, Oxon OX14 4RN

and by Routledge
711 Third Avenue, New York, NY 10017

Routledge is an imprint of the Taylor & Francis Group, an informa business

© 2014 Dilip K. Das

The right of Dilip K. Das to be identified as author of this work has been asserted by him in accordance with sections 77 and 78 of the Copyright, Designs and Patents Act 1988.

British Library Cataloguing in Publication Data
A catalogue record for this book is available from the British Library

Library of Congress Cataloging in Publication Data
Das, Dilip K., 1945- author.
  China and the Asian economies: interactive dynamics, synergy and symbiotic growth/
Dilip K. Das.
    p. cm
  Includes bibliographical references and index.
  Summary: "This book analyzes the emergence of Asian economies, followed by China, as an economic growth pole of enormous significance. Notwithstanding the diversity in the region, rapid growth was instrumental in integrating the Asian economies initially in a market-led manner and this book explores the interactive dynamics and the process of integration in the region"– Provided by publisher.
  1. China–Foreign economic relations–Asia. 2. Asia–Foreign economic relations–China.
3. China–Economic conditions–21st century. 4. Asia–Economic conditions–21st century.
5. Asia–Economic integration. I. Title.
  HF1604.Z4A785188 2014
  330.95–dc23
                 2013022991

ISBN: 978-0-415-72352-7 (hbk)
ISBN: 978-0-415-72353-4 (pbk)
ISBN: 978-1-315-85765-7 (ebk)

Typeset in Bembo
by Taylor & Francis Books

With endless love and gratitude to Vasanti,
my partner and guide in thought and deed

Being and non-being create each other,
Difficult and easy support each other.

Long and short define each other.

High and low depend on each other.
Therefore the Master

acts without doing anything;
and teaches without saying anything.
Things arise and she lets them come;
things disappear and she lets them go.
She has but she does not possess,
acts but does not expect.
When her work is done, she forgets it.
That is why it lasts forever.

——Wisdom of *Tao Te Ching*

CONTENTS

LIST OF ILLUSTRATIONS

Figures

Tables

ABOUT THE AUTHOR

Professor Dilip K. Das has been associated with several prestigious business schools around the globe, including the European Institute of Business Administration (INSEAD), Fontainebleau, France; the International Business School in Europe (ESSEC), Paris; the Graduate School of Business, University of Sydney, Australia; the Australian National University, Canberra; and the Webster University, Geneva, Switzerland. He was Professor and Area Chairman at the Indian Institute of Management, Lucknow, India, and EXIM Bank Distinguished Chair Professor in the International Management Institute, New Delhi. He is presently Professor of International Finance and International Banking and Director of the Institute of Asian Business, SolBridge International School of Business, Woosong University, Republic of Korea. His areas of expertise include international finance and banking, international trade and WTO-related issues, international business and strategy and the Asian economy, including the Chinese and Japanese economies. His most recent interest is globalization and the global business environment.

Professor Das has worked as a consultant for several international organizations, such as USAID, the World Bank, and the World Commission on Development and Environment in Geneva. He has organized 13 large international conferences during the last 10 years.

Professor Das has an immense appetite for research. He has written extensively and published widely. He is author or editor of more than 30 critically acclaimed books. His most recent books are *The Chinese Economic Renaissance: Apocalypse or Cornucopia?* published by Palgrave Macmillan, UK, in 2008 and *Financial Globalization: Growth, Integration, Innovation and Crisis*, published by Palgrave Macmillan, UK, in 2010. The former book was translated into Mandarin for the Chinese market, while the latter was translated into Korean. He has contributed over 90 articles to professional journals of international repute, many of which are EconLit or SSCI-listed journals. Eighty-nine of his papers have appeared in prestigious research and working paper series and 22 of them have also been posted on well-regarded websites of business schools and universities.

The author is regarded as a world-class scholar of the Asian economy. A naturalized Canadian, he has lived and worked in Asia and Australia for long periods and has a long-term interest in the Asian economies, including those of China, Japan and Korea. He has written several books on the Asian economy, including two successful textbooks. He has taught Asian economy-related courses in several Asian and Australian business schools and served a short-term stint at the economic research division of the Asian Development Bank.

Professor Das was educated at St John's College, Agra, India, where he took his BA and MA (Economics) degrees. He went on to study at the Institut Universitaire de Hautes Etudes Internationales, University of Geneva, where he completed an M.Phil. and a Ph.D. in International Economics. He is fluent in French and his other language skills include basic Mandarin, Japanese and Korean.

PREFACE

This is a transformative period for the global economy. Asia has been the most rapidly growing, industrializing and modernizing region in the world economy and has been reshaping its contours in the initial decades of the 21st century. Importance and stature of Asia in the global economy has risen monotonically and it has achieved a meaningful *mise en scène* on global economic and financial stage. Re-emergence of Asia is one of the most significant geo-economic events in modern history. During and after the global financial crisis (2007–09) Asia played the role of a linchpin for global economic recovery. The crisis was little more than a short tumble in economic ascent of Asia. It emerged from the stressful period of the global financial crisis with its global economic standing intact. If anything it strengthened after 2009.

Influence of Asia on shaping the world trade laws and capital, commodities and consumer markets significantly rose; barring the unforeseen it would continue to rise. Asian economies also remained resilient during the implacable Eurozone sovereign debt crisis. According to the World Bank (2013), the developing economies of Asia grew by 7.5 percent in 2012, well above the global average of 3.2 percent and higher than any other region in the global economy. China has become the veritable engine of regional growth. If the new reform programme in China stumbles there are risks of slowing, but otherwise it is likely to remain an engine of growth for Asia.

One of the important reasons behind Asia's resilience was the extensive reforms and restructuring undertaken in the post-Asian crisis (1997–98) period. Many of these reforms were not an easy sell to the people inhabiting in the reforming economies. They *inter alia* made Asian economies not only resilient in a period of global economic and financial turmoil but also an engine of global growth. If the region stays the course its gross domestic product (GDP) will be larger than that of the Group of Seven (G-7) economies by 2030. To enhance its growth potential Asia needs to continue with structural and macroeconomic reforms as well as embrace greater economic and financial integration. The other crucial areas where Asia needs to improve and upgrade include innovation, research and development (R&D), governance, promotion of services and strengthening its social safety nets.

Conceptual foundation of this book is the rise of rapidly-growing Asian and Chinese economies, in that order, their interactive dynamics and symbiotic growth. GDP growth rate in several East and Southeast Asian economies picked up momentum in the 1960s. China was to join the dynamic groups of Asian economies a trifle later. They interacted together and developed a pattern of symbiotic growth and industrialization, which in turn stepped up their pace of industrialization and synergized growth and development in the region. A spontaneous and intricate process of market-led integration ensued. One salient characteristic of it was that it was more organic than mechanistic. Regional integration has had a significant influence on reshaping the regional economies. Asia has re-emerged as a major locus of world economic power in the second decade of the 21st century. This is the principal thematic strand of this book.

Equally important is the theme of China's unparallel growth performance of the last three decades, which made it into the largest regional economy and second largest economy in the world in 2010. As a rule, a large, open and rapidly growing economy influences the performance of the surrounding economies. China had a veritable impact over its surrounding Asian economies. This book also examines how China's vertiginous growth was instrumental in integrating Asian economies with each other and mutually supporting the rise of a dynamic Asia. They have evolved into a vibrant geo-economic space. China's rapid growth in the recent period and its integration with its dynamic neighbors has been paid sufficient attention in this book. The Asian and Chinese economies moved up the value-added chain, continually entering new and higher technology oriented industries. It enabled them to diversify their export base as well as go on shifting their export composition, increasing its technology content, sophistication, and domestic value-added in their exports.

Market-led regional integration of Asia worked essentially through expansion in intra-regional trade and investment and subsequently through the growth and brisk expansion in vertically integrated production networks. Lately the financial channel has also become an instrument of regional integration. If Asian economies succeed in eschewing the middle-income trap, their rapid growth will surely help them graduate into being high-income countries by the middle of the century. The oft-mentioned dream of an Asian century could then become a reality.

Asia is a diverse and heterogeneous region and merely a geographical concept. It is not a political or economic entity. However, when the 21st century dawned, one of the most significant economic events of the first decade was emergence of the dynamic Asia as an economic force reshaping the contours of the global economy. Process of Asian and Chinese economies integrating in a symbiotic manner also ensured steady increase in the heft of the regional economy in the global economy. At this juncture, individually many Asian economies were no longer marginal economies and as a group they made their global presence felt. The status of the region was elevated in the business, economic and financial spheres as well as in global economic governance. Several Asian economies became a part of the venerated and influential Group of Twenty (G-20). Decision makers in the corporate, financial and banking world, particularly those making consequential decisions in the multinational corporations (MNCs), logically began giving extra importance to Asian markets. Few could afford not to. Asian markets became among the largest and/or most rapidly growing for the MNCs in numerous industries and services. As they are a large centre of production and exports, Asian economies began casting large shadows in the commodity and energy markets as well.

An amber signal is necessary here. This book does not deal with the entire region but only with the rapidly growing dynamic economies of Asia. The dynamic Asia has been defined in Chapter 1, Section 1.1. This book provides a detailed analysis of the Asian and Chinese economies in a global context. My objective in this book is to create a clear fact base on how the relationship between the dynamic Asia and China evolved and how it reached the current synergetic state. Notwithstanding the fact that they are a diverse group of economies, they are growing in a progressively symbiotic manner. They have been integrating and turning into a global economic and financial force and business presence. Since the turn of the century, contribution of the dynamic Asian economies to global economic growth discernibly increased. The significance and recognition of this phenomenon escalated in the backdrop of advanced economies moving from the Great Moderation to the Great Recession (2009). Myriad projections by supranational institutions and investment banks like Goldman Sachs demonstrate that in future economic clout of the dynamic Asia will be greater than it is at present.

Asia is sure to be an increasingly important entity in international business. In early 2013 the environment for international business and finance was not buoyant, yet Asian businesses have managed to remain optimistic about their present and future. Dominic Barton (2013), Global managing Director of McKinsey, noted that with approximately a billion middle-class consumers Asia's economic fundamentals, drivers of growth and the gravitational forces are all strong. In addition rapid urbanization and good demographics have strengthened the tail winds for the Asian economies. He also observed that long-term oriented managers and governments in Asia have been investing pragmatically and ambitiously. In 2013 approximately 179 of Fortune 500 companies were domicile in Asia. They are investing in a large array of sectors, from consumer goods to airlines, almost twice the amount of their Western counterparts. Asia would be a significant growth area of international business and finance, although this growth may not be linear.

The number of academic institutions offering courses related to Asian economy as well as Chinese economy is already significant and growing. Several new research centers and institutes in these areas have been born over the period of a decade. The target readership of the book is master's level students in economics, international political economy, international relations as well as MBA students. Ambitious senior level undergraduates as well as policy mandarins in the government and international institutions and researchers can also benefit from the book. Having a background of initial micro-, macro-, international finance and monetary economics should be sufficient to comprehend this book because it provides definitions and explanations of terminology and advance concepts used in the text as footnotes. Decision makers and public-policy makers will find this book an informative and valuable aid.

Dilip K. Das
5 June 2013

References

Barton, D. 2013. "Asia's Titans Play the Long Game." *Global Brief*. March 5. Available online at http://globalbrief.ca/blog/2013/03/05/asia%E2%80%99s-titans-play-the-long-game.

World Bank. 2013. "East Asia and Pacific Economic Update." Washington, DC. April.

PROLOGUE

The essential thematic strand of this book

Economic dynamism and resilience has made Asia an engine of global economic growth. The dynamic economies of Asia have been transformed from the inside out. They continued to post the highest gross domestic product (GDP) growth rates in the post global financial crisis (2007–09) period and became a global growth leader, driving an astonishing two-thirds of global growth in the five years between 2008 and 2012 (Lagarde, 2013). During and after the global financial and Eurozone crises, the dynamic Asian economies maintained relatively stronger fundamentals compared to other regions of the global economy. Although the various sub-groups of Asian economies represent a varied mix of stages of development, the dynamic ones among them began integrating in an essentially market-driven or private-sector-led manner some four decades ago. This process began to accelerate after the Plaza Accord (1985) and further after the early 1990. Since this point in time, Asia saw an efflorescence of regionally based economic initiatives, which accelerated further after 2000. Asian economies are a good deal more productively integrated today than they were at the turn of the century.

In this book we shall see that the economic integration of the various sub-groups of the Asian economies was first *de facto* or private-sector driven. Their policy- or institution- or government-led integration is a relatively recent phenomenon. Trade and foreign direct investment (FDI) were the principal channels of regional integration. In addition, creation of special economic zones (SEZs), vertically integrated production networks and increasing trade in parts, components and intermediate products were also instrumental in integrating them.

The conceptual foundation of this book is the emergence of Asia as a global growth hub centered around the People's Republic of China (hereinafter China). It focuses on the rise of Asian and Chinese economies, in that order, their interactive dynamics, symbiotic growth and regional integration. Rapid growth in the outward-oriented Asian economies not only integrated them in a market-led manner but also transformed patterns of co-operation and competition in the region. During the last decade, China has evolved an important engine of growth for the region. China became not only the major trading partner of all the neighboring Asian economies but it also robustly participated in the Chiang Mai Initiative (2000), the Bali Accord (2003) and the Singapore Declaration (2007). A distinctive trait of Asian economic integration is that it is essentially soft and open and largely uninstitutionalized. It is flexible in nature and has followed an incremental path. It was principally motivated by economic or geo-economic factors.

This book provides a substantial coverage of China, particularly its role in turning the region into an economic growth pole of global consequence as well as in advancing soft-regionalism in Asia. As a large and open economy growing at double-digit pace, China played a defining role in Asia's economic integration—particularly during the post-Asian crisis period. Its World Trade Organization (WTO) accession enhanced this role further. China was instrumental in promoting regional growth and integration in both *de facto* and *de jure* manner.

The principal thematic argument in this book emphasizes the role of China in becoming the driver of wide-ranging transformations in the regional economies through myriad of inter-linkages and inter-dependencies. This book sets a germane regional as well as a global context in which the rising Asian and Chinese economies are discussed. It is a significant contribution in terms of coverage of the issues and approaches in analysis of the issues involved.

Integration of dynamic Asian economies was instrumental in Asia forging ahead at a rapid pace. Even in difficult periods of global financial and Eurozone sovereign debt crises Asia maintained the highest GDP growth rate in the world economy. The development of Asia has been projected to grow by 7.1 percent in 2013 and China by 8.0 percent. This performance is a great deal superior to that of the global economy (3.3 percent) and the advanced economies (1.2 percent) (IMF, 2013). It was made possible by better business opportunities as well as institutional co-operation in the region. Regional integration is one of the driving forces behind the relative strength of the Asian economy.

The rapid pace of GDP growth in Asia is reflected in rising per capita incomes, improving living standards and speedy poverty alleviation. Private wealth has risen to a record level. There are more millionaires, super-rich households and individuals in Asia than ever before. According to the Boston Consulting Group (BCG, 2013), private wealth increased the fastest in Asia (excluding Japan) in recent years. It increased to $28 trillion in 2012, a 17 percent jump on 2011. In 2018 it is projected to nearly double to $48 trillion ($ stands for US$, unless otherwise stated).

Integration of dynamic Asian economies is also responsible for the growing influence of Asia over the global business and economy. In the recent past Asia has been endeavoring to generate domestic demand and domestic demand-driven growth. To the extent Asian economies succeed they will have greater impact over the global economy. It is helping shape the contours of the global economy. It is one of the most significant events in the global economy during the contemporary period. The theme of Asia's growing heft is attracting a great deal of scholarly interest. It is also of enormous direct consequence and value for the public policy mandarins and senior decision maker in the business world.

Until the last quarter of 2012, both the Eurozone and the USA failed to put together credible medium-term plans to resolve the sovereign debt crisis and serious fiscal disorder, respectively. As growth prospects in the other major regions of the global economy diminished since the global financial crisis and the so-called Great Recession, there was higher investment in Asia from both the regional players and the multinational corporations (MNCs) from the advanced industrial economies. Strong economic fundamentals of the regional economies would ensure consistent growth across a range of industries over the medium to longer term.

Asia in this book is defined to include the dynamic sub-groups and economies of East Southeast Asia (Chapter 1). In terms of economic dynamism, rapidity of GDP growth and structural economic transformation they stand apart from the other sub-groups of Asian economies like those of South and Central Asia. According to the latest (2011) available statistical data, this dynamic Asia is now a substantive economic entity in the global economy. With a population of

2.2 billion, GDP of $17.15 trillion at market exchange rates, decadal average annual growth rate of 7.34 percent and sound fundamentals, the dynamic Asia has emerged as a significant geo-economic space.

After the collapse of the dotcom bubble (2000–01), Asia's contribution to the global GDP steadily rose. By 2010 expressions like "engine of global economic growth" began to be frequently used for Asia. Myriad computations were put forward regarding Asia's growing weight in the global economy. On current trends, "Asia's economy will be larger than the Group-of-Seven (G-7) by 2030" (Lagarde, 2012, p. 4). It is apparent that Asia is of enormous and increasing importance in the global economy. Concurrently the global economy has a growing stake in Asia. The global financial crisis accelerated the shift in global economic power to the Asian economies.

There is a notable asymmetry. Notwithstanding the growing goods market integration, the dynamic Asian economies and their sub-groups were (and are) much less integrated financially. Despite recent progress, financial integration in Asia is lagging behind real economic integration. Their stock markets do not show positive correlation. Cross-border capital flows and investments into each other's financial assets have so far been limited. The reason was that Asian governments followed restrictive policies in their respective financial sectors. However, the global financial crisis of 2007–09 has put a question mark on the contribution and helpfulness of financial integration. It contains apparent risks of financial contagion.

Nevertheless, the East and Southeast sub-groups of Asian economies form the globalized and/or briskly globalizing Asia. Other than business and economic, there are soft linkages among them. For instance, many of them share ancient traditions like Confucianism. Geographical proximity, shared borders and linguistic commonalities are some of the other bonds binding them together.

China and Japan, the two largest Asian economies—also the second and third largest in the world—have a special place in Asia. Of the two, China's influence over the regional economy has been augmenting while that of Japan has been on the wane. There have been lasting consequences of Japan's real estate and stock bubbles burst in the early 1990s. It has had two lost decades of anemic growth and weak job markets.

Over the last two centuries, Chinese Diaspora spread over the neighboring Asian economies forming a "bamboo network" of businesses. Large and small business Chinese enterprises conducting their businesses from different Asian bases are a force to reckon with in the Asian business world. These business houses have contributed a great deal to the continuing regional integration. Numerous scholars have predicted that the 21st century will be Asia's century, then China will have a major role in Asia. It has emerged as a leader in a pivotal region of the global economy.

As Table 0.1 shows, over two decades of rapid growth and integration have turned the Asian economy into a dynamic growth pole. It is defined as an economy whose domestic growth helps drive growth process in other economies. A comparison of selected economic indicators shows the favorable position of Asia vis-à-vis the other two major regions of the global economy, namely, the European Union (EU) and the North American Free Trade Area (NAFTA). Various chapters of this book focus on the interactive dynamics of the Asian economies, the synergy created by it and how this country group is emerging into an increasingly more significant geo-economic space. These chapters also delve into the variegated channels of regional integration among the Asian economies as well as emergence of symbiotic growth in them.

The size of the middle-class in the dynamic Asian economies has been expanding rapidly. Therefore domestic demand and intra-regional demand were on the rise. Together they can potentially help Asia in rebalancing its growth towards domestic sources. Although intra-regional trade among the ASEAN-Plus-Three (APT) economies expanded after the Asian crisis (1997–98)

TABLE 0.1 Selected comparative indicators for dynamic Asia and the two other regional economies (for the latest available year)

	Year	Asia	EU	NAFTA
Population (millions)	2011	2,167	332	460
GDP (US$ trillions)	2011	17.15	13.07	17.41
Average decadal GDP growth in percentage (2000–10)	2011	7.34	1.46	2.09
Domestic savings (% of GDP)	2010	39.13	19.31	18.38
Investment (% of GDP)	2010	33.30	19.64	20.63
Imports of goods and service (US$ millions)	2010	4,583,974	6,760,130	3,152,584
(a) Goods imports (US$ millions)	2010	3,831,494	5,356,030	2,682,283
(b) Service imports (US$ millions)	2010	752,480	1,404,100	470,301
Exports of goods and service (US$ millions)	2010	5,296,966	6,722,025	2,565,826
(a) Goods exports (US$ millions)	2010	4,541,012	5,153,225	1,964,587
(b) Service exports (US$ millions)	2010	755,954	1,568,800	601,239
FDI flows (US$ millions)				
(a) Inflows	2011	324,621	420,715	287,423
(b) Outflows	2011	354,088	561,805	455,171
FDI flows (% of GDP)				
(a) Inflows	2011	1.89	3.22	1.65
(b) Outflows	2011	2.06	4.30	2.61
Foreign Exchange Reserve (US$ millions)	2012	5,433,036	999,863	375,075
Current Account Balance (US$ billions)	2010	648	56	(−) 531
Current Account Balance (% of GDP)	2010	5.69	0.31	−2.33
National Indebtedness (% of GDP)	2010	54.25	74	64.50

Sources:

1 The World Bank, *World Development Indicators Data Base*, Washington, DC, July 2012.

2 The International Monetary Fund, *World Economic Outlook Data Base*, Washington, DC, April 2012.

3 The World Trade Organization, *International Trade Statistics 2011*, Geneva, Switzerland, 2011.

and *de jure* regionalization efforts progressed, the region still needs to move towards a wider cross-border free trade regime. Establishing an Asia-wide free trade area (FTA) will enable Asian economies to benefit from the escalating regional domestic demand, which could well become a significant source of regional growth. With their sizeable pool of foreign exchange reserves, Asian economies also have a great deal of financial muscle, which can be utilized for promoting freer intra-regional investments.

As integration of financial markets in the region have so far made conspicuously inadequate progress in Asia, there is a pressing need to take earnest policy initiatives to address this shortcoming. Furthermore, Asian economies have a long way to go with regard to promoting innovation and research and development (R&D), improving governance, promoting growth in services sectors and strengthening social safety nets.

In addition, role and importance of Asia in the arena of international business steadily rose. For MNCs Asian economies are progressively more important because a large part of the next billion customers in the global economy will be based in Asia. MNCs normally have a special significance and strategies for their Asian markets. As the time passes, more and more Asian companies will grow in international status and make their way into the Fortune 500 or the Global 2000.

References

Boston Consulting Group (BCG). 2013. "Maintaining Momentum in a Complex World: Global Wealth 2013." Boston, MA. May.

Lagarde, C. 2013. "Fulfilling the Asian Dream." Speech at the Boao Forum, Hainan, China, 7 April.

——2012. "New Perspectives on Asia's Role in the Global Economy." Speech at the Bank of Thailand Policy Forum, Bangkok, Thailand. 12 July.

International Monetary Fund (IMF). 2013. *World Economic Outlook*. Washington, DC. April.

1

EMERGENCE OF ASIA AND INTEGRATION OF CHINA

1. Introduction

Two relevant and interrelated economic realities are as follows. First, the recent economic transformations in rapidly growing Asian economies and China have been systematic, meticulous, extensive, methodical and far-reaching, although far from uniform and comprehensive. Alan Greenspan (2000) described three decades of Asian economic growth as "phenomenally solid". Asian economies turned into the most dynamic in the global economy. Furthermore, over the last decade Asia emerged as a manufacturing powerhouse. As manufacturing drives innovation and productivity and therefore economic advancement, it matters a great deal. The gross domestic product (GDP) of Asian economies[1] was $17.15 trillion in 2011, not far behind that of NAFTA ($17.41 trillion) (WDI, 2012). Second, from the global business and economic perspective, the People's Republic of China (hereinafter "China") in 2012 is a large economy in both absolute and relative terms. Over three decades of macroeconomic reforms and the resulting dynamism turned it into the largest regional economy in mid-2010. In a short period of time China has established a substantial regional and global presence for itself (Das, 2008a, 2008b). As growth prospects in the other regions of the global economy diminished since the global financial crisis (2007–09) and the Great Recession, there was higher investment in Asia from both the regional players and the multinationals from the advanced industrial economies (EIU, 2012). Strong economic fundamentals of the regional economies would ensure consistent growth across a range of industries over the medium to longer term. This is unlike the Eurozone and the United States of America (USA), where poor economic fundamentals may well result in a period of economic and financial turbulence and structural weaknesses.

The two realities are correlated because China's belated economic ascent has had an appreciable effect over the neighboring Asian economies and it became the driver of wide-ranging transformations in them through myriad interlinkages and interdependences. China is a defining factor behind the rapidly transforming Asian economy. Its role in the Asian economy grew monotonically and is now pivotal. Its soft power has been on the rise, which is not to denigrate its hard power. Although it is an emerging-market economy (EME) by definition, it surpassed Japan, a mature industrial economy, as Asia's leader in many dimensions. China's resurrection to its previous economic role in the regional and global economies as a prominent economic power is "not only the best news for global human welfare in a generation, but promises to raise a variety of geopolitical challenges, which as yet remain unpredictable" (Findlay and O'Rourke, 2007, p. 545).

It is an epochal period for the global economy. Since the beginning of the 21st century, the dynamic Asian economies and China saw an efflorescence of regionally based economic initiatives. A symbiotic and synergetic relationship developed among these economies. The ascent of this group of economies is the single most important force shaping the contours of the global economy. It has become increasingly crucial for global business, finances and economic growth. One of its significant contributions is that it has diversified sources of global economic growth. The question whether Asia is replacing the North Atlantic as the most influential geo-economic space in the global economy has been asked in numerous fora and with good reasons.

Integration among the Asian economies and then their subsequent integration with the Chinese economy occurred for the most part in a spontaneous manner, with the national economic initiatives playing a vital role. It was essentially a soft, open and uninstitutionalized integration, which was motivated by economic factors, both domestic and regional. It followed an incremental path. Regional economies did not plan or work in an orderly-coordinated grand scheme to form an integrated regional economy or a single market. The Asian economies followed a flexible and *ad hoc* method of integration, largely based on the requirements of economic expansion and industrialization (Okamoto, 2011). Thus the integration occurred more in an organic manner than in a mechanistic manner. This movement towards regionalism strengthened since the turn of the century. In a globalizing world economy, it emerged as a megatrend.

It was indubitably facilitated by technological advancements and declining costs of communications and transportation. Policy coordination among the regional governments in all the important areas like trade, finance and investment was indeed indispensable, but "Asia's integration has mostly come from the bottom up" (ADB, 2010, p. 3). It was largely an organic, market-led process (Das, 1993, 2005; Urata, 2004). What remains to be seen is how this group of economies will progress from integrated trade and production networks to the next stage of deeper integration in a real economy sense.[2] The latter stage would entail deeply integrated goods markets which could be created by "lifting behind-the-border barriers to trade in services, allowing a freer movement of labor, especially skilled labor, across regional members, developing deeper, wider, and more crisis-resilient financial markets in Asia that are able to allocate the region's vast savings more efficiently to its huge investment needs" (ADB, 2010, p. 4).

1.1 Conceptualizing Asia

There is an interminable debate on what constitutes Asia. Little wonder that there are myriad definitions. To an informed observer, geographical Asia stretches between Afghanistan and North Korea. This Asia comprises over 4 billion people in more than 40 nation-states. Heterogeneity in Asian economies as well as sub-groups of economies in this region was and continues to be considerable. Economic, social, political, physical and cultural diversity among the Asian countries is breathtaking. Asia in this book comprises only the dynamic countries, which have made concerted endeavors to reform and restructure their macro- and micro-economies. This group of dynamic countries took an overriding interest in economic growth and development. They made commendable efforts and commitment to engender inclusive growth to support social stability and equity.

From the Republic of Korea (hereinafter Korea) to Thailand, they present a rich tapestry of diversity in economic structures, natural resource endowments, stages of development, periods of take-off, degrees of openness, depths of capital markets and financial development, degrees of market-orientation, maturity of markets and their sophistication and sovereign creditworthiness. No region in the world is known for such extraordinary diversity. Besides, most countries in the region are also known for strong nationalism, historical mistrust of each other and economic rivalry, like that between China and Japan. Therefore it would be prudent to identify and recognize an economist or business person's concept of Asia as follows in this chapter.

One familiar observation is that economic developments of the last four decades in Asia were nothing short of arresting. Japan's post-war economic miracle made it the second largest global economy in 1968. In a space of two generations, the four Northeast Asian economies[3] known as the newly industrialized economies (NIEs) became high-income economies, with per caput income higher than $20,000 at current prices and exchange rates. One outcome of this ebullient economic growth is that Japan and the other regional economies of Northeast and Southeast Asia grew more aligned with China and its economic activities in a market-led manner than at any time since 1949. For the most part, this alignment materialized after 1990 and was promoted by the expectations and belief in mutual economic gains. Therefore Asia in this book is defined to include Japan, the four East Asian economies, China and the Southeast Asian economies.[4] That being said, Japan is quite distinct from the rest of the economies named here because it is a matured industrial economy. While the other Asian economies have been vying for this status, they are far from attaining it.

The principal focus in this book is on the East and Southeast Asian economies, namely China, the NIEs and the Association of Southeast Asian Nations (ASEAN) economies. Japan has been included in the analysis when necessary. Why Asia is being defined in this manner needs more explanation. Although the take-off periods for economies in Asia obviously differed, there are noticeable similarities in their growth paradigms. In chronological terms, success of Japan and the East Asian NIEs was later on mirrored in that of Southeast Asia and China. These sub-groups of economies *mutatis mutandis* followed the outward-oriented economic paradigm. Openness to trade and investment was an important policy stance common to all of them. Asia's trade openness is higher than that of the world economy. Trade-to-GDP ratio in Asia was 57.3 percent in 2011, while that for the world economy was 51.9 percent (ADB, 2013). Between 1990 and 2011, rate of growth in the trade-to-GDP ratio in Asia was much higher than that those in the EU, North America and the other regions of the global economy. Strong export demand in the advance industrial economy and increasing intra-regional trade were the two factors that were largely responsible for this.

Other common strategic ingredients in the dynamic Asian economies were high domestic savings and investment rates, which strengthened physical and digital infrastructure in the region as well as improved the quality of human capital. Besides governments had a role to play in the healthy running of the economies. In the post-1990 period China played a vitally significant regional role in economic, business and financial spheres. In the second decade of the 21st century, the East and Southeast Asian economies tended to accept China's growing regional role. Several of them were well on their way to be the "miracle" economies of the future when China launched into its journey to be the largest regional economy.

In contrast, the South and central Asian economies were not nearly as dynamic as the East and subsequently Southeast Asian ones were. The former sub-group remained stuck to inward-oriented growth strategies for a long period and virtually stagnated. Will, commitment and ability of the governments of South and central Asian economies to economic growth was not comparable to those of East and Southeast Asian economies. These countries neither economically integrated with the dynamic Asia nor among themselves. They continued to remain the most mal-integrated group of Asian economies even at present, although some overtures were recently made by India. However, India's success so far has been partial and inadequate.

Asia defined in the above-mentioned manner is universally regarded as a highly successful group of economies in its own right, *a fortiori* after the global financial crisis. Only a couple of generations ago, this region was an impoverished, underdeveloped, agrarian, backwater. It has been transformed out of recognition in two generations. Today this region comprises several prominent competitive economies. Together they form the "global factory". A combination of macroeconomic policy reforms and restructuring on the one hand and outward-oriented macroeconomic policies, largely market-based resource allocation, and business strategies followed by firms in the region on the other underlie their successful status as the global factory. Governments in these countries were proactive partners in development, capable, pragmatic and suffered from relatively lower incidence of corruption.

These sub-groups of Asian economies are geographically close to Japan, a fast-expanding high-income, mature economy, which was also the second-largest in the world until mid-2010. In the post-Plaza Accord (1985) period, efficient Japanese multinationals were eager to relocate their manufacture of medium- and low-technology products to low-cost production sites in Asia. It benefitted the Asian economies in myriad ways (Das, 1992). There is a consensus of sorts over China's steadily growing regional influence, particularly over the last two decades, and with that decline in the regional influence of Japan. That said, there is disagreement over how increase in China's influence has come about and to what extent it will continue to expand.

2 Emergence of Asia and integration of China

Between 1950s and 1990s, four countries or country groups in Asia recorded ebullient GDP growth and displayed superlative economic performance. It began with the post-war reconstruction, recovery and brisk growth of Japan. It was followed by equally brilliant performance of the four NIEs. As alluded to above, the ASEAN-4[5] were the next to pick up the baton. China was to join these high achievers last. One reason why *de facto* (deepening intra-regional trade and investment linkages) integration of the neighboring Asian economies with the Chinese economy proceeded at a brisk pace was that the private sector enterprises in the Asian economies, particularly in Japan and the NIEs, began taking active interest in the Chinese economy at an early stage of its liberalization and reform process. Corporate Asia responded promptly to China's reforms and opening up (Kwon, 2012).

China's liberalization, market-oriented reforms and brisk growth provided a real impetus to *de facto* regional integration. As these economies had adopted an outward-oriented growth strategy, the leading and following country or country-group influenced each other's growth. Recent technological advancements and globalization were the other two imperatives. In the backdrop of ongoing globalization, these high-performers mutually shaped each other's economic evolution as well as economic structure and growth trajectory. Together they are responsible for modernizing, industrializing and revolutionizing the Asian economy in a remarkably short time span. China's regional and global integration caused a regional and global reallocation of economic activities. It also resulted in generating several globally significant externalities.

2.1 Four decades of efflorescence

Four decades of structural reforms and rapid GDP growth, industrialization, urbanization has increased the heft and elevated the role of the Asian economies in the global economy. The size of the Asian economy in 1950 was puny. It was only 13 percent of the total global GDP. At this point in time Western Europe and North American economies along with Japan, Australia and

New Zealand accounted for 62 percent of the global GDP. Rapid regional growth and emergence of China altered this composition of the global GDP. By 1990, Asia accounted for 18 percent of the global GDP and by 2010 33 percent. The post-1990 period was one of exceptionally rapid regional growth when Asia's share in global GDP increased at an exceedingly rapid pace. Projections for 2030 show that Asia will account for 47 percent of the global GDP (Buiter and Rahbari, 2011).

Manufacturing output in several Asian economies grew rapidly in several Asian economies. Measured by gross manufacturing value added, China, Japan and Korea were the second, third and seventh respectively, in the global manufacturing league table in 2010 (MGI, 2012). Asia is in the middle of a historic transformation. If one assumes that Asia continues on its current growth trajectory, a brave assumption by any measure, by 2050, Asia's per caput income would rise sixfold in purchasing-power parity (PPP) terms (Kohli et al., 2011). In the second decade of the 21st century Asian economy was leading the global recovery.

Middle-class consumers are regarded as prominent drivers of consumption and therefore growth. Their number is expanding In Asia. Young populations, which are also growing in terms of productivity, command high disposable incomes. Rising incomes are fueling high spending growth in Asia. A voracious consumer force has emerged in Asia to sustain rapid GDP growth. According to an OECD study Asian, excluding Japan, middle-class spending will surpass that of the European Union (EU), Japan and the USA combined in 2022. China alone will surpass the USA in 2020 (Kharas, 2010). Asian consumer markets have expanded rapidly and their long-term outlook looks promising. For many global brands, Asia is the region that generates the largest proportion of sales. Richemont of Switzerland, Hermes of France, Prada of Italy are prominent among them. In each case, Asian markets beat European revenues. Asian EMEs have powered the luxury retail sector since 2007, as the consumers in the advanced industrial economies were hard hit by the downward economic spiral (Kassel, 2012). For Europe's major brands Asia provides 30 percent to 40 percent of their total revenue (Magnus, 2012).

Japan and the NIEs were, and continue to be, higher up on the economic value chain than China. In the process of regional economic integration they benefited from China's medium and low-end manufacturing prowess. However, the economies of Southeast Asia were and are different in this regard. Many of them resemble China in terms of resource endowments, comparative advantage and technological prowess. They came under pressure when China grew so rapidly and outcompeted them. The process of regional economic integration and development of production-sharing networks changed this state of affairs.

Rapid regional growth and the emergence of China altered the *status quo* in several important global arenas. It clearly enhanced the role and importance of Asia in global business, financial and economic affairs. It now commands the world's attention. Asian demand for minerals, commodities and energy now figures increasingly in these markets and affects global prices in them. For global public concerns like global warming and greenhouse gases, the stance and strategies that Asia is adopting or will adopt are of concern to and debated by the whole world. Asia's trade, particularly its intra-regional trade, is the most important and rapidly growing component of multilateral trade. China has been the biggest source economy making up the chronic current account deficit in the US economy. Along with the USA, China also became the most important destination of foreign direct investment (FDI). Its investment in the energy and raw-material producing sectors in Africa and Latin America has grown large. Growth of vertically integrated supply chains in the region, with China as their hub, has not only integrated the regional economies but also has immensely increased the significance of the region for the multinational corporations (Eichengreen et al., 2008).

As the Asian and Chinese economies integrate to spawn and expand regional economic synergy, the global economy finds itself at the hinge of history. A hinge by its nature is a turning point. It allows a door to swing open and reveal a new dimension. The ascent of Asia is not only influencing the structure and contours of the contemporary phase of globalization but also has become its latest driver. This may well be a new chapter of globalization, having its specific characteristics. Henderson (2008, p. 375) termed it the "Global-Asian era". It will be different from any of the past phases of globalization and will necessarily have larger global footprint of Asia and China in the business and economic arenas.

2.2 Progressively larger contribution to the global GDP

Regional economy not only has steadily magnified and become a larger part of the global GDP but it also succeeded in forging strong bonds with the global economy. It convincingly demonstrated its resilience during the global financial crisis and the ongoing Eurozone crisis (Das, 2012). Until the end of the last century, contribution of Asia's EMEs to the global GDP growth was relatively steady but never exceeded that of the advanced economies of the Western world. The bursting of the dotcom bubble in 2001 and the subsequent recession in the USA was a watershed point in this regard. Since this time, the contribution of the Asian economies to the global GDP growth has been approximately equal to that of the EU and the USA combined.

Another change came in 2006, when the housing boom in the USA was still strong. Since this time the EMEs of Asia contributed more to the global GDP growth than the EU and the USA (Neumann and Arora, 2011). During the global financial crisis and the Eurozone crisis Asian economic growth did moderate, but its contribution to global economic growth remained substantial. Over the three years spanning 2009–11, when output stagnated or declined in the advanced economies, Asian economies accounted for almost half of global growth (WB, 2012). As noted in the Prologue, in the 2008–12 quinquennium Asia accounted for two-thirds of the total global growth.

2.3 China's integration with its Asian neighbors

With rapid growth in China, a new synergy developed among the regional economies. However, until the early 1990s, Chinese political leadership did not display enthusiasm for cultivating close relationship with the region, or for economically integrating into the neighboring Asian economies (Shambaugh, 2005; Ye, 2010). That said, it did remain interested in bilateral relationship with the regional economies. If it is open, a large and rapidly growing economy does impact its neighbors' growth performance through trade and financial flows. It can create complementarities and growth opportunities for its neighboring economies, and also intensify competition for them. Additionally, an important channel of integration for the large economy is supply chain networks made possible by production fragmentation. When with the passage of time they deepen, they strengthen integration among neighboring economies.

In 1980 intra-regional trade in Asia was not particularly high, only 37 percent. With increasing trade in parts, components and intermediate products, it began expanding rapidly. During 2000–09, trade performance in Asia grew increasingly intra-regional. China had a role to play in the strengthening of intra-trade trend because it evolved as the largest destination for regional exports. In 2009 China accounted for more than 50 percent of total regional trade. Exports of Asian economies to the rest of the world (ROW) nearly doubled during this period, but intra-regional exports increased by two-and-a-half times. Intra-regional exports were 49 percent of the total in

2000. They increased to 51.6 percent in 2009 (WTO, 2011a). Thus, Asia became its own most important trade partner. China absorbed 12.3 percent of intra-regional exports in 2009. In 2000 this proportion was only 7.6 percent. China also absorbed almost 50 percent of intra-regional exports of the developing economies of the region. By 2011 intra-regional trade in the region reached 55.5 percent and in the first eight months of 2012 it was 56 percent (ADB, 2013). Also, intra-sub-regional trade share in Asia were stable.

A relevant development in this regard is declining trade partnership of Asia with the two largest global economies, the Eurozone and the USA. According to the Asian Developmemt Bank (ADB) data, Asia's trade with the Eurozone declined from 11.26 percent of the total in 2001 to 10.82 percent in 2011, while with the USA it declined from 21.67 percent of the total to 14.08 percent over the same period. This trend apparently strengthened in the post-2007 period because of the twin crises. Also, Asia's trade with the EMEs has recorded a steady rise during this period, from 9.81 percent to 17.28 percent.

Over the decade of 2000s China's significance for the regional economies increased. Over the 2000–09 period, the role of Japan and the Asian NIEs as major export destinations for the regional exporters declined somewhat. Their intra-regional imports fell. In case of Japan this decline was 2.1 percent and NIEs 3.3 percent. The NIEs recorded the largest (10.8 percent) increase in their exports to China during the period under consideration. In 2009 24.2 percent of their total exports were headed to China. At the same time NIEs' exports to Japan declined significantly (4.2 percent). In 2009 Japan was the destination of merely 5.8 percent of their exports. The ASEAN economies were minor trading partners of China in 2000, exporting only 3.9 percent of their regional exports to it. In 2009 China grew an important trade destination, absorbing 10.4 percent of their total intra-regional exports (UNESCAP, 2011).[6] These statistics demonstrate the increasing centrality of China in Asia's trade flows.

During and after the global financial crisis (2007–09), the Asian economy proved to be a compelling and credible force in the global economy. For structural and policy reasons, it not only led the global economic recovery from what is being termed the Great Recession but also contributed meaningfully to it (Das, 2011). According to Shinohara (2010) it provided an appreciable pull force to the global recovery. Asia emerged from the global financial crisis as a growth driver and an anchor of stability for the global economy. It emerged from what was being referred to as the Great Recession with its standing in the world economy strengthened. Well integrated regionally and with the global economy, Asian economy promises to be the largest economy in the world in the foreseeable future.

Over the preceding three decades, the mutual relationship between China and surrounding Asia has evolved in a pragmatic, productive and constructive manner. This chapter investigates their evolving process of mutual acceptance and progressive economic interaction. The broad objective is to examine how China is influencing its neighboring Asian economies and to see whether their economic relationship developed into a market- and institution-led symbiosis. This chapter examines how China's rapid growth was instrumental in integrating Asian economies with each other and mutually supporting rise of a dynamic Asia. Unquestionably there were apprehensions in some quarters regarding rapidly growing China having a damaging and deleterious economic impact over the neighboring Asia. The bottom line is to explore whether the Asian economies have gained or lost from China's recent rapid growth.

During the reform process, the Chinese economy liberalized both domestically and externally, which enabled its market-led integration with the regional economy. China's market-led integration with its dynamic Asian neighbors took place through trade and FDI as well as vertically-integrated production networks, also known as processing trade. A defining economic occurrence of the last quarter of a century for Asia is China's resurgence as a manufacturing powerhouse. China's economic importance not only grew enormously for the regional economies but it has also been econom- ically influential in a significant manner on an unremitting basis. It has been having a constant and decisive impact over regional institutions and economic structure. In the process it has been influencing the pace of economic growth in the rest of Asia for close to two decades. As the 21st century dawned, China began to appear a major driver of regional economic growth.

Economic events in China have a largely favorable impact on Asia. What cannot be ignored is that the reverse can be equally true. China's vertiginous growth, on the one hand, and its rapid trade expansion and increased inflows of FDI on the other, have influenced the Asian economy massively. There is little element of surprise in it. As noted above, other than trade and FDI, regional production chains or production networks became a mechanism by which Asian econo- mies tangibly influenced each other as well as integrated in a market-led manner. As barriers to the movement of goods, services and factors of production are dropped further, Asian economies would integrate more with each other as well as with the global economy. It would enable higher degree of specialization and integration as well as facilitate exploitation of scale and scope econo- mies. Indubitably both deepening regional integration of China in Asia as well as intensifying regional integration *per se* is sure to stimulate regional growth. Industries and businesses will have more opportunities than they have had so far. In the post-global financial crisis period this boost to regional growth could not be timelier because the advanced economies have been recovering at a tepid pace. The economic challenges in the Eurozone and the USA have been keeping their medium-term growth below potential.

China's rise as a regional economic power, before becoming a global one, was a substantially significant, if a trifle sensitive, economic event. Its policies toward Asia underwent a distinct and striking transformation. In the pre-1978 era, China was not trusted by its neighboring Asian economies. In turn, for quite some time China also regarded its Asian neighbors with mistrust and suspicion. It perceived them as an instrument of US foreign policy, bent on thwarting China's progress and economic ascent. Early during the reform period (post-1978) this mindset and posture of the policy-making establishment in China changed. It dawned on them that China's economic interest lay in engaging and co-operating with the surrounding regional economies. This could be achieved by developing close bilateral economic relationships as well as through multilateral engagement, including proactive promotion of formal regional institutions.

In regional policy-making, the Chinese government adhered to Deng Xiaoping's policy guidelines of remaining passive in exerting regional influence and not being anxious to assume or assert leadership in regional affairs. Not accepting a large regional or global role or responsibility that the society and country might later on find burdensome was another similar policy guideline. These ideas were embodied in Deng's *buyao dangtou* or "not seeking leadership" principle. In his post-1990 public speeches Deng repeated them on numerous occasions. Deng's penchant for exercising self-restraint in regional and international affairs and avoiding being seen as obtrusive and meddlesome by other countries was strong. He implored his country to do likewise. Hindsight demonstrates that Deng was a far-sighted political leader and his strategies served China well for a long period.

3 The Asian crisis and China's strategic policy shift

China was less engaged in Asia until the mid-1990s and was even somewhat aloof (Section 2). A defining moment in China's expression of its policy stance towards its Asian neighbors came at the time of the outbreak of the Asian financial crisis of 1997–98. Until then, economic growth and national security had been regarded as two separate logical policy spheres rather than a single policy domain in China. Economic reform-led growth was given higher priority on the domestic policy agenda. When the Asian crisis 9 struck, it became clear to the policy mandarins that China's economic fortunes and domestic economic stability were impossible to disentangle from what was happening in the rest of the Asian economy (Wang, 2004). This realization led to a significant conceptual and policy transformation. The Asian crisis made Chinese policy-makers rethink the link between domestic and regional, including international, economic policy. Their understanding regarding the value and consequences of engagement with the regional economies grew.

Realizing the importance of interdependence, the Chinese policy mandarins came to conclude that regional economic engagement would eventually be in China's national economic self-interest. After the Asian crisis China began taking its regional role far more seriously than ever before. They also realized that joining and actively participating in the region and global economy had two realistic sides to it: shouldering responsibilities and benefiting from the arrangement. The term *fuzeren de daguo*, or "responsible great power", became endemic in official communications after the Asian crisis.

It was recognized that a regional environment of conflict, stress and tense relationships with small and less powerful neighbors would align them against China. This could be their first reaction. In addition, it may have served US interests vicariously. The USA would get an opportunity to become more active and important in Asia as a counterbalancing power against China. Therefore, maintaining amicable relations with its regional neighbors became vitally important for China. It made strenuous efforts to improve economic and political ties with other Asian countries, and even made strong concessions to achieve improvement in bilateral relations.

3.1 Emergence of a post-crisis policy stance

Based on policy advice proffered by the International Monetary Fund (IMF) and the World Bank, many rapidly growing Asian economies had followed a three-pronged strategy of attracting capital from the global financial markets. It included liberalization of domestic financial sector, maintaining a high domestic interest rate to attract capital and pegging the national currency to the dollar so that foreign investors to reassure foreign investors against currency risk. An excessive amount of short-term capital—notorious for its volatility—found its way to the Asian economies. Indonesia, Korea, Malaysia, the Philippines and Thailand found themselves in dire straits. Transmission mechanism of the Asian crisis worked its way through economic fundamental and financial and trade channels. The crisis-affected Asian economies and the regional economy suffered credit contractions, recessions, stock price bursts, depletion in forex reserves and steep currency depreciations. The real economy was pummeled, leading to serious deterioration in economic fundamentals. The costly bailout packages devised for the crisis affected Asian economies by the IMF during the 1997–98 crisis were perceived by the Asian governments as humiliating. The macro-economic and structural conditionality associated with the IMF's assistance programs that were negotiated with Thailand (August 1997), Indonesia (November 1997 and August 1998), and Korea (December 1997) was seen as overly harsh and intrusive. Disillusionment and disaffection of the Asian governments with the IMF, and in general with the international financial institutions (IFIs), over the handling of the Asian crisis is well documented.

In addition to making the Asian governments feel that they were trivial and inconsequential, the IMF prescriptions made a bad economic and financial situation in the crisis-stricken economies as well as in Asia much worse. The perception of the Asian governments regarding the conditionality prescribed by the IMF was that it was planned by the US Treasury. The crisis response of the IFIs was seen in Asia as the USA defending its own interests in a blinkered and inflexible manner at the expense of crisis-affected Asian economies. One viewpoint in this regard was that the USA was a malevolent hegemonic power reveling in the humiliation of the highly successful Asian economies by imposing its will and power through its influence in the IFIs. IMF policy prescriptions for the crisis-affected Asian economies were evidently wrong. Scholars like Joseph Stiglitz pointed out the erroneous ways and excesses committed by the IMF in this regard (Stiglitz, 2002). Subsequently the IMF publicly admitted its errors of judgment on several occasions.

For Asia, the crisis and its handling, was a defining moment. The US action was seen as detrimental to the regional economy as well as to the crisis-ridden economies. For all appearances, the USA was having a destructive influence on the Asian growth paradigm, which had served Asia well until that point in time. At this juncture Japan was the only country ready with a $100 billion assistance package. This ambiance engendered collective predisposition towards regionalism *per se*, which in turn initiated a change in the institutional ecosystem in the region. In their quest for GDP growth regional economies grew more disposed towards cooperation and collaboration than in the past.

Therefore, many Asian governments reacted by turning to the strategy of not relying on the US-dominated IFIs, particularly the IMF, in future for resolution of the regional economic and financial problems. They acknowledged the need for self-reliance and regional mutual support. There was a strong political support for establishing a self-help mechanism for the regional economies. To that end, Asian policy makers determined to rely more on regional institutions, resources and solutions to solve regional economic and financial problems. For individual economies, self-help mechanism included cautionary measures like balanced or surplus budgets, current account surplus, strengthening foreign exchange reserves, lower and stable inflation rates, lower corporate leverage and robust bank balance-sheets. In addition, Asia's reliance on foreign banks had dwindled. This was their broad strategy of resisting US hegemony in regional and global affairs.

The economies in East and Southeast Asia were united on this strategic stance. This shared position gave an impetus to and strengthened regional economic and financial co-operation. The atmosphere of growing regional cooperation and mutual support provided an ideal opportunity for China to join in with its regional neighbors in their quest for mutual economic reliance. By not allowing the renminbi to depreciate during the Asian crisis China sent a clear signal to its Asian neighbors that it stood ready to help them in their hour of need and economic distress.

Although the Chinese economy was not badly damaged by the Asian crisis, it saw this regional ambience as an opportunity for partnership and collaboration with neighboring economies in designing regional public goods such as the Chiang Mai Initiative (CMI), the Asian Monetary Fund (AMF) and the development of Asian currency-denominated long-term Asian bond markets. It was envisaged that these institutions, if successfully created, would efficiently and credibly help the regional economy in fending off any future regional crises, which in turn would lead to a vibrant Asian economy in the future. Development of the Asian bond market would not only help channel huge amounts of Asian savings into long-term investments in Asian currency-denominated instruments in the region but also remedy their financial systems' excessive reliance on foreign banks. During the Asian crisis China made a decisive contribution to stabilizing regional markets.

3.2 Compelling surge in China's economic role in the region

In the post-Asian crisis period China's standing in the regional neighboring economies increased markedly. China's celebrated rise to the status of the second largest global economy, largest exporter, largest trader[7] and the hub of regional production networks has meaningful ramifications for the Asian economy.[8] By the 2020s it is projected to be the largest economy in the world at current prices and market exchange rates. Growing status of the Chinese economy is sure to create further opportunities for the neighboring Asian economies to upgrade their pattern of growth as well as move up the economic ladder and value chain. As for the recent past, when the global financial crisis (2007–09) struck, China's macro-economic fundamental were strong. It enjoyed a current account surplus and a sizeable accumulation of forex reserves. In addition, its public and external debts were low. China's economic dynamism and fast expanding business firms favorably influenced the regional economies and businesses. It became a driver of growth for them.

China became, and helped Asian economy become, the factory of the world. Electronics and light manufactures are two of the important lines of China's exports, which are split almost equally between processing and non-processing trade. China has evolved into the center of regional and global production chains. This has increased China's importance for the regional economy immensely and significantly affected the structure of manufacturing industries in Asia. This applied *a fortiori* to the high-technology manufactured products. It has enabled them to benefit from China's dynamism.

In the post-global financial crisis period, China appears well placed to enhance its significance in the regional and global production chains, which are likely to be further consolidated in the future. This would be largely because China's manufacturing base is large, diversified and expanding fast. A progressive number of large domestic firms with skilled labor force and R&D capabilities would support such an expansion. Along with that regional and global supply chains will also expand.

Although the USA and Japan are the global leaders in innovation, a range of measures indicate that new nucleuses of global innovation are emerging. China is the most conspicuous among them. This trend is driven first by strong growth in R&D investment in Asia in general and China in particular.[9] Since 2000, China's annual investment in R&D has expanded rapidly. In 2009 it was 580.2 billion RMB. China also has the benefit of the largest R&D workforce in the world. According to Park (2011) 20 percent of world's total R&D brain power resides in China. Both quality and quantity of innovation in China are approaching world-class levels. Recent R&D investment has increasingly been financed by private sector. The second driving factor is the globalization of higher education. China also had medium- and long-term National Plan for Science and Technology Development. The objective of these plans was to enhance the indigenous innovation capabilities, so that the next stage of economic transformation may entail entering capital- and technology-intensive industries.

China's large and diverse imports also materially influence the regional economy. Between 2000 and 2010, China's import volumes increased 4.4-fold. In 2011 its merchandise imports were $1,743 billion and services imports $236 billion (WTO, 2012). During the global financial crisis (2007–09) China devised and implemented a sizable fiscal and monetary stimulus, which supported China's import growth, in the process buttressed regional and global recovery efforts. China is an important trading partner of all the regional economies. As a large trader it has been influencing the regional economy inordinately and it will continue to do so in the medium term. Although China's multilateral trade volumes are likely to grow slowly during the post crisis period, it is sure provide a strong impetus to intra-regional trade. As China's macro-economic rebalancing endeavors continue, China's import composition is likely to change. Imports of intermediate inputs may decline, while more consumer goods may become items of large import, which in turn may well benefit the regional trading partners.

China also sways both the regional and global economies as a large net saving and high-investing economy. At 35.1 percent of GDP its rate of investment was high in 2000. In 2010 it was exceedingly high at 48.6 percent. The rate of gross national saving was even higher. It increased from 36.8 percent of GDP to 54.2 percent over the same period. Consequently, China's current account surplus rose from $20.5 billion to $300 billion during the period under consideration. In 2011 there were 13 capital exporters in the world, five of which were in Asia. Other than China (20.9%), they were Japan (13.3%, Singapore (3.4%), Taiwan (2.8%) and Korea (1.9%). Together they accounted for 42 percent of the total exports (Ito *et al.*, 2011). However China's current account surplus peaked in 2007 (10.8 percent of GDP). In 2011 it declined substantially (to 2.8 percent of GDP) and the downward trend continued in 2012 (2.6 percent of GDP).

3.3 China's investment in Asian economies

In the post-Asian crisis period, China continually reduced restrictions on outbound capital flows. In 2011 its total outward FDI was $65.12 billion (WIR, 2012). It gradually emerged an increasing source of FDI for the Asian economies, which became the latest element in China's integration in the Asian economic system. China's outward foreign direct investment (OFDI) is projected to reach $150 billion by 2015 (Lee, 2013). The government has an overwhelmingly high influence over the direction of China's OFDI.

Consistent OFDI data are available from the Ministry of Commerce for the 2003–10 period. They demonstrate that in the post-Asian crisis period there was a dramatic increase in China's OFDI in the surrounding Asian economies, from $1,505 million to $44,890 million. There were large year to year increases in China's investments in the regional economies. They remained the largest recipients of the Chinese OFDI. There were years when OFDI doubled or more than doubled from one year to the next (see Table 1.1 and Figure 1.1). This helped integrate the Chinese economies with the region. It was evident that for the investing Chinese firms surrounding Asian economies were the most important. A large proportion of their total OFDI went to them. China had a unambiguous bias toward Asian economies. In 2008 and 2009 Asia accounted for close to three-quarters of the total OFDI flows. As 2009 was a global financial crisis year, OFDI flowing to Asia recorded a minor decline. However, in 2010 the old increasing trend returned and Asian economies again received almost two-thirds of the total OFDI.

4. Regional acceptance of China and its soft power status

China had a history of conflict and even war with several of its Asian neighbors. For acceptance and economic integration, it needed to be accepted by them. In attempting to sway the contours of the

TABLE 1.1 Chinese outward FDI flows to Asia, 2003–10 (US$ millions)

Year	Asia	Annual increase (%)	Proportion of total OFDI (%)
2003	1,505.03	–	52.72
2004	3,013.99	100.26	54.82
2005	4,484.17	48.78	36.57
2006	7,663.25	70.90	43.46
2007	16,593.15	116.53	62.60
2008	43,547.50	162.44	77.89
2009	40,407.59	−7.21	71.48
2010	44,890.46	11.09	65.24

Source: MOFCOM, 2010 Statistical Bulletin of China's Outward Foreign Direct Investment (Posted in Sep 16,2011)

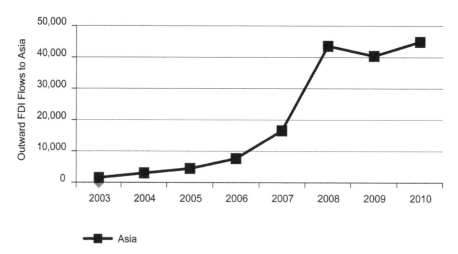

FIGURE 1.1 Chinese outward FDI flows to Asia, 2003–10
Source: MOFCOM, 2010 Statistical Bulletin of China's Outward Foreign Direct Investment (Posted in Sep 16, 2011)

regional economic order, China has utilized the capital of regional acceptance, or what Wang (2008) termed "reputational capital", namely caution persuasion, prudence and skill. China's soft power in Asia was evidently on the rise (Breslin, 2009). The term "soft power" implies the ability to persuade by foreign policy and influence based on a country's culture, values, belief, policies and way of life. It entails persuasion to get what you want rather than force or payment. Rejection of coercion is imperative for the soft power. Chinese policy mandarins believed that soft power would enhance China's comprehensive strength in regional and global affairs by creating a peaceful regional and global environment for securing resources for growth and development (Siow, 2010). The Communist Party of China (CPC) repeated Deng Xiaoping's mantra of "economic construction as the core". The influence of sixth-century-BC sage Sun Tzu was obvious, one of whose aphorisms was, "the highest excellence is never having to fight because the commencement of battle signifies a political failure".

Initially China saw itself as an evolving regional economic power. However, as the regional and global scenario developed, China rapidly emerged a geo-economic and geo-strategic power. As its status rose, China was anxious not to be perceived as a menace to its regional neighbors. Since the early 1990s it actively worked to build an impression and persona of a good regional and global citizen as well as a responsible neighbor. This strategy was actively pursued by the Chinese government. Chinese soft power began in Asia in 1997, when China refused to depreciate the renminbi in response to sharply plunging currency values in the crisis-affected Asian economies. The substantive signal China sent to the Asian economies was that it would stand with them through the period of financial difficulties.

Through constant mild-mannered diplomatic endeavors, a non-threatening, non-confrontational and non-challenging image of a reasonable and responsible power or *fuzeren daguo* was consciously and consistently cultivated by the Chinese government. At every opportunity the Chinese government communicated that it had a strong inclination to promote regional prosperity and that in its economic rise there was no intention to prevent or interrupt any neighboring economy's scheme to thrive, prosper and raise the living standards of its people. Its eagerness to both be and be perceived as a benign power was obvious. In fact, it did not want to be seen as a power of any ilk. It wanted to project itself as a country of opportunity to its regional neighbors, not a threat. This official gesture of the Chinese leadership was statesman-like and had significant regional and international ramifications. One influential Chinese academic strategist, Zheng Bijian, who was Chair of the China Reform Forum, promoted the doctrine of "peaceful rise" or *heping jueqi*. Zheng Bijian famously remarked, "China's economic integration into East Asia has contributed to the shaping of an East Asian community that may rise in peace as a whole" (Zheng, 2005, p. 23).

With the disintegration of Soviet Union and collapse of the bipolar world order, confrontation between blocs of power ended. The USA was the only super- or hegemonic power left. It was also the principal provider of technology and markets to China. In addition, large US companies and multinational firms were an important source of FDI and technology to China. A confrontation or irreparable rupture with the USA would have been wholly gratuitous and not in the economic interest of China. Therefore China adopted a reasonable and level-headed stance and did not show any aversion or active opposition to the USA. It was a rational and pragmatic stance. Why should China, or any other country, be opposed to the USA if the USA does not act in a hegemonic manner and transgress international norms? It would not have been in China's rational self-interest to fritter away its resources in confronting the only remaining geo-economic and geo-political superpower. China's policy-making elite learned from the history of other rising powers. It was determined to peacefully rise within the system, without unduly rocking the boat. Being and remaining part of the global economic system was regarded as essential by it. China's economic and foreign policy-makers did not lose sight of the fact that its intra-system growth would have the benefit of enabling China to influence the system as a whole.

China's proclivity toward soft power was recently obvious during the sixth plenary session of the 17th Central Committee of the CPC in October 2011. It was the first time in two decades that CPC decision-makers focused on cultural issues in the Party's plenary session. China does not lack cultural assets (Pei, 2011). Government continues to fund projects to promote Chinese culture abroad through Confucius Institutes. After successfully achieving building of a modern economy, expanding its physical infrastructure and avant-garde cities, China is aspiring for advancing its intangible soft power as well as international influence of its own culture. However China has incurred losses in this regard. Truculence over fishing rights with Japan in 2010 and Korea in 2011 went counter to China's soft power preference. Also, serious mishandling of the sensitive maritime issues like South China Sea had a high cost in terms of loss of soft power and goodwill of ASEAN neighbors. China surprised them by stepping up its demands for large swaths of the South China Sea. Many of them now demonstrate unconcealed apprehension and uneasiness over China's new assertiveness. China also detained Philippine and Vietnamese boats. This overly assertive conduct put a question mark on China's peaceful rise doctrine and alienated neighboring countries. Tensions between China and the US over how to resolve competing claims spilled over during the Asia Pacific Economic Cooperation (APEC) summit in Indonesia in November 2011.

There is another major incongruous, if not a paradoxical, fact. It cannot be ignored that Myanmar, North Korea and Pakistan are close diplomatic associates of China in the region, while India, Indonesia, Japan, Russia and Vietnam are cautious, if not explicitly distrustful, regarding China's growing influence and power. Since 2009 the regional neighbors became much more guarded and vigilant of an increasingly abrasive China. After the East Asia Summit in Cambodia in November 2012, it appears that there is a probability that the East and issues can exacerbate into a conflict between claimants like Japan, Korea, Brunei, China, Malaysia, the Philippines, Taiwan and Vietnam. Such a conflict will categorically be counterproductive for the growth and integration of the Asian economy and businesses.

5. Essentials of China's regional economic strategy

The Chinese policy-making elite paid attention to developing their economic strategy with its dynamic regional neighbors in mind. It regarded methodical expansion and deepening economic ties with its regional neighbors as a positive means of winning their trust. Developing a symbiotic relationship with the regional economies was another certain advantage. Both of these objectives were paid copious attention by the Chinese policy makers. To them this appeared to be a distinct win-win regional strategy. It could lead to creation of ties that bind Chinese economy with its dynamic Asian neighbors and these relationships could be innovatively nurtured and strengthened in the future. This is not to deny the occasional flare-ups and verbal spats on the prickly Taiwan issue, of course.

An eminent characteristic of the Chinese economy is liberalization. Openness or trade orientation of an economy is measured by trade (exports plus imports) as a percentage of GDP. As seen in Table 1.2, by 1990 openness of the Chinese economy had reached 29 percent and by 2000 44 percent. The opening up process was accelerated after 2000, particularly after China's World Trade Organization (WTO) accession. Between 2000 and 2005, it dramatically increased from 44 percent to 69 percent. China became a proponent of regional trade liberalization. It supported and initiated several regional trade liberalization endeavors. This confirmed China's support to the tenet of free trade and belief in the classical economic principle of gains from trade, rather than in narrow code of mercantilists.

In 2006 China's openness was 70 percent, implying that it was a trade-orientated economy, but when the global economic crisis began in 2007 it declined somewhat to 68 percent (Table 1.2). As the global financial crisis worsened, it declined further to 62 percent (in 2008) and 49 percent (in 2009). However, during 2010, the year of the recovery, it spurted to 56 percent (World Bank, 2012). Trade became one of the prominent channels of integration with the regional economy for China and in turn led to regional economic interdependence in an effective manner. Multilateral trade decelerated in 2011, which affected Chinese trade. Its exports declined in 2011.

As the statistics in Table 1.3 show, the other Asian economies also have an open trade regime, with Singapore and Hong Kong SAR coming at the top due to their huge *entrepôt* trade. Malaysia, Vietnam and Thailand are also highly trade-oriented economies. The trade volume of Taiwan and

TABLE 1.2 Openness of the Chinese economy, 1990–2011

Year	Exports as percentage of GDP	Imports as percentage of GDP	Total (%)
1990	16	13	29
1995	29	19	39
2000	23	21	44
2005	37	32	69
2006	39	31	70
2007	38	30	68
2008	35	27	62
2009	27	22	49
2010	30	26	56
2011	29	26	55

Source: The World Bank. *World Development Indicators Data Base*, Washington, DC, July 2012.

TABLE 1.3 Openness of the other Asian economies, 2011

	Imports of goods and services (% of GDP)	Exports of goods and services (% of GDP)	Total (% of GDP)
Japan	16	15	31
Hong Kong, SAR	226	230	456
Singapore	182	209	391
Korea	54	56	110
Taiwan	69	76	145
Indonesia	26	25	51
Malaysia	76	92	167
Philippines	33	29	62
Thailand	71	78	149
Vietnam	87	81	168

Sources:
1 The World Bank. *World Development Indicators Data Base*, Washington, DC, July 2013.
2 Asian Development Bank (ADB). *Key indicators for Asia and the Pacific 2012*, Manila, Philippines.

Korea are also close to the size of their respective GDPs. This should facilitate regional integration for these economies and China. Indonesia is the least open economy in this group, with trade to GDP ratio at 51 percent. Japan, the only mature industrial economy in the group, is not as open as it was in the past. Its openness indicator is merely 31 percent.

Declining tariff rates are another important indicator that portend to the opening up of an economy. Over the recent decades China's tariff barriers continuously declined. In 1980–84 they were high at 49.5 percent. In 1985–89 they fell to 39.3 percent. They did not show a fall in 1990–94 and remained almost stationary (40.0 percent). However, in preparation to the WTO accession a precipitous fall occurred in 1995–99 to 18.8 percent and further down to 12.8 percent in 2000–05 (Nicita and Olarreaga 2006). Non-tariff barriers were also reduced or eliminated. Although an open economy is a necessary condition, it is not sufficient to make an economy a successful trader. It needs to be supported by complementary policy inputs like efficient infrastructure for production and well-organized logistics that enable firms to connect to international networks of producers and suppliers.

China, like the USA, had adopted a strategy of keeping its economy open to promote global economic interdependence. By keeping its markets open China has managed to provide growth opportunities to the regional economies and to be a welcoming economic partner to them. In the second decade of the 21st century regional economies accept China much more than they did in the past. For the most part, Asian economies began to perceive China as an economy that will provide them with growth opportunities. The likelihood of seeing China as an overbearing menace has been reduced. Thus openness of the economy indubitably was a logical and pragmatic strategy. By following this strategy and by opening its markets for exports from the regional neighbors and targeting their markets for its own export, China could become a veritable locomotive of regional growth. Tang and Zhang (2006, p. 53) succinctly describe the Chinese strategy as, "participate actively, demonstrate restraint, offer reassurance, open markets, foster interdependence, create common interests, and reduce conflict".

With the exception of Japan, the regional economies are much smaller than China in terms of the size of GDP. Adoption of outward-oriented strategy had also helped in integrating the NIEs of

Asia as well as the members of the Association of Southeast Asian Nations (ASEAN)[10] into the Chinese economy. This process received an impetus from China's bilateral economic agreements, which drew the neighboring Asian economies closer to the Chinese domestic markets. China has bilateral agreements with Singapore and Thailand, a Taiwan Economic Cooperation Framework Agreement with Taiwan and a Closer Economic Partnership Agreement (CEPA) with Hong Kong. In 2002 China also entered into a comprehensive framework agreement with ASEAN; its objective was to reach an agreement on an ASEAN–China free trade agreement (FTA) by 2010. Also, emerging multilateral structures were utilized by China for pursuing the objective of coming closer to the regional economies. Being in the multilateral frameworks would enable China to compete for influence with the erstwhile regional powers like Japan and the USA.

As a regional strategy, China also encompassed the political and security dimensions in its relationship with its Asian neighbors. A fully fledged cooperation and partnership relationship with the regional states was not possible without the inclusion of these dimensions. For instance, China began its interaction with the ASEAN economies through the ASEAN Regional Forum (ARF), which was created during the 1992 ASEAN Summit in Singapore after the collapse of the Soviet Union, withdrawal of the USA from its bases in the Philippines in 1991 and the visit of Indonesian President Suharto to China. China elevated its relationship with ASEAN further by strengthening economic and political relationship through the ASEAN–China Free Trade Area (ACFTA). The initial ACFTA agreement was signed in 2002 in Phnom Penh, Cambodia, with the intent to establishing an FTA in 2010. In addition, the Treaty of Amity and Cooperation in Southeast Asia (TAC-SEA) was signed in 1976 by the ASEAN members, which China joined in 2003. Later on a good number of other states also joined the TAC-SEA. The USA became a member late, not until 2009. Thus, developing close relations with the regional neighbors remained an important policy objective for China and it deployed different channels for developing them.

With its northeastern neighbor, Korea, China began its relationship directly on an economic level. Subsequently it grew closer and more cordial and flourished in political and security domains as well. There have been favorable results in terms of China's efforts to improve relationships with East and Southeast Asia. Despite constantly improving the regional economic and political relationships and succeeding in developing strong economic ties, China's relationship with India and Taiwan cannot be called amicable and satisfactory. There have been occasions when it flared into wars of words and stinging public statements in the media. The old regional rivalry between China and Japan is no longer as intense as it was in the past. China has promoted the ideas of an FTA between China, Japan and Korea as well as an ASEAN-Plus-Three (APT). These initiatives reflect China's inclination to ignore the historic bitterness and form a constructive relationship between the two regional economic giants. This bilateral relationship between the largest and second largest regional economies is a significant one for Asia and will always influence the regional economy.

6. China and the Asian growth model

The growth model followed by economies like Japan and the NIEs is acclaimed for being uniquely successful. Although China chronologically followed its energetic Asian neighbors, its rapid GDP growth is comparable in many ways to that of its neighbors. Its recipe for rapid growth found many economic and institutional initiatives in the Asian economies. Therefore, to a cursory observer it appears that China's market-oriented economic transformation benefitted substantially from the Asian growth paradigm and that China followed the Asian growth model. It positively shares many characteristics of the Asian growth strategy. There are many similarities in China's take-off strategy and those of its Asian neighbors. China also exemplifies the success of the Asian growth model, but like the other Asian economies it is *sui generis*.

External sector liberalization and international trade, export-oriented FDI and large imports of technology, which included advance technological knowledge and equipment, were a common thread that ran through all the Asian economies and China. Also, like the other Asian economies, China's intra-regional trade expanded fast. In contrast, among the obvious differences was China not being seriously affected by the Asian crisis. This occurred despite the fact that China shared some of the economic and financial vulnerabilities with the crisis-affected Asian economies. Control over capital movements, inconvertibility of currency, management of short-term external debt, a significant trade surplus and forex reserves and strong FDI inflows were instrumental in keeping China from plunging into the crisis.

Wade's concept of government-guided development is applicable to China and many Asian economies (Wade, 1990). Despite declining importance of the state-owned enterprises (SOEs) in China, they are still important and China is a mixed economy. They are an instrument of government-guided development. Many Asian economies followed the so-called developmental state principle. Under this doctrine a state has a well laid-out industrial policy. It promotes high rates of domestic saving, heavy industries and a "corporatist control over the society" (Baek, 2005, p. 487).

There is little concurrence over what is an Asian model because economies in the region transformed their economic and industrial structures differently and their governments intervened in them in their own idiosyncratic manners. While they pursued generally efficient macro-economic policies, they did not do so in a uniform manner. Strategies also had intertemporal variations. That said, some common elements can be identified. Boltho and Weber (2009) selected four major features that were common as well as imperative for the rapid growth in the Asian economies: (1) emphasis on investment, manufacturing and external competitiveness; (2) belief in promoting micro-economic competitiveness; (3) rational macro-economic policies, including budgetary balance and eschewing high inflationary rates; and (4) socio-economic and political features necessary for reinforcing economic growth, such as high-quality human capital formation, capable and reliable bureaucracies and authoritarian governments. China also followed many of these strategic traits in its growth model.

If China's development model is compared to different sub-groups of Asian economies, it appears "closer to the experience of some South-East Asian countries than to that of the North-East Asian ones" (Boltho and Weber, 2009, p. 277). That is not to deny that it also has close resemblance to the North-East Asian economies in several respects. "In particular, Chinese policy mandarins regarded 'Singapore model', which essentially entailed authoritarian state-capitalism, as valuable. It competes with the market-based liberal democratic model. Deng Xiaoping was taken with the 'Singapore model' and in 1994 he exhorted the Chinese government to learn from the economic miracle in the city-state. Singapore had one dominant party, soft-authoritarian state and an efficient incorruptible government. Together they were responsible for its economic miracle. Many Chinese policy makers saw Singapore as a successful developmental stage and an apt example to follow, While in Japan, Korea (Republic of) and Taiwan the developmental state concept came under pressure and was modified, it persisted in Singapore, where the government continued to play a strong role in the economy."

7. Summary and conclusions

This chapter has explored the relationship between China and the surrounding Asian economies and their growing role in shaping the contours of the global economy. It begins with defining

Asia. It delves into the economic interaction and dynamics of the Asian and Chinese economies and also examines how China's rapid growth was instrumental in integrating Asian economies with each other and mutually supporting rise of a dynamic Asian economy. It analyzes how Asia and China peacefully accepted each other, and how China was/is influencing its neighboring Asian economies in a synergetic manner.

This chapter also attempts to establish whether the economic relationship between the Asian economies and China is synergetic and a market- and institution-led symbiosis. Of the two, the symbiotic relationship has been more market-driven than institution-driven. In following this trend, Asian economies conformed to their past pattern and predilection. That said, the political factors have recently begun reinforcing this trend and their impact is on the rise in enhancing the interaction between Asia and China. One of the conclusions is that China has been influencing the pace of economic growth in the rest of Asia for close to two decades. As the 21st century dawned, China began to appear to be a major driver of regional economic growth.

When the Chinese economy began its resurgence to become the largest regional economy, some of its smaller neighboring Asian economies were on their way to being among the "miracle" economies of the future. As Chinese GDP growth gained momentum, it began influencing its Asian neighbors in a significant manner. The two groups that were affected most due to China's rapid growth were Japan and the NIEs on the one hand and the ASEAN economies on the other. China becoming a regional economic powerhouse was unquestionably a significant and sensitive issue. Although during the pre-reform era China did not have close economic and political relations with its Asian neighbors, during the reform period Chinese political leadership consciously decided to engage and cooperate with the surrounding regional economies.

China regarded soft power as important and its status as a soft power in the region was on the rise, with the result that its intentions were no longer mistrusted by its regional neighbors as they had been before 1980. The Asian crisis (1997–98) proved to be an opportune period for China to cultivate close economic ties with the neighboring Asian economies. Mishandling of the crisis and bail-out packages by the IMF had made the Asian governments resentful. They were disaffected with the IFIs, particularly the IMF. As an alternative to the IFIs and IMF, they were anxious to create regional frameworks for handling any future crises. They clearly saw a pressing need for self-reliance and regional mutual support. The Asian crisis was also a reminder to China that its economic fortunes and domestic economic stability could not be dissociated from what happened in the rest of Asia. The importance of regional interdependence dawned on the Chinese policy mandarins. China joined its regional neighbors in their quest for mutual economic reliance. Its partnership and collaboration endeavors with them escalated. China methodically expanded and deepened economic ties with its regional neighbors. This served to win their trust and helped to develop a market-driven symbiotic economic relationship between them.

To that end China adopted an open trade policy stance. It also unilaterally reduced its tariffs rates and non-tariff barriers. Keeping the economy open was instrumental in cultivating regional and global interdependence. Developing a close APT grouping and strengthening it was another policy measure that brought China close to the regional economies. The APT network was instrumental in developing a sense of regional identity. This regional framework also made it feasible to seek regional solutions for regional economic and financial problems. It was a functional and valuable regional public good.

This chapter also examines how the Chinese policy-making elite paid attention to developing their economic strategy with its dynamic regional neighbors. Taking a long-term perspective, it developed a strategy of methodical expansion and deepening economic ties with its regional neighbors. Chinese leadership saw clear advantages in developing a symbiotic relationship with the regional economies.

Notes

1 Asia is defined as China, Japan, the four Asian NIEs and the ASEAN group. GDP of the two regions has been calculated from the WDI statistics, in July 2012.
2 The term real economy, or real economic activity or real-side activity refers to the physical part of the economy that is concerned with actually producing goods, services and resources. This facet of the economy deals with using resources to produce goods and services that make satisfaction of wants and needs possible. It entails creation of jobs, incomes and consumer spending. It excludes the paper economy and the financial side of the economy.
3 Namely Hong Kong, SAR, the Republic of Korea, Singapore and Taiwan.
4 Those that are members of the Association of Southeast Asian Nations (ASEAN).
5 The ASEAN-4 economies comprise Indonesia, Malaysia, the Philippines and Thailand. Three of these are resource-based countries.
6 See Table 5, p. 9 of UNESCAP (2011).
7 Trade is measured as exports plus imports. In 2012 China ($3.87 trillion) eclipsed the USA ($3.82) in trade in goods, although if services are added the USA was still ahead.
8 See Das (2008a, 2011) and Vincelette *et al.* (2011) for a current account of China's pre-crisis growth.
9 Global innovation landscape is changing. The US and Japan are still the leaders in innovation in science and technology, but competition from Asian economies has been on the rise. China is the leading competitor. According to a study by Goldman Sachs, R&D spending in Asia exceeds EU levels and is likely to overtake the US levels by 2015. China is the most important player in this area. At $100 billion R&D investment, China is the third leading R&D investor in the world. Both the USA (at $325 billion) and Japan (at $123) made higher investments than China. The Chinese government's target of 2.5 percent of GDP on R&D by 2010 would triple China's R&D investment, reaching $300 billion by 2010 (Gilman, 2010).
10 ASEAN was founded by five Southeast Asian economies, namely, Indonesia, Malaysia, the Philippines, Singapore and Thailand in August 1967. Since then its membership has expanded to include Brunei, Myanmar (Burma), Cambodia, Laos and Vietnam.

References

Asian Development Bank (ADB). 2013. *Asian Economic Integration Monitor*. Manila, the Philippines. March.
——2010. *Institutions for Regional Integration*. Manila, the Philippines.
Baek, S. W. 2005. "Does China Follow 'the East Asian Development Model'?" *Journal of Contemporary Asia*. Vol. 35. No. 4, pp. 485–98.
Boltho, A. and M. Weber. 2009. "Did China follow the East Asian Development Model?" *The European Journal of Comparative Economics*. Vol. 6. No. 2, pp. 267–86.
Breslin, S. 2009. "Understanding China's Regional Rise: Interpretations, Identities and Implications". *International Affairs*. Vol. 85. No. 4, pp. 817–35.
Buiter, W. H. and E. Rahbari. 2011. "Global Growth Generators: Moving Beyond Emerging Markets and BRICs." *Policy Insight*. No. 55. London. Center for Economic Policy Research. April.
Das, Dilip K. 1992. *The Yen Appreciation and the International Economy*, London: Macmillan Press, and New York: New York University Press.
——1993. *Market-led Integration in the Asia-Pacific Region*. Fontainebleau, France. Euro-Asia Centre. European Institute of Business Administration (INSEAD), Research Series, No. 24. April. pp. 45.
——2005. "Market-Driven Regionalization in Asia." *Global Economy Journal*. Vol. 5. Issue 3. Article 2. The Berkeley Electronic Press. Berkeley, CA. Available online at www.bepress.com/cgi/viewcontent. cgi?article=1082&context=gej.
——2008a. *The Chinese Economic Renaissance: Apocalypse or Cornucopia*. Basingstoke: Palgrave Macmillan.
——2008b. *The Chinese Economy: Making a Global Niche*. Working Paper No. 239, March. Centre for the Study of Globalization and Regionalization, University of Warwick.

——2011. "China: Epitome of an Emerging Market." *Journal of Emerging Knowledge on Emerging Markets*. Vol. 3. No. 1, pp. 57–81.

——2012. "The Eurozone Financial Crisis and the Resilience of Asia's Economies." Daejeon, Korea. SolBridge International School of Business. Institute of Asian Business. Research Paper No. 2012–02. 15 April.

Economic Intelligence Unit (EIU). 2012. "Asia Competition Barometer." London. January.

Eichengreen, B., Y. C. Park and C. Wyplosz. 2008. "Introduction", in B. Eichengreen, Y. C. Park and C. Wyplosz (eds). *China, Asia and the New World Economy*. Oxford: Oxford University Press, pp. xv–xxii.

Findlay, R. and K. H. O'Rourke. 2007. *Power and Plenty: Trade, War and the World Economy in the Second Millennium*. Princeton, NJ: Princeton University Press.

Greenspan, A. 2000. "Global Challenges." Paper presented at the conference on *Financial Crises* by the Council on Foreign Relations, New York, 12 July. Available online at www.federalreserve.gov/boarddocs/speeches/2000/20000712.htm.

Henderson, J. 2008. "China and Global Development: Toward a Global-Asian Era?" *Contemporary Politics*. Vol. 14. No. 4, pp. 375–92.

Ito, T., A. Kojima, C. McKenzie and S. Urata. 2011. "Developments in Asian Finance." *Asian Economic Review*. Vol. 6, No. 1, pp. 157–75.

Kassel, J. 2012. "Asia's Lust for Labels Tempts Brands to Tap the Markets." *Financial Times*. 31 May, p. 5.

Kharas, H. J. 2010. "The Emerging Middle Class in Developing Countries." Paris: Organization for Economic Cooperation and Development. The Development Center. Working Paper No. 285. January.

Kohli, H. S., A. Sharma and A. Sood. 2011. *Asia 2050: Realizing the Asian Century*. New Delhi: Sage Publications India.

Kwon, H. J. 2012. *SERI Economic Report*. Samsung Economic Research Institute. Seoul. 30 July. Available online at www.seriworld.org/01/wldContV.html?mn=A&mncd=0301&key=20120730000004.

Lee, E. Y. 2013. "It May be Time to Lower the FDI Sluice Gate." *China Daily on Line*. Available online at http://europe.chinadaily.com.cn/epaper/2013–01/11/content_16104826.htm.

McKinsey Global Institute (MGI). 2012. *Manufacturing the Future*. San Francisco, CA: November.

Magnus, G. 2012. "Will Asia Shake or Shape the World Economy?" Brussels, Belgium: The European Center for International Political Economy. Policy Brief 05. July.

Neumann, F. and T. Arora. 2011. "Chart of the Week: Can Asia Save the World?" Hong Kong: HSBC Global Research. 26 August.

Nicita, A. and M. Olarreaga. 2006. *Trade, Production and Protection, 1976–2004*. Washington, DC: World Bank.

Okamoto, J. 2011. "Flexible Process for Integration in East Asia." *East Asia Economic Forum*. 30 January. Available online at www.eastasiaforum.org/2011/01/14/flexible-processes-for-integration-in-east-asia/.

Park, C. S. 2011. "China's Innovation Capability is Catching Korea's." *Weekly Insight*. Seoul: Samsung Economic Research Institute, 25 July, pp. 9–13.

Pei, M. 2011. "China's Cultural Devotion." *The Wall Street Journal Asia*. 9 November, p. 15.

Shambaugh, D. 2005. "The Rise of China and Asia's New Dynamics", in D. Shambaugh (ed.). *Power Shift: China and Asia's New Dynamics*. Berkeley, CA: University of California Press, pp. 1–18.

Siow, M. W. 2010. "Chinese Domestic Debates on Soft Power and Public Diplomacy." *East-West Center Asia Pacific Bulletin*. No. 86. 7 December.

Stiglitz, J. E. 2002. *Globalization and its Discontents*. New York and London: W. W. Norton.

Tambunan, T. 2006. "The Likely Impact of the ASEAN Plus China on Intra-ASEAN Trade." Paper presented at the conference held on *WTO, China and the ASEAN Economies*, in Beijing, 24–25 June.

Tang, S. and Y. Zhang. 2006. "China's Regional Strategy", in D. Shambaug (ed.). *Power Shift: China and Asia's New Dynamics*. Los Angeles, CA: University of California Press, pp. 48–68.

Vincelette, G. A., A. Manoel, A. Hansson and L. Kuijs. 2011. "China: Global Crisis Avoided, Robust Economic Growth Sustained", in M. K. Nabli (ed.). *The Great Recession and the Developing Countries: Economic Impact and Growth Prospects*. Washington, DC: World Bank, pp. 110–35.

United Nations Economic and Social Commission for Asia and Pacific (UNESCAP). 2011. *Asia-Pacific Trade and Investment Report 2011*. New York.

Urata, S. 2004. "The Shift from 'Market-Led to Institution-Led' Regional Economic Integration in East Asia." Tokyo: The Research Institute of Economy, Trade and Industry. Discussion paper No. 04-E-12.

Wade, R. 1990. *Governing the Market*. Princeton, NJ: Princeton University Press.

Wang, Y. 2008. "Public Diplomacy and the Rise of Chinese Soft Power." *Annals of the American Academy of Political and Social Sciences*. Vol. 616. No. 1, pp. 257–73.

Wang, Z. 2004. "Conceptualizing Economic Security and Governance: China Confronts Globalization." *The Pacific Review.* Vol. 17. No. 4, pp. 523–45.

World Bank (WB). 2010. *World Development Indicators 2010.* Washington, DC.

——2012. "East Asia and Pacific Data Monitor." Washington, DC. October.

World Development Indicators (WDI). 2012. Washington, DC: World Bank.

World Investment Report (WIR). 2012. United Nations Conference on Trade and Development. Geneva and New York. October.

World Trade Organization (WTO). 2011a. *International Trade Statistics 2010.* Geneva, Switzerland.

——2011b. "Trade Patterns and Global Value Chains in East Asia." Geneva, Switzerland. July.

——2012. "Trade Growth to Slow in 2012 after Strong Deceleration in 2011." Press Release. Press/658. Geneva, Switzerland. 12 April.

Ye, S. 2010. "China's Regional Policy in East Asia and its Characteristics." Nottingham: University of Nottingham. China Policy Institute. Discussion Paper No. 66. October.

Zheng, B. 2005. "China's 'Peaceful Rise' to Great Power Status." *Foreign Affairs.* Vol. 84. No. 5, pp. 18–24.

Zhou, Y. and S. Lall. 2005. "The Impact of China's FDI Surge on FDI in South-East Asia: Panel Data Analysis for 1986–2001." *Transnational Corporations.* Vol. 14. No. 1 pp. 41–65.

2

LAUNCHING ECONOMIC TRANSITION IN CHINA

Macroeconomic reforms and restructuring

> I think that when somebody writes the history of our time 50 or 100 years from now, it is unlikely to be about the great recession of 2008. It is also unlikely to be about the fiscal problems that America confronted in the second decade of the twenty-first century. It will be about how the world adjusted to the movement of the theatre of history towards China.
>
> Lawrence H. Summers (2010)

1. Introduction

In a short span of three decades the Middle Kingdom has come a long way. It has been transformed from a marginal economy to a global giant. The scale and quality of the People's Republic of China's (hereafter China) achievements deserve an accolade. Economists, public policy mandarins and decision-makers in the business community the world over have been awestruck by China's vertiginous gross domestic product (GDP) growth, relentless economic ascent, sustained capital accumulation, large changes in the sectoral composition of output, increasing urbanization, escalating regional and global heft and integration with the regional and global economies. The re-emergence of China represents the most profound economic event of the last three decades.

A crucial fact is that real GDP growth in China averaged 9.9 percent a year during 1978–2010. Such rapid, long-term growth without an episode of hyperinflation or recession was unimaginable by any academic scholar or policy mandarin when the Chinese economy began its fêted U-turn in 1978. A growth target of doubling the GDP between 1978 and 2000 was taken by external observers with considerable skepticism. It was achieved in 1995, well before the target year. To put this accomplishment into perspective, it should be mentioned that during 1950–78, the pre-reform era, China's average annual growth rate of real GDP was a mere 4 percent (Brandt and Rawski, 2008). The rapid post-1978 GDP growth rate has had the predictable impact on society and living standards. If compound annual growth is measured, this vigorous GDP growth rate can be seen as doubling the Chinese GDP every seven years. Contemporary China is an indomitable economic force in the global arena. It contributed to the recovery from the global financial crisis (2007–09). Subsequently when many advanced economies suffered from weaknesses and slow growth, it contributed to regional and global GDP growth. Notwithstanding the setbacks, it was putting up with the ongoing Eurozone crisis resiliently.

The objective of this chapter is first to provide an exposition of the fact that instituting market-oriented macro-economic reforms, liberalizing the economy and institutional upgrading turned China, a centrally planned command economy, productively and profitably toward market mechanism and a free-enterprise economy.[1] These strategic measures created immense synergy and opened prosperous vistas of economic transformation for the Chinese economy. The second theme is to highlight China's stupendous economic achievements following reforms and liberalization. The end result of these measures drew approbation of academics, policy mandarins and business leaders in the rest of the world. Initially this transformation was slow but it accelerated since the early 1990s, albeit state control of the economy has not been abandoned. It continued to operate in several important areas and state-owned enterprises (SOEs) are a significant part of the economy. Several largest ones among them have turned into multinationals. Factor prices continue to be an important part of one of the state controls. Continued government intervention in the economy and financial markets gave rise to the term "Beijing Consensus". It may be taken for economic authoritarianism, which is the antithesis of neo-liberal and market-oriented economic concepts. However, as explained in Section 2.1, it was China's unique path to growth and development.

1.1 Three purposeful decades of meritorious achievements

The post-1978 economic transformation and modernization of China was essentially the consequence of the marriage of thoroughgoing macro-economic reforms, foreign technological know-how, domestic labor and globalizing markets and economies. Sustained rapid growth not only transformed the economy but also the society. The so-called China model of growth portends to a distinctive relationship between markets and government, or even market, government and society. In its growth process China evolved a system of complex interaction of inter-related processes of becoming a market economy, the process of technology transfer and innovation, and the process of learning and adapting to new economic realities (Jefferson, 2008). It bears repeating the cliché that in close to three decades, in terms of real economic activity, China achieved a position of immense significance and became an ascendant economic power in the global economy.[2]

The China model has produced successful economic growth. A valid question is whether it is a replicable model. Although there is no dearth of admirers of the China model in the developing world, it needs to be noted that China has followed several neo-classical, neo-liberal, economic policies. An identical strategy was also adopted by the dynamic Asian economies with commendable outcome. The most important ones are adopting market-oriented reforms, liberalization of the economy and encouraging domestic and foreign investment, adopting flexible labor laws, lightening the regulatory burden, taking a conservative fiscal stance and improving economic infrastructure. This went hand-in-hand with an authoritarian system of one-party government.

As the largest emerging market economy (EME), the largest creditor country, the largest exporter, the largest trader, the largest exporter of high-technology manufactured products, the fastest growing economy, the oldest continuous civilization and still run by a one-party communist bureaucracy, China occupies a unique position. As a political unit, China is the oldest continuously existing entity in the world. It was founded by Qin Shi Huangdi, meaning the first emperor, in 221 BC. For a large part of its existence it was known as *Zhonguo* or the Middle Kingdom. For a large part of its history China held the position of the largest economy in the world, notably between 1300 and 1820 (Maddison, 2006). Until the beginning of the 19th century China and

Western Europe had comparable living standards (Pomeranz, 2000). After almost two centuries of conflict and humiliation by foreign powers, China is on its way to returning to the center of the global economy. Its re-emergence as a regional and global power has been extraordinarily rapid.

Reforms and restructuring measures had a deterministic effect on China's rate and pattern of growth. China rose from a marginal and systemically insignificant economy in 1980 to the sixth largest in 2000 and the third largest in 2007. At market exchange rates, it became the second largest in the world in mid-2010 (Table 2.1; Figure 2.1).[3] Since 1968, Japan was the second largest economy in the world. After 42 years it ceded its high perch to China. This was a real economic

TABLE 2.1 China's GDP, 1978–2011, at current prices and exchange rates and in terms of PPP (current international $)

Year	GDP (billions of nominal $)	GDP in PPP (current international $)
1978	148.2	n/a
1979	176.6	n/a
1980	189.4	245.5
1981	194.1	282.4
1982	203.2	326.9
1983	228.5	376.9
1984	257.4	450.5
1985	306.7	526.9
1986	297.8	586.1
1987	270.4	673.2
1988	309.5	775.4
1989	344.0	837.6
1990	356.9	902.4
1991	379.5	1,018.9
1992	422.7	1,188.1
1993	440.5	1,384.1
1994	559.2	1,597.3
1995	728.0	1,812.6
1996	856.1	2,029.2
1997	952.7	2,260.7
1998	1,019.5	2,471.2
1999	1,083.3	2,698.0
2000	1,198.5	2,987.9
2001	1,324.8	3,309.3
2002	1,453.8	3,669.1
2003	1,641.0	4,121.0
2004	1,931.6	4,664.8
2005	2,256.9	5,364.3
2006	2,713.0	6,240.5
2007	3,494.1	7,333.3
2008	4,521.8	8,215.0
2009	4,991.3	9,066.2
2010	5,930.5	10,124.4
2011	7,318.5	11,379.2
2012	n/a	n/a

Source: World Bank. 2013. *World Development Indicators Online Database, 2013*. Washington, DC.

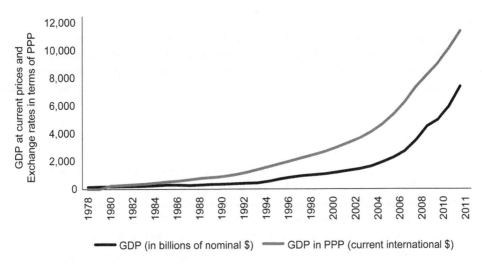

FIGURE 2.1 China's GDP, 1978–2011
Source: World Bank. 2013. *World Development Indicators Online Database, 2013*. Washington, DC.

miracle. In 2011 China's GDP at market prices and exchange rates reached $7,318.5 billion, although the National Bureau of Statistics (NBS) has a slightly different figure. The size of the GDP cake according to the NBS was $7,301.06 in 2011 and per caput GDP $5,432 (NBS, 2012). In a succinct manner, this chapter traces the myriad stages, events and structural transformations along China's growth path. Not ignoring the downside of rapid growth, this chapter also highlights the structural and macroeconomic imbalances created in the Chinese and the global economies. It contends that after three decades of meritorious economic performance and GDP growth, it is imperative that China change its growth model and move to a different and more sustainable growth trajectory. The methodology used in this chapter is descriptive analysis.[4]

While turning from the non-market economic system to the free-market doctrine, the government emphasized prudent fiscal policy, privatization, maintaining a balanced budget and aiming for low inflation. Switching from a centrally planned, command economy framework to a market mechanism was not only a momentous policy change but also "was the single most important cause of the on-going expansion in productivity" (Bernanke, 2006). Turning to the free-market system also explains China's export success "much more than the principle of comparative advantage" (Rodrik, 2006a). It should, however, be clarified that China is not a free-market economy but a mixed economy, with strong market economic features.

That being said, market-oriented reforms were not conducted in the proper sequential manner that a neoclassical economist would recommend. They were not only carried out in an unorthodox and asymmetric manner but there were also inordinate delays in reforming some important sectors. An important example is the reform of the trade regime. In the initial phase of reforms when the government abandoned quantitative planning of trade, it began by adopting a heavily protectionist trade regime.

However, market-oriented macro-economic reforms triggered a shift in the utilization of human resources from agriculture to manufacturing and service sectors. The reforms were essentially based on changes in the price system. *Inter alia*, they brought about the market-determined pricing system in China, which in turn was instrumental in efficient resource allocation in the economy. It increased the overall level of efficiency in the economy and gave birth to a dynamic private sector. The rapid expansion of this sector, brisk GDP growth and continuing economic transformation over the preceding three decades altered China's economy structurally in a striking manner. Current economic expansion, driven largely by growth of the private sector, is expected to continue over the medium term. As China adopted an outward-oriented growth strategy, supported by institutional innovations like the special economic zones (SEZs), it began summarily integrating both regionally and globally. This process in turn began to significantly influence the regional and global economies, their growth rates, growth patterns and growth dynamics. As China's integration deepened, its influence on the regional and global economies intensified. China's accelerated integration into the regional and global economies led to significant relocation of labor-intensive industries in China from other parts of Asia and the advanced economies.

With the prompt and timely support of counter-cyclical macro-economic policy measures, China weathered the global financial maelstrom of 2007–09 resiliently, which indisputably accentuated its importance in the regional and global economies. Although China's GDP growth decelerated during the crisis period, the economy never suffered a recession. Chinese demand helped to pull a number of economies into recovery. It led the global recovery and contributed to the recovery efforts of the Asian EMEs. Without China's support the so-called Great Recession would have been more severe, deeper and lasted longer (Das, 2011). Although in the 1990s it was a commonplace EME, that is no longer true. It has become an obvious exception because it figures so prominently among global policy makers, business executives and investment officials. Although still an EME, which is not a member of the reputable and esteemed Organization for Economic Cooperation and Development (OECD), by some measures China was a wealthy country in the second decade of the twenty-first century. Vying to be a space power, its technological competence is comparable to more advance economies. In September 2011 China launched a space station, *Tiangong-1*. It has also publicized a plan for upgrading its Long March rockets so that it can have high-resolution earth-observation satellites and put a man on the moon.

During the Great Recession and recovery China, in collaboration with some of the other Asian EMEs, continued to drive global growth (Das, 2011). During the global recession of 2009, the Chinese economy displayed an astounding ability to grow at 9.2 percent. In 2009 China's share of global growth was almost the same as all the advanced industrial economies put together. In 2010 the year of global recovery, China accounted for about a third of global growth (Makin, 2011). After growing at the rate of 10.4 percent in 2010, the Chinese economy was showing no signs of slowing down or descending to a lower growth trajectory in 2011. The International Monetary Fund (IMF, 2011) has projected its 2011 GDP growth rate at 9.6 percent and 2012 growth rate at 9.5 percent.[5] However, due to sovereign debt crisis in the Eurozone these projections were subsequently pared down to 8 percent (IMF, 2012a and 2012b). At this juncture, China's economic boom has entered into its fourth decade.

While the global financial crisis and recession (2007–09) left deleterious effects over other economies, particularly over the advanced industrial economies, they managed to enhance China's relative regional and global economic and financial prominence. The post-global financial crisis Chinese economy is widely regarded as the principal engine of regional and global growth. Furthermore, while affected by the ongoing Eurozone crisis through the trade channel, China was putting up with it in a practical and pliant manner (Das, 2012).

While China had unique achievements, not everything was *sui generis*. China's striking growth performance motivated a search for an alternative growth path for the developing economies and EMEs. In its success there are numerous lessons for the other developing economies, particularly in the areas of local initiatives, integrating with the regional and global economies, making foreign direct investment (FDI) an effective instrument of development and importing and adjusting to new technologies and building quality infrastructure.

2. Macro-economic reforms and restructuring

Although Hua Guofeng initiated the economic reforms after the death of Mao Zedong, Deng Xiaoping, who served as the paramount leader between 1978 and 1992, was the principal force behind implementing them (Vogel, 2011). Under his leadership macro-economic reforms and the so-called "open-door policy" were adopted at the historic Third Party Plenum of the Communist Party of China (CPC) in December 1978.[6] The new party leader was determined to modernize China and open it to the world. Politically skillful, Deng provided clear direction to reforms. He had the judgement to pace them and maintain the support of the senior cadres in the CPC, many of whom sincerely mistrusted them. He earnestly urged top officials to chart a new course of development. Under his leadership China reversed its course and decided to embrace globalization. By the time Deng stepped down in 1992, China was well on its way to being a prosperous and modern economy. The economic surge that began in 1992 was significant (Table 2.1; Figure 2.1). It rendered China free from its planned-economy straitjacket.

Deng Xiaoping was widely considered the intellectual father of the liberal and pragmatic economic strategy that China adopted in the post-1978 era, but Zhao Ziyang, the Secretary-General of the CPC, was the one who had originally conceived it.[7] His economic thinking and policies were progressive for their time and place. He had visualized and developed what became known as the "preliminary stage theory", which in fact was the course for transforming the Chinese socialist non-market system and set the stage for much of the economic liberalization that was undertaken subsequently.[8] It laid the groundwork for the prosperity that China enjoys at present. To convince the CPC top-brass about the assured superiority of progressive liberal economic concepts, Zhao Ziyang had first implemented his liberal and pragmatic economic theories, which included macroeconomic reforms and restructuring, in Sichuan province in the early 1970s. He had favorable results to show to the CPC leadership, which was eventually convinced regarding the adoption of the market economy route to economic prosperity.

Deng had little experience in economic affairs and in 1978 did not have a plan regarding how to improve the impoverished Chinese economy. He did have a framework for thinking about how to proceed. He wanted to open the country for science, technology and premium economic ideas and management systems from anywhere in the world. He was suitably impressed with the economic performance of Japan and the newly industrialized economies (NIEs) of Asia,[9] but was also aware that he could not import an entire economic system. It needed to fit the unique needs of China. He also realized that free-market economies did not always succeed and that one needed to build institutions to support them. He encouraged senior officials to "expand their horizons, to go anywhere to learn what brings success, to bring back promising technology and management practices, and to experiment to see what would work at home" (Vogel, 2011, p. 3).

As China did not have knowledge and experience in conceiving and devising reforms, local initiatives sprung up and were subsequently encouraged officially to play an increasing role in market-oriented experiments. Coase and Wang (2012) argued that Chinese leaders did not make a concerted attempt to create a capitalist society. They contend that it was the so-called "marginal revolutions" that introduced market mechanism and entrepreneurship to China. Adam Smith's concept of market economy was guided by the traditional Confucian principle of "seeking truth from facts". By turning to capitalism, China returned to its own cultural roots.

A familiar fact is that macro-economic reforms, liberalization and institutional changes in China started without a well laid-out blueprint. They were based on gradual, incremental, exploratory and somewhat experimental changes. Deng Xiaoping's metaphor "crossing the river by feeling the stones" (*mozhe shitou guohe*) became well known. This aphorism not only strongly influenced the early reform measures but also was applicable to reforms during the latter years. China's gradualist reforms eventually proved to be radical and deep.

The experimental nature of reforms was reflected in their implementation first of all on a trial basis in some locations particularly the SEZs (as noted below). After learning from that trial, dispelling the deficient policies and subsequently implementing them on economy-wide basis. This approach provided time for preparing and changing institutions. Secondly, following an inter-mediate method for transforming the economy to a market-oriented path in a phased manner represented the same experimental approach. An excellent example is the creation of SEZs for gradually introducing foreign capital and technology as well as adopting the market mechanism in a gradual manner.

Those who implemented Deng's reforms believed in his dictum of "doing what works" or "seeking truth from fact" and assigned a high premium to pragmatism. That said, the Five-Year Plans focused on economic development and did provide the direction of change and targets of sectoral growth. Economic reforms began in the agricultural sector in the countryside and were not initiated in the urban-industrial sector until 1984. In China's economic transformation highly effective agricultural reforms had an important place (Arrighi, 2007). When China embarked on its transition path from a centrally planned economy to a market economy, it combined three for-midable tasks of structural transformation, economic liberalization and institutional transition into one (Lin and Wang, 2008). China managed this three-in-one transition with enormous skill, efficiency and alacrity, although the extent of transition differed in these three areas. Government intervention during the reform phase was both heavy and extensive. Many EMEs and developing economies have been trying to emulate China's stellar success in macro-economic reforms and liberalization.

The political elite did come to the realization that a thorough macro-economic reform program was the only feasible way to alleviate abject poverty, modernize the economy, boost its efficiency and make it competitive. Adopting a dual-track approach in its economic reforms enabled China to achieve "both stability and dynamic transformation simultaneously" (Lin, 2011a, p. 3). The expediency of their policy direction and earnestness of implementation were the keys to their success. They were also cognizant of the value of upgrading their institutions. They realized that post-war Japan had succeeded in catching up with the advanced economies of the West by, *inter alia*, upgrading its institutional structure through emulative learning (Ozawa, 2009).

SEZs were effectively used as an instrument for promoting reforms. Conditions for market economy were tested and tried in the SEZs first. Once this experiment showed that a market economy tended to be dynamic, a domestic constituency was formed that not only supported reforms but also wanted their countrywide expansion (as alluded to above). The achievement of SEZs was to be the early reform zones in the Chinese economy and demonstrate the benefits of good economic governance. To that end, an environment of sound physical infrastructure, enabling services and market-friendly institutions was created in the SEZs before it was done in the other parts of the economy. The resulting high productivity in the SEZs and special export-processing zones (EPZs) had the demonstration effect.[10] It spilled over into the non-SEZ regions and into the

SOEs. By 1994, the special economic and business environment that was carefully and painstakingly created in SEZs and EPZs was essentially expanded to the rest of the economy. As the market-oriented economy developed in SEZs and EPZs, firms began demanding greater property rights, independent courts and less government interference.

2.1 Rejecting the Washington consensus

The Washington Consensus was an attempt to specify a list of ten institutional arrangements that would optimize economic growth in a developing milieu (Williamson, 1990). Many countries following it recorded poor growth. Both proponents and critics of Washington Consensus concur that the policies spawned by it did not produce the desired results (Rodrik, 2006b, 2008; Henry, 2007; Estevadeordal and Taylor, 2008; Stiglitz, 2008a). Subsequently the consensus in Washington shifted from getting policies right to getting institutions right. The fact that China rejected certain aspects of the conventional wisdom of Washington consensus cannot be ignored.[11] While macro-economic reforms and liberalization were undertaken to institute, advance and synergize the market forces in the economy, it was never forgotten that the state plays a role in the development of an economy. The macro-economic reforms and restructuring were so successful because the state participated in the reform process in a methodical manner. China is a developmental state.

Like Japan and the NIEs of Asia, wisely China did not reject several policy strands prescribed by the Washington Consensus, namely, the neoliberal policies like macro-economic stabilization, responsible fiscal policies, trade liberalization, attracting FDI and partial privatization. Free market reforms became the growth engine for China. There also were strategies that were not compatible with the Washington Consensus.

Like Japan and the NIEs of Asia, China rejected some aspects of the Washington Consensus. In Japan, the NIEs and subsequently in China, the so-called industrial policy was regarded as an intrinsic ingredient of the development process. Selective government was a part of it. These economies firmly believed in guided development, where the government had a decisive role in the economy. Industrial policy had actively supported and promoted successful industrialization in the Republic of Korea (hereinafter Korea), Singapore and Taiwan. One little-known fact is that in the past it played the same role in Germany, Japan and the USA as well.[12] Broadly considered, industrial policy is taken to encompass government policies relating to trade, science and technology, policies affecting FDI, allocation of financial resources and supporting infant industry. These government policies also govern and shape developmental institutions and economic actors and are the ultimate adjudicator of what can be managed by market forces and what cannot (Cimoli et al., 2009).

The so-called Beijing consensus is not a growth principle or theory but merely socialistic implementation of market economy ideas. This is a definitional issue. Beijing consensus is a blend of the two seemly contradictory doctrines. Under the Beijing consensus, Chinese policy makers adopted the path of macro-economic reforms and restructuring. While they liberalized domestic economy and integrated it regionally and globally, it was done under firm government control. The state's role in guiding economic development continued to remain an accepted maxim. While the market mechanism is of importance, the government's strong macro-regulatory function cannot be ignored. Chinese policy mandarins believed that the government needs to actively guide the economy. This strategy assured political stability and eventually improved living standards in society.

In addition, while markets are the basic mechanism for effective resource allocation, the process of development requires industrial upgrading and improvement in hard and soft infrastructures. This is where government has a decisive role to play (Lin, 2011b). China succeeded in achieving something of an economic miracle by pursuing this growth paradigm in which both markets and state mutually play a role in the economic growth process. Lin (2010, p. 23) went on to note that Government intervention in an economy is "indispensable for helping economies move from one stage of development to another". Since the global financial crisis (2007–09) a supportive ambiance has been created for the role of government in an economy. It has become heterodox wisdom of the post-global financial crisis period.

2.2 Stages of economic reforms and liberalization

As the reforms had begun in an experimental manner, the dual-track price system was adopted in 1984, which was helpful in the progress of their implementation. It opened the door for economic incentives to play a constructive role in the decision-making process in the SOEs. Lau *et al.* (2000) contended that the dual-track price system brought Pareto improvements to the Chinese economy. Many other researchers also believe that to be true (Yao, 2009). This is not to deny that the dual-track system had some serious drawbacks as well.

Both reforms and developments in China's trade and investment regimes conformed to the basic patterns of Chinese comparative advantage, which yielded important benefits to China and its trading partners. By 2007, when the global financial crisis broke out in the US financial market and subsequently spilled into the real economy, China had devoted close to three decades to broad-based, market-oriented, macroeconomic reforms and restructuring as well as regional and global integration.[13] The reforms had an enormous macroeconomic impact. They unleashed a large amount of entrepreneurial energy and propelled continuous capital accumulation. Productivity gains of large proportion in the economy are attributed to them. Most importantly, they helped to make both labor and capital more productive. The rising productivity was reflected in accelerating GDP growth rate. This is not to deny the role of the other driving forces behind GDP growth, however. During the three decades of reforms virtually every indicator of economic well-being improved, in many cases appreciably.

Chronologically the reforms occurred in four broad stages:

- The first stage (1978–84) involved the reforms of collective farming, the hallmark of all the non-market economies of the erstwhile era. Farming was decentralized to household units. This was the stage of rural reforms. Prices for the farm products were adjusted upwards. Rural industrialization was spearheaded by township and village enterprises (TVE) that operated outside state control. During the first two decades of reforms, they were the most dynamic sector in the Chinese economy. Some SOEs were allowed to retain their profits.
- Orderly reforms of SOEs began around 1985 and continued into the 1990s. Workers and managers were given incentives to improve efficiency. Subsequently through a combination of management and worker buyouts, a significant part of the public sector was transferred into private hands. In 1995 the State Council endorsed a policy of retaining the large SOEs and allowing the small one to be released. In 1997 it further envisaged a large shift of ownership from the central government to municipalities, with the explicit goals of expediting privatization. In the late 1990s many of the SOEs were closed and also allowed to go bankrupt. During the mid-1990s, small and medium-sized SOEs in the rich coastal provinces were privatized and the government began selling stakes in the large ones.
- Deng Xiaoping's celebrated historic visit to Guangdong province and Shenzhen in 1992 motivated an innovative round of macroeconomic reforms, liberalization measures and privatization.

The CPC officially accepted Deng's stance that market economy system is not incompatible with the ideals of socialism. The economy was opened up further and the inflows of FDI accelerated. Also, exports from the manufacturing sector picked up momentum. Deng's tour also created an investment rush in the economy and excess capacity in several industrial sectors resulted. SOE reforms continued. Over the 1995–2001 period the number of SOEs fell from 1.2 million to 468,000 (*The Economist*, 2011a). However, during this period other SOEs were created with different forms of state-support. Experiments on incentives and structures persistently continued. Foreign investment was also sought for privatization of large SOEs.

- The post-Asian Crisis (1997–98) reforms, which essentially represented the second generation of economic reforms for which the economy was ready. During this phase broader and general liberalization of the economy took place. World Trade Organization (WTO) accession (in December 2001) was a crucial milestone in China's journey towards transformation to a market economy. Valiant reforms and restructuring measures were implemented during this period, making 2001 a defining moment in reforms. Trade and foreign investment liberalization measures were further broadened. For accession to the WTO China had to relax more than 7,000 tariffs, quotas and other kinds of trade barriers. Also, following the WTO accession, agriculture and services sectors were speedily opened up. During the post-WTO accession phase, growth became heavily dependent on export and investment. Specific accession commitments were largely met in the first five years.

    A lot of credit for carrying out major macro-economic reforms is deservedly given to Premier Zhu Rongji (1998–2003), a pragmatic political leader who demanded a strong work ethic from his followers. His contribution to China's economic transformation was nothing short of momentous. A gifted political leader, he was courageous, far-sighted and enterprising enough to pull the plug on thousands of SOEs as well as endorse and promote measures for opening up the SOEs for foreign capital and for trying to inculcate market discipline in them.

One of the most significant consequences of the market-oriented reforms, domestic price liberalization and growing integration with the world economy was increasing the market determination of prices in the Chinese economy. In particular, traded goods prices achieved substantial convergence with world market prices. Thus, reform implementation helped link the Chinese economy to the world market prices, which in turn led to a dramatic conversion in its economic structure.

However, it must be mentioned that not all prices in China are market determined and that China's transition to a market economy is still incomplete. On the positive side, an important lesson for the developing economies is that China took a pragmatic and meticulous approach to economic reforms and liberalization. The economic agents displayed an admirable adaptive capacity to the economic reform process. Political leadership in China was unique and astute in choosing a practicable and result-oriented economic path. It enabled China to succeed in the inordinately complex task of integrating with the ever-evolving regional and global economies.

3. Unilateral trade liberalization and export expansion

Perhaps the most important of the liberalization measures was the adoption of export-led growth. This one policy move enabled China to integrate in the regional and global economies through trade and investment. It facilitated exploitation of comparative advantage, which included a comparative advantage stemming from an abundant labor supply. Although it was delayed, China undertook a great deal of imaginative unilateral trade liberalization. In this China moved with the surrounding Asian economies, which often moved ahead of WTO obligations. According to Lardy (2003, p. 3) China continuously adopted policy measures to "transform its economy from one of the most protected to ... the most open among the EMEs". The consequences were obvious. Since 1988, China's exports grew at an annualized rate of 17 percent, more than twice the rate of growth of world exports.

To put it in perspective, in 1977 on the eve of launching economic reforms, China's total trade was $20 billion. At this point, it was the 13th largest trader in the world and its share of world trade was a trifling 0.6 percent. However, in 2000 its total trade was $475 billion and it was the seventh largest trading economy in the world. Although the growth rate of multilateral trade expansion decelerated after 2000, Chinese trading performance continued to be robust. In 2001 and 2002 China overtook Canada and the United Kingdom (UK) in terms of the value of multilateral trade, respectively, to hold the position of the sixth and the fifth largest trading economy. At this juncture China had become a major trading economy of global significance. In 2003 it surpassed France to be the fourth largest.

The rate of trade growth in China was much faster than that of multilateral trade. Between 1978 and 1990, both its exports and imports soared, growing at more or less similar pace. What is noteworthy is that in the 1990s rate of export growth picked up and after 2000 they accelerated at even higher rate. The long-term (1978–2010) average annual growth of foreign trade was 16.3 percent. In 2007 the year in which global financial crisis struck, they were 9 percent of total multilateral trade and 38 percent of China's GDP. This was a small, 1-percent decline from the previous year when they were 39 percent of GDP. The global financial crisis caused the collapse of multilateral trade and China's exports declined to 36 percent of GDP in 2008 and further down to 27 percent in 2009. Likewise, China's imports also contracted (WB, 2011a). In current dollars, China's annual average trade growth rate for the 1990–2010 period was a remarkable 17.6 percent. In 2010 China accounted for 10.4 percent of total merchandise exports and 9.1 percent of imports. In 2011 while the share of exports remained the same, but the share of exports edged up to 9.5 percent (WTO, 2012). It is the largest trading partner of almost every other country. For obvious reasons, Canada and Mexico are two exceptions to this rule.

A significant point in this regard is that throughout the reform period both exports and imports increased steadily and simultaneously. Thus, China is not only a seller of goods and services to the regional and global economies but also a buyer from them. In 2010 a recovery year, China's exports of goods and services were 29.8 percent of the GDP and imports 25.9 percent of the GDP (WB, 2011a).

China achieved regional and global integration in its own, somewhat unconventional, manner. The appropriate neoclassical strategy to achieve this objective entails swift dismantling of quantitative restrictions on imports, sharp reduction in import tariffs as well as their dispersion, convertibility of currency for the purpose of current account, the truncation of bureaucratic formalities and eradication of red tape and other barriers to FDI inflows, and improvement in the efficiency of customs procedures. China disregarded these policy guidelines. It did liberalize its economy, but the opening-up process was exceedingly slow. Although state monopoly of trade was removed early, in the late 1970s it was initially not supplanted with a liberal free-trade regime. Instead a complex policy structure of a highly restrictive set of tariffs and non-tariff barriers (NTBs) and licenses began operating. Tariffs were in fact raised in the early 1980s. The average statutory tariff rate in 1982 was 56 percent, high by any norms. Even in 1990 average unweighted tariffs in China were 44 percent, among the highest in the world. The standard deviation of dispersion of tariff rates was also exceedingly high and maximum tariffs were above 200 percent. Dismantling of this complicated and restrictive trade regime did not begin until the early 1990s (Rodrik, 2006a).

China's trade growth was more rapid than its GDP growth. While GDP grew between 1995 and 2005 by approximately 100 percent, export growth outstripped GDP growth by 62 percent (WB, 2010a). Over the 1995–2005 decade, export-to-GDP ratio rose by 59 percent (Harris and Robertson, 2009). Export steadily rose from a low base and in the post-2000 period they reached more than a third of GDP and they became a major driver of economic growth. Also, evidence is available to prove that productivity growth was higher in the export sectors than in the non-tradable goods sectors (Perkins, 1997; Amighini, 2005). In 2009 China's total trade was $2,208 billion and in 2010 it was $2,973 billion (WTO, 2010a and 2011). In 2009 it beat Germany to reach the top of the WTO league table. This spectacular rise as the largest trader was certainly a momentous development, more surprising than the impressive rise of Germany and Japan. In 2011 value of China's merchandise trade increased to $3,642 billion, when it accounted for 10.4 percent of total multilateral exports and 9.5 percent of imports (WTO, 2012).

A significant source of dynamic gains from opening up of an economy to international trade is increased competition in the domestic market created by large imports. They in turn contributed to a radical transformation of the economy—particularly in the manufacturing sector. Trade liberalization would not have been successful without *pari passu* implementation of supportive policies changes. They included liberalization of the old rigid system of exchange controls, reform of the pricing and allocation of foreign exchange system and correcting the overvaluation of renminbi. In real terms the currency depreciated by 70 percent over the 1980–95 period. Government began providing rebate on indirect taxes which reduced the profitability of exporting firms. Also, current-account transactions were made convertible, while the inconvertibility of capital account was maintained.

3.1 Effects of vertical fragmentation of trade

Although China was slow to open its trade regime, opening the import regime was given an impetus by rapid expansion of processing trade, also known as vertical specialization or international production fragmentation. Production process is fragmented or "unbundled" into distinct tasks, which are then located in different countries to minimize costs. An array of alternatives terms like production fragmentation, production networks, network trade, value-added processes, vertical specialization, vertical integration, supply chain, slicing the value chain (Krugman, 1995), outsourcing (Hanson et al., 2001), international production sharing (Ng and Yeats, 2001) and off-shoring are used to describe it. Peter Drucker (1977) coined and used the term "production sharing". Over the post-1990 period this activity became very important for Asia and the Asian economies.

An identical term, "processing trade", implies importing inputs and components and assembling them for export. It has been rendered possible by rapid advances in production technology and technological innovations in transportation and communications, which have enabled firms to unbundle the stages of production so that different tasks can be efficaciously and competitively performed in different locales. It makes a firm more productive and profitable. Proximity facilitates formation of value chains and integrates real sector of the neighboring economies. Processing trade enhances productivity all participating countries benefit from gains in productivity (Johnson and Noguera, 2012). An excellent example is Japanese electronics firms, which continued to prosper and grow because they have moved their assembly lines to China and other parts of Asia. Given the high Japanese cost structure, they could not be run in Japan.

Network production or processing trade radically transformed the nature of global trade. It became a defining characteristic of economic globalization. It essentially relied on declining costs of transportation and communication (Feenstra, 2010). Under this innovative method of production, the manufacturing process is sliced thinly into many stages. The fragmented production process is then carried out in different locations in different countries. Product fragments typically go through multiple border crossings before being incorporated in a final product. The final production of the finished product involves the collaboration and participation of many firms dispersed in different countries, which in turn are at different stages of development. Each country specializes in different segments of the vertical production chain. Therefore international competition takes place not at the industry or firm level but at the level of individual tasks. These value chains are the centerpiece of regionalization and globalization of economies. Regionalization is an important facet of globalization. It waxes and wanes with regionalization. In a seminal paper Yi (2003) established that vertical specialization of trade is more sensitive to changes in trade costs than regular trade. Vertical fragmentation of trade has grown into a global phenomenon.

Owing to the fragmentation of production, contemporary international trade is increasingly dominated by trade in parts, components, intermediate products and subassemblies. Processing trade originated in electronics and then spread to a wide array of industries. Principal among them are autos, cameras and watches, clothing, chemicals, electrical machinery, machine tools, office equipment, pharmaceuticals, printing and publishing, radio receivers, sewing machines and sports footwear. Processing trade began in electronic and garments in the 1960s. It continued to be prominent in information and communication technology (ICT) products, which was an important line for the Chinese exporters. In 2004 China became the biggest exporter of ICT goods ($180 billion), surpassing the US ($149 billion) (OECD, 2010a). Fragmentation of the production process refined the classical economic concept of comparative advantage.

Rapid export growth in East and Southeast Asian economies was the result of the fast expanding intermediate goods trade. As different sub-regions of Asia have significant diversity in labor supply conditions and wages, labor-intensive tasks could be easily moved to lower-wage economies. In addition, the general liberal trade and investment environment in the Asian economies and efficient ports and communication systems made it possible to run well-organized and economical production chains. Also, rapid GDP growth in the Asian economies led to fast structural transformation in them and swift expansion in their market size as well as outsourcing (ADB, 2012).

As noted above, transformation of policy structure in this manner had far-reaching macroeconomic implications. After these reforms were implemented and the Chinese domestic price structure was linked to that of the world market, Chinese firms found that they could specialize in accordance with their comparative advantage. Consumers could realize the resulting gains from trade. The principle of comparative advantage is as valid today as it was in 1817 when David Ricardo conceived it.

The trade in parts and components has been particularly prominent in China's business dealings with its neighbors. The Chinese firms involved in processing trade had the privilege of duty-free imports of raw materials, intermediate inputs, and parts and components they needed for producing the exportable products. In 1987 the government further expanded these incentives for the exporting firms. A duty drawback system was instituted that supported China's massive export processing industries. Export-processing firms were treated as privileged firms. In addition, joint ventures and wholly foreign-owned enterprises were allowed to import capital goods duty-free. China emerged as a low-cost assembly center and manufacturing hub, which contributed to trade integration in the region.

In the latter half of the 1980s China became involved in the vertically integrated production networks with the other Asian economies. Firms from Hong Kong, Taiwan and the other Asian economies began relocating their labor-intensive industries and processes into China. To promote exports, government provided tariff-free imports for processing and re-exporting. This resulted in a dual trade regime, namely, processing trade that entailed export based on imported parts and components and customary non-processing exports based on local inputs. The latter was dominated by domestic firms. Imports for processing increased rapidly during the 1990s. The foreign-invested enterprises (FIEs) played an imported role in China's processing trade—or vertical specialization. In 2001 they accounted for 50 percent of China's exports and 52 percent of imports (Lemoine and Unal-Kesenci, 2004). A high degree of duality of Chinese trade remained a persistent feature for a long time.

This trend of assembling and processing of imported inputs went on intensifying. By the mid-2000s foreign firms and their affiliates dominate the network production in China. Close to 60 percent of China's total trade and 80 percent of processing trade was controlled by them (Gaulier et al., 2007). The manufactured goods exported by China have a high import content (OECD, 2010b). Using a new Chinese dataset, Dean et al. (2007) measured the degree of vertical specialization in China's exports. Their results showed that vertical specialization in China's exports to the world was more than 30 percent in 2002. In some product lines, like plastic products, steel processing, communication equipment, industrial machinery, metal products and computers, it was much higher, more than 50 percent. There was "strong evidence of the importance and persistence of an Asian supplier network to China. About 58 percent of China's vertical specialization in 2002 was attributable to imports from Japan, Taiwan, Korea and other Southeast Asian countries" (Dean et al., 2007, p. 13). Vertical specialization of China's trade with the USA the European Union-15 (EU-15) and Canada was found to be 30 percent. Trade with Singapore and Taiwan also had a comparable degree of vertical specialization. A recent calculation by the World Bank (2011) puts division between processing and non-processing activities for 2010 as equal.

An important benefit of processing trade was that the skill content of Chinese manufacturing export increased markedly. This was essentially due to the imported inputs that went into assembling exports. The skill content of China's manufactured exports remained unchanged once processing trade is excluded (Amiti and Freund, 2010). China's exports did become increasingly sophisticated, which could partly be the result of the learning externalities in processing trade. As production networks in Asia grew, sharing of production processes between China and its neighbors increased, which in turn led to a marked reorganization of industrial production in Asia. Growth in production networks also propelled China to the top of the world export league.

Production networks have enabled China to maintain its competitive edge in the global markets. Although the renminbi appreciate by more than 5.5 percent between June 2010 and June 2011, yet export figures for the first half of 2011 were $874 billion, 20 percent higher than a year earlier. Other than gainfully using production networks, Chinese manufacturers adjusted to changing realities by moving production to cheaper inland labor markets and expanding into higher value goods (Frangos, 2011).

3.2 Changing trade structure

The progressive openness of the multilateral trading system under the sponsorship of the GATT/WTO system benefited the Chinese economy enormously. Trade made a critical contribution to China's vertiginous growth, which was trade-biased. Growth rate of exports was faster than that of the GDP. During the reform period a dramatic structural transformation in China's trade was observed. At the time of launching the reforms, China had a negligible role in multilateral trade. Its meagre exports were limited to primary goods and processed primary goods. These categories accounted for over 75 percent of China's exports. As China was a labor-abundant economy, in the *initial stages* exports were concentrated in the labor-intensive light-manufacturing sector. It successfully mobilized low-wage labor in the export sector.

This was logical and squarely premised on the Heckscher-Ohlin theory. At this stage of economic development in China, textiles and apparel, footwear and toys, the so-called soft manufactures, were its major export lines. Over the 1980–98, period this category of exports steadily increased. They rose from $4.3 billion to $53.5 billion, a hefty 10.22 times increase. Over this period, the share of total exports accounted for by these product lines soared from 6.9 percent of the total to 29.1 percent.[14] In each one of these product lines China succeeded in capturing a progressively rising share of world markets. Price competitiveness of its exports enabled it to capture new world markets for its exports. It has also become a global competitor in terms of technology. Such enviable growth was seen by some observers as posing a threat to China's trading partners. Even scholars of towering pedigree—like Samuelson (2002)—argued that China's success could harm the USA if its export success continues in the industries where the USA has a comparative advantage.

Textiles and apparel continued to be a strong industrial and export industry. Domestic Chinese firms are both competitive producers and exporters. This industry exports half of its output. It has maintained the basic characteristics of a traditional export-oriented industrial sector. For instance, all the production chains are domestically located. Therefore, the amount of local value-added in this industry is large, close to 70 percent (Koopman and Wang, 2008). Therefore, currency appreciation will affect this industry more unfavorably than those that have supply chains dispersed in other regional economies.

As exports grew, so did their specialization. The structure of exports shifted rapidly towards sophisticated industries. With an increase in specialization, market forces "work to attract resources into main sectors where relative cost advantages are the greatest" (Amiti and Freund, 2010, p. 43). If China's export basket was determined *only* by the traditional forces of comparative advantage, it would have been dominated by labor-intensive products suitable for production in a low-income economy. However, in the post-1990 period the principle of comparative advantage was not the main determinant of export products. Although the principle did not become irrelevant, it worked in a more dynamic manner. The growing sophistication of exports was found to be positively correlated to the share of wholly foreign-owned enterprises from the advanced economies and the share of processing exports of FIEs (Xu and Lu, 2009).

Beginning in 2001, significant industrial upgrading took place, which led to both sophistication and diversification of exports. Government policies played an active role and helped in nurturing production capabilities in advanced technology industries. Therefore, its export structure was not compatible with China's resource endowment and stage of economic development. Rodrik (2006a, p. 1) noted that "China has ended up with an export basket that is significantly more sophisticated than what would be normally expected for a country at its income level". Its export basket resembles a country that is that is three or four times as rich as China (Rodick, 2010). The level of export sophistication falls when exports of FIEs are removed. Chinese firms produced less sophisticated products for exports.

Since the early 1990s, particularly after 2001, an increasing proportion of exports diversified towards capital- and skill-intensive products. China successfully penetrated product markets traditionally dominated by advanced economies (Wang and Wei, 2008). Schott (2008) observed that in terms of sophistication China's export structure increasingly resembled the collective export structure of advanced economies, not with that of countries that have similar factor endowments as China. Its export similarity index is comparable to those of Japan, the Eurozone and the US economies (IMF 2011a, Table 5, p. 27).

Research and development (R&D)-intensive industries like consumer electronics and automotive products became prominent export lines.[15] Yang *et al.* (2009) contended that in its exports China's adopted a limited catch-up strategy, rather than only following its comparative advantage. That is, it exported products with technological content higher than justified by its comparative advantage. They computed a limited catch-up index (LCI) and found it positive for China. Cross country comparisons revealed that countries, like Korea and Taiwan, with higher LCI grew faster than those with lower LCI.

One intuitive explanation that could clarify this incongruity is the role played by FIEs and processing trade. Foreign capital and technology lent a helping hand in technological upgradation of China's trade. Wang (2010) disagreed and argued that it is important to focus on both export structure and the unit value of exports. According to him neither FIEs nor processing trade were responsible for the sophistication of Chinese exports and their similarity with those of the advanced economies. The two principal contributing factors were improvement in human capital and the policies of the government which promoted tax-favored high-technology zones to contribute significantly to the rising sophistication of China's exports. Economic policy measures were consciously adopted to absorb existing technology. It was sagacious because it was cost effective.

Since the early 1990s, China's export structure shifted towards hard manufactures, which include machinery, electronics goods and computers. Of these, the broad category of exports of machinery became the strongest overall growth sector. Within this category the most important product lines were telecommunications, electrical machinery and appliances and office machines. Large growth in this category of exports is essentially attributed to processing trade. The R&D intensity of Chinese manufactured exports went on increasing steadily. High-technology exports increased from 6 percent of the total manufactured exports in 1992 to 29 percent in 2008 (World Bank, 2010b).

Large foreign firms, multinational corporations (MNCs) and their affiliates played a dominant role in China's exports of high-technology manufactured products. They were responsible for some 80 percent of these exports. A large part of this trade took place with the neighboring Asian economies. Trade in high-technology products overwhelmingly reflected international fragmentation of production. It was not an indicator of domestic upgradation of manufacturing capabilities, although domestic technological upgradation did take place. Particularly noteworthy was China's success as the exporter of manufactured products covering an impressive range of technological level. Since 2001, its share in global manufactured exports increased by almost 1 percent per year. In 2010 its share in global manufactured exports was 13.7 percent (EIU, 2011a). This trend is more than likely to continue.

A great deal of China's exports is the product of the operations of supply chains in numerous industries. China became the "hub" for regional and global production networks. The term hub stands for the final assembly center. Approximately half of China's exports presently represent domestic value-added (DVA). Horn *et al.* (2010) computed the DVA of Chinese exports. To calculate the DVA of exports, imports used in production of goods and services that are subsequently exported are subtracted from the value of exports. Over 2002–08, imported goods accounted for 40 percent–55 percent of the value of total exports. The DVA share of exports rose over time, denoting that China was becoming progressively less of a mere assembler of imported products. This was a publicized government policy objective.

Although China achieved export dominance in a significant range of industrial sectors, it cannot be regarded as immutable. As wages rise, labor-intensive, low-value-added manufacturing sectors will need to be abandoned. In the recent past they rose at a high rate. As technological advancement progresses, China's manufacturing sector will undergo further transformation in the coming decade. China's price and technological competitiveness in numerous new sectors has been increasing, which is sure to continue. With that exporters will move up the value chain. Chinese firms' competition with the firms from the advanced economies in their core product markets will rise.

China's active participation in the vertical integration of production and becoming a regional assembly center rapidly expanded its trade in parts and components, in turn favorably influencing the volume of intra-regional trade. In fact, China began playing an important role in parts and component trade not only regionally but also globally (Kim et al., 2010). Trade statistics show that there has been a secular and rapid increase in China's trade in parts and components. It increased from around $16 billion in 1992 to almost $430 billion in 2008. This was a 24-fold increase. As a proportion of the total Chinese trade, parts and components were only 10 percent of the total in 1992. In 2006 their share peaked at 21 percent. After that there was a sharp decline in trade in parts and components owing to the global financial crisis (2007–09) and it did not recover for the next two years. However, it remained an important part of China's overall trade. What is noteworthy is that China's imports of parts and components far exceeds its exports. This fact corroborates China's role as a major regional production center. There also has been an increase in the exports of parts and components, which in turn reflects China's increasing importance as a manufacturing base of parts and components. Trade statistics demonstrate that SITC 77 (which is essentially electrical machinery and apparatus) has remained the pivotal sector in China's parts and component trade. This category shows a large increase in both exports and imports. This trade has a relatively high degree of regional concentration (Lee et al., 2011).

There has been a steady rise in the technology composition of exports from the EMEs, conspicuously from China. The contribution of high-technology exports to overall exports during 1995–2008 was 30 percent for China, compared to 26 percent for the USA, 17 percent for Germany and 11 percent for Japan. However, if exports are adjusted for foreign contents to reflect their domestic content, the contribution of high-technology exports to overall exports declined for China (24 percent), whereas it rose for the USA (29 percent) and Germany (20 percent) (IMF, 2011a).

According to an Economic Intelligence Unit (EIU) (2011b) white paper heavy equipment, like the construction machinery sector, is one of the many such areas. In this sector China is slated to overtake Germany and Japan in 2011 and be the second largest exporter in the world. The USA is the largest exporter of construction machinery and will continue to be so. Exporting firms in China are deliberately and purposefully trimming down their reliance on the Western markets and increasing their engagement with the markets in the EMEs and other middle-income developing economies. The global financial crisis of 2007–09 sparked this trend. Although the global economy recovered in 2010, the trend continued to gain momentum. China's future export growth and increase in market share will be essentially driven by the strengthening demand in the non-OECD countries, in particular the fast-growing EMEs.

Growing sophistication of China's manufacturing industries will have substantial impact over the global trade, particularly when Chinese firms are backed by scale economies. Chinese firms will begin competing with their counterparts in the advanced economies in the global market place as well as in their domestic markets. They would begin to chip away the dominant market shares of the established firms in the advanced economies. The EIU (2011b) white paper identified 37 industrial sectors, representing global market value of $927 billion in 2010, which would come under pressure. Between 2007 and 2010, China's market share in these sectors increased from 8.5 percent to 14.0 percent. These industrial sectors entail capital equipment and related components, reflecting improvements in precision levels of metal-cutting and metal-shaping facilities in metal-lurgical processes. In the past, Chinese companies could not produce many components that required high levels of strength, durability and precision, or only produce with difficulty at high costs. This has changed. They can now mass produce them. In many cases reverse-engineering of imported components was helpful.

4. Reforms and strategies aimed at attracting FDI

When the reforms were launched, China was not a favorite destination for FDI inflows, although it did receive trivial amounts. FDI is regarded as significant because it is a package of capital, technology, managerial skills and international networks. A developing economy benefits from it in myriad of ways. Over the 1984–88 period, FDI flows increased to $2.2 billion annually. This uptick disappeared in 1989 because China was blamed universally for its poor human rights record. Thereafter the first watershed year was 1992 when FDI flows spurted to over $10 billion. After this time the sources of FDI became more important for the economy. FDI inflows became diversified and FDI from the EU economies and the USA increased markedly. It should, however, be noted that as China was, and continued to be, a high- or very high-saving economy, the bulk of its investment was financed domestically (Table 2.2 and Figure 2.2). As a proportion of GDP, FDI remained between 3 percent and 4 percent (Vincelette *et al.*, 2011).

More comprehensive economic and social transformation of China took place after 1992. In this context, a significant event was Deng Xiaoping's early 1992 tour to the Pearl River delta (see Section 2.2), known as *Nanxun*. He made this tour because he believed that his successors were overly cautious and in promoting growth and expanding the role of markets in China (Vogel, 2011). The Fourteenth Party Congress occurred in November 1992. At this point, economic reforms entered a new era. Call for GDP growth escalation and modernization was renewed. The economy maintained growth momentum during and after the Asian economic crisis of 1997–98. The decadal average of GDP growth for the 1991–2000 period was 10.1 percent.

After 1992, China became a veritable magnet for FDI, receiving the largest annual inflows among the EMEs year after year. In 1993 FDI crossed the $30 billion mark. This was an important time for China's FDI inflows. This spurt was partly the result of the selective opening up of China's capital account. *Nanxun* was regarded as symbolic of the commitment of the top political leadership to liberalization and global integration of the Chinese economy. It was also instrumental in creating business-friendly policy environment for attracting increased inflow of FDI. By the mid-1900s China became the largest recipient of FDI in the developing world. Although FDI flows to the other three BRIC economies also increased, but China was the largest recipient among the BRICs economies. It used a number of activist policies to attract and retain FDI. Important among them was a 57.2 percent depreciation of the renminbi between mid-1986 and early 1994. In line with Article VIII of the IMF Agreement, the renminbi became fully convertible on current account transactions in 1996.

The so-called *Nanxun* effect is credited for the development of the coastal provinces of China. They involved two globalized delta economies, namely, the Pearl River Delta (PRD) and the Yangtze River Delta (YRD). Rapid growth in these two delta regions continuously out-performed all the other regions in China. In the mid-1990s China became the largest developing-country recipient, when FDI flows hovered around $40 billion per annum. This was the time-point when

TABLE 2.2 Gross savings and gross capital formation (% of GDP)

Year	Gross savings	Gross capital formation
1980	n/a	35
1981	n/a	33
1982	36	34
1983	36	34
1984	36	35
1985	35	38
1986	36	38
1987	37	37
1988	37	38
1989	36	37
1990	40	36
1991	40	36
1992	39	37
1993	42	44
1994	43	42
1995	42	42
1996	41	40
1997	42	38
1998	40	37
1999	38	37
2000	37	35
2001	38	36
2002	40	38
2003	44	41
2004	47	43
2005	49	42
2006	52	43
2007	52	42
2008	53	44
2009	53	48
2010	52	48
2011	53	48

Source: World Bank. 2013. *World Development Indicator Online Database 2013*. Washington, DC.

liberalization of trade and FDI regimes dramatically accelerated.[16] This acceleration was instrumental in deepening China's regional and global integration. China acquired the reputation of being an FDI magnet. FDI was concentrated in the manufacturing sector because the services sector was not liberalized until China's WTO accession[17] in 2001.

Manufacturing sector and assembly operations were the destination of an overwhelmingly large part of FDI inflows. They caused a radical shift in China's industrial structure, which altered from low-skill intensive to high-skill intensive products and services. In 2005 FDI inflow was $72 billion. This spurt in FDI made China the third largest recipient of FDI in the world, after the UK and the USA, in that order. In 2008 China received $92.4 billion in FDI and in 2009 $95 billion in FDI (UNCTAD, 2010a). These statistics demonstrate that FDI flows during the global financial crisis period did not plummet sharply. China became a bit of an oasis for the MNCs during the global financial maelstrom (Tse, 2009). When the Eurozone sovereign debt crisis was raging in

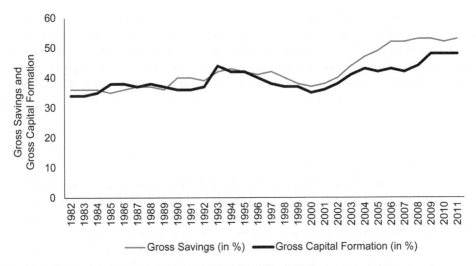

FIGURE 2.2 Gross savings and gross capital formation (% of GDP)
Source: The World Bank (2013). World Development Indicator Online Database 2013. Washington DC.

2011, China's FDI receipts were $123.99 billion (WIR, 2012). By 2010, according to the World Bank, China had accumulated $574 billion in FDI.

The gradual opening of FDI in the banking sector took place in 2004 and 2005. Driven by major investments in Chinese banks, FDI flows into the financial services sector surged to $12 billion in 2005. Foreign banks entered into Chinese financial markets, acquiring ownership stakes in some banks. By the end of 2005, 18 foreign financial institutions had invested in 16 Chinese banks. The biggest four banks were the largest recipients. The real estate emerged as another attractive sector; in 2005 it received $5.4 billion in FDI (UNCTAD, 2007). However foreign banks did not make much headway and accounted for less than a stake of 2 percent in total banking assets in 2010 (Goodstadt, 2012).

Macro-economic and institutional reforms and liberalization continuously improved China's foreign investment climate. The indicators of investment environment constantly improved (Tuan *et al.*, 2009). These improvements, along with external factors, made China's increasingly attractive for FDI inflows. The very fact that China transformed and integrated its centrally planned economy into the regional and global economies made it a uniquely appealing for FDI, which played a crucial role in the development of manufacturing sector in China. A long-term perspective of FDI flow shows that China is the largest developing country recipient of FDI over the last three decades, and the third largest globally after the USA and the UK (Xing, 2010). In three decades China received $940 billion in FDI stock (Chen, 2001). While devising its FDI strategy, policy makers paid attention to joint venture requirements and technology transfer policies. Skillful handling of these policies enabled China to develop "national champions" in several prominent sectors, including high-speed railways, ICT, automobile and the fast growing commercial aircraft industry.

The largest amount of FDI came to China from Hong Kong, SAR, which should not be taken to mean that business firms in Hong Kong were the source of this FDI. Business firms based in China may be from any part of the world. There also was a good deal of what has become known as "round tripping". A large proportion of FDI came from China's Eastern and Southeast

Asian neighbors. The OECD economies, particularly the USA and the EU, also played a large role in investing in China. These flows were biased towards the manufacturing sector. They played a pivotal role not only in China's economic development, productivity growth and industrialization but also in export promotion, employment generation and integrating with the regional and global economies. FDI has a major presence in leading trade and investment sectors. FIEs both joint ventures and wholly owned foreign enterprises accounted for 55 percent of China's exports and 68 percent of its trade surplus in 2010 (MoC, 2011). While FDI inflows augmented investment only to a limited degree, they had other favorable macro- and micro-economic effects, particularly on the volume of production and multilateral trade and on upgrading technology and the general production efficiency of the economy.

Using panel data from Chinese Industrial Surveys of medium-sized and large firms for 2000–06, Hale *et al.* (2010) found positive technological spillover effects of FDI. However, these spillovers were distributed unevenly across industries, origin of FDI and ownership structure of the firms. Spillovers were found to be higher from FDI that came from outside the greater China region. Also, FDI contributed to both the range and quality of manufactured goods produced in China. It expanded China's depth and breadth of manufacturing capabilities and accelerated its regional and global integration. It also promoted market integration of the Chinese firms and economy with the global economy and diversified markets for suppliers to them. That is, it strengthened the links of Chinese firms with global markets and companies. Although the coastal and other regions, where FDI flows were concentrated, made faster economic progress, they also created regional disparities in China.

Another major strategy that yielded rich dividends in terms of attracting FDI, transfer of technology and export promotion was the methodical setting up of SEZs in the coastal provinces and delta regions, alluded to above.[18] The SEZs are more liberal in terms of economic and other legislation than the rest of the country. A legal framework for inviting FDI and operations of foreign firms was created early, in 1979. Subsequently the FDI regime was further liberalized in several pragmatic stages. The SEZ was not a homogeneous concept. There were several kinds including free-trade zones, export-processing zones, industrial parks, high-technology industrial development zones, free ports, enterprise zones and others of the similar kinds. They are functionally diverse and cover large land areas (Zeng, 2011). The top political leadership remained strongly committed to the success of SEZs and EPZs. Local and provincial authorities were given increasing autonomy to make their own plans, laws and administrative procedures for attracting FDI.

Public–private partnership in the SEZs and EPZs was pragmatically encouraged. A major change came in 1986, with the so-called 22 regulations, which liberalized FDI further and eased the procedures for making foreign investment. With the passage of time, investment procedures were increasingly truncated and simplified. The SEZs not only made a decisive contribution to China's rapid industrialization and growth but they also tested the market economy concepts and strategies and new institutions in the initial stages of China's structural transformation and macroe-conomic restructuring. They became the role models for the rest of the country to follow.

Economic activity in the two delta regions of China is dominated by foreign-owned and family run private companies that generate remarkable growth. These regions are known for operating a free-market form of capitalism. Two kinds of FDI projects, namely, export-oriented and advanced technologically projects, were unambiguously offered more welcoming treatment by authorities by offering them additional benefits. Foreign firms making FDI in advanced technologically projects were given the mandate of upgrading domestic production capacity and technology standards. This astute FDI management regime had far-reaching ramifications.

FDI that originated in other parts of the world than Hong Kong, SAR, Macau and Taiwan had a positive effect on individual firm-level productivity (Du *et al.*, 2012). It also helped in significantly increasing inbound technology transfer, which in turn extensively improved the growth potential of the economy by strengthening the manufacturing sector and enhancing the competitiveness of the economy. The two delta regions attract almost 70 percent of China's FDI and contribute over 70 percent of its exports, particularly the high-technology exports (Walter and Howie, 2011).

4.1 Impact and future prospects for FDI inflows

FDI is widely regarded as a major driving force promoting regional economic growth (Lee, 2007). Analysts have found evidence of foreign affiliates of multinational corporations (MNCs) having higher levels of productivity in an FDI-recipient economy. The overall productivity effect of FDI was found to be positive (Lin *et al.*, 2011). Transfer of technology is regarded as one of the important effects of FDI. Seminal research by Findley (1978) developed a theoretical model that demonstrated that the rate of technology transfer through FDI is positively related to the technology gap between the sourcing and host countries. Higher productivity is essentially driven by firm-level assets of MNCs which favorably influence the operations and performance of its affiliates as well as FDI receiving domestic firms (Aitken and Harrison, 1999; Egger and Pfaffermayer, 2001). Conventional FDI theory posits that firm-level intangible assets—technological expertise, managerial and marketing skills, close functional relationships with suppliers and large customers and brand name—combine to act as a tangible economic force that works to the benefit of the MNC affiliate, or an FDI receiving business firm in the host economy. Thus, FDI flows directly enhance the performance of the recipient firms and economies, when performance is measured by either productivity or labor productivity. In addition, favorable economic impact of FDI in the host economy is also caused by spillovers to other firms. Evidence of productivity and technological spillovers was found by Aitken and Harrison, 1999, and Buckley *et al.*, 2002. Technologically advanced MNC affiliates in the host economy tend to stimulate the performance of and productivity of domestic firms (Buckley *et al.*, 2010a).

FDI made by MNCs and large foreign firms results in the movement of factors of production and factor services to the host economy. Therefore FDI can potentially influence both the volume and pattern of trade of the host economy. China is a useful and appropriate case for studying the changes in trading pattern when factors of production and services are mobile. China receives FDI from both the neighboring Asian economies as well as the advanced economies. The latter group of countries is far ahead of China in terms of factor endowments, technological advancement, management skills and headquarter services. FDI made by them accompanies these factors to China. They stimulate exports from the labor-abundant China.

Role of FDI in first improving the performance of the manufacturing sector and then exports in China has been the focus of several empirical studies. They found evidence of generally positive and significant role of FDI in promoting Chinese exports (Buckley *et al.*, 2002; Sun, 2001). Earlier empirical studies by Sun (2001) and Zhang and Song (2000) found evidence of MNCs promoting export growth in China. Empirical results of Wang *et al.*, (2012) also confirmed that coefficient on FDI variable is positive and statistically significant, which proves that FDI contributed to China's overall export expansion. Every 1 percent increase in FDI resulted in 0.2 percent increase in exports after a one-year lag during the time period considered.

MNC affiliates and large foreign business firms that have chosen the FDI as an entry vehicle to China are usually considered much better placed to serve the international markets than their domestic counterparts. The principal advantages for the MNC affiliates are information and knowledge about the global market conditions and access to the international marketing networks, through their parent companies at home. In addition, MNC affiliates and foreign firms operating in China are generally much larger in terms of resources and managerial knowhow than their domestic counterparts. They can easily afford high fixed costs associated with establishment of a large export operation.

Taking aggregate data for various years from the *China Statistical Yearbook* and the *Foreign Economic Statistical Yearbook*, Wang *et al.* (2010) conducted an empirical study. They took 20 years (1983–2002) of export and FDI data to show that the rapid increase in Chinese exports went together with increasing share of exports by MNC affiliates and foreign firms operating in China. The strategy of officially promoting industries that support the production of exportables was partly responsible for it. A significant proportion of FDI was flowing into the industrial sectors that produced exportable products. In particular, export expansion in the early 1990s was directly or indirectly related to the activities of MNC affiliates and large foreign firms. Domestic firms also exported a substantial volume, but they were slower and less successful than the MNC affiliates.

Wages in China have been rising. In 2010 the average annual wage of an urban worker reached $5,487, which was comparable to those in the Philippines and Thailand, but significantly higher than those in India and Indonesia (Li *et al.*, 2012). According to Ceglowski and Golub (2007), in 2002 China's relative unit labor cost was 63 percent that of Malaysia and 70 percent that of Korea. If the gap between wages and productivity in China continues to close at the rate of 2.5 percent per year, China's lower labor cost advantage relative to Korea will disappear by 2018 and relative to Malaysia by 2022.

However, China still possesses the compelling advantage of having a large, low-cost, educated as well as fairly industrious and productive labor pool.[19] This is a significant advantage that China has over the other EMEs and the neighboring Asian economies. The labor pool is presently large enough at various skill levels, even in capital- and knowledge-intensive industries. One defense of rising wages in China is that labor productivity has also risen. However, these advantages are partially offset by thinness in the availability of managerial personnel, particularly the middle managers. Despite dilution in incentives, overall investment climate is still favorable. China's implementation of its WTO commitments is another favorable factor which led to improvement in its market access for foreign firms and upgradation in its investment climate vis-à-vis other economies vying to attract FDI.

FDI flows favorably influenced technological standards, particularly in the manufacturing sector. China's technological capability in several sectors grew discernibly over the years. Technological spillovers from FIEs assisted in technological advancement. Efforts in this vital area are being strengthened by China's rapidly modernizing educational system, students and professionals returning from the advanced economies and the high-skill personnel leaving FIEs. According to Buckley *et al.* (2010b), in the recent past higher value-added, market-oriented FDI from the advanced economies in China has been rising. The other plausible hosts for this kind of FDI are the Southeast Asian economies. However, structural impediments in this group of economies are preventing its FDI flows into them.

A large change in direction in China's FDI flows was in the services sectors that are being liberalized for the first time after the WTO accession. Between 1999 and 2005 the service sector received around 25 percent of the total FDI inflows. In keeping with the WTO accession agreement, this sector was liberalized since 2006 and FDI inflows began to increase dramatically. R&D was an important sector that became an impressive draw of FDI from MNCs. In the first 11 months of 2011 the service sector received more ($48.8 billion) than the manufacturing sector ($47.3 billion) (Yongjian and Jiechang, 2012).

In this regard, achievements of Chinese automobile sector are particularly striking. Energized by technology transfer and spillovers from foreign auto companies, China emerged as the world's largest automobile-producing country in 2009. With the rise in consumer income and production volume, the Chinese auto market recorded exceedingly rapid growth. In 2013 China's auto production is projected to be ten times higher than in 2000, when its share of global car manufacturing was a paltry 3.5 percent. It is projected to rise to 23.8 percent in 2013 (Marsh, 2013). This important and large size industrial sector was designated a "strategic" sector by the government. In the post-2004 period, it successfully introduced a full spectrum of advanced technologies in production and management. A variety of industries are closely related to and dependent upon the automobile industry. Therefore it is regarded as representing industrial and managerial advancements of a country. Chinese auto firms not only succeeded in absorbing a great deal of foreign technology but also grew independently (SERI, 2013).

The well-off eastern seaboard regions benefitted more from large FDI inflows over the preceding two decades. They contributed to rising regional income disparity in China. However, geographical distribution of FDI inflows has shown signs of shifting. Of late, the inland provinces that had failed to attract FDI seemed to be set to receive higher volumes of FDI. The proportion of FDI going to the favored eastern provinces declined from 80 percent of the total inflows to 60 percent over the 2000–10 decade (EIU, 2012). Foreign investors showed a preference to move to inland provinces. This trend is likely to continue and by 2015 the share of eastern provinces will decline to less than half of the total FDI inflows. Recent trends indicated that southwestern cities like Chongqing are set to receive more FDI in comparison to traditional FDI destinations like Shanghai.

Similarly the northeastern region recorded gains of 31 percent in FDI receipts during 2006–10 due to joint ventures made by large automakers (EIU, 2012). The three important ones among them were BMW, Volkswagen and Audi. A4 and A6 models of Audi are valued highly and are the model of choice of the well-heeled Chinese. They have enjoyed strong sales in recent years. Central provinces also started attracting a growing proportion of FDI. This draw was largely driven by domestic demand. Unilever, a world-class consumer goods MNC, located its production facility in Anhui essentially to cater for the domestic market. Indubitably the inland provinces will take a while to catch up with the seaboard provinces, although the process is underway. In 2010 the province of Liaoning overtook Guangdong as the second largest recipient of FDI. In 2014 it is forecast to leave Jiangsu behind as the largest FDI recipient. Cities of Shenyang and Dalian succeeded in attracting large projects in manufacturing sectors, particularly in auto and high-end electronics. For instance, Toshiba made a recent announcement that its TV manufacturing facility in Dalian will supply to the domestic Chinese market in collaboration with a local Chinese supplier TCL.

The A. T. Kearney FDI Confidence Index provides a trustworthy indication of the future prospects of FDI flows. It is calculated by surveying the 1,000 largest FDI-making MNCs, spanning 44 countries and 17 industries. Together these firms comprise more than $2 trillion in annual global sales and are responsible for more than 75 percent of global FDI. According to the 2010 survey results, the A. T. Kearney FDI Confidence Index is the highest for China (1.93), followed by the USA (1.67) (A. T. Kearney, 2010). In the 2010 survey foreign investors were more positive about China than in the 2007 survey. The amount of FDI inflows in 2010 was $114.7 billion (UNCTAD, 2012).

The optimism of investors' was driven more by search for new markets than by producing in a cost efficient manner. According to the 2012 survey results, China maintained its top position with a score of 1.87 in FDI Confidence Index. In the backdrop of tepid recovery and turbulence in the advanced economies, there was little surprise in it. The USA fell two places to the fourth position in 2012 with a score of 1.52. Political gridlock on fiscal policy in the USA and continued uncertainty about economic outlook weighed heavily on investor sentiment (A. T. Kearney, 2012).

After increasing in 2011 to $123.9 billion, FDI flows into China fell in 2012 to $111.7 billion, which was a 3.7 percent fall (UNCTAD, 2012). This contraction was partly the result of rising costs for producers in China and increasing relative attraction of other Asian economies. FDI inflows to Cambodia, Myanmar (Burma), the Philippines, Thailand and Vietnam grew in 2012. Indonesia alone attracted 66 percent more FDI in its manufacturing sector. Textiles and apparel sector recorded the largest, contraction of FDI in China, 19 percent. Asian firms accounted for much of the investment drop in China in 2012. However, China still is the second largest FDI recipient in the world after the US.

Since April 2012 foreign institutional investors can invest more in China's capital markets. Credit controls persist in Chinese financial markets and China stringently controlled cross-border capital flow. Foreign institutional investors needed to apply for the status of a qualified investor and then invested only the agreed amount. In a large liberalization move, China more than doubled the quota to allow foreign institutional investors to invest in China. This major financial reform and liberalization move was a part of China's next phase of development and could also help in internationalizing the Chinese currency. China was required to open its capital markets further under its WTO commitments. The China Securities and Regulatory Commission (CSRC) increased the quota under the Qualified Financial Institutional Investors (QFII) scheme, which was started in 2002. The investment quota was raised from RMB 30 billion to RMB 70 billion ($7.95 billion). As regards the pattern of financial investment, foreign investors invest a large part (almost 75 percent) of their assets in Chinese stocks and the balance in bonds and deposits. In addition, foreign investors can raise more RMB in Hong Kong for investment in mainland China. This limit was increased from RMB 20 billion ($3.2 billion) to RMB 70 billion. Together these policy liberalization moves will allow global financial institutions to play a more active role in China's largely closed equity and financial markets, increasing global capital inflows into the capital markets.

5. Growth in total factor productivity

Total factor productivity (TFP) is an important indicator of growth because it measures the overall efficiency of an economy. TFP is also referred to as the Solow residual, or multi-factor productivity (MFP), and is defined as increase in output growth not accounted for by increase in factor inputs. Although sources of TFP growth are inherently difficult to quantify, the principal ingredients that determine TFP growth are labor, physical capital and human capital. While macro-economic and financial reforms or outward-orientation make a decisive contribution to TFP growth, determining their impact is a complex affair.

A contribution of TFP to economic growth is necessary for improving living standards in general and the overall competitiveness of the economy in particular. A growing body of research warns that while physical and human capital accumulation are necessary conditions for economic growth, TFP accounts for the bulk of cross-country differences in the level of growth (Easterly and Levine, 2001). China's saving and investment rates have been exceedingly high and they have had an increasing trend. A corollary of this fact is the frequent assertion that the high GDP growth in

China was essentially based on capital accumulation. This direct logical link may or may not be correct.

The question of whether China's growth was based on factor accumulation or TFP ignited an impassioned debate among academics. During the pre-reform decades China's growth was sustained almost entirely by the increase in capital and labor inputs, while the TFP remained negative. To be sure, macroeconomic reforms and restructuring *inter alia* led to TFP growth in China. Several empirical and econometric studies were conducted to assess the sources of Chinese growth. Estimates based on production function reveal that before 1978, almost all output growth could be sourced from capital accumulation, with a small contribution made by labor-force growth (Heytens and Zebregs, 2003). Although conclusions and estimates differ owing to differences in methodologies and assumptions, many studies concurred on some of their crucial conclusions. There was an agreement among many researchers on TFP growth contributing to real GDP growth during the reform era.

In the post-reform era, sizable physical accumulation took place in China. It is still continuing. Using the data series for the 1980s, several researchers pointed out that growth in China was brought about essentially by physical capital accumulation (Chow, 1993; Borensztein and Ostry, 1996; Sachs and Woo, 1997). According to Lau and Park (2003) for the 1965–95 period "tangible input" or physical capital accumulation explained 86 percent–95 percent of output growth, while increase in labor accounted for between 5 percent and 14 percent. Their conclusion was that the TFP growth was nil during the period under consideration. Krugman (1994) agreed with the conclusions of these researchers and warned that if China's TFP did not rise during the 1990s, the mere accumulation of factors of production would not be sufficient to sustain brisk growth.

A subsequent generation of empirical studies (e.g. Hu and Khan, 1997; Wang and Yao, 2003; Wu, 2004; Arayama and Miyoshi, 2004) used the translog production function and focused on the estimation of factor input shares in the process of computing aggregate productivity growth. This set of studies found compelling evidence of positive TFP growth in the reform period, although estimates of TFP growth ranged between 2 percent and 4 percent. Liang (2005) refuted the conclusions arrived at by Lau and Park (2003) and found that their estimated share of capital at 60 percent was too high to be supported by either national income statistics or bottom-up analysis of enterprise financial data.

More recent studies have used different methodologies to ascertain whether China recorded TFP increases or merely accumulated factors of production to grow rapidly. In the post-reform era China's real GDP growth rate remained close to 10 percent, which was a good three times higher than that in the pre-reform period. It was also almost three times the long-term average growth rate of the global economy. Heytens and Zebregs (2003) concluded that this GDP growth was largely the result of TFP growth. The studies that used the frontier production approach for measuring TFP growth decomposed TFP growth into two components: efficiency change and technological change. Using this methodology, Chen (2001) concluded that positive TFP growth occurred during the 1992–99 period. Also, technological improvement contributed more to TFP growth than any other factor. Zheng and Hu (2006) concurred with this conclusion and found that, while there were ups and downs in TFP growth, for a large part of the 1979–2001 period technological progress contributed to TFP growth.

Kuijs and Wang (2006) used the Cobb–Douglas technique and estimated the contribution of accumulation of factors of production and TFP for the 1978–2004 period. They inferred that since the launching of the reforms, TFP growth contributed significantly to GDP growth. Their estimates show that while growth in capital stock contributed about a half of GDP growth, TFP growth contributed an average 3.3 percent per annum to the growth rate during the period under consideration. The balance contribution was made by increase in employment. They divided the sample period into two and compared TFP growth in 1978–93 to that in 1993–2004. They concluded that the contribution of factor accumulation to GDP was larger in the former period than in the latter.

Dekle and Vandenbroucke (2006) argued in favor of TFP supporting GDP growth. According to them it resulted from the movement of labor from agriculture and public non-agriculture sectors to private non-agriculture sectors was a major contributor to China's TFP growth. Perkins and Rawski (2008) concluded that during 1978–2005 TFP was the principal driver of growth, affecting growth both directly and indirectly. Their results show that during the period under consideration average annual TFP growth was 3.8 percent, with the pace slackening somewhat during the final decade. According to them TFP growth also helped in the acceleration of physical growth.

Another recent study (Vincelette et al., 2011) that used the same methodology as Kuijs and Wang (2006) reported respectable TFP growth. It inferred that the contribution of capital accumulation to labor productivity growth increased from 2.9 percent out of 6.4 percent per annum in 1978–94 to 5.5 percent out of 8.6 percent in 1994–2009. It was categorical in its assertion that China's TFP growth was higher than that in most other countries.

From 2003 to 2008 average annual GDP growth in China was 10.8 percent. This was an indubitably exceptionally high growth performance. During this quinquennium capital stock expanded rapidly and annually contributed 6 percent of GDP growth. Because of the one-child policy labor-force growth continued to remain subdued. This means that the more than 4-percentage-point growth per annum was not the result of factor accumulation but was owing to "extremely vigorous growth efficiency" (OECD, 2010c, p. 25). This efficient use of the available resources was partly due to the reallocation of the labor force from the low-productivity agriculture sector to manufacturing and services, where factor productivity is much higher. The TFP for the period under consideration came to 4.1 percent per annum.[20]

China's success in attracting FDI was another factor that stimulated TFP growth. An empirical study by Tuan et al. (2009) confirmed a positive link between FDI and TFP. They demonstrated that FDI flows affected TFP favorably in China. FDI had a spillover effect and TFP progressively increased in the two globalized delta region economies, namely, the PRD and the YRD. FDI affected both output growth and productivity process in these two regions. Future growth in FDI and more foreign firms entering China will further stimulate TFP growth.

The above exposition indicates that while earlier empirical studies concluded that the primary source of growth in China was essentially accumulation of physical capital, the later ones concurred that it was largely TFP growth. The primary source of growth shifted from accumulation of physical capital in the initial stages of growth to TFP growth. This occurred as the Chinese economy evolved from a low-income, capital-deficient economy to a middle-income, capital-abundant economy. A possible explanation of this is that as capital accumulation continued, the law of diminishing marginal returns on capital set in and it was followed by an increase in TFP. The empirical literature cited above in this section concluded that capital accumulation had driven growth in Asia until around 1990. Park and Park (2010) found empirical evidence of a structural shift in this trend around 2002. The TFP growth began playing a much greater role in Asia, including in China, at this point in time and continued thereafter.

An obvious inference of this analysis is that policy-makers in China need to pursue policies that foster high productivity. Policies that promote the productivity growth of all inputs to production will be crucial to sustaining growth after the global financial crisis period. For instance, the labor force cannot increase very much in the foreseeable future in China. Its productivity can be increased by better education standards, however. Education levels in China have steadily improved since 1980; these endeavors need to continue in earnest. They will contribute tangibly to future productivity growth. In addition, policy measures that make the labor market more flexible will result in more efficient allocation of labor across industries and firms. In addition, non-market institutional developments are also required so that China can complete its shift to a market economy, with sustained TFP growth. Furthermore, at the current stage of economic development China will need to rely on its innovation and R&D policies for TFP improvements. Policy making community is aware of it and China's investment in R&D has been on the rise since the mid-1990s. Technological advancement will result in moving the production possibilities frontier outward, leading to higher TFP growth. Policy moves on the microeconomic front cannot be ignored either. Better and professionalized management would enable a firm to be more productive without augmenting inputs and moving up to the next technological level.

For shifting to a new growth trajectory and for achieving the objectives delineated in the 12th Five-Year Plan (2011–15), economy's reliance on and ability to innovate will have to increase. Innovation enhances productivity, promotes sustained economic growth, which in turn leads to welfare gains. Policy makers in China believe that innovation is necessary for upgrading the economy, so that wages and living standards can be improved. So far China's performance on this score is mixed. No doubt economy is progressing towards growing more innovative instead of merely mass-producing items that were designed elsewhere. Since 2000 China's rate of investments in R&D accelerated. It increased at an average rate of 10 percent per annum (Battelle, 2010). Among the non-OECD countries, China makes the largest contribution to total global R&D investment. It accounts for half of the total non-R&D share of R&D expenditure. In 2008, China's R&D spending was 1.5 percent of the GDP, up from 1.25 percent in 2004. This was impressive because this period was a high GDP growth rate period. The Eleventh Five-Year Plan (2005–10) the rate of R&D investment increased further, albeit target of R&D spending of 2.5 percent of GDP was not met in 2010. The achievement was only 1.4 percent of GDP. However, China still accounted for 12.3 percent of global R&D spending in 2010 (Orr, 2011). In 2010, China's R&D spending was equal to that of Japan. They were bracketed at the second position, with the USA having the largest (34.4 percent) share in global R&D expenditure (Battelle, 2010).

Large increases in R&D expenditure led to important development in China's innovative system. A noteworthy attribute in this regard was R&D spending shifting from government-controlled research institutions to medium- and large-sized private business firms. The latter group began playing an active role and accounted for 60 percent of total R&D spending in China in 2010. Creation of an enterprise-centered innovation system is indeed an impressive achievement. The driving forces behind this structural shift were a combination of restructuring of research institutions, expansion of higher education and strengthening of R&D and innovation capabilities of business enterprises. The ambition underlying this systemic shift is to make R&D capability respond to market mechanism. By commercializing R&D it can be linked closely to the business sector and its needs. Research institutions and academia can still focus on basic research. Interestingly, FIEs accounted for a small segment (7 percent) of this spending. It was spread over 1,500 R&D centers established by MNCs. The number of PhDs in science and engineering is on the rise and China has become one of the leading countries in science and technology publications (Ernst, 2011).

China does not presently rank high in innovative thinking. Therefore political leadership in China appreciates R&D and emphasizes its value. Eight of the nine members of China's Standard Committee of the Political Bureau have engineering degrees. President Hu Jintao is also a trained engineer. The Chinese government has an indigenous innovation policy to encourage Chinese companies to originate and own technology.[21] China's ambition is to become an innovation leader by 2020. In the recent past many of the high-technology products produced in China came out of the manufacturing facilities operated by the multinational enterprises. The objective of the policy makers is to change this scenario effectively.

During the decade of the 2000s, to encourage technology transfer from abroad Chinese policy makers persuaded foreign companies to transfer their R&D operations to China. In exchange these companies were offered access to China's large-volume markets. China's growing R&D capabilities and its large domestic market are strong attractions for many multinationals. Large multinationals, such as IBM, Intel and Samsung, saw benefits in such an offer and responded by establishing large R&D facilities in China. In its quest for sophisticated technology, China has been frequently accused of coercing Western and Japanese firms (Hout and Ghemawat, 2010).

For enhancing TFP, the government adopted a new innovation policy in 2006. Accordingly, government-led research consortia brought together leading business firms, universities and R&D institutions run by the state. The new government strategy continues to favor SOEs as the main platform of indigenous innovation, albeit the fresh strand in the policy is that the private-sector enterprises have become significantly more important than ever in the past. In recent years mega-projects developed by government-led research consortia have become important (Liu and Cheng, 2011). However, the role of the private sector in TFP improvement and innovation at the technology frontier is quite critical. It is different in nature from catching up technologically. It is a process of trial and error, fraught with uncertainties. While it cannot be achieved by government planning, the role of the government needs to change to supportive and facilitating (WB/DRC, 2013).

6. The Asian crisis and the WTO accession as catalysts of reforms

In the reform process, the Asian crisis of 1997–98 cast a large shadow. It was a confluence of currency and banking crises. It provided China with an opportunity to adopt the next generation of macro-economic reforms. A meaningful development of the post-Asian crisis period was the concerted attempt to alleviate infrastructure-related bottlenecks by channeling large investments in upgrading and constructing the road network[22] as well as ports and airports expansion programmes. Promotion of a high-speed railway system was also taken up. A large proportion of the post-Asian crisis investments helped to remove critical obstructions to the growth process and promote high rates of returns on investments.

Tariff and non-tariff barriers had come down significantly during the decade prior to joining the WTO, in 2001. At this time, unweighted tariffs declined to 15.3 percent (see Section 3), standard deviation of dispersion came down to 12.1 and maximum tariffs to 121.6 percent. Special importing privileges were introduced for export processing firms and foreign-owned enterprises (FOEs) as well as jointly owned businesses. A significant degree of trade liberalization had taken place, particularly in manufactures, prior to WTO accession (Branstetter and Lardy, 2008). The WTO accession negotiations continued for 16 years. During this period China opened domestic markets further. It helped, *inter alia*, in opening up important segments of the service sector. In the post-WTO accession period, exports became a major driver of economic growth. As a percentage of GDP exports of goods and services hovered in the vicinity of 20 percent in 2000, but they rose precipitously to 39 percent in 2006. In 2007, when the global financial crisis began, they were still 38 percent of the GDP, albeit they plunged to 27 percent in 2009. There was a small uptick (29 percent) in 2010, the recovery year (WB, 2011a).

The WTO accession negotiation took 16 long years. This is an indication of the complexity of the negotiations. The WTO members expected China to conform to international rules and norms. In the process, China made myriad commitments to liberalize its domestic markets, which included the banking, insurance and financial sectors. Both the office of the US Trade Representative and the EU Chamber of Commerce in China believe that China did a good job of implementation of numerous commitments it made to liberalize its trading regime, domestic markets and other regulatory regimes. Most major commitments were met in the first five years after the accession (Ikenson, 2006). However, there are areas in which China did not adhere to the spirit of the WTO accession protocol, while complying with the letter of the law. For instance China has not joined the government procurement agreement. Services trade regime, particularly financial services, and protection for intellectual property rights are two areas where fulfillment of the WTO requirements is inadequate. China's currency policy and export restrictions are the other contentious areas (WTO, 2010b).

During the WTO accession negotiations, China had to acquiesce to the entry of foreign firms in its markets. This was a first for China. The foreign firms were to have full trading and direct distribution rights. Other important WTO commitments were in the areas of relatively better management of rural–urban labor migration, facilitating and supporting the urbanization process, general improvement of macro-economic management of the economy and long-awaited financial sector reforms. Financial markets were known for financial repression and a lack of depth (Allen et al., 2007; Huang, 2012). This was one important area in which reforms had lagged badly. The influential World Bank (WB/DRC, 2013) study stressed on loosening the state's grip on the financial sector.

Accession to the WTO enhanced the role of market forces in the domestic economy. Trade liberalization and entry of foreign firms also increased pressure on Chinese business firms to globalize. Official encouragement and financial support was provided to the domestic firms trying to globalize. They sought new global markets for their products and learned to grapple with the competition in the global marketplace. They also adjusted to and learned from operating in the global marketplace.

Since its accession to the WTO, China carefully complied with its obligations. According to the Trade Policy Review of the WTO, its tariff lines are bound and its applied tariff rates are close to most-favored-nation (MFN) rates. This tendency imparted a high degree of predictability to China's trade regime. In addition, NTBs were also brought down. The general objective of its trade policy does seem to be acceleration of opening its economy to multilateral trade. In 2009 average tariffs were down to 9.8 percent (WB, 2011b). After joining the WTO, China liberalized its trade regime and domestic regulations more rapidly than in the past. It changed or eliminated 2,300 laws and regulations in 2002. In all 30 federal ministries were involved in this large scale change of domestic bureaucratic, procedural and regulatory regime. The changes were far more at the provincial level, where over 100,000 local laws and regulations had to be changed or eliminated (Yu, 2009). Accession to the WTO helped China deepen its regional and global links.

During the WTO accession negotiations, it was made clear that China has to increase the pace of the reform process in several other significant areas of the economy. Important among those were, first, thorough revamping of the legal system so that it complied with esteemed international norms and, second, SOE reforms and the state-owned bank restructuring. Construction of the legal sector was undertaken in a highly concerted manner (Ambler et al., 2009).[23] The same can not be said regarding the SOEs reforms. China had promised a hands-off policy during the accession negotiations. Accordingly the government was to give up directly or indirectly influencing

SOE operations. Apparently, as discussed below, this commitment was not kept. New ways of influencing and controlling the SOEs evolved after China's WTO accession. Government provided them with five-year guidance plans and they became instruments of achieving the most important economic goals of the government.

7. Restructuring and rise of the state-owned enterprises

With progress in market-oriented reforms, a private sector was born in the 1980s and became increasingly active. Gradually the contribution of the SOE sector to GDP declined and that of the private sector went on increasing. Reforms and restructuring of SOEs fell behind the market-oriented economic reforms. The stance of gradualism, vigilance and caution in reforming the SOEs was deliberate and premeditated. The reason was that the economy's dependence on them, particularly during the early stages of market-oriented reforms and restructuring, was heavy. By any measure SOE reforms were a massive policy step because their political and economic impact was going to be large. They were going to affect the social welfare system, financial institutions and conditions in the labor market. Besides, SOEs played the role of stabilizers in an economy that was briskly adopting economic reforms and restructuring measures. Some of these policy measures could potentially have adverse short-term effects over the macro-economy. Stability in the SOE sector was essential for success of reforms in other sectors of the economy. The macro-economy could remain anchored to the SOEs during the implementation of reforms, which was taking place at a rapid pace.

The challenging task of restructuring of SOEs began in the 1980s when attempts were made to reinvigorate them by providing increasing autonomy and incentives to managers. Although these measures had favorable results, they were meager. The SOEs were neither restructured nor did they initiate any reforms in corporate governance. In addition, there was little change in ownership and corporate structure. Consequently, the performance of SOEs deteriorated and they recorded plunging profits in the 1980s and 1990s.

A major step in the area of SOE reforms was taken in 1992, when the government adopted the "Socialist Market Economy" stance during the 14th National Congress of the CPC. Building up a socialist market economy became an officially pronounced objective. Accordingly SOEs needed to be transformed into economic entities suitable for a market economy. Their identity as state production units had to alter to incorporated business entities. In 1994, at the third plenary session of the 14th central committee, Modern Enterprise System was proposed as a corporate form compatible with the socialist market economy. Internal management of SOEs was modified, so was the relationship between the government and SOEs. The new system entailed the following: (1) clarification of property rights; (2) clarification of rights and responsibility; (3) separation of bureaucracy and business; and (4) adoption of modern practices of management. SOEs were impelled to behave like corporate entities.

In 1997 out of 22,000 SOEs of large and medium size, 6,599 recorded losses (OECD, 2009). At this time the SOEs sector suffered from over-capacity and was also not able to compete with the newly established private enterprises and FIEs. A majority of them also suffered from unfavorable prices in their product lines. Low margins of profitability in SOEs made it clear to the policy mandarins that there was a pressing need for broad-based reforms in the SOE sector. It was in the mid-1990s that SOE reforms became a priority policy area. This time the policy measures aimed first at improving efficiency and second at SOEs catching up with the on-going market-oriented transformation of the macro-economy. Government action was freely taken to close or merge unviable SOEs.

Premier Zhu Rongji's Three-Year Reform Plan of 1998 had a central place in the chronicles of SOE reforms. This is when government began adopting business practices commonly used in market economies like layoffs, buy-outs, and action against corporate insolvency. Under the Three-Year Reform Plan huge layoffs, debt-reduction, debt-equity swap and technology improvement support were undertaken. These were bold and radical policy measures taken to improve the financial performance of SOEs in within three years (Li and Putterman, 2008).

At present several SOEs are among the largest companies in the world. They are a potent economic force and China has become more vulnerable to the allegation of state capitalism. It entails hybrid corporations, which are either owned or backed by the state but behave like a private-sector MNC.[24] As the economic strategy adopted by China is socialism with Chinese characteristics, SOEs will continue to play an important role in future as well. Thus viewed, the assumption of China turning into a capitalist economy dominated by private-sector enterprises is of dubious credibility. What seems more likely is that the private sector will coexist with the SOEs. In many industrial sectors, SOEs have been playing a diminishing role, yet they overwhelmingly dominate core industries like petroleum, coking, nuclear fuel, raw chemicals, transport equipment and mining. The state is determined to maintain a presence in these key industries, finance and high-technology sectors but moved away from the labor-intensive and competitive industries. They were opened for the private sector.

SOEs have complex ownership structures and are linked with the power of the state. They are owned by, or report to, three tiers of the government, central or national, state and local (Woetzel, 2008).[25] The 150 or so SOEs that report directly to the central government are huge conglomerates. They are large holding companies that have been climbing the world's league tables in every industry from oil to banking. They in turn own multiple firms as their subsidiaries. These first-tier SOEs are fully owned by the central government through the State-owned Assets and Supervision and Administration Commission (SASAC).

When the SASAC was set up in 2003, it had a total of 196 SOEs under its winds—the majority of them large and important. Subsequently, the smaller and less viable enterprises were either disbanded or merged into the larger ones. In May 2011 it was supervising 121 of the largest SOEs (Wang *et al.*, 2012). Since the inception of the SASAC, power and profitability of firms under the SASAC went on increasing. The SOEs owned by the SASAC provide public goods like defense, communication, transportation and utility as well as firms that specialize in natural resources. Enterprises owned by the SASAC are the largest among the three tiers of SOEs. The SASAC has identified an array of industries that are necessary for growth and national security. It is likely that these industries will remain under whole or partial state control. Managing large SOEs was not the only objective of the SASAC. It was to reform and modernize them and create profitable "national champion" firms. The concept of "national champion" has been described below. It did a commendable job of consolidation of Chinese steel mills. This industry was once plagued with small and uneconomical units of doubtful viability. Mergers planned by the SASAC created "emperors" and "kings", which have a high probability of viability and profitability. In 2007 the SASAC established a system of after-tax profit sharing. A part of the profits earned by SOEs under the SASAC supervision now goes to it.

The large (4 trillion renminbi or $590 billion or €640 billion) fiscal stimulus package designed and delivered during 2008–09 to alleviate the economic and financial stress created by the global financial crisis and the Great Recession worked favorably for the SOEs, particularly the large ones. A group of the largest 121 SOEs, which was selected for consolidation and strengthening, was the recipient of large dosages of credit from the four state-owned banks. The *Trade Policy Review* report of the WTO disapprovingly mentioned the SOE sector benefitting decidedly disproportionately from the stimulus package (WTO, 2010b).

To calculate the economic footprints of SOEs, the simplest method is to compute the contribution of SOEs to GDP. However, no such published estimates are available. Calculating the significance of SOEs in the economy is not free of data availability problems. Besides, the opaque nature of SOE ownership made assessing their contribution to GDP difficult. In the Chinese government's published estimates definition of SOEs includes only wholly state-funded SOEs. These estimates do not cover SOEs in which state-ownership is less than 100 percent, therefore leave out a massive part of the SOE sector. These data grossly understate the contribution of SOE sector and therefore incorrect. In 2010 SOEs produced 40 percent of China's non-agricultural GDP. To this, if firms that are indirectly controlled and those that benefit from government subsidized credit are included, this proportion rises to half the non-agricultural GDP (Report to Congress, 2011).

Employment statistics and official policy proclamations did reveal that their overall significance in the economy has declined. It is borne out by the statistics of industrial SOEs. According to the estimates made by OECD (2009) share of output of industrial SOEs in total industrial production declined from 49.6 percent 31.2 percent over the 1998–2006 period, value added declined from 57.0 percent to 35.8 percent, assets from 68.8 percent to 46.4 percent and employment from 60.5 percent to 24.5 percent. However, it was logical to expect the overall role of SOEs to decline after China's WTO accession in 2001. It did not (Wang et al., 2012). Assets and revenues of the SOE sector substantially increased since then. Data published in the National Bureau of Statistics show that the total assets of SOEs owned by the SASAC were 3 trillion RMB Yuan ($360 billion) in 2003 and shot up to 20 trillion RMB Yuan ($2,9 trillion) in 2010.

SOE restructuring was implemented with the financial restructuring of state-owned commercial banks (SOCBs). China's Big Four state-owned commercial banks, which dominate the banking system, were heavily saddled with non-performing loans (NPLs) that the SOEs had declined to service. The SOCBs were technically insolvent in the mid-1990s. Sector-wide NPL ratio was as high as 50 percent according to some estimates (Anderlini and Parker, 2011). These banks were recapitalized after 1998. To deal with the SOCBs' NPLs four Asset Management Corporations (AMCs) were set up. By 1999, four AMCs took over 1,394 billion RMB Yuan NPLs from the corresponding four SOCBs. For 580 large SOEs, a total of 404 billion RMB Yuan debt was swapped into equities (OECD, 2009). Also, a comprehensive reform program was implemented and the People's Bank of China (PBC) tried to instill market discipline in the state-owned banks. This was opposed by the Ministry of Finance, even though Premier Zhu Rongji was fully supportive of professionalization of the big four banks. Zhu Rongji handled the demanding task of economic and financial restructuring brilliantly during his tenure. PBC's banking reforms continued in the early 2000s after Zhu Rongji departed from the political scene. His leadership saved China from a potentially crippling financial crisis.

The initial recapitalization of the banking sector yielded encouraging results. It led to the impressive recovery of banks, and yet key weakness in the allocation of investable resources persist (Farrell et al., 2006; WB/DRC, 2013). Banking reforms transformed China's banking system. It is no longer a state monopoly. A wide range of non-state banking institutions now operate with the large SOCBs. The two segments of the banking industry are responsive to market signals and discipline. As a result of banking reforms banks' balance sheets and corporate governance have improved and with that compliance with international best practices. Yet, to develop a market-based banking sector, further retreat of the influence of the state is essential (Kwong, 2011). Problems have evolved in the post-global financial crisis period. After the large monetary stimulus of the post-global financial crisis period, volume of NPLs in the Chinese banks grew alarmingly large. In addition, in search of decent returns, retail investors snapped up a large volume of wealth management products, which may trouble Chinese banks in the same way that structured products plagued Western banks (WSJ, 2011; Orr, 2013).

During the decade after joining the WTO in 2001, China took numerous comprehensive measures to liberalize the economy. These measures were mandatory as China's accession obligations. However, of late the process seems to have reversed and the public policy makers in China give an impression of keeping large parts of the economy under the command of the government. What the CPC called the "Socialist Market Economy" is state-guided capitalism, where the government plays an active role in guiding the markets by supporting industries and enterprises that have a potential of becoming winners. State-ownership of banks is instrumental in implementing this strategy. This was the strategy followed by Japan and the NIEs in the past and China is taken a leaf from their strategy book (Baumol *et al.*, 2007). Other than favourable access to credit, the government also provides the SOE sector a variety of subsidies. This occurs at the expense of the private sector enterprises because they are crowded out of the financial access (WB, 2010a).

8. Outward foreign direct investment

The gradual liberalization of China's outward foreign direct investment (OFDI) occurred over 1986–91, when non-state firms were allowed to invest abroad. A total of 891 projects, with total outward investment of $1.2 billion were approved by the government during this period. Liberalization of OFDI progressed and Chinese business firms began investing in Asian stocks and real estate. However, when the Asian financial crisis precipitated, China's Ministry of Foreign Trade and Economic Co-operation (MOFTEC) discouraged OFDI and made approval procedures stringent for any OFDI over $1 million. During the 1992–98 period OFDI added up to $1.2 billion (Hong and Sun, 2006; Salidjanova, 2011).

When the recovery from the Asian crisis began in 1999, China's OFDI strategy was reconstituted, with an emphasis on "going global". To this end, legislation to promote and facilitate OFDI was enacted in 2000 (Rosen and Hanemann, 2009 and 2011). At the beginning of the 10th Five-Year Plan (2001–05), the government formulated the "go overseas" or *zouchuqu* policy. Starting from a low base, China's OFDI began to grown at a steep rate.[26] Its growth occurred both regionally and globally. OFDI became the latest element in China's integration in the Asian and global economic system. China's huge stash of forex reserves were an opulent source of mobile capital. Institutional support for OFDI was strengthened by the National Development and Reform Commission (NDRC) and the Export-Import Bank of China (EIBC). In 2004 they provided joint guidelines to encourage overseas investment by Chinese business firms. Government regarded regional and global expansion of Chinese firms as a key element of ensuring continued economic growth (Hong and Sun, 2006). Given the official encouragement and double digit growth of the Chinese economy, OFDI began to grow at a swift pace.

The government decided on the magnitude of the OFDI flows. The areas of investment are determined in accordance with the developmental goals of the economy and so were the geographical directions. The first wave of OFDI was essentially the resource-seeking OFDI and was made by large SOEs. Chinese business firm now regard OFDI as an instrument of acquiring equity stake around the world to diversify supply risks, dilute foreign bargaining power and gain a foothold in highly profitable upstream businesses. Interest in market-seeking OFDI has remained understandably low because of a large domestic consumer base. Foreign markets can be served by exporters, without the need for OFDI. However, when OFDI was made by private firms, it was more from market-seeking perspective (Ramasamy *et al.*, 2012). Using firm-level OFDI data, Tian and Yu (2012) concluded that during the recent years, a trend has emerged that shows that highly productive Chinese business firms have a greater tendency to make OFDI. They also tend to make larger volumes of OFDI.

Business firms regarded the government approval procedure for OFDI a trifle too long as well as complicated and cumbersome. In an effort to simplify the process and encourage OFDI, the State Administration of Foreign Exchange (SAFE) eliminated quotas of restrictions on the purchase of foreign exchange for foreign investment in 2006. Several other policy measures were taken to shorten the OFDI approval procedure by Chinese firms. These measures facilitated the outward investment of China's overseas companies moving capital outward across a broad spectrum of sectors. It needs to be mentioned that SOEs continued to be the dominant Chinese investors.

According to the statistics compiled by the Ministry of Commerce (MOC) of China the OFDI is still not large. The OFDI is small in comparison to its massive inward FDI. It was merely $12.26 billion in 2005, but more than quintupled by 2010, at $68.81 billion (MOC, 2010). At this juncture China's OFDI was merely 4.4 percent of world total global FDI and it was the fifth largest direct investor in the world. In 2011 OFDI increased to $65.11 billion, making China the sixth largest direct investor (UNCTAD, 2012). It stood at $77.2 billion in 2012. However, notwithstanding the rapid growth China's OFDI volume is not large in relative terms. It is only a fraction of OFDI made by the USA, UK or Germany and almost half of what Hong Kong, SAR makes. China is not even the largest OFDI-making EME, it is Russia.

In September 2012 China's foreign exchange reserves stood at $3.29 trillion and in March 2013 at $3.44 trillion. Supported by China's enormous foreign exchange reserves, continuing trade surpluses and receipts from existing global investments, China's has become the largest capital surplus economy in the global economy. Consequently, in the post-global financial crisis (2008–09) years, China's OFDI bucked the global trend in FDI flows. While global FDI flows suffered an understandably sharp decline (by 43 percent), China's OFDI recorded a small increase (1.11 percent), as indicated in the preceding paragraph. As the large accumulation forex holdings are a part of China's government policy, OFDI are not only likely to continue and but also strengthen.

Although both SOEs and private business make OFDI, SOEs have played a principal role in the expansion of OFDI. The four large entities that dominated the OFDI were the two oil giants China National Petroleum Corporation and Sinopec and China Investment Corporation (CIC), which is a sovereign wealth fund (SWF) and metals conglomerate Chinalco. In the latter half of the 2000s Chinese firms and investors increasingly explored opportunities for investment in a wide range of industries (Ming and Williamson, 2007). As regards the areas of investment, they ranged from natural resources to telecommunications. Sectors like business services attracted the largest part of the OFDI followed by mining and petroleum, wholesale and retail trade, transportation and storage and manufacturing. In 2008 and 2009 when the global FDI flows were declining, China's OFDI flows were still increasing. The government has a long-term strategy of OFDI and the Chinese business firms follow that. The government plays a role in selecting the industries and markets where OFDI should go. This control over OFDI is largely exerted through the SOEs.

Towards the end of 2011, CIC expected to receive fresh injections of capital. It was exploring investment opportunities in infrastructure development in advanced economies, starting with the UK. The government in the UK was looking for funds from UK pension funds and SWFs in Asia and the Middle East to help finance upgrades of roads, railways, ports and social housing. The CIC was eager to team up with fund managers or participate through a public–private partnership in the UK infrastructure sector as an equity investor. So far Chinese companies' involvement in overseas infrastructure projects was limited to the role of contractors. This is changing. Chinese companies and investors not only want to help build infrastructure in the advanced economies but also own and operate it (Anderlini and Parker, 2011).

China grew into an FDI-making economy in a sort span of time. Its OFDI is considered idiosyncratic. Current international business theories, such as Dunning's ownership–location–internalization (OLI) model of investment development path hypothesis does explain China's OFDI (Li, 2007). One unique feature of Chinese OFDI is government support and encouragement and policy innovation.[27] To explain the Chinese OFDI, this idiosyncratic feature should be added to the much-admired OLI hypothesis. Besides, China's rapid economic maturation as well as its integration into the regional and global economies is another reason that fast growth in OFDI reflected. Also, as brisk industrial development progressed in China, it became a huge consumer of natural resources, which included oil. China's OFDI had to increase because of the growing need for natural resources. The strategy of acquisition of advanced technology provided another impetus to OFDI. Additionally, China made a large foreign investment in iconic industrial takeovers like Zhejiang Holding Group's purchase of Volvo from Ford Motors. Due to several such high-profile acquisitions, China has attracted a lot of international attention.

Asia was the largest recipient region of Chinese OFDI. This region accounts for over 70 percent of Chinese OFDI. The amounts of annual outflows have picked up in the recent years and the OFDI is becoming an instrument of regional and global integration. It soared from $2.9 billion in 2003 to $17.6 billion in 2006 and further to $68.8 billion in 2010 (Table 2.3; Figure 2.3). In future China's OFDI is likely to continue and it is likely to influence regional and global economies through its rapidly increasing OFDI. Regional bias of China's OFDI flows is partly due to the fact that Hong Kong, SAR has been the largest beneficiary of OFDI flows. However, Chinese companies have also been busy expanding their production base in the region. They regard OFDI an instrument of expanding exports and capturing larger market shares in the neighboring economies (Salidjanova, 2011).

Chinese companies tend to invest in foreign companies in their own industries but they ensure that these foreign companies have higher technology and management as well as brand names. They also invest in service companies that could facilitate exports from the domestic bases. Cost minimization is not a motivation for Chinese OFDI because China is a successful low-cost producer.

TABLE 2.3 Chinese outward FDI flows by region, 2003–10 (US$ millions)

Region	2003	2004	2005	2006	2007	2008	2009	2010
Total	2,854.65	5,497.99	12,261.17	17,633.97	26,506.09	55,907.17	56,528.99	68,811.31
Asia	1,505.03	3,013.99	4,484.17	7,663.25	16,593.15	43,57.50	40,407.59	44,890.46
Africa	74.81	317.43	391.68	519.86	1,574.31	5,490.55	1,438.87	2,111.99
Europe	145.03	2,046.77	2,166.65	597.71	1,540.43	875.79	3,352.72	6,760.19
Latin America	1,038.15	1,762.72	6,466.16	8,468.74	4,902.41	3,677.25	7,327.90	10,538.27
North America	57.75	126.49	320.84	258.05	1,125.71	364.21	1,521.93	2,621.44
Oceania	33.88	120.15	202.83	126.36	770.08	1,951.87	2,479.98	1,888.96

Source: MOFCOM, 2010 Statistical Bulletin of China's Outward Foreign Direct Investment (Posted in September 16, 2011)

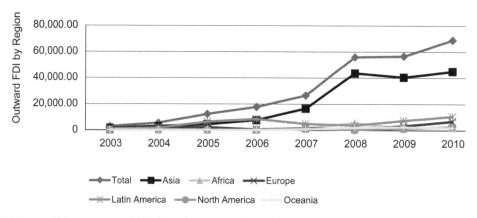

FIGURE 2.3 Chinese outward FDI flows by region, 2003–10
Source: MOFCOM, 2010 Statistical Bulletin of China's Outward Foreign Direct Investment (Posted in September 16, 2011)

Resource exploration has been an important motive behind Chinese OFDI. Mergers and acquisitions (M&As) by the Chinese firms with foreign business firms were an effective means of enhancing the international competitiveness of Chinese business firms. M&As serve to accelerated Chinese business firms' entry into foreign markets. In recent years the predominant areas of China's M&As were energy, mining, infrastructure, financial services, auto, high-end manufacturing, pharmaceuticals, medical and health care. OFDI was also a functional instrument of regional and global integration of the Chinese economy. It was consistent with the growing Chinese trade surplus and a gap between savings and investment.

As a global strategy, Chinese companies accelerated their M&A operations. The total number and transaction value of M&As deals by Chinese companies reached an all time high in 2012. In all 229 M&A deals were made abroad during the year and their disclosed transaction value was $53 billion. The average turnover rate per deal posted was $330 million. To become global leaders competitive Chinese companies have been making adroit use of M&As. For instance Lenovo took over NEC of Japan and Medion of Germany. It became the largest PC selling company in the world in the third quarter of 2012, acquiring 15.7 percent of the global PC market. Also, Haier acquired the white goods business of Sanyo electronics in 2011, which would become a leading global firm in 2012, when its market share was 8.6 percent. Haier entered new markets in 2012 by taking over Fisher & Paykel, a home appliance maker in New Zealand (SERI, 2013).

9. Summary and conclusions

A remarkable, perhaps even astonishing, economic event of the early part of the 21st century is that China has become the second largest economy in the world in a short span of three decades. Its stature in the global economy continued to increase and it contributed significantly to the recovery of the global economy from the global financial crisis (2007–09) and, despite setbacks, put up a resilient performance during the on-going Eurozone crisis. From a long-term perspective China can convincingly be presented as a clear winner of globalization.

In a succinct manner, this chapter traces the growth path of the Chinese economy during its market-oriented macro-economic reform era. China's reforms and restructuring process were unorthodox and implemented in a manner that a neo-classical economist will not regard as ideal.

In many ways China's policies ignored the Washington Consensus. The government continued to play a vital role in guiding the economy to its market-oriented transformation.

In approximately three decades, instituting sequential macro-economic reforms and institutional upgrading turned China into a dynamic, market-oriented economy. The synergy produced by this switch from a centrally planned economic framework to a market economy was enormous. It increased economic efficiency and productivity many times over. This momentous transfer explains China's success as an exporting economy much more than the principle of comparative advantage. China started its reforms and restructuring without a carefully drawn plan and assigned high priority to pragmatism, experimentation and improvisation.

China was slow to open up its trade regime but its participation in export processing, also known as vertical or international fragmentation of production, provided an impetus to opening its import regime. Chinese firms that were involved in export processing enjoyed the privilege of duty-free imports. During the decade of the 1990s, China undertook a good deal of trade liberalization and unilateral tariff reduction. As noted earlier, the Asian crisis and the WTO accession catalyzed the reform and liberalization process of the trade regime.

During the reform period, the trade structure of China underwent a dramatic transformation. Since the early 1990s, China's export structure has shifted towards hard manufactures, which include machinery, electronic goods and computers. Another important transformation was in FDI flows. When the reforms were launched China was not a favorite destination for FDI. However, macroeconomic and institutional reforms and liberalization continuously improved China's foreign investment climate. Methodically setting up SEZs in the coastal provinces and delta regions in order to attract FDI was another major strategy that yielded rich dividends in terms of FDI. It not only became the most attractive EME destination but also the 2010 investors' confidence index was the highest for China.

The Asian crisis of 1997–98 and the WTO accession of 2001 proved to be veritable catalysts to the reform process. They provided China with the next generation of macroeconomic reforms. The prolonged WTO accession process was responsible for ushering in a significant transformation in the restructuring of the Chinese economy. Increasing openness of multilateral trading system benefited the Chinese economy enormously, which was trade-biased. Expanding trade made critical contribution to China's vertiginous GDP growth. In its exports China adopted limited catch-up strategy. Rather than merely following its comparative advantage. Therefore, R&D-intensive industries like consumer electronics and automotive products became prominent export lines. China's trade regime was skillfully designed for rapid expansion of processing trade, also known as vertically integrated production networks or international production fragmentation. Network production not only integrated Chinese economy regionally and globally but also transformed the nature of multilateral trade. In the post-1992 period China became a veritable magnet for FDI, receiving the largest amounts of inflows among the EMEs year after year. It was the result of a proactive and well-considered FDI promotion strategy. Manufacturing sector and assembly operations were the destination of an overwhelmingly large part of FDI inflows.

With the progress in market-oriented reforms, a private sector was born in the 1980s and became increasingly active. Gradually the contribution of the SOE sector to GDP declined and that of the private sector went on increasing. Reforms and restructuring of SOEs fell behind the market-oriented economic reforms. The challenging task of restructuring of SOEs began in the 1980s, although the measures taken were meager. Therefore their performance deteriorated. Premier Zhu Rongji's Three-Year Reform Plan of 1998 had a central place in the chronicles of SOE reforms. This is when the government began adopting business practices commonly used in market economies like layoffs, buy-outs and action against corporate insolvency. Their performance improved over the years and at present many of them are among the largest companies in the world.

After the Asian crisis, starting from a low base, China's OFDI began to grown at a steep rate. Its growth occurred both regionally and globally. OFDI became the latest element in China's integration in the Asian and global economic system. China's huge stash of forex reserves were an opulent source of mobile capital. Institutional support for OFDI was strengthened by the National Development and Reform Commission and the EIBC. In 2004 they provided joint guidelines to encourage overseas investment by Chinese business firms. Government regarded regional and global expansion of Chinese firms as a key element of ensuring continued economic growth. Given the official encouragement and double digit growth of the Chinese economy, OFDI began to grow at a swift pace.

Notes

1 Also see WB/DRC (2013) for a detailed discussion on this subject.
2 The terms real economy, or real economic activity or real-side activity refer to the physical part of the economy that is concerned with actually producing goods, services and resources. This facet of the economy deals with using resources to produce goods and services that make satisfaction of wants and needs possible. It entails the creation of jobs, incomes and consumer spending. It excludes the paper economy and the financial side of the economy.
3 It needs to be mentioned that in purchasing-power parity (PPP) terms, China was the second largest economy in the world in 2002. The PPP-based computations adjust the different purchasing power of the dollar across countries.
4 Hu (2011) provides a rich and lucid insider's perspective on China's re-emergence to be a regional and global economic power and a window over where it is headed over the next decade. Supported by a plethora of facts and up-to-date economic and social statistical data, the book provides a nuanced story of China's modern economic development.
5 The source of statistical data used here is IMF (2011).
6 At this point Deng Xiaoping was the chairman of the central military commission. Despite his domineering position during the reform era, he still had to mobilize political support from important leaders like Chen Yun, Peng Zhen, Bo Yibo *et al.*
7 Chen Yun was another prominent political leader who played an important role in economic reforms.
8 The so-called preliminary stage theory dealt with the ideological challenges of how to integrate market instruments into a socialist planned economic system.
9 The NIEs comprise Hong Kong, SAR, Korea, Singapore and Taiwan.
10 These institutional innovations had produced meritorious results in other high-performing Asian economies. The first export promotion zone was established in 1966 in Kaoshing, Taiwan. Its success motivate motivated Korea to establish two large EPZs. They contained 200 bonded warehouses. In the 1980s Malaysia set up several of them and they became the principal producers of its exports. The Philippines followed closely and turned Subic Bay and Clark into EPZs. Their successful operation was a lesson for China and the first Chinese EPZs were created in Shenzhen.
11 The Washington Consensus was beginning to lose its sheen in the late 1990s. Aggressive criticism by Joseph E. Stiglitz (1998a and 1998b) saw its demise.
12 It should however be clarified that the nature of the state-market relationship of Germany and Japan on the one hand and the USA on the other represent opposite ends of capitalism.
13 Several scholarly accounts of the reform process are available. For instance, see Das (2008a), Lardy (2002), Lau *et al.* (2000), Murphy *et al.* (1992) and Naughton (2007).
14 These statistical data have been sourced from Lardy (2003).
15 See Wignaraja and Olfindo (2009) for a detailed analysis how automotive and electronics became successful export sectors in China.
16 See Branstetter and Lardy (2008) for a detailed account of liberalization of China's trade and FDI regime.
17 On 11 December 2001 China became the 143rd member of the WTO.
18 Das (2008a) and Naughton (2007) provide a detailed account of the setting-up process of SEZs and the benefits that Chinese economy received from them.

19 In the recent past, wages has increased at a steep rate in China. Year-on-year rise in wages was 10.4 percent in 2008, 12.4 percent in 2009 and 9.7 percent in 2010.
20 See OECD (2010b), Chapter 1, p. 25, Table 1.2.
21 The innovation policy is laid out in the *Medium- and Long-Term national Plan for Science and Technology Development* issued by China's State Council in February 2006.
22 China's 41,000 km of National Expressway Network (NEN) is second in size to the US Interstate Highway System.
23 See in particular Ambler *et al.* (2009), Chapter 5.
24 State directed capitalism is not a new phenomenon. East India Company (1600–1874) was granted a Royal Charter by Queen Elizabeth I in December 1600.
25 There are thousands more SOEs that fall into a grey area. For instance, the subsidiaries of these 150 SOEs come under this category. In addition, there are SOEs owned by provincial and municipal governments. There also are SOEs that have been partially privatized but the state has continued to be a majority shareholder or influential shareholder.
26 OFDI is defined to include all investment where a foreign investing firm exerts control over domestic assets. Usually portfolio investments are not included. Contrary to this convention, the Ministry of Commerce (MOC) of China aggregates both the financial and non-financial OFDI.
27 As a strategy, the Chinese government encourages OFDI that helps in securing scarce resources, stimulate exports, promote state of the art technology transfer, enhance technological capabilities of Chinese firms and advance management skills of Chinese firms.

References

Aitken, B. and A. E. Harrison. 1999. "Do Domestic Firms Benefit from Direct Foreign Investment?" *The American Economic Review*. Vol. 89. No. 3, pp. 605–18.
Allen, F., J. Qian and M. Qian. 2007. "China's Financial System", in L. Brandt and T. Rawski (eds). *China's Great Economic Transition*. Cambridge: Cambridge University Press, pp. 429–86.
Ambler, T., M. Witzel and C. Xi. 2009. *Doing Business in China*. 3rd edition. London and New York: Routledge.
Amiti, M. and C. Freund. 2010. "An Anatomy of China's Export Growth", in R. C. Feenstra and S. J. Wei (eds). *China's Growing Role in World Trade*. Chicago, IL: University of Chicago Press, pp. 35–62.
Anderlini, J. and G. Parker. 2011. "China Fund Targets Big Projects in the West." *Financial Times*. London. November 28, p. 1.
Arayama, Y. and K. Miyoshi. 2004. "Regional Diversity and Sources of Economic Growth in China." *The World Economy*. Vol. 27. No. 7, pp. 1583–607.
Arrighi, G. 2007. *Adam Smith in Beijing: Lineages of the Twenty-First Century*. London: Verso.
Asian Development Bank (ADB). 2012. *Asian Economic Integration Monitor*. Manila, the Philippines. July.
A. T. Kearney. 2012. *Cautious Investors Feed a Tentative Recovery. A. T. Kearney FDI Confidence Index*. Vienna, VA: Global Business Policy Council.
——2010. *Investing in a Rebound: The 2010 A.T.Kearney FDI Confidence Index*. Vienna, VA: Global Business Policy Council.
Battelle. 2010. "2011 Global R&D Funding Forecast." *R&D Magazine*. Vol. 28. Available online at www. battelle.org/aboutus/rd/2011.pdf.
Baumol, W. J., R. E. Litan and C. J. Schramm. 2007. "Sustaining Entrepreneurial Capitalism." *Capitalism and Society*. The Berkeley Electronic Press. Vol. 2. No. 2. Article 1.
Bernanke, B. S. 2006. "The Chinese Economy: Progress and Challenges." Paper presented at the Chinese Academy of Social Sciences, Beijing, 15 December.
Borensztein, E. and D. J. Ostry. 1996. "Accounting for China's Growth Performance." *American Economic Review*. Vol. 86. No. 6, pp. 224–28.
Branstetter, L. and N. Lardy. 2008. "China's Embrace of Globalization", in L. Brandt and T. G. Rawski (eds). *China's Great Economic Transformation*. Cambridge: Cambridge University Press, pp. 633–82.
Buckley, P. J., J. Clegg and C. Wang. 2010a. "Inward FDI and Host Country Productivity", in P. J. Buckley (ed.). *Foreign Direct Investment, China and the World Economy.*" Basingstoke: Palgrave Macmillan, pp. 216–38.

Buckley, P. J., J. Clegg, A. Cross and H. Tan. 2010b. "China's Inward Foreign Direct Investment Success", in P. J. Buckley (ed.). *Foreign Direct Investment, China and the World Economy*. Basingstoke: Palgrave Macmillan, pp.239–69.

Buckley, P. J., J. Clegg and C. Wang. 2002. "The Impact of Inward FDI on the Performance of Chinese Manufacturing Firms." *Journal of International Business Studies*. Vol. 33. No. 4, pp. 637–55.

Ceglowski, J. and S. Golub. 2007. "Just How Low are China's Labor Costs?" *The World Economy*. Vol. 30. No. 4. pp. 597–617.

Chen, Y. 2001. "Evidence of the Effects of Openness Policy on TFP and its Components: The Case of Chinese Provinces." Paper presented at the Third International Conference on the Chinese Economy in Clermont-Ferrand, France, 21 May.

Chow, G. 1993. "Capital Formation and Economic Growth in China." *Quarterly Journal of Economics*. Vol. 108. No. 4, pp. 809–42.

Cimoli, M., G. Dosi and J. E. Stiglitz (eds). 2009. *Industrial Policy and Development: The Political Economy of Capabilities Accumulation*. New York: Oxford University Press.

Coase, R. and N. Wang 2012. *How China Became Capitalist*. Basingstoke: Palgrave Macmillan.

Das, Dilip K. 2011. *Asian Economy: Spearheading the Recovery from the Global Financial Crisis*. London and New York: Routledge.

——2008. *The Chinese Economic Renaissance: Apocalypse or Cornucopia?* Basingstoke: Palgrave Macmillan.

Dean, J. M., K. C. Fung and Z. Wang. 2007. *Measuring the Vertical Specialization in Chinese Trade*. Working Paper No. 2007/01/A. January. Washington, DC: US International Trade Commission.

Dekle, R. and G. Vandenbroucke. 2006. "A Quantitative Analysis of China's Structural Transformation." *Proceedings*. Federal Reserve Bank of San Francisco. June.

Drucker, P. 1977. "The Rise of Production Sharing." *The Wall Street Journal*. 15 March, p. 8.

Du, L., A. Harrison and G. H. Jefferson. 2012. "Testing for Horizontal and Vertical Foreign Investment Spillovers in China, 1998–2007." *Journal of Asian Economics*. Vol. 23. No. 3. June, pp. 234–43.

The Economist. 2011a. "Capitalism Confined." 3 September, pp. 62–4.

The Economic Intelligence Unit (EIU). 2012. "China in Focus: Spreading the Wealth." London. February.

——2011a. "Heavy Duty: China's Next Wave of Exports." London. October.

——2011b. "Multinational Companies and China: What Future?" London. December.

Egger, P. and M. Pfaffermayer. 2001. "A Note on Labor Productivity and Foreign Inward Direct Investment." *Applied Economic Letters*. No. 8. pp. 229–32.

Easterly, W. and R. Levine. 2001. "It's Not Factor Accumulation: Stylized Facts and Growth Models." *World Bank Economic Review*. Vol. 15. No. 2, pp. 177–219.

Ernst, D. 2011. "China's Innovation Policy is a Wake-up Call for America." *Asia Pacific Issues*. No. 100. Honolulu, HI: East-West Center. May.

Estevadeordal, A. and A. M. Taylor. 2008. "Is the Washington Consensus Dead? Growth, Openness and the Great Liberalization." Cambridge, MA: National Bureau of Economic Research. Working Paper No. 14264. August.

Farrell, D., S. Lund and F. Morin. 2006. "How Financial System Reform Could Benefit China." *The McKinsey Quarterly*, pp. 92–105.

Feenstra, R. C. 2010. *Offshoring in the Global Economy*. Cambridge, MA: MIT Press.

Findley, R. 1978. "Relative Backwardness, Direct Foreign investment and Transfer of Technology." *Quarterly Journal of Economics*. Vol. 92. No. 1. pp. 1–16.

Frangos, A. 2011. "China Boosts Export Edge." *The Wall Street Journal Asia*. 11 July, p. 1.

Gaulier, G., F. Lemoine and D. Unal-Kesenci. 2007. "China's Emergence and Reorganization of Trade Flows in Asia." *China Economic Review*. Vol. 18. No. 2. pp. 209–43.

Goodstadt, L. F. 2012. "China's Financial Reforms: Why Dysfunctional Banking Survives." Hong Kong: Hong Kong Institute of Monetary Research. Working Paper No. 02/2012.

Hale, G., C. Long and H. Miura. 2010. *Where to Find Productivity Spillovers from FDI in China?* Working Paper No. 14/2010. Hong Kong: Hong Kong Institute for Monetary Research. June.

Hanson, G. H., R. J. Mataloni and M. J. Slaughter. 2001. "Expansion Strategies of US Multinational Firms", in S. M. Collins and D. Rodrik (eds). *Brookings Trade Forum*. Washington, DC: Brookings Institution Press, pp. 120–48.

Harris, R. G. and P. E. Robertson. 2009. "Trade, Wage and Skill Accumulation in the Emerging Giants." Adelaide: University of Western Australia. Discussion Paper No. 09–19.

Henry, P. B. 2007. "Capital Account Liberalization: Theory, Evidence and Speculation." *Journal of Economic Literature*. Vol. 45. No. 4, pp. 887–935.

Heytens, P. and H. Zebregs. 2003. "How Fast Can China Grow?", in W. Tseng and M. Rodlauer (eds). *China Competing in the World Economy*. Washington, DC: International Monetary Fund, pp. 8–29.

Hong, E. and L. Sun. 2006. "Dynamics of Internationalization and Outward Investment." *The China Quarterly*. No. 187, pp. 610–34.

Horn, J., V. Singer and J. Woetzel. 2010. "A True Picture of China's Export Machine." *McKinsey Quarterly*. September. Available online at www.portugalglobal.pt/PT/PortugalNews/EdicaoAicepPortugalGlobal/Documents/China041010.pdf

Hout, T. M. and P. Ghemawat. 2010. "China Vs the World: Whose Technology Is It?" *Harvard Business Review*. Vol. 88. No. 12, pp. 95–103.

Hu, A. 2011. *China in 2020: A New Type of Superpower.* Washington, DC: The Brookings Institution Press.

Hu, Z. and M. S. Khan. 1997. "Why Is China Growing So Fast?" Washington, DC: International Monetary Fund. *Economic Issues Paper No. 8*. April.

Huang, Y. 2012. "Time for China to Give Up Financial Repression." *The Financial Times*. 2 May, p. 9.

Ikenson, D. J. 2006. "China: Mega-Threat or Quiet Dragon." Paper presented at the American Institute of International Steel conference in Chicago, IL, on 6 March. Available online at www.cato.org/pub_display.php?pub_id=10912.

International Monetary Fund (IMF). 2012a. *World Economic Outlook Update*. Washington, DC. 24 January.

——2012b. *Financial Sector Assessment: People's Republic of China*. Washington, DC. March.

——2011. *World Economic Outlook*. Washington, DC. April.

Jefferson, G. H. 2008. "How Has China's Economic Emergence Contributed to the Field of Economics?" *Comparative Economic Studies*. Vol. 50. No. 1, pp. 167–209.

Johnson, R. C. and G. Noguera. 2012. "Proximity and Production Fragmentation." *American Economic Review*. Vol. 102. No. 3, pp. 407–11.

Kim, S., J. W. Lee and C. Y. Park. 2010. "The Ties that Bind Asia, Europe and the United States." Manila, the Philippines: Asian Development Bank. Working Paper No. 192. October.

Koopman, R. and Z. Wang. 2008. "How Much Chinese Exports Is Really Made in China? Assessing Domestic Value-Added." Cambridge, MA: National Bureau of Economic Research. Working Paper No. 14109.

Krugman, P. 1995. "Growing World Trade: Causes and Consequences." *Brookings Paper on Economic Activity*. 25th Anniversary Issue. pp. 327–77.

——1994. "The Myth of Asia's Miracle?" *Foreign Affairs*. Vol. 73. No. 1, pp. 62–78.

Kuijs, L. and T. Wang. 2006. "China's Pattern of Growth: Moving to Sustainability and Reducing Inequality." *China and World Economy*. Vol. 14. No. 1, pp. 1–14.

Kwong, C. C. L. 2011. "China's Banking Reform: The Remaining Agenda." *Global Economic Review*. Vol. 40. No. 2, pp. 161–78.

Lardy, N. R. 2003. "Trade Liberalization and Its Role in Chinese Economic Growth." Paper presented at the International Monetary Fund conference on *A Tale of Two Giants: India and China*, New Delhi, 14–16 November.

——2002. *Integration of China in the Global Economy*. Washington, DC: The Brookings Institution Press.

Lau, L., Y. Qian and G. Roland. 2000. "Reform without Losers: An Interpretation of China's Dual-Track Approach." *Journal of Political Economy*. Vol. 108. No. 1, pp. 120–43.

Lau, L. J. and J. Park. 2003. "The Sources of East Asian Economic Growth Revisited." Paper presented at Tsinghua University, Beijing, 26 March.

Lee, G. 2007. "Long Run Equilibrium Relationship between Inward FDI and Productivity." *Journal of Economic Development*. Vol. 32. No. 1, pp. 183–92.

Lee, H. H., D. Park and J. Wang. 2011. "The Role of People's Republic of China in International Fragmentation and Production Network." Manila, the Philippines: Asian Development Bank. Working Paper No. 87. September.

Lemoine, F. and D. Unal-Kesenci. 2004. "Assembly Trade and Technology Transfer: The Case of China." *World Development*. Vol. 32. No. 5, pp. 82–850.

Li, H., L. Li, B. Wu and Y. Xiong. 2012. "The End of Cheap Chinese Labor." *Journal of Economic Perspective*. Vol. 26. No. 4, pp. 57–74.

Li, P. P. 2007. "Towards an Integrated Theory of Multinational Evolution: The Evidence of Chinese Multinationals." *Journal of International Management*. Vol. 13. No. 3, pp. 296–318.

Li, W. and L. Putterman. 2008. "Reforming China's SOEs: An Overview." *Comparative Economic Studies*. Vol. 50. No. 2, pp. 353–80.

Liang, H. 2005. "*China's Ascent: Can the Middle Kingdom Meet Its Dreams?*" *Global Economic Papers*. No. 133. New York: Goldman Sachs.

Lin, C. H., C. M. Lee and C. H. Yang. 2011. "Does Foreign Direct Investment Really Enhance China's Regional Productivity?" *The Journal of International Trade & Economic Development*. Vol. 20. No. 6, pp. 741–68.

Lin, J. Y. 2011a. "China and the Global Economy." *China Economic Journal*. Vol. 4. No. 1, pp. 1–14.

——2011b. "New Structural Economics: A Framework for Rethinking Development." *The World Bank Research Observer*. Vol. 26. No. 2, pp. 193–221.

——2010. *New Structural Economics: A Framework for Rethinking Development*. Washington, DC: World Bank. Policy Research Working Paper No. 5197. December.

Lin, J. Y. and Y. Wang. 2012. "China's Integration with the World: Development as a Process of Learning and Industrial Upgrading." *China Economic Policy Review*. Vol. 1. No. 1, pp. 1–33.

Liu, X. and P. Cheng. 2011. "Is China's Indigenous Innovation Strategy Compatible with Globalization?" Honolulu, HI. East-West Center. Policy Study No. 61.

Maddison, A. 2006. "Asia in the World Economy 1500–2030." *Asian Pacific Economic Literature*. Vol. 20. No. 2, pp. 1–37.

Makin, J. H. 2011. "Can China's Currency Go Global?" *Economic Outlook*. Washington, DC: American Enterprise Institute. February.

Marsh, P. 2013. "China Looks to Drive the Car Industry." *The Financial Times*. 2 January, p. 14.

Ministry of Commerce (MOC). 2011. "Ministry of Commerce." The Government of the People's Republic of China. Available online at http://english.mofcom.gov.cn/statistic/statistic.html.

Ming, Z. and P. J. Williamson. 2007. "Dragon at Your Door", Boston, MA: Harvard Business School Press.

Murphy, K., A. Shleifer and R. Vishny. 1992. "The Transition to a Market Economy." *Quarterly Journal of Economics*. Vol. 107. No. 2, pp. 889–906.

National Bureau of Statistics (NBS). 2012. *National Economy Maintained Steady and Fast Development in 2011*." Beijing. 17 January. Available online at www.stats.gov.cn/english/newsandcomingevents/t20120117_402779577.htm.

Naughton, B. 2007. *The Chinese Economy: Transition and Growth*. Cambridge, MA: MIT Press.

Organisation for Economic Co-operation and Development (OECD). 2010a. *OECD Information Technology Outlook*. Paris. December.

——2010b. *China in the 2010s: Rebalancing Growth and Strengthening Social Safety Nets*. Paris. March.

——2010c. *Economic Survey of China 2010*. Paris.

——2009. "State-Owned Enterprises in China." Paris. 26 January.

Orr, G. 2011. "Unleashing Innovation in China." *McKinsey Quarterly*. January. Available online at www.mckinseyquarterly.com/Unleashing_innovation_in_China_2725.

——2013. "What's in Store for China in 2013?" San Francisco, CA: McKinsey. January.

Ozawa, T. 2009. *The Rise of Asia*. Northampton, MA, CA and Cheltenham: Edward Elgar.

Perkins, D. 1997. "Completing China's Move to the Market." *Journal of Economic Perspectives*. Vol. 8. No. 1, pp. 23–46.

Perkins, D. H. and T. G. Rawski. 2008. "Forecasting China's Economic Growth to 2025", in L. Brandt and T. G. Rawski (eds). *China's Great Economic Transformation*. Cambridge: Cambridge University Press, pp. 829–86.

Pomeranz, K. 2000. "Locating China in the Twenty-First-Century Knowledge-Based Economy." *Journal of Contemporary China*. Vol. 21. No. 73, pp. 113–30.

Rodrik, D. 2010. "Making Room for China in the World Economy." *American Economic Review*. Vol. 100. No. 2, pp. 89–93.

——2008. "The New Development Economics: We Shall Experiment, but How Shall We Learn?" Cambridge, MA: Harvard Kennedy School, Harvard University. Working Paper Series No. 08–0555. October.

——2006a. *What's So Special about China's Exports?* Working Paper No. 11947. Cambridge, MA: National Bureau of Economic Research. January.

——2006b. "Goodbye Washington Consensus, Hello Washington Confusion?" *Journal of Economic Literature*. Vol. 44. No. 4, pp. 969–83.

Rosen, D. H. and T. Hanemann. 2009. *China's Changing Outward Foreign Direct Investment*. Washington, DC: Peterson Institute for International Economics.

——2011. *Outward FDI from China: Dimensions, Drivers Implications*. Washington, DC: Peterson Institute for International Economics.

Sachs, J. D. and W. T. Woo. 1997. *Understanding China's Economic Performance*. Working Paper No. 575. Cambridge, MA: Harvard Institute of Economic Research, Harvard University.

Salidjanova, N. 2011. "Going Out: An Overview of China's Outward Foreign Direct Investment." Washington, DC: US-China Economic & Security Review Commission. Research Report. 30 March.

Samsung Economic Research Institute (SARI). 2012. "Foreign Car Companies' Technology Transfer." Beijing, China. Available online at www.seriworld.org/01/wldContL.html?mn=E&natcd=KR&mncd=03 05& listopt=L&sortopt=D&gubun=00&pagen=1.

Samuelson, P. A. 2002. "Where Ricardo and Mill Rebut and Confirm Arguments of Mainstream Economists Supporting Globalization." *Journal of Economic Perspectives*. Vol. 18. No. 3, pp. 135–46.

Schott, P. K. 2008. "The Relative Sophistication of Chinese Exports." *Economic Policy*. Vol. 53. No. 1, pp. 5–49.

SERI., 2013. "China's Overseas M&As in 2012." Beijing: Samsung Economic Research Institute. 22 March.

Stiglitz, J. E. 1998a "More Instruments and Broader Goals: Moving Towards the Post-Washington Consensus." WIDER Annual Lectures No. 2. Helsinki, Finland. 7 January.

——1998b. "Sound Finance and Sustainable Development in Asia." Keynote address to the Asian Development Forum, Manila. 12 March.

Summers, L. H. 2010. "Parting Words." *The Wall Street Journal*. New York. 22 November, p. 11.

Sun, H. 2001. "Foreign Direct Investment and Regional Export Performance in China." *Journal of Regional Science*. Vol. 41. No. 2, pp. 317–36.

Tian, W. and M. Yu. 2012. "Outward Foreign Direct Investment and Productivity: Firm-Level Evidence from China." Social Science Research Network. Available online at papers.ssrn.com/sol3/papers.cfm?abstract_id=1985130& http://www.google.com/url?sa=t&rct=j&q=tian%20and%20yu%202012%20outward%20foreign%20direct%20investment%20and%20productivity&source=web&cd=2&ved=0CCcQFjAB&url=http%3A%2F%2Fpapers.ssrn.com%2Fsol3%2FDelivery.cfm%3Fabstractid%3D1985130&ei=ntuhT7LRLc7mmAWz_7n7Bw&usg=AFQjCNFCqLHpsEjpmSMBTcsFpLijSbsS7Q. 25 February.

Tse, E. 2009. "China as an Oasis amid the Global Economic Crisis." New York: Booze. Available online at www.booz.com/media/uploas/China_An_Oasia.pdf.

Tuan, C., L. Ng and B. Zhao. 2009. "China's Post-Economic Reform Growth: The Role of FDI and Productivity Process." *Journal of Asian Economics*. Vol. 20. No. 2, pp. 280–93.

United Nations Conference on Trade and Development (UNCTAD). 2012. *World Investment Report*. Geneva and New York. June.

——2010. *World Investment Report*. Geneva and New York. July.

——2007. *Rising FDI into China: Facts Behind the Numbers*. UNCTAD Investment Brief No. 2. Geneva and New York.

US-China Economic and Security Commission. 2011. *Report to Congress*. Washington, DC: US Government Printing Press. November.

Vincelette, G. A., A. Manoel, A. Hansson and L. Kuijs. 2011. "China: Global Crisis Avoided, Robust Economic Growth Sustained", in M. K. Nabli (ed.). *The Great Recession and the Developing Countries: Economic Impact and Growth Prospects*. Washington, DC: World Bank. pp. 110–35.

Vogel, E. F. 2011. *Deng Xiaoping and the Transformation of China*. Cambridge, MA: Harvard University Press.

Wall Street Journal (WSJ). 2011. "China's Self-Reforming Banks?" New York. 6 December, p. 11.

Walter, C. and F. Howie. 2011. *The Weakness beneath China's Rise*. Singapore: John Wiley & Sons (Asia).

Wang, J., D. Guthrie and Z. Xiao. 2012. "The Rise of SASAC: Asset Management and Ownership Concentration." *Management and Organization Review*. Vol. 8. No. 2, pp. 253–281.

Wang, Z. 2010. "What Accounts for the Rising Sophistication of China's Exports?", in R.C. Feenstra and S.J. Wei (eds). *China's Growing Role in World Trade*. Chicago, IL, and London: University of Chicago Press, pp. 63–108.

Wang, Z. and S. J. Wei. 2008. "What Accounts for the Rising Sophistication of China's Exports." Cambridge, MA: National Bureau of Economic Research. Working Paper No. 13771. February.

Wang, Y. and Y. Yao. 2003. "Sources of China's Economic Growth, 1952–99: Incorporating Human Capital Formation." *China Economic Review*. Vol. 14. No. 1, pp. 32–52.

Williamson, J. 1990. *Latin American Adjustment: How Much Has Happened?* Washington, DC: Institute for International Economics.

Woetzel, J. R. 2008. "Reassessing China's State-Owned Enterprises." *McKinsey Quarterly*. July 2008. Available online at www.mckinseyquarterly.com/article_print.aspx?L2=21&L3=33&ar=2149.

World Bank and the Development Research Center (WB/DRC). 2013. *China 2030: Building a Modern, Harmonious and Creative High-Income Society*. Washington, DC.

World Bank (WB). 2011a. *World Development Indicators 2010*. Washington, DC.

——2011b. "East Asia and Pacific Economic Update 2011." Washington, DC. March.

——2010a. *China: Quarterly Update*. World Bank Office, Beijing. June.

——2010b. *World Development Indicators 2010*. Washington, DC.

World Investment Report (WIR). 2012. *United Nations Conference on Trade and Development*. Geneva and New York. October.

World Trade Organization (WTO). 2012. "Trade Growth to Slow in 2012 after Strong Deceleration in 2011." Press Release. Press/658. Geneva, Switzerland. 12 April.

——2011. *International Trade Statistics 2011*. Geneva, Switzerland.

——2010a. *International Trade Statistics*. Geneva, Switzerland. September.

——2010b. *Trade Policy Review of China*. Geneva, Switzerland. 26 April. (WT/TPR/S/230).

Wu, Y. 2004. *China's Economic Growth: A Miracle with Chinese Characteristics*. London and New York: Routledge.

Xing, Y. 2010. "Facts about and Impact of FDI on China and the World Economy." *China: An International Journal*. Vol. 8. No. 2, pp. 309–27.

Xu, B. and J. Lu. 2009. "Foreign Direct Investment, Processing Trade and Sophistication of Chinese Exports." *China Economic Review*. Vol. 20. No. 2, pp. 425–39.

Yao, Y. 2009. *The Disinterested Government*. Research Paper No. 2009/33. Helsinki, Finland: World Institute for Development Economic Research. May.

Yang, R., Y. Yao and Y. Zhang. 2009. "Technological Structure and Its Upgrading in China's Exports." *China Economic Journal*. Vol. 2. No. 1, pp. 55–71.

Yi, K. M. 2003. "Can Vertical Specialization Explain the Growth of World Trade?" *Journal of Political Economy*. Vol. 111. No. 1, pp. 52–102.

Yu, K. 2009. *Democracy is a Good Thing*. Washington, DC: The Brookings Institution Press.

Zhang, J. 2011. "China Backpedals." Stanford, CA: Hoover University. 12 January.

Zhang, H. K. and S. Song. 2000. "Promoting Exports: The Role of Inward FDI in China." *China Economic Review*. Vol. 11. No. 2, pp. 385–96.

Zeng, D. Z. 2011. "How Do Special Economic Zones and Industrial Clusters Drive China's Rapid Development?" Washington, DC: World Bank. Policy Research Working Paper No. 5583. March.

Zheng, Y. and A. Hu. 2006. "An Empirical Analysis of Provincial Productivity in China (1979–2001)." *Journal of Chinese Economic and Business Studies*. Vol. 4. No. 3, pp. 221–39.

3

ECONOMIC GROWTH IN THE CHINESE ECONOMY

An *ex-post* perspective

1. Introduction

The objective of this chapter is to take account of what and how the Chinese economy achieved following its post-1978 turn-around. It scrutinizes the structural transformation of the economy and enumerates its superlative achievements. Rapid growth and transformation altered the People's Republic of China's place on the global economic stage from marginal to central. Among the important changes taking place in China were the growth and steady rise of private-sector enterprises, although it is still a mixed economy where the state-owned enterprises (SOEs) play a salient role. For the first time China succeeded in creating a substantial middle class—a driver of economic growth—and also a prosperous class. China's domestic demand strengthened and began to matter for the regional and global economies. As it grew into the second largest importing economy in the world, it global significance increased markedly. It became the center of the world economic affairs essentially through manufacturing-led growth.

2. Economic growth and transition: Tangible achievements

In the early 1980s, China was an agrarian, abjectly impoverished, inward-looking, low-income, deliberately isolated and a near autarkic economy. At the time of launching its market-oriented macroeconomic reforms in 1978 its per caput income was $182 and trade-to-GDP ratio 9.7 percent. At this juncture, China's exports amounted to $9.8 billion, or 0.6 percent of the multilateral exports. China's total trade in 1978 was $20.6 billion (Lin, 2010). Quantitative planning of trade was done by a handful of foreign trade corporations and it had no relation to China's comparative advantage. These statistics attest that China was an absolutely marginal economy and that it began its rise to global prominence from a very low base. Summers (2007) pointed out that in a span of three decades China has experienced the same degree of industrialization that took two centuries to occur in Europe.

2.1 Superlative growth performance

Few parallels are available for China's rapid GDP growth performance in economic history. This applies more to China's growth performance during the post-World Trade Organization (WTO) accession period. China established itself as an economy with the highest long-term average GDP growth rate in real terms in the fastest growing region of the global economy. It achieved this distinction without suffering from any major crisis or sharp interruption in the growth process, which were common in the other emerging market economies (EMEs). Beyond any shadow of doubt it is an exceedingly dynamic economy, which has successfully integrated deeply both regionally and globally. During the decade following its WTO accession China's GDP in dollar terms quadrupled, while its exports nearly quintupled.

A prominent recent development in the arena of international economy was China storming up the league tables to overtake Japan in the second quarter of 2010. It reached the second place in the table of the world's largest economies. Japan was the second largest global economy for over four decades. This was a symbolic moment for China, because in terms of dynamism and economic influence China had outpaced Japan a long time ago. At market prices and exchange rates, the annual 2010 GDP figures were as follows: Japan's GDP was $5.5 trillion, while China's was $5.9 trillion. It was almost impossible to visualize in 1978 that China would achieve this enviable distinction in a short time span of three decades. This was the time when the Communist Party of China (CPC) adopted its renowned Deng doctrine, the *Gai Ge Kai Fang*, or "change the system, open the door" strategy, which in turn incited the Chinese economy's celebrated U-turn.

Various time points have been computed for China to become the largest global economy. According to *The Economist* (2010a) China will surpass the USA and be the number one economy in 2019. According to an Australian government white paper, "by some measures, China has the potential to overtake the USA as the world's largest economy around 2020".[1] In an upgraded forecast, Goldman Sachs' chief economist Jim O'Neill reported that China will overtake the USA economy by 2027 (*The Economist*, 2010b). However, the renowned economic historian Angus Maddison projected 2030 as the time point for China reaching the top (Maddison, 2001). In April 2011 projections on this issue were made by the International Monetary Fund (IMF, 2011a), stating that China would be the leading economy in 2016. These projections included adjustments for the domestic purchasing power of the two countries' currencies (Rachman, 2011). Public perception regarding who is leading at present is interesting. According to the Gallup's *World Affairs* survey of February 2011, 52 percent of the Americans responded that China is the leading global economy, while 32 percent perceived the USA as the largest (Gallup, 2011). No matter when China equals or overtakes the US to be the largest global economy, its per capita income will still be a fraction of the average in the advanced economies.

During the recent periods of global recession China was an important source of growth. It holds true for 2001–3[2] and 2009 and also during the recovery of 2010. During the 2009 when the global economic growth was in the negative (–0.5 percent), China's GDP growth was 9.2 percent. This was a robust growth performance during a recession year. In 2010 while global economy recovered from the global financial crisis and grew at the rate of 5.2 percent, China grew at 10.4 percent contributing 31.6 percent to global growth. It increased after this point in time. In the backdrop of the Eurozone crisis China's GDP growth for 2011 was 9.2. Its projected growth rate for 2012 is 8.2 percent. China's contribution to global growth was 36.8 percent in 2011 and estimates for 2012 put it at 36.4 percent (IMF, 2012; CB, 2012).

China succeeded in sustaining a near 9.8 percent real GDP growth rate over 1978–2010. It represented 9.5 percent of global GDP at nominal exchange rates. Rapid growth also sharply reduced the proportion of the population living in absolute poverty. A recent World Bank (2009) report testified that between 1981 and 2004, the fraction of China's population consuming $1 a day in today's purchasing power fell from 65 percent to 10 percent. The absolute number of poor people declined from

652 million to 135 million. As a consequence half a billion people were lifted out of poverty. This magnitude of decline in poverty in such a short time span has no historical precedent. If poverty line is taken as $1.25 per day, poverty in China dropped from 40.77 percent in 1991 to 12 percent in 2002 and 2 percent in 2007 (Yuan *et al.*, 2011). In rural China, the poverty rate plummeted from 18.5 percent in 1981 to 2.8 percent in 2004 (Chaudhury and Ravallion, 2007).

China has either achieved most of the Millennium Development Goals (MDGs) or is close to doing so. Human development indicators have improved remarkably. Compared to the late 1970s, improvement in the quality of life and economic development has been nothing short of phenomenal. Therefore, by the second decade of the 21st century China had reached a vastly different stage of development than in the early 1980s, when the macro-economic reforms were in their infancy. In 2011 its medium-term growth prospects were ranked high by the Bloomberg Economic Momentum Index for Asia. China was ranked first among 22 Asian EMEs as the country most likely to maintain steady growth over the next quinquennium (Bloomberg Businessweek BB, 2011). This ranking was based on 16 indicators, including economic competitiveness, education level, urban migration, high-technology export products and inflation. They measure an economy's ability to continue delivering high GDP growth.

2.2 Structural transformation

During the three-decade comprehensive reform period China's economy underwent a profound transformation, which included a major alteration in the structural composition of the output. Traditionally the structure of an economy is divided into primary (agriculture and extractive activities), secondary (industry and manufacturing) and tertiary (services) sectors. The earlier theorists on economic growth regarded structural transformation an essential condition for attaining high rate of per caput income growth and growth of output per worker (Lewis, 1954; Kuznets, 1979). Structural transformation essentially implies that the factors of production are reallocated from less productive sectors or industries to more productive ones. It was regarded as a source of growth by the eminent scholars of the early post-World War II period. The concept of structural change and factor reallocation was the basis of Chenery *et al.*'s (1986) theory of economic development. They regarded factor reallocation as vitally important in explaining economic growth and performance. Lucas (1993) and Verspagen (1993) also constructed models of industrial development in developing economies. The former took supply side variables, while the latter demand-side variables. Both laid a great deal of emphasis on the importance of structural changes for GDP growth as well as for total factor productivity (TFP) growth.

From this perspective the Chinese economy presented an interesting research proposition for economists. Sectoral reallocation of the factors of production and resources as well as their reallocation across manufacturing firms has been a key source of sustained return to capital and productivity growth for the Chinese economy. In addition, reallocation from law- to high-productivity firms became another source of high return on investment in China (Hsieh and Klenow, 2009). The rate of return on investment remained well above 20 percent in China (Song *et al.*, 2011). This was impressively higher than that in most advance industrial and developing economies.

China's total GDP and industrial output increased several times over the three-decade comprehensive reform period. The manufacturing sector expanded even at a faster pace than the GDP. The manufacturing sector recorded robust growth and maintained its dominance of the Chinese economy throughout the reform period (Table 3.1; Figure 3.1). In 2008 it was the largest sector,

TABLE 3.1 GDP at constant prices

Year	Gross Domestic Product (100 million yuan)	Primary/ Agriculture (%)	Secondary/ Industry (%)	Manufacturing (%)	Construction (%)	Tertiary/ Services (%)
			Price Base Year = 1970			
1978	3,548.2	26.4	49.8	93.1	6.9	23.8
1979	3,816.9	26.0	50.1	93.5	6.5	23.9
1980	4,116.2	23.8	52.7	92.8	7.2	23.5
			Price Base Year = 1980			
1980	4,567.9	30.0	48.5	91.2	8.8	21.5
1981	4,807.4	30.5	46.9	91.1	8.9	22.6
1982	5,242.8	31.2	45.4	91.2	8.8	23.4
1983	5,811.8	30.5	45.2	90.7	9.3	24.3
1984	6,693.8	29.9	44.9	91.0	9.0	25.2
1985	7,595.2	26.8	46.9	90.7	9.3	26.2
1986	8,267.1	25.5	47.5	90.2	9.8	27.0
1987	9,224.7	23.9	48.4	89.9	10.1	27.7
1988	10,265	22.0	49.8	90.5	9.5	28.1
1989	10,682	21.8	49.7	91.6	8.4	28.5
1990	11,093	22.5	49.4	91.7	8.3	28.1
			Price Base Year = 1990			
1990	18,548	27.3	41.6	88.9	11.1	31.1
1991	20,250	25.6	43.4	89.3	10.7	31.0
1992	23,134	23.5	46.0	89.3	10.7	30.5
1993	26,365	21.6	48.4	89.5	10.5	30.0
1994	29,813	19.8	50.7	89.9	10.1	29.5
1995	33,071	18.8	52.0	90.0	10.0	29.2
1996	36,380	17.9	53.0	90.3	9.7	29.1

TABLE 3.1 (CONTINUED)

Year	Gross Domestic Product (100 million yuan)	Primary/ Agriculture (%)	Secondary/ Industry (%)	Manufacturing (%)	Construction (%)	Tertiary/ Services (%)
1997	39,763	17.0	53.6	91.0	9.0	29.5
1998	42,877	16.3	54.1	91.0	9.0	29.6
1999	46,145	15.6	54.4	91.3	8.7	30.1
2000	50,035	14.7	54.9	91.6	8.4	30.4
			Price Base Year = 2000			
2000	99,215	15.1	45.9	87.9	12.1	39.0
2001	107,450	14.3	46.0	88.1	11.9	39.7
2002	117,208	13.5	46.3	88.2	11.8	40.2
2003	128,959	12.6	47.4	88.2	11.8	
2004	141,965	12.1	47.8	88.6	11.4	
2005	158,021	11.5	48.2	88.2	11.8	40.4
			Price Base Year = 2005			
2005	184,937	12.1	47.4	88.2	11.8	40.5
2006	208,381	11.3	47.7	87.8	12.2	
2007	237,893	10.3	48.0	87.6	12.4	41.7
2008	260,813	9.9	48.1	87.7	12.3	42.0
2009	340,903	10.3	46.2	85.8	14.2	43.4
2010	401,202	10.1	46.8	85.8	14.2	43.1
2011	n/a	10.0	46.6	n/a	n/a	43.3

Source: China Statistical Yearbook 2012. Beijing, China: China Statistics Press.

Notes

a There are two figures at the base switching year, one at the former base year prices, another at the latter.

b Please refer to the brief introduction for the definition of gross domestic product at constant prices.

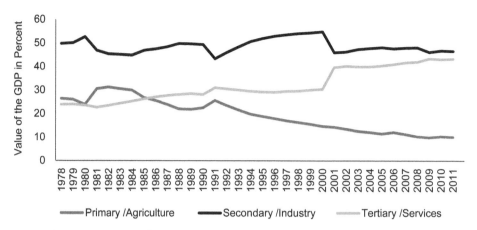

FIGURE 3.1 Sector-wise vision of GDP at constant prices
Source: China Statistical Yearbook 2012. Beijing, China: China Statistics Press.

accounting for 48.1 percent of GDP, although it declined somewhat (46.6 percent) in 2011. Except for the early 1990s, manufacturing accounted for around 50 percent of the GDP. The only exception to this was the 1994–2000 period, when the industrial sector produced more than 50 percent of the total GDP.

Chen *et al.* (2011) estimated the stochastic frontier sectoral production function and concluded that TFP growth exceeded the quantitative growth of inputs since 1992. Using a decomposition technique, they also found that the structural transformation in the Chinese economy substantially contributed to TFP and output growth but decreasingly over time. This empirical analysis inferred that the market reforms and changes in industrial structure significantly accounted for the overall trend and the sectoral heterogeneity of factor allocative efficiency during the process of rapid industrial growth. The industrial sector in the Chinese economy may continue to remain dominant in the foreseeable future because of extensive investment that has been made in the manufacturing capacities. It needs to be mentioned that during the Eleventh and 12th Five-Year Plans the emphasis has shifted to tertiary-sector development.

Although the level of education in the Chinese society has improved in the recent past and according to the Program for International Student Assessment (PISA) of the OECD (2012)[3] and the Grattan Institute Report (Jensen, 2012), an average 15-year-old in Shanghai was found to be two to three years ahead in mathematics than students in Australia, the UK and the USA. Notwithstanding these achievements education standards so far have not progressed so much as to carve out and support a robust and dynamic services sector of the kind that the advanced industrial economies have developed. This group of economies is known for their knowledge-intensive business services.

One prominent sectoral transformation occurred in the shifting roles of the primary and tertiary sectors. The primary sector was close to a quarter of the GDP in the late 1970s. It rose first in importance to approximately one-third in 1984, but after 1991 went into a steady decline. In 2008 it contributed a paltry 9.9 percent of the total GDP. In contrast, the tertiary sector demonstrated a gradually bolstering trend. In the late 1970s it accounted for only a quarter of the GDP, but in 1990 its contribution climbed to 31.1 percent. Its contribution to the GDP remained stationary for some time and in 2000 it was 30.4 percent. Tertiary-sector activities expanded sharply after this juncture and in 2008 it accounted for 42 percent of the GDP. In 2010 they edged further to 43.1 percent (Table 3.1; Figure 3.1). These transformations in the structure of the Chinese economy present a vivid picture of the dynamic growth in an economy that started from a low base and grew to be the second largest in the world. China's transformation to a tertiary-sector-dominated economy cannot occur in the short term. However, given the swift stride of development in the tertiary sector, it could unavoidably become a dominant sector in about a decade.

The present stage of China's industrialization is far from maturity. It is still in its initial stages. With the passage of time the economy will absorb more labor from the agricultural sector. It may go into labor-intensive industrial and other sectors. Parallel to the structural transformation indicated in the preceding paragraphs, the proportion of industrial value-added went on increasing from an exceedingly low level of 17.6 percent in 1952 to a high level of 44.1 percent in 1978. In the pre-1978 period, China's industrial development was heavy-industry based. During the post-1978 reform era it changed to a mix of light and heavy industry. China's industrial value-added during this period stabilized around 40 percent (Chen *et al.*, 2011). This level has been sustained until the present.

Other major areas of structural transformation were the burgeoning of a *de novo* private sector and paring of the SOE sector which was a distinguishing trait of the non-market economy period and turning a nearly autarkic economy into an outward-oriented economy. In a short time span, China opened up to trade and investment flows in large measures. During the first decade of the 21st century China's trade-to-GDP ratio was 70 percent or above, much higher than that of other comparable EMEs. Since it acceded to the WTO in 2001, trade and FDI made larger contributions to China's GDP growth than before (Lawrence, 2008). Given its outward orientation, its rapid expansion and the fact that it is the second largest economy in the world, China is likely to have a large impact on the global trading system and pattern as well as its policies. It will be a force to reckon with in the future evolution of the global trading system. So far China has promoted multilateral trade liberalization as well as at regional level through free trade agreements (FTAs).

2.3 Dramatic change in global economic stature

Long-term GDP growth statistics are available for 119 economies. Of these, Korea and Taiwan recorded long-term average GDP growth rates comparable to that of China in the post-1970 period, but they did not equal that of China. Diamond-rich Botswana also fared well. During the three decades of reform (1978–2008), "China's total gross domestic product (GDP), industrial output, foreign trade and importantly, its per capita income increased respectively by factors of 16, 27, 124, and 12" (Golley and Song, 2011, p. 1). With the passage of time, China inaugurated an unambiguous shift in the contours of its regional and global economic power balance. Its heft in the global economy increased at a swift pace. In terms of aggregate GDP it overtook Japan and began to close in on the USA. In terms of purchasing-power parity (PPP), China's share of global GDP increased from 2.0 percent in 1980 to 12.52 percent in 2009. Computed in nominal dollars and market prices, this increase was from 2.6 percent to 8.3 percent over the same period (Dahlman, 2010).

Japan (in the 1950s and 1960s) and the four Asian newly industrialized economies (NIEs, in the 1960s and 1970s) were also high performers during similar stages of their development and they won an accolade from the global academic and policy-making establishment for their export-and-FDI-led rapid industrialization. However, owing to the sheer size of China's GDP, its global economic impact is, and will be, much higher than that of any of the NIEs. In terms of systemic significance, it is far more important. The Japanese economy had a great deal of systemic significance and global impact during its high-growth period, but it entered a "deep slump" in the fourth quarter of 1991 (Bernanke, 2000, p. 149). Its real GDP growth rate in 1991 Q4 through 1999 Q4 was less than 0.9 percent per year. It has yet to recover from its self-induced paralysis. Japan's share in global GDP has been in decline since 1991.

At the time of launching the reforms in the late 1970s, China's contribution to the growth of the world economy was less than 0.1 percent. In 2010 China became the main driver of global growth. It contributed 33 percent to the global growth (OECD, 2010c). This reflected both the catch-up momentum in China and slower trend growth in the advanced industrial economies. It has also begun to have wide-ranging ramifications over global economic and financial architecture as well as in the areas of international business and investment. In November 2008 in the context of the severe global financial crisis, the first Group-of-Twenty (G-20) summit took place in Washington, DC. China and the USA, as the two most important members of the G-20, were expected to propose initiatives to support the global economy and stabilize financial markets. For the record, it must be mentioned that according to the *World Development Indicators 2013*,[4] China's GDP in current dollars was $6.07 trillion in 2012. Its gross national product (GNP) per caput, also in current dollars, was $4,940 in 2011. In terms of PPP, its per caput income in 2011 was $8,390 (Table 3.2; Figure 3.2). Growth rates of these two vital indicators accelerated in the 21st century.

From a completely peripheral economy approximately three decades ago, China became the third largest in the world in 2007, measured in market prices and exchange rates, and the second largest in 2010. By 2009, it had become the largest exporter, when the value of its exports was $1,202 billion (or 9.6 percent of the total multilateral exports). China edged out Germany and the USA to be world's biggest trading power. In 2009 those countries followed China with 9.0 percent and 8.5 percent shares in total, respectively (WTO, 2010). In 2011 China's total trade was $3.64 trillion and it accounted for 10.4 percent of total merchandise exports, notably larger than the USA (8.1 percent) and Germany (8.1 percent, WTO, 2012).

Since 2005, measured by cargo tonnage Shanghai has been the world's busiest port. In 2010 China also became the largest energy consumer, surpassing the USA. This includes all the sources of energy including fossil oil, coal, natural gas, nuclear power and renewable. Since early 1900s the USA was the largest energy user (Swartz and Oster, 2010). It is the largest consumer and importer of iron ore, aluminum, copper, nickel, potash, timber products and zinc. It consumes 37 percent of world's cotton (Das, 2011a). China also became one of the world's most wired retail markets. In 2013 China's e-commerce market was well on its way to be the largest in the world, overtaking the USA's. By some measures Alibaba was the world's largest e-commerce firm (*The Economist*, 2013). According to Forbes Global 2000 list for 2013, the Industrial and Commercial Bank of China and the China Construction Bank are the largest two banks in the world. The Agricultural Bank of China and the Bank of China were eighth and 11th on that list, respectively. Rising prosperity has ushered in dramatic lifestyle changes in China.

Little exposure to the so-called toxic assets and a partially closed capital account protected China from the initial global financial market turmoil in 2007–08. Supported by a large fiscal and monetary stimulus package, which was 12.9 percent of the GDP in 2008, China emerged from the global financial crisis with flying colors. It sustained rapid growth and played a decisive role in the recovery of the regional and global economies (Fardoust et al., 2012). While the global economy was in recession in 2008, China grew by 8.8 percent. In 2009 when the global economy

TABLE 3.2 Per caput GNP (in terms of PPP and market exchange rate, US$)

Year	PPP	Market exchange rate
1980	250	220
1981	280	220
1982	320	220
1983	370	220
1984	440	250
1985	500	280
1986	550	310
1987	620	320
1988	700	330
1989	750	320
1990	800	330
1991	890	350
1992	1,020	390
1993	1,180	410
1994	1,340	460
1995	1,480	530
1996	1,650	650
1997	1,820	750
1998	1,960	790
1999	2,120	840
2000	2,340	930
2001	2,560	1,000
2002	2,840	1,100
2003	3,180	1,270
2004	3,590	1,500
2005	4,090	1,740
2006	4,750	2,040
2007	5,580	2,480
2008	6,230	3,040
2009	6,840	3,620
2010	7,520	4,240
2011	8,390	4,940

Source: The World Bank. 2013. *World Development Indicator Online Database April 2013*. Washington, DC.

contracted by 0.7 percent the Chinese economy grew by 9.2 percent. Although global economy bounced back to 5.1 percent growth in 2010, China grew by 10.3 percent (IMF, 2011b). It was bolstered by a strong fiscal position, recently recapitalized banking sector, enormous forex reserves and low short-term debt. Overall status of the Chinese economy improved in the post-global financial crisis period because, as alluded to in Section 1, it helped shorten the so-called Great Recession and quickened the regional and global recoveries (Das, 2011a).

3. Growing middle class

For having a mass-consumption market it is indispensable to have a middle class. Three decades of rapid clip growth has propelled China into the ranks of upper-middle-income countries with a swiftly emerging middle class (WB, 2011b).[5] One imminent impact of rapid GDP growth was the

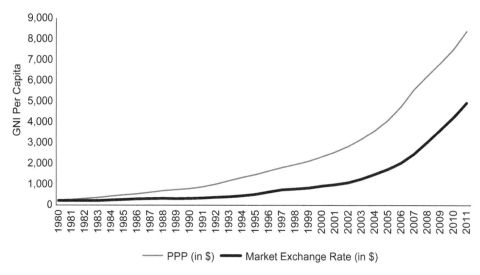

FIGURE 3.2 GNI per caput income in PPP and market exchange rates
Source: The World Bank. 2013. World Development Indicator Online Database 2013. Washington DC.

transformation of a low-income but largely egalitarian society of the past into one with distinct income classes. China's middle class was born in the late 1990s. Emergence of a consuming class in China and the other Asian EMEs augurs well for the global economy. The size of the middle class grew both rapidly and significantly. It seems that the middle class made a conscious political choice for growing prosperity and improving living standards.

One direct consequence of the growth in its middle class is that China, like the other large EMEs, is evolving from the factories of the world to the markets of the world. By 2012, these EMEs had emerged not only as strong hands in the low-end market, but also in the luxury goods and premium markets. That being said, the size of the middle class in China does not match that in the EU or the USA. The size of the middle class in an economy is important because it is the source of economic growth. Middle-class households not only possess high levels of human capital but also provide a highly sought-after commodity to the economy, entrepreneurs.

As there are few well-defined and internationally accepted thresholds identifying the middle class, there are widely varying estimates of its size in China. On the lower side, Kharas (2010) computed its size at 157 million in 2007, less than 12 percent of the total population. Ravallion (2009) calculated that 61.5 percent of the population belonged to middle class in 2005. Evidently they used different definitions of the middle class. An esteemed think tank, the Chinese Academy of Social Sciences (CASS), published its estimates in its *2011 City Blue Book* in August 2011. It estimated that the size of the middle class in 2010 was 230 million of urban population, which was 37 percent of urban population. Its definition of middle class was a disposable income of RMB 16,300 to RMB 37,300 per year per caput. In dollar terms the corresponding range was between $2,400 and $5,500. CASS estimated its middle class on the basis of Engel's coefficient ranging between 0.30 and 0.373.

The members of the CASS middle class are educated, own their own houses, earn fairly high and stable incomes and enjoy a relatively better standard of living. Although these middle-class consumers have neither the consumption pattern and level rivaling that of the Western world, nor those of the NIEs when they were going through their period of rapid growth in the 1990s, they definitely have the capability of discretionary spending. In 2010 the average disposable income of the urban population was RMB 19,109 or $2,995. In China the kind of people who comprise the middle class largely come from the following professions: civil servants, professors in universities and institutions of higher education, high- and middle-ranking executives in high-technology business firms, foreign-invested enterprises, financial institutions and large private-sector enterprises. This class of people consists not only of large consumers but it also acts as a social stabilizer.

A detailed statistical study was conducted by Yuan *et al.* (2011) that obtained macro-economic data from National Bureau of Statistics (NBS) and well-cited Chinese Household Income Project Survey (CHIPS). They defined middle class differently. According to their perception it encompassed those whose daily income per caput fell between $2 and $20 in PPP terms. Their estimates regarding the size differ dramatically from the two mentioned above. According to their profile of the middle class in China, growth of per caput real income was exceedingly rapid over the 1991–2002 period, which led to a swift shift of households into higher income brackets. This shift into higher income groups occurred for both rural and urban households. It has been noted above that high GDP growth rate was also instrumental in exceedingly fast poverty elevation in China.

As can be expected, the proportion of the middle-class population was larger in urban China than in rural. To draw a more realistic picture, Yuan *et al.* (2011) employed a different consumer price index (CPI) and PPP for rural and urban areas. Based on this amendment, they concluded that in 1995, 84 percent of urban households and 30 percent of rural could be classified as middle class. The rapidity of the rise in the middle class was historically unprecedented. The rate of its expansion was 6 percent per annum. According to the results of this statistical exercise, it was 39.3 percent of the total population in 1988, 55.6 percent in 1995, 71.3 percent in 2002 and 89.1 percent in 2007.[6] Another technique of sizing up the middle class was using durable goods owned by the households. According to this measure, 58.88 percent of the Chinese households belonged to the middle class in 2007.

If the above statistical analyses are correct, China will be able to avoid being a "barbell economy" (Farrell *et al.*, 2006, p. 2.). Common in developing economies, it implies that majority of the population is at two extremes of income distribution, with only a few in the middle. Many global business enterprises are aiming at serving this rapidly growing comfortable segment, particularly the well-off urbanites whose disposable income is significant. Early movers into the Chinese markets, like Coca Cola, GM, IBM and P&G, have begun making models to target this segment profitably.

As McKinsey's 2011 survey of Chinese consumers for 2011 delineated, the Chinese middle class has adopted consumerism with enormous ease, enthusiasm and alacrity. In a short time they have embraced thousands of new products, services and brands. Three principal findings of this survey are as follows: first, even in the face of high inflation in 2011, consumers were more confident than in the previous years. Although on a decline, the rate of inflation in China continued to be high. It was 9.4 percent in 2009, 8.5 percent in 2010 and 6.1 percent in September 2011. The level of consumer confidence was at an all-time high (58 percent) in 2011. Second, among the urban consumers the number of first-time buyers has begun a decline. This group of consumers is regarded as a major driver of category growth in China. Third, although brand awareness among the middle class is on the rise, there was little evidence of brand loyalty. This survey estimated that by 2020, real consumption will have doubled to $4.8 trillion. At this juncture, China will be the second largest consumer market after the USA (McKinsey, 2011a).

As China is now in a transformation phase from an export-driven to a domestic-demand-driven economy, its middle class has a definite role to play by increasing domestic consumption of both goods and services. The development and growth of the middle classes in North America and Europe provided them with economic strength. If it does not mean that growth in China will be on the early 20th-century pattern and will have environmental and ecological sensitivity, development of a middle-class market in China will indeed be a virtuous and awaited development. China is the largest automobile market in the world as well as a large market in luxury goods, which is good news for foreign firms and MNCs. However, they need to take a closer look at the idiosyncratic evolution of the Chinese middle class. In 2010 the two fastest growing markets were religious tourism, revival of an ancient tradition and pet care products (Li, 2011). The fast growing services areas were healthcare, consulting and environmental services.

3.1 Dawn of an affluent class

Japan is world's largest premium market. While in China and other large EMEs per caput incomes are still not very high, they have a large population of luxury goods consumers. Increasing market demand for premium products, or premiumization of the Chinese market has gone a long way. The McKinsey Global Institute has identified the rise of another well-heeled urban middle class whose spending power will soon redefine the Chinese market. These urban affluent consumers earn more than RMB 100,000 (or $12,500) a year and command RMB 500 billion, which is approximately 10 percent of urban disposable income (Farrell *et al.*, 2006). This segment of consumers has cultivated a taste for globally branded luxury goods. They regard them as the necessary symbol of social status. This class of well-off customers is swelling by the year. According to the March 2011, Forbes list of billionaires, China has 115 on the mainland alone.

Income elasticity of demand for luxury goods is usually regarded as very high, much higher than one. Therefore, confident Chinese consumers have become a key factor for the global luxury goods market. China's big cities now have gleaming new high-end shopping malls and glitzy boutique. The global financial crisis did not adversely affect the super-rich segment of the Chinese market. The luxury goods market in China bucked the trend during 2009; while global sales fell by 8 percent across the globe China recorded an estimated growth of 12 percent (KPMG, 2010).

Disposable incomes have been rising, and with that taste for luxury brands is percolating and more *nouveau riche* Chinese consumers can afford pricey and prestigious luxury brands now than ever before. Prosperous customers in China have sybaritic taste, which has created a large and growing market for luxury goods. As anywhere in the world they are regarded as the *de rigueur* symbols of wealth and social status. Unlike Europe or the USA, in China three-quarters of the luxury goods consumers are the young adults. Young people known as the "moonlight clan" spend all their monthly income, often on luxury brands. Together with increasing conspicuous consumption by young people, women's purchasing power has risen, which accelerated luxury consumption. Recent popularity of online transactions also worked as a catalyst in increasing consumption of luxury products. This trend has grown exceedingly fast in the recent years and is expected continue.

The global size of the luxury brand goods market is $80 billion; Chinese consumers shopping at home and abroad accounted for 10 percent of total global sales in 2009. According to a KMPG (2010) study, China was the second largest luxury market in the world after Japan in 2010. According to a McKinsey (2011b) survey, sales in 2009 were $10 billion and growth in luxury goods market is on track to reach $27 billion by 2015. By this time, China is projected to be the largest market for luxury goods (Chadha and Husband, 2007). It is also the second-largest market for Rolls-Royce cars, the perennial financial status symbol, accounting for 20 percent of total sales in 2010 (*Daily Telegraph*, 2011).

In 2010 China was world's second largest air travel market, trailing only the USA (Cliff *et al.*, 2011). Chinese market in executive jets is booming. In 2011, half of all new orders for Dassault Aviation's Falcon jets came from China. Experiences of other manufacturers, Boeing, EADS, General Dynamics and Hawker Beechcraft were similar. Each one of these jets typically sells for upward of $65 million (Pearson, 2011). Largely owing to Chinese customers, 2010 recorded a 57 percent sales increase in luxury brands of Swiss watches, like Cartier, Piaget and Vacheron Constantin. China is the fastest growing market for the high-priced, classic, ultra-thin dress watches manufactured in Switzerland. In 2009 China accounted for 5.3 percent of total Swiss exports, compared with 0.2 percent in 2000, and 2.7 percent in 2005.

Omega has 180 stores in China, including 15 directly owned ones. Some of the Omega watches, like the Constellation line, are enormously popular with the prosperous Chinese. Although Omega is a global company and does not design its products according to markets, in 2009, Omega redesigned an entire line to appeal to Chinese taste and launched it in Shanghai (Koresnikov-Jessop, 2010). More luxury products customized to Chinese taste would hit the market. Hermes, a renowned French fashion designer, launched a distinctive new brand Shang Xia. Levi Strauss designed dENiZEN jeans to fit slim Chinese body type. BMW 5 Series was redesigned to suit the Chinese preference for big sedans.

For China's *nouveau riche* Château Lafite has become a drink of choice, which has been driving its prices into the stratosphere (Stimpfig, 2011). Some of the "toniest" luxury brands are scrambling to establish substantial retail outlets in urban shopping districts of Chinese cities. Louis Vuitton has 36 stores in 29 cities in China, Gucci 39 and Hermes 20 (McKinsey, 2011b). By April 2011, the well-known fashion brand Burberry had 57 stores in China. Its 57th store in Beijing was 12,500 sq ft, the largest in Asia. Driven by its high sales in China, Burberry had an excellent year in 2010; Chinese sales jumped by 30 percent over its 2009 figures. China is expected to become the largest market for Burberry by 2015 (Friedman, 2011). In 2010 a global recovery year, luxury goods market became revitalized in China. According to a market survey in 17 Chinese cities by McKinsey (2011b), this market was on track to reach RMB 180 billion ($27 billion) by 2015. At this point in time, China will account for over 20 percent of the global luxury goods market, surpassing Japan as the world's largest luxury goods market.

The increase in buying power of the population is also reflected in the growing consumption for electronics. In the second quarter of 2011, China became the largest market for consumer electronics, particularly personal computers (PCs). Manufacturers shipped 18.5 million PCs in China compared to 17.7 million in the USA. Normally PC shipments in the USA rise in the fourth quarter. Projections for the entire year still show that the USA would be the largest market in 2011, with 73.5 million PC shipments versus 72.4 million in China. However, in 2012 China is expected to be the market leader (Kopytoff, 2011).

3.2 Second largest importing economy

As rapid growth continued and industrialization progressed, China became a huge market for other countries' exports. It became an insatiable consumer and large importer of industrial raw materials, commodities, intermediate inputs, technology and consumer goods (Das, 2011b). Between 1998 and 2010, China's imports soared 128 times in nominal dollar terms. They increased 16.4 percent annually. Between 2000 and 2010 China's import volumes grew 4.4 times. With $1,006 billion worth of imports in 2009 and 1,395 billion in 2010, and $1,743 billion in 2011, China has been the second largest importer in the world after the USA (WTO, 2010, 2011 and 2012).

China is the largest importer of energy and several other important industrial raw materials and resources. Owing to its housing boom and infrastructure investment boom, its demand for commodities surged over the last decade. During 2000–10, in value terms China's imports of iron ore surged 42.5 times, thermal coal 248 times and copper 16.2 times. In 2012 it became the largest consumer of all commodity categories in the world (Anderlini, 2012) As China's commodity imports increased, their world market prices firmed up, which in turn benefited the commodity exporting economies. The US Federal Reserve squarely blamed China's rampant appetite for the soaring prices of industrial raw materials in 2011 (Denning, 2011). Australia and Brazil, two commodity-exporting countries, benefited most from China's commodity-importing boom.

China's role as a large importer influences both the regional and global economies. China needed capital goods, that is, heavy machinery to build its factories. Japan and Germany were major machinery exporting economies to China. In addition, its rapidly rising imports of parts, components and subassemblies from the neighboring East and Southeast Asian economies are of enormous significance to them. They supported strong economic expansion in these economies. These countries have become a part of China's export ecosystem. China's imports from these Asian countries rose much faster than its exports to them. For many developing economies and EMEs, rapid growth in exports to China became an important contributor to growth. In particular, for several Asian economies, notably Korea and Taiwan, Chinese imports were responsible for one-half of their export increase in the recent years.

China is also credited with helping the long-moribund Japanese economy. Its large imports contributed to the firming of oil and commodity prices. China's status in the domains of multilateral trade, global financial markets and manufacturing output catapulted it over its rival economies. China has recorded very high import growth rates for consumer goods—about 15 percent annually for the last 15 years. This is much higher than the world average of 10 percent (IMF, 2010). Therefore China has gradually acquired the status of the locomotive of growth for the regional as well as global economies. When the Chinese economy suffered from high inflation and a real estate bubble during the 2011, there were realistic concerns about its slowdown. This understandably caused anxiety for the regional economies.

4. Manufacturing behemoth

Until the 18th century China was a large and well-developed manufacturing economy, but it went into a precipitous decline in the 19th century (Maddison, 1991). Its resurrection began in the post-1978 period, when the manufacturing sector became a significant driver of Chinese economic growth. China succeeded with its unorthodox strategy in rapid industrialization. Its industrial sector is the end result of a gradualist transition and incremental marketization. It not only turned from an agrarian to a vigorous and internationally competitive manufacturing economy but it also integrated well into regional and global manufacturing products and services markets, carving an imperious niche for itself in the regional and global production networks. What is atypical and somewhat surprising is that China was able to do this despite the initial lack of financial-sector development.

Even when structural transformation to market economy was underway the Chinese government did not lose faith in guided development. It adopted a wide array of industrial policies in an unorthodox manner to support and invest in what it referred to as a "national champion" or "national team", which were large SOEs. The ultimate objective of this strategy was to create large firms that would be more capital-intensive and technologically sophisticated than the common businesses and eventually will become globally competitive. This policy was in direct contrast to the prevailing trend of liberalization and globalization and against the grain of what is known as the Washington Consensus. Instead of the "invisible hand", the visible hand played a decisive role in China's development strategy, in particular development of the manufacturing sector. These national team enterprise groups and subsidiaries performed well with respect to a number of performance measures (Sutherland, 2007; Ernst and Naughton, 2008).

China's transformation from a primarily agrarian economy, with large employment of labor force in the agricultural sector, to an economy with a large manufacturing sector was exceedingly rapid. The momentum of this transformation during the last three decades was impressive. If growth of value-added in manufacturing is taken as a yardstick, during the first three decades of their take-off China's dynamic neighbors Korea and Taiwan were faster than China. However, China was faster than Japan in expansion of value-added in manufacturing (Brandt *et al.*, 2008). In terms of sheer volume, industrial development in China was matchless. Consequently, China's industrial economy is large and diverse. High-technology industrialization is an important part of China's success story. Given its size, it is difficult to make a meaningful assessment of it in its entirety. Its manufacturing enterprises are a formidable competitor in the global markets. Interestingly, they successfully compete with those from all the three groups of economies: namely, the advanced industrial economies, the EMEs and developing economies. McKay and Song (2010, p. 2) contend that China was able to move to the "center of the world (economic) affairs through manufacturing-led development".

Its gigantic manufacturing economy is frequently referred to as a "manufacturing juggernaut" or "world's factory" in the economic and financial press. It occupies a large share of global production in an array of industries such as toys, bicycles, microwave ovens, shoes, textiles and apparel, televisions, air conditioners, mobile phones, washing machines, refrigerators. It is also a large supplier of manufactured products to all the major global markets. In this category of exports China's share in all the major markets doubled between 2001 and 2009. It accounted for 35 percent of all manufactured imports into the Japanese market in 2009, 30 percent in the EU and 26 percent in the US market (Mattoo *et al.*, 2011).

China has the largest manufacturing workforce in the world, more than 112 million (*The Economist*, 2010c). Although wages steadily rose in the manufacturing sector, in terms of production cost structure Chinese workforce is still cheap. Many MNCs resisted moving to the other Southeast Asian economies because productivity of Chinese workers was also on the rise, although some did adopt China+1 strategy (*The Economist*, 2012). In comparison to the advanced economies the hourly compensation of Chinese workforce is exceedingly low. According to the US Bureau of Labor Statistics (2011) hourly compensation cost in the manufacturing sector is $1.36 in 2008, or 4.2 percent of the hourly cost in the USA.[7] A law introduced in 2008 gave workers more contractual rights, and consequently the labor force in China is growing more assertive. Workers in China will grow less docile and bolder, demanding higher wages. The most conspicuous case is that of Foxconn, which gives an inkling of future developments. Headquartered in Taiwan, Foxconn has 13 large factories in nine Chinese cities, employing 1.2 million workers. The world's largest maker of electronic components, it is one of the main contractors of Apple and produces iPad as well as other products for Microsoft, Dell and Hewlett-Packard. Faced by acute international criticism for maltreatment of workers Foxconn increased wages three times in three years over 2010–12. Annual increases ranged between 16 percent and 25 percent. For some categories of workers, wages more than doubled in two years.

Large FDI inflows were instrumental in shifting China's manufacturing base drastically. FDI from large business firms from the advanced industrial economies and MNCs in manufacturing sector is known to transform the developing host economy through several important channels. The ability of FDI to bring in modern technology, production processes and managerial skills to the host economy are well known. It also helps develop supplier networks in a vertical direction and "provides export externalities, introducing indigenous firms to international buyers and outlets" (Moran, 2011, p. 2). MNCs and their affiliates played a vital role in the development of China's high-technology manufactures, whose R&D intensity went on increasing steadily. About one-third of the value-added of the Chinese manufacturing sector is exported and the rest is considered substitutable with foreign goods in the domestic economy. In 2010 China accounted for 15 percent of the world value-added in the manufacturing industries. This proportion is the same as that for Japan (OECD, 2010b). Productivity growth in the manufacturing sector has been high. Growth-accounting analysis by Bosworth and Collins (2008) led to the conclusion that TFP growth in the manufacturing sector contributed 55 percent of output growth in the manufacturing sector between 1995 and 2005.

Rapid industrialization progressed with greater spatial concentration and increasing regional specialization of industrial activities. Long and Zhang (2010) show increasing interconnections among firms in the same industry as well as those in the same region. Industries have become increasingly spatially connected and regions have become increasingly specialized. Industrializing firms followed Michael Porter's industrial cluster concept (Porter, 2000). The manufacturing sector in China has emerged as strong and globally competitive. It is difficult to compete with in a large range of manufactured products. In 2010 the USA held the top spot in manufacturing output, however it was poised to relinquish this distinguished status to China in 2011. According to a study released by HIS Global Insight, a Boston-based economics consultancy firm, China accounted for 19.8 percent of world manufacturing output in 2011, fractionally ahead of the USA with 19.4 percent (Marsh, 2010 and 2011).[8]

According to *The Economist* (2011a), in value-added measured in current prices, China became the largest manufacturing economy in 2010. Thus, a 110-year run of the US as number one nation in factory production has ended. According to the *Global Wind Energy Outlook* (2010), China overtook the USA as the world leader in wind power in 2010. According to the 2010 report, China's installed wind capacity has grown exponentially, from 0.3 GW in 2000 to 42.3 GW in 2010; it accounted for 22 percent of the world's total wind power capacity (GWEC, 2010). It is the largest exporter of solar panels and has the world's largest private solar research facility. China consumed 41 percent of total consumption of refined metals in the world in 2010, making it the largest consumer of refined metals. China's sovereign risk is rated on par with Japan, after Standard and Poors (S&P) downgraded Japan to BB in January 2011 (WB, 2011b).

A significant fraction of exports are products that are designed in other parts of the world, frequently by firms in the advanced industrial economies. As discussed earlier, this is called a processing trade. China's development of this kind of contract manufacturing capability has been extraordinary. Contract manufacturing enabled Chinese industrial firms to develop close relations with those in the advanced economies. This means that China's own industrial success is tied to that of its business partner firms and countries. The contract manufacturing activity ranges over a wide array of industrial products, from toys manufactured by Mattel, or PCs by Lenovo to highly sophisticated components for the Airbus. Although China has emerged as a manufacturing base for firms around the globe, the sheer size of its industrial sector and its rapid growth has caused challenges for many business firms and even economies (Feenstra and Wei, 2010). In several major industrial subsectors, China became the largest producer during the 2000s. It is set to pass several milestones in the foreseeable future.

Comparative advantage is a dynamic concept. It is affected, *inter alia*, by changing factor prices. Owing to rising wages and a tightening labor market, unit production costs in China have been rising for some time (Sternberg, 2011). The consequences for low-skill and low-wage industries are obvious. China is slowly relinquishing its position as the world's manufacturer of low-cost consumer items, although China is still a major exporter of these goods. By 2010, low-value-added manufacturing products (textiles, shoes, etc.) and hard goods (like furniture and consumer electronics) had begun slipping away from China's export basket. In addition, higher logistics costs are forcing large importing firms to look at closer-to-home markets for imports. While China is no longer the lowest cost producer, it continued to be competitive due to the completeness of its supply chains. Countries like Bangladesh and Vietnam, as their infrastructure is in a better shape now, have started producing and exporting apparel and footwear on a much larger scale. They are successfully exploiting economies of scale and competing with China. Indonesia and Thailand were also picking up orders that went to China in the past (KPMG, 2011a). By 2020, Chinese companies may well be out of the low-end, low-wage industries and be building a market share in the middle-end manufactures.

As globalization progresses, China's status as a manufacturing colossus is sure to change. The principal change agents would be rising wages and benefits. The narrowing wage gap may reduce China's cost advantage over costs in the EU and the USA. According to Sirkin *et al.* (2011), it may decline from 55 percent in 2011 to 39 percent in 2015, when adjusted for the higher productivity of workers in the EU and USA. The EU is likely to rely on China as a manufacturing base for at least a quinquennium longer than the USA. Second, by 2015 cost savings in China for firms in the advanced economies would be minimal owing to rising transportation costs, duties, industrial real estate and supply chain risks. Third, automation and other measures to improve productivity in China may not be enough to preserve China's cost advantage. Fourth, as the disposable incomes in China and the surrounding Asian economies have been rising, the multinational enterprises producing in China are likely to devote their production capacity in China to serve the rapidly expanding local and regional markets. Fifth, some manufacturing production may relocate to other low-cost Asian locations. Principal among them are Bangladesh, Indonesia and Vietnam. In fact, this relocation has begun and is in an early phase. Its rate will vary from industry to industry and product to product, depending upon the labor content.

4.1 Trade in manufactured products

China's manufactured export structure had shifted from largely light industrial and textile products to principally mechanical and electronics products in the 1990s. Since the turn of the century exports of high-technology products had expended fast. This category was led by electronics and information technology (IT) products. Although China sat out much of the early development in the IT industry in Asia, at present it is one of the major manufacturer of IT hardware in the world. With expansion of its manufacturing sector, China became a major trader of manufactured products. Since its WTO accession exports to all the major markets in this sector recorded notable increases.

MNCs were responsible for producing a substantive proportion of Chinese exports. Besides, it cannot be doubted that spillovers from FDI and operations of MNCs played a role in the exports of manufactured products. However, Moran (2011) contended that while these spillovers led to externalities that favorably influenced export performance in manufactures, the horizontal and vertical spillovers from them were relatively limited.

Mattoo and Subramanian (2011) identified 10 of the largest markets in the world and for each of them identified the largest supplier in the manufacturing sector. They found that China's share in these markets doubled over 2001–09. In some of the largest import markets, China accounted for more than 20 percent of total imports of manufactured products in 2009 or more. In the total imports of manufactures in Japan, 35 percent originated in China. For the EU this proportion was 30 percent and for the USA 25 percent.

In the highly protected sectors in its major trading partners, China's export penetration was found to be large. In the protected sectors in the 10 largest trading partner economies, China's share of total imports was significantly larger in 2009 than it was in the total imports in these markets. Mattoo and Subramanian (2011) found that China's share in protected sectors in Japan was over 70 percent, in Korea over 60 percent, in Brazil about 55 percent and in Canada, the EU and the USA about 50 percent each. In addition, China succeeded in increasing its import shares in manufactures in economies that were located close to large economies and had free trade agreements (FTAs) with them. Principal among them are Canada, Mexico and Turkey.

5. China in the global trading system

Even before its accession to the WTO in 2001, China was emerging as a major participant in multilateral trade. It was obvious in the 1990s that it was going to be a huge market access opportunity. It loomed particularly large as a major exporter of labor-intensive manufactured products, parts and components as well as a major importer of capital goods, parts and components, sub-assemblies, energy, primary commodities and industrial raw materials. Even at this point in time, it was obvious that given its size, unusually high degree of openness and rapid trade expansion it was going to make a large impact over global trade and the multilateral trading system's evolution (Subramanian, 2011).

After accession China became an active participant in the WTO activities. China adopted a dual track trade strategy, that is, while complying with its multilateral obligations it participated and promoted in regional integration endeavors. It negotiated bilateral trade agreements (BTAs) with Chile, Hong Kong, Macao, Pakistan, Peru, New Zealand, Singapore and Thailand, although the most important one of them was with the Association of Southeast Asian Nations (ASEAN). It was also working on agreements with Australia, Costa Rica, Korea, Norway and Switzerland.

When China acceded to the WTO, some considered it a negative development (Mallon and Whally, 2004). As China had not fully converted into a market economy, it has continued to be a mixed economy it was believed that it will not be able to adhere to the WTO regulations. The accession protocol for China had demanding terms and conditions. Therefore it was believed by some that China will inadvertently or deliberately be in breach of WTO rules and parameters. If China failed to comply, the other members might retaliate or impose sanctions on China, in the process weakening the world trading system. Another concern was that China's participation in the WTO may not be constructive. As the largest EME, it may throw its weight around and try to basically change the WTO system. China's regional integration initiatives were also seen as a possible attempt to undermine the multilateral trading order.

When China assumed the membership of the WTO, it first tried to assume the WTO obligations at the level of large developing economies. As a developing economy it was in principle entitled to take the benefit of the "enabling clause" and therefore to special and differential treatment. However, many members in particular the USA insisted on China entering the WTO on "commercial terms". This implies that at the time of accession it had to assume obligations "that went far beyond those expected of existing members at their stage of development. These commitments involved not simply reducing border barriers but undertaking detailed changes in internal policies" (Lawrence, 2008, p. 151).

During the accession negotiations China committed to substantially reducing its trade barriers in agriculture, manufactures and services. In compliance with the requirements of the WTO accession protocol and in eagerness to be a responsible and active part of the global trading system, China bound all of its tariff lines by 2004. This high degree of discipline was not accepted by other developing economies, even those from Asia. Usually developing countries have a large gap between their bound rates and applied rates of tariff, the former far exceeded the latter. In case of China the two were almost the same. In 2004 its average applied rates were 10.4 percent, close to bound rates of 10 percent. China's services trade liberalization was impressive. Liberalization commitments were made for 93 sectors. This was much higher than a typical developing country. The member countries of ASEAN had a much lower number.[9] Important sector like banking was to be opened by 2006.

The current (2011) trade statistics testifies to China's trade ascendency. China's merchandise exports were $1.89 trillion, which was 10.4 percent of the total multilateral exports in 2011. Its merchandise imports were $1.74 trillion, which was 9.5 percent of the total multilateral imports. To put these trade statistics in perspective, comparing them to those in 2001, when China acceded to the WTO would be relevant. China's share in world exports in 2001 was merely 3.9 percent and in world imports only 3.3 percent. In merchandise trade, China was the largest exporter in the world in 2011 and the second largest importer, after the USA. China was also the fourth largest exporter of commercial services ($182 billion) in 2011 and the third largest importer ($236 billion) (WTO, 2012). In 2010 China overtook the EU as major exporter of telecom equipment. Its exports of integrated circuits increased by 57 percent in 2010. Also, its exports of textiles became the largest in the world in 2010, it pushed the EU into second place (WTO, 2011). Overall it was a good year for China's success in global trade.

China's interest in supporting and continuing the global trading system squarely depends on the fact that it is an extraordinarily open economy. There is a rule of the thumb that large countries tend to trade less than the small ones. Bearing that in mind, if one compares the openness of Chinese economy with those of the UK and the USA during comparable time periods, one can see that it is an extremely open economy. At the height of its empire (in 1870) the trade to GDP ratio for the UK was 12.2 percent, while for the USA (in 1975) was 13.3 percent. Compared to these, China's openness in 2008 was 56.5 percent (Mattoo and Subramanian, 2011). Unlike the other two, the Chinese economy is overpoweringly trade dependent. Therefore its stake in a stable and open global trading system is far greater. As its per caput income is still not high, its interest in this system might be more existential and strong than that of the other large economies.

Another fact that portends to the same conclusion is that lately China has made deliberate and clean up endeavors to internationalize its currency. One of the goals of the 12th Five-Year Plan (2011–15) is to slowly realize the goal of internationalizing the renminbi and to make it convertible. To this end, the People's Bank of China (PBC) took several measures to promote international use of the renminbi for trade and financial transactions. Premised on these lines of logic, there is little surprise in seeing China becoming a normal and routine participant in the WTO dispute settlement proceedings, both as a plaintiff and a defender. As China's dependence on the global trading system is so high, the probability of it trying to keep it intact and becoming a leading preserver of the trading system is high.

6. A burgeoning *de novo* private sector

Small and medium-sized private-sector enterprises began to be established in the late 1970s. With progress in reforms in the 1980s, the government began downgrading the role and significance of the SOEs. A large number of them were performing poorly and incurring losses, some of them heavy. In 1984 SOEs were asked to devise shape-up strategies, strengthen their management capabilities and be commercially viable. Growth of private sector enterprises was officially encouraged more after 1990. The state sector had to abandon food and beverages, textiles and apparels, home appliances and the other consumer goods industries for the private sector. Former state monopolies in finance, electricity, telecommunications, railroads, civil aviation and petroleum were also legally opened for private-sector business firms.

Over the preceding three decades, private-sector enterprises had made a large contribution to rapid GDP growth and employment generation. In the post-1990 period this sector became more dynamic and is nominally regarded as responsible for a growing proportion of economic activity in China. Not only have a large number of them established themselves well but they are also devising new business models, production processes and management systems. They are also known for training personnel, nurturing talent and increasingly adopting management skills in vogue in Western business firms and multinationals. Accession to the WTO provided a large stimulus to the private sector. Private enterprises also pressured the SOEs to become more efficient. The long-term trend is that in terms of production and assets the weight of private-sector enterprises has steadily increased and that of the SOEs declined. The share of private-sector enterprises in industrial production was 80 percent in 2008 (WB, 2010a).[10] Their share in GDP was also approximately 50 percent in 2010 (Szamosszegi and Kyle, 2011).

A recent influential study by the World Bank concluded that private-sector enterprises need more space to thrive (WB/DRC, 2013). Establishing private-sector enterprises in China is still onerous and calls for a lot of business acumen, determination and perseverance. The reason is that despite the constitutional amendment of 2002, which gave them rights equal to those of the public sector, they are still frequently discriminated against. Several major markets and industrial sectors have still been regarded as off-limits for them. They have limited access to bank credit and the risk-averse banks show little interest in servicing their credit needs. State-owned banks, which dominate the banking system, particularly shun smaller firms. Even in 2009, 80 percent of bank credit went to the SOEs (Zhang, 2011).

Private-sector firms increasingly rely on informal financial markets or grey market institutions. They are becoming progressively more mature. These markets include a variety of trust companies, finance companies, leasing companies and underground banks. Operations of shadow banking in China are large. According to one estimate annual flows could be as large as RMB 2,000 billion or $305 billion, close to one-third of the GDP (Sender and Hiller, 2011).

Private-sector firms tend to save costs through maintaining lower inventory and have to rely on retained earnings. Undoubtedly a great deal of variationexists in financial access among private firms; usually smaller private firms face more financial constraints than the larger ones. The access of large and established private firms to bank finance is usually equal to their SOE counterparts (Hale and Long, 2011). Private-sector enterprises also do not enjoy many official benefits that the SOEs do. Their inputs of land energy and credit are artificially cheap. Private-sector business firms need financial and policy support. They frequently have to maintain close ties with the SOEs and survive and prosper on their periphery. The most critical financial difficulty that private-sector enterprises face in China is in the area of long-term funds to make investments for growth. Future financial reforms need to make this their high priority.

Often the credit for China's successful private manufacturing sector is assigned to its bureaucracy. According to this line of thinking, it is the heavy role of the so-called visible hand that made China a successful manufacturing giant. Terms like "developmental state" or "state-directed capitalism" are frequently used to describe China's brand of capitalism. The important role played by the state cannot be denied. It has tried earnestly to eliminate both physical and technological obstacles commonly faced during the early and middle stages of industrialization. To eliminate the former state built physical infrastructure and to remove the latter, it facilitated transfer of foreign technology. Although this imperative role of the state should be acknowledged, China's industrial vigor and dynamism owes much to what has been happening from the bottom up. Comparable to the celebrated *Mittelstand* of Germany, China has a multitude of vigorous private enterprises. *The Economist* (2011b, p. 11) christened it "a fast-growing thicket of bamboo capitalism". This bamboo capitalism "lives in a laissez-faire bubble". Liu and Siu (2010) applied the Generalized Method of Moments (GMM) estimator derived from a structural investment model to a large sample of Chinese industrial firms. They found robust evidence of listed private companies being more profitable than similar listed SOEs. The results from their benchmark estimation indicated that the return on capital for a private-sector firm was more than 10 percentage point higher than that of a similar SOE. The highest returns on equity were reported by unlisted private enterprises.

Notwithstanding the problems and scarcity of credit, the private sector did well during the 11th Five-Year Plan (2006–10) period. According to the statistics released by the State Administration of Industry and Commerce, the number of private business firms increased from 4.3 million to 8.4 million during the 11th Five-Year Plan years. This was an average annual rate of growth of 14.3 percent and total growth of 93 percent. At the end of 2010, private enterprises accounted for 74 percent of all enterprises in China. They made a significant contribution to the generation of employment. Employment in the private sector exceeded 180 million at the end of 2010, 60 million more that at the end of 2005. Private-sector enterprises employed approximately 7.87 million workers laid off by the SOEs in the last five years (Gang, 2011). Private-sector investment also increased at a remarkable pace. These enterprises moved into new fields such as biological medicine, new energy, information technology and other strategic areas. Large private enterprises were also active in strategic acquisition of globally acclaimed foreign brands. Lenono's acquisition of IBM's PC division and Zhejiang Holding Group's acquisition of Volvo are cases in point.

7. Rapid urbanization

In 1980 China's rate of urbanization was merely 19.6 percent, less than that of India (23.1 percent) and Indonesia (22.1 percent). With its rapid clip economic transformation, China embraced the urbanization process. As the old restrictions on mobility of labor were dismantled, labor began moving from rural to urban areas in search of jobs, or better-paid high-productivity jobs, in the rapidly expanding industrial and services sectors. Consequently Chinese society urbanized at an exceedingly brisk pace during the reform era. Between 1978 and 2010, China experienced huge internal migration, with approximately 160 million people migrating from the rural areas to the coastal cities. Rapid pace of urbanization is part of the success story of China.

In 2005 42.9 percent of Chinese population lived in urban areas. By 2010, according to the *National Bureau of Statistics 2011* this proportion increased to 49.68 percent, or half of the Chinese population, was urban. This proportion was almost the same as the global average (50 percent), but it was higher than that for East Asia (41 percent) and much higher than that of some of the Asian

EMEs, like India (28.7 percent). Population of the wealthier coastal regions increased at the expense of that in the inland and poor western regions. Owing to rapid urbanization roughly one out of every 10 people in the world in 2011 lived in a Chinese city (Lall and Wang, 2011). China's modern-day coastal areas are dominated by large cities, while the hinterland is characterized by small and medium-sized cities. In 2011 China's urbanization rate surpassed 50 percent. A significant proportion of urban population is moving towards "several key focal points across the country" (EIU, 2012, p. 1). Number of megalopolises in China has been projected to grow from three in 2000 to 13 in 2020. A swelling urban population is expected to spend more in a more highly concentrated retail environment. By 2025 China has been forecast to have added 400 million to its urban population, which will make 64 percent of its total population urban (Dobbs and Sankhe, 2010). Markets that are likely to benefit most from this trend are transportation and communications, housing and utilities, personal products, health care and recreation and education.

The ratio of urban population in the total population soared rapidly during the latter half of the 2000s (Golley and Song, 2011). This movement coincided with a surge in the proportion of working-age population, resulting in a "demographic dividend". Rural–urban migration is expected to continue, with 200 million projected to migrate over 2006–20 (Das, 2008). It results in approximately 20 million workers annually moving from underdeveloped rural areas and agrarian economy to the modern industrial sector in the urban areas. Their impact is equal to adding another medium-sized industrial economy to the global economy each year (Eichengreen *et al.,* 2007). As between 200 million and 300 million rural workers are waiting to be reallocated from the rural areas, this process can be expected to continue for more than a decade. By 2020, urbanization could pass the 60 percent mark (Yusuf and Nabeshima, 2008). At this stage, urbanization in China will dwarf that in the other Asian EMEs. Such a large movement of population will have a major effect on the domestic economy as well as spillover effects for the region and the global economy.

With an objective of amplifying the gains from urbanization process, institutional foundation of urbanization has been methodically improved by the authorities. To that end, an urban land market has been created by standardizing regulations applicable to land use rights. While the basic intention of the original urban planning laws of 1980s was to control the size of large cities, in the 10th Five-Year Plan (2001–05) this objective was abandoned. Instead emphasis was laid on the synergetic development of large, medium and small cities. The new planning strategy and guidelines enforced land use rights and promoted intensive development of the central areas of cities. In this context, large investments in expressways, rapid transit systems and high-speed railways enabled and improved connectivity among cities as well as the rural hinterlands (Lall and Wang, 2011). Simultaneous endeavors have been made to qualitatively improve the rural life. In line with the broad poverty reduction and human development agenda of the 11th Five-Year Plan (2006–10), investment programs targeted the development of the countryside. The purpose of this strategy was to reduce the rural–urban gap in the delivery of public services.

8. Summary and conclusions

The transformation that took place in the Chinese economy over the preceding three decades was nothing short of a sea change. With good reason it is credited for a superlative economic growth performance, something for which the NIEs were admired in the past. Economic growth during the post-WTO accession period was particularly noteworthy. After this point trade and FDI made a larger contribution to GDP than before. In the second quarter of 2010, China became the second largest economy in the world and various time points have been computed for China to take the top spot. In the post-2000 era, China and Asia became important sources of global growth. It has either achieved all its MDGs or is close to it. During its structural transformation, its structural composition of the output changed dramatically.

Such rapid and sustained GDP growth led to an increasing share of China in global GDP as well as dramatic change in its global status. As China is an open economy, its share in multilateral exports and imports also increased rapidly and substantially. In order to have a mass consumption market, it is necessary to have a middle class. Three decades of rapid clip growth has propelled China into the ranks of upper-middle-income countries, with a swiftly emerging middle class. Various estimates of the size of the Chinese middle class have been made, both in dollar terms and the renminbi. As the economy is in a transformation phase and it going from an export-led to a domestic-demand driven economy, its middle class has a definite role to play by increasing both domestic consumption of goods and services. China also is becoming a large premium goods market. Although per caput income of China is not high, it has a large population of luxury goods consumers. The urban affluent Chinese consumers are a large group of buyers of branded and designer products. Income elasticity of demand for luxury goods is generally regarded as high.

As industrialization progressed, China became a huge market for other countries' exports. It became an insatiable consumer and large importer of industrial raw materials, commodities, intermediate inputs, technology and consumer goods. Between 1998 and 2010, China's imports soared 128 times in nominal dollar terms. China has acquired the status of a large manufacturing economy. It became the largest manufacturing economy in 2010 and is frequently referred to as a "manufacturing juggernaut" or "world's factory" in the economic and financial press. It occupies a large share of global production in an array of industries like toys, bicycles, microwave ovens, shoes, textiles and apparel, televisions, air conditioners, mobile phones, washing machines and refrigerators. It is also a large supplier of manufactured products to all the major global markets.

Since the late 1970s, small and medium-sized private-sector enterprises began developing. As reforms progressed, the government began downgrading the significance of the SOEs. A large number of them were performing poorly. The state sector was made to abandon certain sectors for the private sector. The contribution of private sector to the GDP went on increasing. In post 1990 period it became more dynamic. The constitution was amended in 2002 to give the private sector the same rights and status as the SOEs. However it is frequently discriminated against.

China's rate of urbanization was traditionally slow, but by 2005 it picked up a great deal of speed. During the latter half of the 2000s, urbanization progressed fast. By 2010, almost half of the Chinese population was urban. This growth in urbanization was much faster than that in the other EMEs.

Notes

1 Quoted in *The Australian*, 2 May 2009.
2 Prasad and Rumbaugh (2004) show that during 2001–03 China accounted for 22.77 percent of global growth measured in purchasing power parity terms. See also the discussion in IMF (2005) on this issue.
3 Since 2000 the Organization for Economic Cooperation and Development (OECD) has rated the school performance of 15-year-olds in different countries.
4 See World Bank on-line data base at http://data.worldbank.org/country/china. [Accessed April 2013].
5 According to the World Bank (2011a) the per caput income range for the upper-middle-income group of countries is $3,976 through $12,275.
6 See Table 7, p. 9, in Yuan *et al.*, (2011).
7 See Table 1, on page 2, the US Bureau of Labor Statistics, 4 April 2011.

8 According to the IHS Global Insight, a Boston-based research and forecasting company, in 2009 the USA was responsible for 19.9 percent of world manufacturing output, compared with 18.6 percent for China. The USA managed to stay ahead despite a steep fall in factory production owing to the global recession. In 2011 on the basis of HIS Global Insight's estimates, China's factory output edged past that of the USA. It accounted for 19.8 percent of the total whereas the USA for 19.4 percent (cited in Marsh, 2011; see also World Bank, 2011b, p. 6). *The Economist* (2011a) also stated that China surpassed the USA in manufacturing in 2011. Until 1850 China was the world's biggest producer of manufactured products. Economic historians believe that China's share of world manufacturing output in 1830 was 30 percent. In 1900 it was low at 6 percent and in 1990 mere 3 percent. China's reversion to the top position marked the closing of a 500-year cycle in economic history.

9 Statistical data in this paragraph come from Lawrence (2008).

10 See World Bank (2010b), Box 1, p. 3.

References

Anderlini, J. 2012. "China's Growth Model Running Out of Steam." *Financial Times*. London. 5 March, p. 9.

Bernanke, B. S. 2000. "Japanese Monetary Policy: A Case of Self-Induced Paralysis", in R. Mikitani and A. S. Posen (eds). *Japan's Financial Crisis*. Washington, DC: Institute of International Economics, pp. 149–66.

Bloomberg Businessweek (BB). "China Tops India as Asian Economy Best Placed for Growth." 27 May. Available online at www.businessweek.com/news/2011–05-27/china-tops-india-as-asian-economy-best-placed-for-growth.html.

Bosworth, B. and S. M. Collins. 2008. "Accounting for Growth: Comparing China and India." *Journal of Economic Perspectives*. Vol. 22. No. 1, pp. 45–66.

Brandt, L. and T. G. Rawski. 2008. "China's Great Economic Transformation", in L. Brandt and T. G. Rawski (eds). *China's Great Economic Transformation*. Cambridge: Cambridge University Press, pp. 1–34.

Chadha, R. and P. Husband. 2007. *The Cult of the Luxury Brand*. Hong Kong: NB Publishing.

Chaudhury, S. and M. Ravallion. 2007. "Partially Awakened Giants: Uneven Growth in China and India", in L. A. Winters and S. Yusuf (eds). *Dancing with Giants: China, India and the Global Economy*. Washington, DC: World Bank, pp. 175–210.

Chen, S., G. H. Jefferson and J. Zhang. 2011. "Structural Change, Productivity Growth and Industrial Transformation in China." *China Economic Review*. Vol. 22. No. 1, pp. 133–50.

Chenery, H., S. Robinson and M. Syrquin. 1986. *Industrialization and Growth: A Comparative Study*. New York: Oxford University Press.

Chinese Academy of Social Sciences (CASS). 2011. *2011 City Blue Book*. Beijing, China. August.

Cliff, R., C. J. R. Ohlandt and D. Yang. 2011. *Ready for Takeoff: China's Advancing Aerospace Industry*. Santa Monica, CA: RAND Corporation.

Conference Board (CB). 2012. *Global Economic Outlook 2012*. New York. March.

Dahlman, C. J. 2010. "Global Challenges from the Rapid Rise of China." Oxford: Oxford University. Department of International Development. RMD Working Paper Series No. 41. 13 July.

Daily Telegraph. 2011. "Rolls-Royce Sets Record Car Sales in 2010." 11 January.

Das, Dilip K. 2008. *The Chinese Economic Renaissance: Apocalypse or Cornucopia?* Basingstoke: Palgrave Macmillan.

——2011a. *Asian Economy: Spearheading the Recovery from the Global Financial Crisis*. London and New York: Routledge.

——2011b. "China in the Domain of International Business." *Human Systems Management*. Vol. 30. No. 1, pp. 71–83.

Denning, L. 2011. "US and China Play the Blame Game." *The Wall Street Journal Asia*. 12 April, p. 30.

Dobbs, R. and S. Sankhe. 2010. "Comparing Urbanization in China and India." *McKinsey Quarterly*. July.

Ernst, D. and B. Naughton. 2008. "China's Emerging Industrial Economy", in C. McNally (ed.). *China's Emergent Industrial Economy: Capitalism in the Dragon's Lair.*" London and New York, pp. 39–59.

Economic Intelligence Unit (EIU). 2012. "Supersized Cities: China's 13 Megalopolis." London.

The Economist. 2013. "The Alibaba Phenomenon." 23 March, p. 13.

——2012. "Manufacturing: The End of Cheap China." 10 March, p. 45.

——2011a. "How to Get a Date." 31 December, p. 57.

——2011b. "Bamboo Capitalism." 12 March, p. 11.

——2011c. "Rising Power, Anxious State." Special Report. 25 June.

——2010a. "The World's Biggest Economy: Dating Game." 16 December, p. 40.

——2010b. "Jim O'Neill Looks at the Global Economy of 2036." 22 November, p. 64.

——2010c. "The Next China." 31 July, pp. 46–48.

Eichengreen, B. S., Y. Rhee and H. Tong. 2007. "China and the Export of Other Asian Countries." *Review of World Economics*. Vol. 143. No. 2, pp. 201–26.

Fardoust, S., J. Y. Lin and X. Luo. 2012. "Demystifying China's Fiscal Stimulus." Washington, DC: World Bank. Policy Research Working Paper No. 6221. October.

Farrell, D., U. A. Gersch and E. Stephenson. 2006. "The Value of China's Emerging Middle Class." *McKinsey Quarterly*. Available online at www.mckinseyquarterly.com/The_value_of_Chinas_emerging_middle_class_1798.

Feenstra, R. C. and S. J. Wei. 2010. "Introduction", in R. C. Feenstra and S. J. Wei (eds). *China's Growing Role in World Trade*. Chicago, IL: University of Chicago Press, pp. 1–31.

Friedman, V. 2011. "Britain's Global Brander." London. *The Financial Times*. 23/ss24 April, p. 7.

Gallup. 2011. *World Affairs*. February. Available online at www.gallup.com/poll/146099/China-Surges-Americans-Views-Top-World-Economy.aspx?version=print.

Gang, X. 2011. "Boosting the Private Sector." *The China Daily*, 12 February, p. 5.

Global Wind Energy Council (GWEC). 2010. *Global Wind Energy Outlook 2010*. Brussels. October.

Golley, J. and L. Song. 2011. "China's Rise in a Changing World", in J. Golley and L. Song (eds). *Rising China: Global Challenges and Opportunities*. Canberra: ANU Press, pp. 1–8.

——2010. "Chinese Economic Reforms and Development", in R. Garnaut, J. Golley and L. Song (eds). *China: The Next Twenty Years of Reform and Development*. Canberra: ANU Press, pp. 1–15.

Hale, G. and C. Long. 2011. "What are the Sources of Financing for Chinese Firms?" in Y. W. Cheung (ed). *The Evolving Role of Asia in Global Finance*. Bingley: Emerald Group, pp. 313–39.

Hsieh, C. T. and P. J. Klenow. 2009. "Misallocation and Manufacturing TFP in China and India." *Quarterly Journal of Economics*. Vol. 124. No. 4, pp. 1403–48.

International Monetary Fund (IMF). 2012. *World Economic Outlook Update*. Washington, DC. 24 January.

——2011a. *Changing Pattern of Global Trade*. Washington, DC. 15 June.

——2011b. *World Economic Outlook*. Washington, DC. April.

——2005. *World Economic Outlook*. Washington, DC. April.

Jensen, B. 2012. *Catching Up: Learning from the Best School Systems in East Asia*. Carlton: Grattan Institute.

Kharas, H. J. 2010. "The Emerging Middle Class in Developing Countries." Paris: Organization for Economic Co-operation and Development (OECD). The Development Center. Working Paper No. 285. January.

Kopytoff, V. G. 2011. "China Overtakes US in PC Shipment." *The New York Times*. 23 August, p. 9.

Koresnikov-Jessop, S. 2010. "Swiss Makers Reward the Chinese Market." *The New York Times*, 17 March, p. 16.

KPMG. 2011. "Product Sourcing in Asia Pacific." Beijing, China. October 4. Available online at www.kpmg.com/Global/en/IssuesAndInsights/ArticlesPublications/Documents/product-sourcing-asia-pacific.pdf.

——2010. "Refined Strategies: Luxury Extends its Reach across China." Beijing, China. 13 August. Available online at www.kpmg.com/Ca/en/IssuesAndInsights/ArticlesPublications/Documents/Refined%20Strategies%20-%20Luxury%20extends%20its%20reach%20across%20China.pdf.

Kuznets, S. 1979. "Growth and Structural Shifts", in W. Galenson (ed.). *Economic Growth and Structural Change in Taiwan*. London: Cornell University Press, pp. 115–31.

Lall, S. and H. G. Wang. 2011. "Balancing Urban Transformation and Spatial Inclusion." *China Urbanization Review*. Washington, DC: World Bank.

Lawrence, R. Z. 2008. "China and the Multilateral Trading System", in B. S. Eichengreen (ed.). *China, Asia and the New Global Economy*. Oxford: Oxford University Press, pp. 145–67.

Lewis, W. A. 1954. "Economic Development with Unlimited Supplies of Labor." *Manchester School of Economic and Social Studies*. Vol. 22, pp. 139–91.

Li, C. 2011. "China in Transition." Washington, DC: Brookings Institutions. Available online at www.brookings.edu/interviews/2011/0919_china_li.aspx.

Lin, J. Y. 2010. "The China Miracle Demystified." Paper presented at the Econometric Society World Congress in Shanghai on 19 August.

Liu, Q. and A. Siu. 2010. "Institutions, Financial Development and Corporate Investment: Evidence from an Implied Return on Capital in China." Hong Kong, SAR: Hong Kong Institute of Economic and Business Strategy. University of Hong Kong. Paper No. 1162. July.

Long, C. and X. Zhang. 2010. "Patterns of China's Industrialization: Concentration, Specialization and Clustering" (unpublished manuscript).

Lucas, R. E. 1993. "Making a Miracle." *Econometrica*. Vol. 61. No. 2, pp. 251–72.

Maddison, A. 1991. *Dynamic Forces in Capitalist Development: A Long-Run Comparative View*. New York: Oxford University Press.

——2001. *The World Economy: A Millennial Perspective*. Paris: Organization for Economic Co-operation and Development (OECD).

Mallon, G. and J. Whally. 2004. "China's Post WTO Stance." Cambridge, MA: National Bureau of Economic Research. Working Paper No. 10649. August.

Marsh, P. 2011. "China Noses Ahead as Top Goods Producer." *The Financial Times*, 13 March, p. 9.

——2010. "US Manufacturing Crown Slips." *The Financial Times*, 20 June, p. 14.

Mattoo, A., F. Ng and A. Subramanian. 2011. "The Elephant in the "Green Room": China and the Doha Round." Washington, DC: Peterson Institute for International Economics. Policy Brief No. BP 11–13.

Mattoo, A. and A. Subramanian. 2011. "China and the World Trading System." Washington, DC: World Bank. Policy Research Working Paper No. 5897. December.

——2011b. *Understanding China's Growing Love for Luxury*. Shanghai, China. April.

McKay, H. and L. Song. 2010. "China as a Global Manufacturing Powerhouse." *China and the World Economy*. Vol. 18. No. 1, pp. 1–32.

McKinsey & C. 2011a. "2011 Annual Chinese Consumer Study: The New Frontier of Growth." Shanghai, China. October.

Moran, T. H. 2011. "Foreign Manufacturing Multinationals and the Transformation of the Chinese Economy." Washington, DC: Peterson Institute of International Economics. Working Paper No. WP.11–11. April.

Organisation for Economic Co-operation and Development (OECD). 2012. "PISA 2012 Mathematics Framework." Paris. Available online at www.oecd.org/dataoecd/8/38/46961598.pdf.

——2010b. *Economic Survey of China 2010*. Paris.

——2010c. *China in the 2010s: Rebalancing Growth and Strengthening Social Safety Nets*. Paris. March.

Pearson, D. 2011. "Private-Jet Firms Look to China's Affluent." *The Wall Street Journal Asia*. 27 May, p. 10.

Porter, M. E. 2000. "Location, Competition and Economic Development: Local Clusters in a Global Economy." *Economic Development Quarterly*. Vol. 14. No. 1, pp. 15–34.

Prasad, E. S. and T. Rumbaugh. 2004. "Overview", in E. S. Prasad and T. Rumbaugh (eds). *China's Growth and Integration into the World Economy*. Washington, DC: International Monetary Fund, pp. 1–4.

Rachman, G. 2011. "When China Becomes Number One." *The Financial Times*. 6 June, p. 16.

Ravallion, M. 2009. "The Developing World's Bulging (but Vulnerable) Middle Class." *World Development*. Vol. 38. No. 4, pp. 445–54.

Sender, H. and K. Hille. 2011. "CIC Seeks Funds out of China Reserves." *The Financial Times*, 16 January, p. 13.

Sirkin, H. L., M. Zinser and D. Hohner. 2011. *Made in America, Again*. Boston, MA: Boston Consulting Group. August.

Song, Z., K. Storesletten and F. Zilibotti. 2011. "Growing Like China." *American Economic Review*. Vol. 101. No. 1, pp. 202–41.

Sternberg, J. 2011. "China's New Competitors." *The Wall Street Journal Asia*. Hong Kong. 22 September, p. 14.

Stimpfig, J. 2011. "The New Red Army." *The Financial Times*. 2 April, p. 10.

Subramanian, A. 2011. *Eclipse: Living in the Shadow of China's Economic Dominance*. Washington, DC: Peterson Institute for International Economics.

Summers, L. H. 2007. "The Rise of Asia and the Global Economy." *Research Monitor*. Special Issue 4–5.

Sutherland, D. 2007. *China's 'National Team' of Enterprise Groups: How Has It Performed?* Discussion Paper No. 23. Nottingham: China Policy Institute, University of Nottingham.

Swartz, S. and S. Oster. 2010. "China Hunger for World's Fuel." *Wall Street Journal*. 21 July, p.19.

Szamosszegi, A. and C. Kyle. 2011. "An Analysis of State-Owned Enterprises and State Capitalism in China." Washington, DC: Capital Trade Incorporate. 26 October.

United States Bureau of Labor Statistics. 2011. *International Labor Comparisons*. Washington, DC. 4 April.

Verspagen, B. 1993. *Uneven Growth between Interdependent Economies*. Aldershot: Avebury.

World Bank (WB). 2011a. "Country and Leading Groups." Washington, DC. Available online at data.worldbank.org/about/country-classifications/country-and-lending-groups#Low_income.

——2011b. "East Asia and Pacific Update." Washington, DC. March.

——2010a. *World Development Indicators 2010*. Washington, DC.

——2010b. *China: Quarterly Update*. World Bank Office, Beijing. June.

——2009. *From Poor Areas to Poor People: China's Evolving Poverty Reduction Agenda*. Washington, DC. March.

World Trade Organization (WTO). 2012. *International Trade Statistics 2012*. Geneva, Switzerland.

——2011. *International Trade Statistics 2011*. Geneva, Switzerland.

——2010. *International Trade Statistics*. Geneva, Switzerland. September.

Yuan, Z., G. Wan and N. Khor. 2011. "The Rise of the Middle Class in the People's Republic of China." Manila, Philippines. Asian Development Bank. Working Paper Series No. 247. February.

Yusuf, S. and K. Nabeshima. 2008. "Optimizing Urban Development", in S. Yusuf and T. Saich (eds). *China Urbanizes*. Washington, DC: World Bank, pp. 1–40.

Zhang, J. 2011. "China Backpedals." Stanford, CA: Hoover University. 12 January.

4

CONTEMPORARY STATE OF THE CHINESE ECONOMY AND ONGOING TRANSITION TO A NEW GROWTH TRAJECTORY

1. Introduction

Major transformations have occurred in the Chinese economy. Should this be taken to imply that all is in apple-pie order? Perhaps not. As the economy was in a state of rapid change and in flux, several structural and policy issues could not be satisfactorily resolved. Others had to be delayed because the time for reforms to them was not considered ripe. The process of structural transformations was far from smooth. A litany of problems and distortions in the economy persist. The economy faces myriad domestic and external imbalances. The focus of this chapter is the existing state of the Chinese economy. It deals with its strengths, weaknesses and incongruities. It also examines the transformations in China's growth trajectory, ongoing adjustments and amendments, as well as the emerging future trends. Among the important transformations, one that attracts immediate attention is the current soft landing of the Chinese economy.

A tepid global economic environment and tighter domestic policies for cooling the overheated property markets were largely responsible for the deceleration in gross domestic product (GDP) growth in China. It declined from 10.4 percent in 2010 to 9.2 in 2011. This was the slowest quarterly GDP growth rate in three years. However, policy mandarins need not raise their hackles over it because this is a deceleration of the growth rate from above the potential level in a context where the potential growth rate itself is gradually slowing (WB, 2012a). In 2012 GDP growth rate declined to 7.8 percent, while the first two quarters of 2013 recorded growth rates of 7.7 percent and 7.5 percent, respectively. The faltering export demand was a major causal factor. In particular, exports of manufactured products weakened markedly, causing the trade balance to fall into deficit in the first quarter of 2012. This was the principal factor behind the softening of the balance of payments. A sustained reduction in China's external surplus is taking place. The growth rate of forex accumulation also dampened. The flip side of the coin was that as wage and household income growth were strong, consumption growth also remained robust. Another favorable development was the abatement of inflationary concerns in 2012 because it demonstrated a declining trend.

2. Structural and economic imbalances and asymmetric liberalization

Periods of heady growth often mask deep-seated economic problems. Among the imbalances and asymmetries in the Chinese economy, financial sector is commonly named first. The process of liberalization and structural transformation of the Chinese economy was far from methodical, logical and smooth. It was not only *ad hoc* but in some vital sectors it was also immensely retarded. Until the early 1980s, the financial system in China was far from developed by any existing norms. Reforms were overly delayed in the financial sector. Progress in reforms of the financial sector and banks is still regarded as disappointing. Little wonder that until recently it was regarded as on the verge of collapse (Goodstadt, 2012; Garcia-Herrero and Santabarbara, 2013). The financial sector is still bank-dominated and the so-called "big four" commercial banks tower over it. Attempts were made to gradually make them autonomous. The conventional wisdom is that a well-developed financial system is a major prerequisite for industrial development. The rapid industrialization in China disproves it.

Privately owned small and medium enterprises had little access to formal credit from the state-owned banks. Reforms in the financial sector did not go into full swing until 1994, a good 16 years after the reform process began. The commercial banking law was enacted in 1995. Although the regulation and supervision of China's banking system have improved in the past few years, China lags far behind the advanced industrial economies in the area of financial development.[1] Its large banking system is still owned by various levels of government. Persisting limitations in its financial system are widely regarded as the Achilles' heel of the Chinese economy. This is not to ignore the significant progress made in finance and banking since 2005 (Herd *et al.*, 2010).

Another conspicuous incongruity in the liberalization process is that the product markets in China are nearly completely liberalized, while factor markets continue to remain distorted. This asymmetry is significant and has had far-reaching macro-economic ramifications. The consequence of factor market and institutional distortions is the repression of prices of land, labor and capital and environmental pollution, which in turn lowers the cost of production. Their eventual outcome is equivalent to a subsidy for producers, exporters and investors. According to Yiping (2010, p. 283) these subsidies "artificially raise profits from production, increase investors' returns and improve the international competitiveness of Chinese goods. They also surely help contribute to China's extraordinary growth performance". This subsidy effect promotes and reinforces investment and export, causing imbalances and inefficiency problems in the domestic and global economies. Exports and investment, measured as a proportion of GDP, continued to remain unusually high in China. They partly explain China's large, somewhat disproportionate, influence on the global economy.

Financial repression has been a problematic issue and a source of serious economic imbalance. It led to distortions in the domestic economy and a substantial increase in the national savings rate. Bank deposits yielded negative real rate of return for the depositors, particularly since 2003. Negative real returns adversely affect consumption expenditure by depressing household incomes. Besides, many households responded to it by increasing their savings in other forms, which further depressed the proportion of disposable income going to consumption. A popular alternative mode of saving was investment in housing. It accounted for 5 percent of GDP in 2003 but doubled to 10.7 percent by 2010. This level far exceeds the average level of housing investment in economies having comparable per caput income. Also, this sharp rise accounted for almost half of the increase in the share of investment in GDP between 1997–2003 and 2004–10 (Lardy, 2012). China now faces a risk of overinvestment in residential property, another imbalance in the economy.

On the road to economic expansion and historic transformations, several structural problems emerged. Among the myriad challenges that China faces are excessive and unsustainable dependence of economic growth on export and investment, malaise of skewed income distribution between urban and rural populations and weak oversight of product safety standards. Largely because it is partially reformed, the economy has a built-in inflationary tendency. High inflation in 2010 and 2011 had both domestic and external causal factors. The Gini coefficient continued to worsen.

Although China has rapidly become a global economic power, its household incomes have risen but not commensurate to GDP growth. In recent years the economy has suffered from domestic and external imbalances partly as a result of the heavy emphasis on industrial development. The rural–urban income divide was large and continued to widen. During the reform period, urban real incomes increased at the rate of 12 percent annually, while in the rural areas this rate was a mere 5.5 percent (Das, 2008a). In 2005 real rural income per caput was only 39 percent of real urban income per caput (Park, 2008). Presently urban income in China is three times higher than rural. This rural–urban income gap in China is one of the largest in the world and has triggered massive rural to urban migration. This gap partly reflects the institutional legacies of socialism.

The distributional impact of the growth process in China has caused legitimate concerns. Gains from growth-promoting reforms were found to be exceedingly uneven. This unevenness was easy to see across provinces in China as well as sectorally. Primary-sector growth lagged considerably behind secondary and tertiary growth. There has also been uneven growth at the household level. Incomes at the top of the distribution increased much faster than those at the bottom (Chaudhury and Ravallion, 2007).

As stated above, China has been experiencing the world's most rapidly rising income inequality and a worsening Gini coefficient with rising incomes. The maldistribution of income reached dangerous proportions by international standards. The Gini coefficient in China rose from 0.28 to 0.39 between 1980 and 2006 (Ravallion and Chen, 2007). However, the contrary view is that this increasing income inequality and worsening Gini did not have a reliable causal impact on growth. Using panel data that track household incomes, Benjamin et al. (2010) concluded that income inequality was not found to impede growth. One reason behind rising income inequality was that the unemployment rate increased sharply as the SOE sector was restructured. Employment in SOEs declined by nearly 50 million (Overholt, 2005). Regional economic disparities continued to intensify and deep disparities within and between sectors persisted. Coastal cities in the south-eastern part of China have a much higher per capita income than those in the northwestern and interior parts. Earlier cases of rising income inequality in the NIEs and the present experience in China indicate that an unfettered free market is not likely to generate economic growth with equitable income distribution. According to Feng (2011, p. 7), "[g]rowth with equity does not just occur naturally in a political and social vacuum". Governments need to address the issue of inequality adequately to improve income distribution.

A recent econometric study has concluded that most regional income disparities measures are erroneous and biased. The sources of error are as follows: using registered population as a denominator, the abrupt and uncoordinated switch to using a resident denominator and the double-count introduced by the partial and inconsistent way in which residents were counted by different provinces in any given year. This study shows that much of the apparent increases in inter-provincial income inequalities disappear once a consistent series of GDP per resident is used (Li and Gibson, 2012).

Throughout the reform era Chinese households recorded exceedingly high savings levels. The savings rate was exceedingly high from a historical perspective and by international standards. Also, it rose over time. The household sector's propensity to save in China is the highest in the world and it has kept on rising over the last few years. Several recent studies have focused on the high-saving propensity of Chinese households.[2] Since 1990, approximately 40 percent or more of the GDP was annually saved (see Chapter 2, Table 2.1, Figure 2.2). After 2000, savings rates increased further and surpassed those achieved by Japan, Korea and the other East Asian miracle economies during a similar stage of their development. After 2004 more than a half of the GDP was saved. Between 2006 and 2010, gross saving in the economy was higher than 50 percent of GDP for every year. Measured as a percentage of GDP, China was the highest saving economy in the world in late 2000s. The net saving of the corporate sector is negative. The behavior of the corporate sector is not unusual. In the neighboring Asian economies it shows the same trend (Bayoumi *et al.*, 2010).

The marginal propensity to save (MPS) approached 60 percent during the 2000s (ADB, 2009; Zhou, 2009). There was a strong penchant for precautionary savings, particularly by elderly households, owing to an inadequate healthcare system and a lack of old age pension and education benefits. What really set China apart is a rising aggregate savings trend in all the three sectors, household, corporate and government. High savings rates affected domestic consumption rate adversely. They have had ramifications for both internal and external balances. If there was a problematic issue that stemmed from high savings rates, it was that they led to persistent current account surpluses. While China still is a medium-level per caput income country, it has been forced to export its savings to advanced economies.

The high investment rate went *pari passu* with high savings (see Chapter 2, Table 2.2, Figure 2.2). In recent years it remained higher than 40 percent of GDP, one of the highest in the world. It was often wondered whether China was over-investing. Such a high investment can lead to skepticism regarding the return on capital in China. Estimates based on national accounts data reveal that the aggregate rate of return on capital averaged 25 percent over the 1978–93 period, declined somewhat during the 1993–98 period and thereafter hit a plateau at about 20 percent. Also, the standard deviation of the rate of return on capital across Chinese provinces fell after 1978 (Bai *et al.*, 2006; Sun *et al.*, 2011). Thus, the rate of return on capital in China is much higher than in the Organization for Economic Co-operation and Development (OECD) countries (Song *et al.*, 2011).

One direct consequence of high savings and investment was low consumption. China became a consumption-deficient economy. That its consumption is low for the level of its income is a well-recognized and much-examined fact. Besides, with the passage of time its household consumption-to-GDP ratio worsened. The consumption-to-GDP ratio declined from 55 percent in the early 1980s, to 47 percent in 1995 and further to 36 percent in 2005. In 2008 it stood at 35.3 percent (Prasad, 2011a). In the first half of 2011 this ratio was 34 percent. The low domestic consumption led to a declining share of consumption in GDP. Among its Asian peers, China has the lowest consumption-to-GDP ratio. This proportion is also the lowest among any major economy in the world.[3] The population of Italy is 60 million, less than one-20th of China. Yet the size of the consumer economy in these two countries is almost the same. Since the turn of the century, the government has made endeavors to boost domestic consumption. Increasing by an average of 8 percent per year or more between 2000 and 2008, China's rate of consumption growth has been strong. However, in 2009 owing to the global financial crisis this trend reversed (IMF, 2010). Increase in consumption continued in China and notably, in 2011, consumption contributed more to GDP than investment for the first time ever (WB, 2012b).

Although the rates of investment in the economy also rose, they increased at a slower pace than the rate of savings. One valid reason for high rates of investment was technological absorption. Much of the existing technology and innovation can be acquired by procuring new machinery, making it imperative to have high rates of investment. The flip side of the coin is that a high investment rate not only crowded out consumption but also led to overcapacity in several industrial sectors as well as in housing, which plagued the economy. In addition, the environmental pollution created by rapid industrialization has been increasing at an alarming rate. In 2007 China became the world's largest producer of greenhouse gases.[4] This list of serious imbalances and disparities is far from exhaustive. Policy makers in China are aware of these imbalances and discrepancies and have publicly acknowledged them. Premier Wen Jiabao candidly noted that the economy suffers from structural problems. At an important policy-planning forum he remarked, "[t]he biggest problem in China's economy is imbalances in the structure. That kind of economic development is not stable, balanced, harmonious and sustainable". He derisively criticized China's growth model as "unstable, unbalanced, uncoordinated and unsustainable".[5]

Another flagrant imbalance in the Chinese economy is its oft-discussed regional imbalance. The eastern and southern coastal provinces grew at a much faster pace than the inland central and western ones. Such disparities are not unknown at the early stages of development. To promote social harmony, since 2002, the present government has actively pursued the policy of redressing this eye-catching regional disparity. One important measure was encouraging industries to relocate from the coastal provinces to the inland ones. This was like applying the famous Akamatsu's doctrine of "the flying geese paradigm" domestically. To encourage industries to relocate to central and western provinces the Ministry of Commerce implemented a project in 2006 called "10,000 Businesses Going West". To make these regions alluring to the industries the Ministry of Commerce developed infrastructure and economic development zones in the central and western provinces. Also, 31 priority locations were designated for this purpose in 2007 and 2008. This strategy has begun to bear fruit and show results. Some of the high-growth industries have moved to the central and western provinces. These regions could therefore start to catch up and the regional disparity may start to be reduced (Kwan, 2009).

The recent rapid GDP growth performance was largely based on the performance of the manufacturing sector. Investment and external demand were the other two major drivers of growth. China has benefitted enormously from regionalization and globalization. Regionalization has given rise to and constitutes an important aspect of globalization. China exploited regionalization and globalization as a fuel for its growth. However, they were not an unalloyed blessing for China. Their downside was that the economy became dependent on external demand, which in turn made China vulnerable to external shocks.

China's rising current account surpluses peaked at 10.8 percent of GDP in 2007, although the figure was a mere 1.7 percent in 2000. The acceleration in saving rates in recent years contributed to China's current account surpluses. The reason is that according to the basic national income identity current account surplus of an economy equals the surplus of savings over investment. The large and continuing imbalance in the current account positions of the USA on the one hand, and China and the other Asian economies on the other, is seen by many analysts as a threat to an orderly development of the global economy. No doubt these imbalances are not sustainable for an indefinite period and call for some rebalancing in demand and exchange rate changes, among other measures. By 2012 China's current account surplus pared down to 2.6 percent of GDP, which led many investors to believe that China's exchange rate was close to an equilibrium.

Since the 1980s China continually enjoyed the "twin surplus", that is, the surplus in both current and capital accounts.[6] This is an idiosyncratic feature of China's imbalances. The usual pattern for a developing country is to run a current account deficit and a capital account surplus. China is different. The explanation for this atypical behavior is that, first, as China is a booming exporter its current account remains in surplus. Second, as it is one of the most attractive destinations for FDI a lot of countries invest in China. Therefore, capital flows into China through both current and

TABLE 4.1 Foreign exchange reserves, 1977–2012 (end-of-year data)

Year	Billions of US$	Year	Billions of US$
1977	2.35	1995	75.38
1978	1.56	1996	107.04
1979	2.15	1997	142.76
1980	2.55	1998	149.19
1981	5.06	1999	157.73
1982	11.35	2000	168.28
1983	15	2001	215.61
1984	17.37	2002	291.13
1985	12.73	2003	408.15
1986	11.45	2004	614.5
1987	16.3	2005	821.51
1988	18.54	2006	1,068.49
1989	17.96	2007	1,530.28
1990	29.59	2008	1,949.26
1991	43.67	2009	2,399.20
1992	20.62	2010	2,847.30
1993	22.39	2011	3,181.10
1994	52.91	2012*	3,290.00

Sources:
1 The World Bank. 2012 *World Development Indicator Online Database 2012*. Washington, DC.
2 People's Bank of China. 2011. *China's Foreign Exchange Reserves*. State Administration of Foreign Exchange. Beijing, China.
3 *National Bureau of Statistic*, Beijing, China.
Note: 2012*: September 2012.

capital accounts. These twin surpluses coalesced to make China the largest holder of forex reserves. Its foreign exchange (forex) reserves continuously rose. In 2007 total reserves soared to $1.5 trillion (Table 4.1, Figure 4.1). At this time they surpassed that of Japan and became world's largest. At the end of 2011 they reached $3.18 trillion. This amount could finance approximately 24 months of imports and was almost half of the 2010 GDP. Such a large size of forex reserves became a bone of contention in the international arena. China is opens to allegations of quasi-mercantilism owing to the volume of its forex reserves (*Financial Times*, 2011a). As a result of heavy capital inflows forex reserves reached $3.44 trillion in March 2013.

The rapid rise of the reserves is a relatively recent phenomenon. In 1990 total forex reserves were merely $29.59 billion and in 2000 $168 billion. China's current account surpluses—rising from 1.7 percent of GDP in 2001 to 10.1 percent in 2007—contributed to the building up of large stash of forex reserves.[7] They increased at an exceedingly rapid rate. In 2010 forex reserves they increased by $448 billion, reaching $2.85 trillion. This indicated massive intervention in forex markets by the PBC to keep the renminbi from appreciating substantially. China was blamed for creating and exacerbating global imbalances by the advanced industrial economies. As the forex reserves grew, it came under increasing pressure from Japan, the USA and other EMEs to allow its currency to appreciate. In March 2013 they stood at $3.44 trillion.

While a healthy level of forex reserves provides safety for an external crisis and contagion, an excessively large level of reserves can have problems: First, the so-called Dornbusch problem, which suggests that the developing economies should use their resources for domestic consumption and domestic investment. The reason is that the return on investment is much higher in the

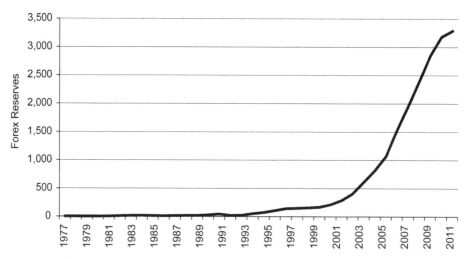

FIGURE 4.1 Foreign exchange reserves
Sources:
1 The World Bank 2013. World Development Indicator Online Database 2013. Washington DC.
2 People's Bank of China 2011. China's Foreign Exchange Reserves. State Administration of Foreign Exchange. Beijing. China
3 National Bureau of Statistic, Beijing China

domestic economy in comparison to the return on the Treasury bills. Second, the Williamson problem, which points out that when a developing country receives resources from an advanced industrial economy it should be spent on buying capital goods, technology and managerial skills so that the current account is in deficit. Third, the Krugman problem, which notes that the USA has accumulated a large debt, so the possibility of a dollar devaluation is high. A dollar devaluation will mean great losses for China. Fourth, the Rogoff problem, a country with high debt is tempted to inflate away the debt burden. If this comes to pass, it will severely reduce the purchasing power of the Chinese Treasury bills (Yongding, 2011).

3. The immediate future: transitioning again to a new growth trajectory

As a high-saving and therefore high-investing economy, it was logical for China to initially adopt a "capital-intensive industry-led growth model", which is outward-oriented like those of the four NIEs of East Asia (Vincelette *et al.*, 2011, p. 116). One benefit of adopting this growth model was that it provided logical support to high productivity in the industrial sector. By the middle of the last decade the economy had reached a significantly higher stage of economic development and structural transformation. There was recognition at the highest political level in China that the economic paradigm that had served China so well thus far was no longer fit-for-purpose. No strategy lasts forever. Every successful development strategy needs to be flexible and change with the changing circumstances (WB/DRC, 2013). The Chinese policy-making establishment has been concerned about high savings and investment rates and low household consumption, high resource and energy intensity, adverse environmental impact, income inequality and large external imbalances. For continued rapid growth, China pressingly needs policy reforms and an appropriate policy paradigm.

As noted in the brief discussion above, the priority objectives of the policy-makers had gone on changing in a pragmatic manner as the economy grew from one stage to the next. For instance, in

TABLE 4.2 Current account balance (current US$)

Year	Billions of US$	% of GDP
1982	5,599	1.99
1983	4,144	1.37
1984	1,944	0.63
1985	−11,508	−3.75
1986	−7,233	−2.43
1987	0.3	0.09
1988	−3,802	−0.94
1989	−4,317	−0.96
1990	11,997	3.07
1991	13,271	3.24
1992	6,402	1.31
1993	−11,902	−1.94
1994	7,657	1.37
1995	1,618	0.22
1996	7,243	0.85
1997	36,962	3.88
1998	31,472	3.09
1999	15,669	1.45
2000	20,519	1.71
2001	17,405	1.31
2002	35,422	2.44
2003	45,875	2.8
2004	68,659	3.55
2005	160,818	7.19
2006	253,268	9.53
2007	371,833	10.99
2008	426,107	9.3
2009	283,756	4.9
2010	305,374	4.0
2011	201,700	2.8

Source: International Monetary Fund, 2012. *IMF Data Base and Forecast*. Washington, DC.

the post-World Trade Organization (WTO) accession era China's economy became increasingly export-oriented and therefore export-dependent. Although the current account surplus was not large until 2001, when China acceded to the WTO, after this juncture the current account surplus rose at a dramatic rate (Table 4.2, Figure 4.2). It was also partly responsible for a sharp rise in the forex reserve. This growth trajectory contributed to domestic and global imbalance and became unsustainable. Recognizing the need for a change in strategy, the 11th Five-Year Plan (2006–10) attempted to provide a new direction to the economy and change China's growth trajectory. Such a transformation was essential for making the economy resilient to large shocks and to ensure sustainability of its growth.

This was a major turning point in the thinking and priorities of the CPC leadership. At this juncture, their most prominent objective was to build a "harmonious socialist society" (*shehui zhuyi hexie shehui*). The less advantaged groups among the population and regions were to be the focus of the 11th Five-Year Plan, so that economic and social inequalities could be addressed. Three decades ago it was pragmatic to follow Deng's dictum of "getting rich first" (*xianfu lun*). After that goal was achieved during the 10th Five-Year Plan (2001–05) to a measureable degree and the

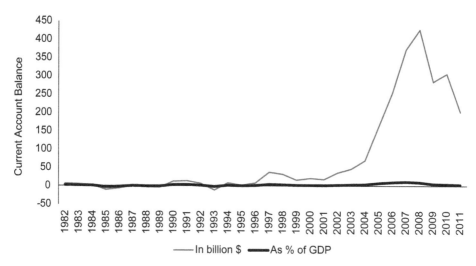

FIGURE 4.2 Current account balance (current US$)
Source: International Monetary Fund (2012). IMF Data Base and Forecast. Washington DC.

economy became stronger both in relative and absolute terms, the time had come to switch focus to achieving "common prosperity" (*gongtong fuyu*). As both domestic and external circumstances were favorable, this was an opportune moment for making bolder reforms to address deep-rooted problems without causing much economic disruption.

As the domestic economy is weighed down with imbalances, there is an imperative need to rebalance it. It is a positive signal that the country's top political leadership has given the impression of will and commitment to adjust the economic structure in such a manner that it improves the quality of growth. To that end, it needs to switch to a new growth trajectory. Researchers in this area have recommended policy adjustments for achieving the twin objectives of sustaining growth and balancing the economy. A precise adjustment strategy was proposed by Blanchard and Giavazzi (2006) under the rubric of a three-handed strategy. The specific measures they suggested were, first, a reduction in the high savings rate, particularly household saving, so that domestic demand can be bolstered; second, an increase in the supply of services, particularly essential services like health; third, an adjustment to generate a gradual if steady appreciation of the renminbi.

However, there are those who are opposed to such *ad hoc* and precisely specified adjustments on the grounds that they are short-term oriented and regard broad macro-economic adjustments to dispel fundamental imbalances as indispensable. The economy imperatively requires a basic shift from export-dependence to dependence on domestic demand as well as changes that contribute to improvement in the efficiency of investment (Dunaway and Prasad, 2006). There are others who recommend continuing with broad reforms, particularly putting the financial and banking sectors and the SOEs in order. The investment share of GDP needs to be reduced. These reforms are, *inter alia*, needed to make the economy more resilient to external and internal shocks (Prasad, 2009). Also, this has been a period of sustained capital inflows in China despite the global financial crisis and there has been a constant pressure to appreciate the renminbi. Such periods are considered ideal for managing a move towards greater exchange rate flexibility. Capital account liberalization can also be adopted.

One major causal factor of structural imbalances in the domestic economy is a distorted incentive structure. Factor prices in China are distorted and depressed. Until decisive corrective measures are taken to liberalize factor markets, structural distortions in the economy cannot be eliminated. Factor inputs include capital, labor, land, energy and environment. Correcting these distortions is a huge challenge because powerful interest groups have come to expect and rely on underpriced factor inputs. Correction in factor price distortions cannot be undertaken without compensating these interest groups.

As stated above, China's consumption-to-GDP ratio has usually remained low. It has had a declining trend and is by far the lowest in Asia. Since the beginning of the 11th Five-Year Plan (2006–10) period, the government made it a publicized policy priority to rebalance growth by stoking private consumption.[8] There is a serious need for improvement in the consumption infrastructure so that Chinese consumers can purchase a wider range of products and services. Expanding the availability and improving the quality of products on the one hand, and increasing the availability and uptake of consumer credit on the other, would contribute to a long-sought-after increase in the consumption-to-GDP ratio. These changes would encourage households to save less of their disposable incomes.

A McKinsey Global Institute (MGI) study inferred that "consumption- and service-led economies tend to create more jobs per unit of investment, accompanied by higher wages per dollar invested" (MGI, 2009, p. 10). Higher consumption would indubitably make growth more sustainable in China. It would boost job creation which in turn would provide an increase in "average household incomes of 10 to 20 percent, and a strong fillip to domestic firms and entrepreneurs, particularly in the retail and services sectors" (MGI, 2009, p. 10). The long-lasting imbalance of low consumption and high investment can also be rectified by banking-sector reforms and further development of the financial markets. Together they would drive out the distortions in pricing capital, which, *inter alia*, promoted excessive investment at the cost of consumption in the economy (Aziz, 2006).

In keeping with a realistic vision of the future, the objective of the 12th Five-Year Plan (2011–15) continues to be the theme of rebalancing. The objective of this plan is not only to address the short-term macroeconomic challenges that China faces but also the long-term structural transformation and reorientation of the economy so that it moves to a steadier and more stable trajectory.[9] A strategic shift from an investment-driven, export-led growth to one that is domestic demand-led has been enshrined in the 12th Five-Year Plan. Emphasis on the quality, balance and sustainability of growth makes the twelfth plan different. Emphasis on reducing the greenhouse gas (GHG) missions per unit of GDP by 40 percent to 45 percent by 2020 in comparison to 2005 levels is continuing in the 12th Five-Year Plan period (2011–15). During the 11th Plan period, China achieved a 19.1 percent energy consumption reduction, narrowly missing the 20 percent target. Investment in the low-carbon economy and sustainable development has been increased in the 12th Plan period. Both provincial and sector-level targets have been fixed and resources are being devoted to monitoring the progress in achieving the well-publicized targets (KPMG, 2011).

The 12th Plan may well herald a turning point in China's economic development and be another valuable opportunity to shift growth trajectory. This shift would entail the development of higher value-added manufacturing sectors and synergizing small and medium, predominantly private, firms. This would also be an opportune time to focus on the growth of the interior provinces in place of the coastal ones (Overholt, 2010). By prioritizing expansion of the services sector the 12th Plan is likely to turn the economy away from capital-intensive economic growth to labor-intensive growth. Raising labor income is one of the important emphases of the 12th Five-Year Plan (2011–15). Putting more people to work would indeed increase labor income and enhance consumption. The economy could also be rebalanced by increasing reliance on imports, both from the regional economies and global economy. Moving to a market-based exchange rate regime is another important part of the rebalancing theme. Expectations of the Chinese policy-making elite are that these alterations would make China's growth trajectory more stable and suitable for its long-term growth (Li and Woetzel, 2011).

3.1 Shifting into a lower economic gear

During the fourth annual meeting of the 11th National People's Congress (NPC) in China in March 2011 pronouncements Premier Wen Jiabao made the fundamental policy shift clear.[10] His statements augur a major transition in China's economic growth strategy. The quality of growth has become a high priority for the top Chinese policy makers. They no longer plan to target high GDP growth rate at the cost of environmental degradation. They evidently regard it as unsustainable. In his opening speech on 5 March Premier Wen Jiabao understandably assigned the top priority to the objective to reining in inflation and the second priority to raising the household consumption share of the GDP.

For the first time maintaining high economic growth was not listed as the top priority objective. A notional GDP growth target of 7 percent per annum was determined for the 12th Plan period. This was lower than 7.5 percent for the previous plan, although actual GDP growth during the 11th Plan period was close to 10 percent. The government has planned for inclusive growth during the 12th Five-Year Plan and to achieve that objective by devoting more resources to rural areas so that the much-maligned rural–urban income gap can be mitigated. Healthcare, energy and technology were singled out as the three priority sectors of the 12th Five-Year Plan. It was not merely a matter of domestic policy but a downturn this time was being supported by external and internal economic factors, global economic environment and financial trends.

China has been making gradual headway in rebalancing its domestic economy by increasing its reliance on domestic consumption. According to the projections of the WB/DRC (2013) study rebalancing of the Chinese economy will be gradual and will take two decades. This cannot be achieved merely through administrative measures. China's policy-making establishment appears to be convinced in this regard. Major adjustments to the growth strategy are being considered for some time. In the past, attempts were made to boost consumption of autos and white goods by subsidizing their purchase. They did increase the consumption of these consumer items without increasing overall consumption in the economy. The basic issue is the low share of Chinese household income that is spent on consumption. This is the appropriate variable to be addressed to increase the consumption share of the GDP (Pettis, 2011).

Driven by the weak global economic environment, early in the second decade of the 21st century, China's high-octane economy shifted into lower gear (Section 1). With that it entered a difficult transition phase. Its two important elements were lower GDP growth rate and a different growth paradigm. China's period of "extensive growth", which was driven by higher rates of capital investment and labor input was ending. It needed to switch to "intensive growth" which entails skills- and technology-based growth (Wolf, 2012). In addition, China's highly elastic supply of low-cost labor is likely to end soon. In the parlance of development economists, China is at the Lewis turning point (Lewis, 1954). That is, its labor surplus is soon to be absorbed in the economy. Arthur Lewis had posited that during the early phases of development the subsistence income of surplus labor in agriculture sets a low ceiling for wages in the industrial and other modern sectors of the economy. This tends to make industrial and modern services sectors highly profitable. If the high profits were then reinvested, as they were in China, the rate of growth in the industrial and modern sectors of the economy would be very high and have large welfare effects in the economy. At this juncture, China was at the tail end of this effect. Therefore, for any future investment the ratio of capital to labor will rise faster. Also, the rate of return on this investment will decline faster.

The implacable sovereign debt crisis in the Eurozone, weak recovery in the USA, curbs on the property market in the domestic economy and general weakening of domestic demand told on the GDP growth rate in 2012. The first and second quarters of GDP growth rate were 8.1 percent and 7.6 percent, respectively, the worst economic performance since the beginning of the global financial crisis. The January 2013 update of the *World Economic Outlook* reported China's 2012 GDP growth rate at 7.8 percent (Section 1). Part of the deceleration in GDP is policy induced. In the first two quarters of 2013 GDP growth declined to 7.7 percent and 7.5 percent, respectively (Section 1), and the economy seemed to be settling around its new growth potential.

Although this soft landing reflected China's shift to a more sustainable development pattern, it entailed pain of lowered hiring, sliding real estate prices and mounting stockpile of unsold inventory. The HSBC/Markit survey of June 2012 reported a rapid rise in inventories, an unfamiliar problem for the Chinese businesses (Bradsher, 2012). Retail sales were flat or sharply declining. Large stockpiles of unsold goods, clogged car dealerships and overflowing factory warehouses became a common sight. Overcapacity soared and there was a glut in many markets ranging from steel to housing appliances to apartments. Owing to rapid expansion of credit, rising debt and structural weaknesses China's sovereign credit rating by Fitch was cut in April 2013. High debt levels in China faced concern since 2009, when the state-owned banks stepped up credit to power the economy through the global financial crisis. Its long-term local currency rating was cut from AA− to A+. Fitch's rating was slightly below those of Moody's and Standard and Poor's (Noble and Rabinovitch, 2013).

Although 2012 GDP growth decelerated, there was an interesting regional disparity. The remote inland provinces moved up the growth rankings as the former successful coastal provinces slid. The economic performance of Tianjin (13.8 percent), Chongqing (13.6 percent), Guizhou (13.6 percent), Yunan (13.0 percent) and Shaanxi (12.9 percent) was far superior to the national average (EIU, 2013). In 2013 it became evident that after an exhilarating growth period of over three decades, China was entering a period of economic slowdown. There are several reasons behind it. First, the share of infrastructure investment in fixed assets declined from 30 percent to 20 percent over the last decade. The return on investment has been falling, and with that the incremental capital-output ratio has been rising. It was 4.6 in 2011, the highest since 1992. This implies that the economy is achieving less growth from its investment (Wolf, 2013). Also, the growth rate of labor supply has declined sharply and wages have been rising incessantly.

3.2 Effect on the Asian economies

When this opportunity for transforming the growth trajectory in China is taken, major economic changes are sure to occur in the region. They in turn would influence the regional economies and the global economy would not remain unaffected. Given the size of the Chinese economy and the extent of its regional and global integration, any structural changes in China would have far-reaching consequences over both, the regional and global economies (Golley and Song, 2011). When the GDP growth rate in China began to slow (Section 1), its impact on the Asian economies was clearly visible. In early 2012 Korea, Taiwan and Malaysia posted weak export numbers (WSJ, 2012).

Indonesia was a substantive exporter of ores and natural resources to China and its economy recorded a robust GDP growth until 2011. Weakening Chinese demand will be reflected in relatively weaker growth in Indonesia over the next few years. Thailand recovered from the disastrous floods of 2011 and rebuilding provided a growth pop, but was expected to be frittered away by a slowing China, which has been Thailand's important export market (WSJ, 2012). China's trade with its Asian neighbors has grown over the years. It included both, trade in inputs to be assembled into final goods for the global export markets and trade in final products to be consumed in China. As emphasis on domestic consumption increased in China, the proportion of the latter grew. If the Chinese economy continues to cool, Asian economies will need to come up with formulas like programs for government spending or further liberalization to immunize themselves from a slowing Chinese economy.

3.3 Approaching the transformation phase

To transform itself from a middle-income country into a high-income country, China will need to adopt numerous deep-seated structural reforms so that it is able to eschew the well-known middle-income trap. A well-researched recent report jointly produced by the World Bank and the Development Research Center (DRC) of the State Council of the Government of China casts light on the need for this difficult set of reforms so that growth trajectory can be sustained over the next two decades and the economy is able to eschew the so-called middle-income trap. Although economic fundamentals are strong, they alone cannot take China to the next level of development. Further essential economic changes of a crucial nature are needed. One of the most important ones is the need for the state to progressively withdraw from the economy. The state sector is too strong in China and distorts the market mechanism. There is also a pressing need to increase its investment in social services to strengthen its human capital. During the approaching economic transformation phase, China needs to accelerate the pace of innovation and seize the opportunity to "go green". Environmental protection policies need high priority. Other priority policies include strengthening the fiscal system, and promoting social security so that the rising inequality in the society is reversed. Lastly, China needs to proactively intensify its trade, investment and financial links with the regional and global economies over the next two decades (WB/DRC, 2013). The release of this report is an indication that the constituency of reforms in China is strong.

That China is not shying away from sensible reforms is obvious from the fact that in the early months of the 2012 government announced a string of new liberalization measures focused on the financial sector. They included increasing the size of the Qualified Foreign Institutional Investor (QFII) scheme, widening the trading band of the renminbi and doubling the previous limit and tariff reductions on some raw materials and luxury products. Also, the top political leadership endorsed bolder financial-sector reforms. In a speech on 13 April, Premier Wen Jiabao told a national audience that the government has plans to eliminate the monopoly of the country's big state-owned banks. He noted, "to break the monopoly we must allow private capital to flow into the financial sector". In the same speech he supported liberalization of interest rates and loosening government control over them, a factor that hurts both consumers and depositors (McMahon et al., 2012).

Competition in the financial sector is likely to increase. To that end, smaller state banks may be expanded and more private capital may be invited in the financial sector. These measures were included in the 2012 program of the National Development and Reform Commission. A pilot project was being run in Wenzhou, in Zhejiang province, to determine the role of the private sector in the financial sector. Promoting establishment of private financial services companies is a practical concept. This would effectively legalize the region's substantial grey market.

3.4 Transformation through innovation

China successfully became the world's factory but frequently the high value work of innovation, product development and design was not being dome at home. Therefore, as alluded to in the preceding section, accelerating pace of innovation may well be a means of transitioning from being an EME to being something like an advance economy in the medium-term. Chinese business firms need to move up the value chain by developing new technologies and expertise in China. History shows that China was a global innovation leader, but lost on innovation owing to bureaucratic feudalism around the 14th century (Needham, 1954).

To promote innovation and raise the level of technology in the economy, former Premier Wen organized the Leading Group on Science, Technology and Education in 2003. He brought toge-ther two important science and technology organizations, namely, Chinese Academy of Sciences (CAS) and the Ministry of Science and Technology (MOST) so that innovation can be given a big push. CAS is justly regarded as an elite science and research center. Using its global network it can call on the talent of ethnic Chinese scientists in the US universities and research institutions for advice. Some 2,000 scientists, bureaucrats and managers from the business community were mobilized and organized into 20 working groups to conduct studies and make detailed plans for promoting technological advancement and innovation (McGregor, 2012). Efforts were made to revamp science and technology bureaucracy. For approval of research projects, importance of peer review was increased and the role of government officials diluted.

One of the objectives of the 12th Five-Year Plan (2011–15) is to engender a transition from a manufacturing power house to an innovation engine, so that instead of "made in China" products, "created in China" products are produced. Under the "Thousand Talents" program Chinese sci-entists working in advanced countries are being encouraged to return. To achieve this objective, expenditure on education has increased by 20 percent since 1999 and universities have increased their knowledge exchanges with the business community. National-level research programs sup-port the development of new technologies in a wide range of fields. The Science and Technology Development Plan calls for 2.5 percent of the GDP spent on R&D (CEIBS, 2012). Recent progress in areas like the space program, high-speed trains and commercial aircrafts was impressive. Over 100 leading Chinese and multinational companies were surveyed by the Benelux Chamber of Commerce and China Europe International Business School. The results of a *China innovation survey* came to a surprising conclusion. Many global MNEs perceived that Chinese companies are a major innovation powers. Of the MNCs interviewed, 45 percent reported that their Chinese competitors were as competitive or more then themselves (CEIBS, 2012).

The fact that many MNCs, such as GE, IBM, P&G, Pepsi Co., Nokia and Siemens, have their R&D and innovation centers in China proves that China's capabilities in these areas have been on the rise. These centers provide research and innovation support and create products for both the domestic and international markets of these MNCs. In 2013 there were over 1,500 such centers in operation in China. Pressure to innovate has been driving Chinese companies to focus more management time on it. In the past companies competed successfully on the basis of cost, but this changed to competing on the basis of product innovation. China is catching up in terms of its commercial innovation with competitors from Japan and Korea. A few Chinese companies, like Lenovo, Huawei, SANY and Xiaomi, have begun displaying a proven ability to innovate (Andrews and Kemper, 2013).

4. Debate on China eclipsing the USA

In 2012 China became the largest food and grocery market in the world, overtaking the USA. It has been projected to overtake the USA to become the largest retail market in 2016 (EIU, 2012). In the second decade of the 21st century economists no longer talk about China taking a more important place on the global economic stage, although they did until a short time ago. This debate transformed into when China will be the largest global economy, not only in PPP terms but also at market prices and exchange rates. The global financial crisis, the Great Recession and the sovereign debt crisis in the Eurozone contributed to this change in the debate and assessment of emerging global profile. In 2011 China exported 30 percent more than the USA and its fixed capital investment was 40 percent higher (*The Economist*, 2011).

In the financial media and in institutions of global governance, like the IMF, a game is played of forecasting when China's GDP cake will be larger than that of the largest global economy, the USA. Periodically forecasts are made and their plausibility debated. *The Economist* has set up a website (at economist.com/chinavusa) for this purpose. Although the US economy losing its pre-eminence was predicted a couple of times in the past, it never materialized. This time the probability seems real. In a thoroughly well-researched study, Subramanian (2011) quantitatively established that relative economic dominance of China over the USA is not only more imminent but may well have started. Economic dominance has numerous dimensions. China's dominance over the USA may be more broadly based, entailing more economic domains than previously visualized. It is well within the realm of probability that in a couple of decades, China's geo-economic primacy and dominance may rival that of the UK in the halcyon era of the Pax Britannica or the post-World War II USA. A valuable and useful instrument, economic dominance can be deployed for achieving economic and non-economic outcomes.

In an engaging exercise of computing the index of economic dominance, Subramanian (2011) came up with results that were both instructive and intuitive. His results are as follows: In 1870 the UK was the most dominant global economic power, with index values between 15 and 20. These values were substantially higher than those for France and Germany, the two close rivals. In 1913, the gap between the UK and close rival the USA shrank markedly, it was almost eliminated. At this point, the global economy was no longer unipolar in terms of economic fundamentals. In 1950 this scenario was dramatically different. The USA had become the new economic hegemonic power, with its index values rising to between 20 and 25. The value for Soviet Russia, the closest competitor, stood at seven. In 1990 Japan mounted a serious challenge to the US economic dominance and Soviet Russia had faded from the scene. What was noteworthy was that compared to the past the US hegemonic status had noticeably declined, with the index value down to 16. It was nine for Japan and China's index value had begun rising. In 2010 Japan's challenge to the USA economic dominance had disappeared, while that of China was on a steady rise. Consistent with the historic trend, economic dominance of China was based on its rapid GDP growth, trade expansion and financial dominance, which in turn was closely related to its recurring current account surpluses. The index values for China and the USA were in close proximity, both hovered around 12.[11]

The decade of 2000s saw many imperative developments in this regard. In several major industrial subsectors, China became the largest producer during the 2000s. For instance, in ownership of mobile phones and beer guzzling China overtook the USA around the turn of the century. Similarly around the same time in steel production it overtook the USA and the European Union (EU) in 2003. Since 2006 it is also the largest steel exporter in the world. In 2009, its steel production was 10 million tons more than all the OECD countries combined. It surpassed Korea in 2010 to be the world's largest shipbuilder in terms of shipbuilding capacity and new orders. Also, in 2010 China ploughed more than $1 trillion into new buildings projects. This construction boom propelled it to the top of global construction, surpassing the USA for the first time (PwC, 2011). In terms of the external financial clout, China and the USA are incomparable. In 2011 China's net foreign assets were $2 trillion, while the USA had net debt of $2.5 trillion. The size of the GDP in an economy is always a helpful and revealing indicator of the economic prowess. In PPP terms China's GDP will equal that of the USA in 2016, while in terms of market prices and exchange rates in 2018 (*The Economist*, 2011).[12]

Another notable industry where China is a confirmed global leader is passenger cars, excluding light commercial vehicles. China overtook the USA in 2006. By 2010, it was producing between one-fifth and one-quarter of total global auto production. It is world's largest market for air conditioners and LCD TVs. As domestic household income rises further, the manufacturing sector output is bound to grow larger. However, given the background of global imbalances, China needs to change its trajectory of industrialization. As noted below, efforts are afoot to turn its external-demand-biased industrialization towards domestic demand. During the first half of the 21st century, regional and global economies may well bear the imprint of China's manufacturing-led economic development. Their growth patterns may be shaped by it.

Forecasts by *The Economist* (2011) make 2014 a notable year because at this point China is set to be the largest importer in the world. This is a huge change from 2000, because at this point US imports were six times larger than China's. Domestic retail sales in China are also projected to exceed those in the USA by 2014. Comparisons of the two GDP data for 2000 and 2011 produce interesting an observation. While at present the US GDP is twice as large as that of China, in 2000 the US GDP was eight times greater.

As the GDP in an economy grows and makes it a dominant global economy, the status of the economy as a trader and a debtor is also enhanced. This pre-eminence translates into the dominance of the currency of this economy in the arena of international business. Based on the current trend, the renminbi may well surpass the dollar in a couple of decades to be an important international currency. By 2025, it may also supplant the dollar as the principal reserve currency. The progress in these transitions may be accelerated if China decides to undertake financial sector reforms in the near future. When the renminbi does acquire the status of premier international reserve currency, China will naturally guard the prestige that comes with this new status. Its own interests would lie in preserving and strengthening the global financial and trade order and relations.

It would be a miscalculation to see China's future dominance as a zero-sum game. China's high growth rate benefits both the regional and global economies. In all probability China will not become a threat to the contemporary open and rule-based global economic, financial and trading system. One cannot disregard the fact that China has an open and regionally and globally integrated economy. In the policy-making circles in China there is a growing constituency that is cognizant of China's dependence on the well-functioning regional and global economies. It has high stakes in preserving them and keeping them operating and in perpetuating the global economic order.

5. Economic transformations and China's brand of globalization

The time period of evolution of the Chinese economy coincided with the advent of the modern era of globalization, which arguably began in the 1970s (Bordo *et al.*, 2003; Das, 2009). The modern era of globalization is characterized by between-country integration of three principal markets, namely trade in goods and services, labor markets and capital markets. This correspondence of the two time periods was significant. It had far-reaching consequences for the Chinese economy. In the absence of this coincidence, the Chinese economy would have grown and globalized much less rapidly. Globalization has had its winners and losers; China is widely regarded as a clear and undisputed winner (Das, 2008b).

While the macro-economic reform-led transition process is still continuing, the Chinese economy has undergone multiple and sizable transformations. To enumerate some of the large and fundamental ones, it has changed from a command economy to an economy where market forces are active and functional, although they have not permeated the entire economy as yet and the SOEs still play a role in the economy. The EU and the USA have not accepted China's market economy status (MES), although by 2010 some 81 countries had. Other major economic transitions include transitions from a rural-agrarian to an urban-industrial society, from a low-income to a middle-income economy (as defined by the World Bank) and from a near-autarkic to a highly open economy.

China's ascent as a major player in the global economy reflects the success of globalization. In comparison to the other EMEs of comparable size China's pace of economic and financial integration with the global economy was discernibly swifter. It became an archetype of economic and financial globalization. Other EMEs, like India, belatedly learned lessons from China's successful global achievements (Das, 2006). As a society, the Chinese were more convinced regarding the macro-economic synergy that globalization generates than any other economy, developed or developing. Impressed by the growth performance of the NIEs, China borrowed and adapted many strategies from them, which supported its regional and global integration. For instance, taking a leaf from the NIEs China adopted the growth plan of the development state. Foreign investment regulations in China were styled after those in Taiwan. Also, the penchant of balancing debt with equity in Chinese businesses was built on the success of such a practice followed by companies in Hong Kong, Singapore and Taiwan. Like Japan and the NIEs, China sought to learn best practices in several areas of economics and business by sending missions to different countries around the globe. Their enthusiasm to learn, adopt and adapt modern technology from the West was always immense. That being said, in many ways China remains *sui generis*.

According to a survey conducted by the School of Management, Fudan University (2005), Chinese business firms were motivated to expand globally for a range of reasons, the most important of which was for tapping new markets for growth. Securing natural resources and acquiring advanced technologies and management skills were the other two most important motivating factors. China was also eager to integrate into the global economy and financial markets. In its endeavors to go global, China has lately been crafting its own brand of post-US globalization. Without hesitation, it has begun recasting the rules, institutions and economic relationships that have been functional in guiding the current wave of globalization. With the official encouragement to go global, Chinese firms' outward FDI flows have increased at an accelerating pace since 2000. FDI accelerated from $1 billion a year in 2000 to $57 billion a year in 2009. Relatively larger investments went to the primary and tertiary sectors, with manufacturing attracting a small part. Financial services received the largest proportion, close to a fifth, of China's total outward FDI. Wholesale and retail trade were the other two activities where outward investment was significant. Although an overwhelmingly large part of the outward FDI went to the Asian economies, it is now spreading globally. At the end of 2009, the value of the stock of outward investment reached $246 billion, which was far above the niggardly $4 billion in 1990 (Davies, 2010). Such a large outflow is intensifying China's global integration endeavors. It is beginning to reshape the world economy, presaging a new wave of globalization. A China-led Asian global era is no longer a remote possibility but is in the making.

As it is the most important trading partner of an increasing number of regional and global economies and is the largest creditor economy in the world, China is deepening its economic and financial relationships with them. It is increasingly selling high-value and sophisticated products to them. A case in point is China's sale of $10 billion worth of power generation equipment in October 2010 to India. Shanghai Electric successfully out-competed General Electric with the help of a generous financing deal offered by China Development Bank (CDB) for the purchase of this equipment. State involvement in firm activity is a characteristic of Chinese globalization. However, the positive aspect of state involvement is that it did not protect its firms or markets. Policy-makers in their wisdom did not protect their markets from foreign competition as much as they were by the governments in the NIEs. Using its economic leverage, China is skillfully crafting close economic and financial partnerships with both the advanced industrial economies and the EMEs. These countries see the benefits of developing symbiotic relationships with China. Its strong growth momentum may well contribute to their success.

Full of ample liquid resources, China's banks have been helping in the expansion of infrastructure and energy sector development in other EMEs and developing economies in ways that will accelerate their growth. This also enlarges two-way trade and brings them closer to the Chinese economy. Gradually but purposefully, PBC is also striving to enhance the role of its currency in the international capital markets and the international monetary system. In 2010 the renminbi made a debut as a currency for bond financing by a multinational corporation, McDonald's. Countries like Indonesia have availed themselves of trade credit in the renminbi. These are some of the initial small steps towards future internationalization of the currency (*Financial Times*, 2011b).

To be a strong contender for a global reserve currency status, the renminbi should be a vigorous currency, backed by a deep and liquid financial market. China still lacks the latter. Also, for advancing towards a global currency status the renminbi will need to be unpegged from the dollar and its value should be determined by market forces. It should also be a currency that is not only freely convertible but traded in a deep and liquid financial market. To that end, China will need to abandon exchange controls as well as liberalize its capital account and financial system. These developments and advances do not seem to be happening at present or in the short term and may take some time (Wolf, 2011).

6. The "China factor" in international business

In the first decade of the 21st century, China emerged as a force to be reckoned with in the arena of international business (Das, 2011). There were few businesses in which the so-called 'China factor' was not regarded as vital. For countries like Australia, geographically situated at the edge of Asia, China factor has unique implications. China's imports of ores and metals from Australia soared from 13.3 percent of the total in 2000 to 55.1 percent in 2009 (Huang and Wang, 2011). The scale and speed with which the Chinese economy and business corporations are transforming the international business world are unprecedented.

Multinational firms and large business firms in the advanced industrial economies see China as a land of promise and opportunities on the one hand and as a serious rival to compete with on the other. The initial attraction of China for businesses around the world was its size. For a long time it was eyed by multinational corporations (MNCs) for being a market of a billion-plus potential customers. In the post-1978 it also became the fastest growing market for their products. Although Coca-Cola's fabled China dream was regarded as preposterous by many, General Motors fell back on its Chinese profits during difficult times. In 2009 China became the largest mobile phone market in the world and therefore a battleground between the MNCs like Nokia, Apple and China Mobil, the world's largest mobile operator by subscribers.

General Electric (GE), a global high-technology giant, takes its China market seriously. Measured by market value, it is the largest American industrial group in China. It enjoyed solid double-digit sales growth for many years in the Chinese market (Cooks, 2011). GE established a large technology center in Shanghai in 2010 and in January 2011 it announced a series of deals with Chinese business firms, including an avionics joint venture with Aviation Industry Corporation of China (Avic). The joint venture will produce the central electronics system for the C919 aircraft. This is a single-aisle aircraft that is being built by Comac (Commercial Aircraft Corporation of China) to challenge the duopoly of Airbus and Boeing.

Chinese companies have grown a lot in the recent years and competition in China's domestic market has been escalating. Chinese firms have become fierce competitors for the MNCs operating in China. Some of these domestic rivals of MNCs in China's domestic markets were firms that were established recently, or were very small until recently. Essentially due to superior knowledge of local customers, domestic rival firms have begun slicing away the market share of the MNCs.

Chinese business firms have been learning fast from the MNC operations in their domestic markets. They are also known to have taken "a leaf out of the foreign rivals' books, poaching their staff and ramping up their own research, development and marketing" (Lucas, 2011). The large domestic rival Chinese firms usually have deep pockets. Occasionally they are government-backed. Chinese firms not only can successfully compete with MNCs but also make them play second fiddle in important markets. For instance, in the powdered and liquid detergents market, global leviathans like Unilever and P&G have merely 17 percent of the total Chinese market share against 35 percent by the Nice Group and Guangzhou Liby Enterprise. Both are former SOEs. Competition between the Chinese firms and MNCs is intense in attracting employees, supply of raw materials, advertising and distribution.

China, followed by India, is regarded as a valuable economy by the MNCs and they have been rebalancing their activities towards it. Relatively newer MNCs from the EMEs like China have become serious competitor to the older and well-established MNCs in any industrial and services sectors. Ghemawat and Hout (2008 and 2009) compiled data for systematically analyzing the ability to compete by the new MNCs from China with the old ones. They covered companies in 33 modern industrial sectors. In the Chinese market, and found that Chinese companies occupied the top two or three spots in 10 of these industrial sectors. Old MNCs occupied leading positions in 10 and overseas Chinese business firms in three. In the remaining 10, leadership was a matter of market segment. Chinese MNCs typically led in the lower performance and lower price segments, while the old MNCs led in the higher price and higher performance sectors. The leadership status depended on the type of industry. Industries in which R&D and advertizing expenditure represented a high proportion of sales revenue, old MNCs dominated. Conversely, Chinese MNCs dominated in industries in which these measures were low. As a rule, the Chinese companies could successfully lead in industries where business moved slowly, product capability and design change occurred less frequently, customers demanded less product development and production cost was a high proportion of the price.

As the economy opened, China became an appealing and rewarding market for many multinational and large business firms of differing sizes in a vast production range. Cross-border production networks and supply chains also intensely integrated China with the regional and global economies. These supply chains are increasingly global. In many products, particularly in electronics, information and communication technology (ICT) and computer areas, China has emerged as a hub for regional and global production networks. Multinational firms regard it as a primary location for manufacturing products to be sold globally. Thus, China has become one of the principal and most conspicuous beneficiaries of economic and financial globalization during the contemporary period.

6.1 Financial weight-enhancing status in the global business arena

A large part of China's forex reserves are managed by State Administration for Foreign Exchange (SAFE). They were $3,181.10 billion in December 2011. As a large part of forex reserves are invested in the US public and private securities, downgrade of the USA's long-term sovereign credit from AAA to AA+ by Standard and Poor's in August 2011 caused valid concern in Chinese financial policy-making circles.[13] With a degree of virtuous indignation, the Chinese media excoriated financial and monetary policy making in the USA.

Its sovereign-wealth fund (SWF), the China Investment Corporation (CIC), was established in 2007 with $200 billion as initial capital. The objective was to deploy China's massive forex reserves better by moving away from low-yielding US treasury securities and diversifying into more gainful assets.[14] In January 2011 its assets were $410 billion. The CIC has made substantial investments in financial firms. Initially it invested an overwhelmingly large proportion (85 percent) of its investments in the matured industrial economies, but in 2010 it began turning towards the EMEs (Sender and Hille, 2011). China's credit-rating agency, Dagong Global Credit Rating, employs quite different norms and standards from those utilized by veteran firms like Standard and Poor's, Moody's and Fitch in assessing the creditworthiness of sovereign countries. International businesses need to adapt to the new evolving business milieu, where China will also have a say in global economic and financial governance.

China's trade surplus jumped from 2 percent in 2004 to 7.3 percent in 2007, which was the peak. Owing to chronic economic woes in the EU and the USA, China's trade surplus began shrinking. In 2011 it shrank for the third straight year to $155 billion, which was 2.1 percent of its GDP. This *prima facie* implies that a global shift in demand to the surplus economies has begun. Chinese firms sold less foreign currency for renminbi because of reduced expectation of currency appreciation in 2012. Higher global risk aversion and valuation effects associated with a stronger dollar were the other reasons behind the shrinkage. In the last quarter of 2011 China's forex reserves shrank for the first time in more than a decade. They dropped by $20.55 billion in the fourth quarter of 2011. Not only growth in China's forex reserves slowed in 2011 but also the share of reserves allocated to the US securities declined.

China's shifting away from the dollar and its diversification into another currency were expected. It aggressively diversified the currency composition of its reserve portfolio. The dollar share of forex reserves fell from 74 percent in 2006 to 65 percent in 2010 to 54 percent in June 2011 (Orlik and Davis, 2012). The yield on a 10-year US Treasury note was declining. In the first quarter of 2012 it was a paltry 2 percent. The euro was chosen the main avenue for diversifying reserves. China ramped up purchase of European debt. Strong official statements about the crisis-ridden Eurozone being the main investment destination were made. Buying undervalued Euro assets during the sovereign debt crisis was indeed a canny move. Other highly rated sovereigns like the Australian dollar and the Canadian dollar also benefited from China's diversification, but to a lesser degree.

The global financial crisis and the Great Recession (2007–09) altered the direction of the on-going wave of globalization of business, although they have not shaken the key trend. First, the recovery in China and the other Asian EMEs has been rapid. Second, the populations in China and the other large EMEs are young and growing. Therefore, they have become the focus of rising consumption and production. Increasingly they are also major providers of capital, talent and innovation. This evolving trend has made it imperative for most companies to succeed in countries like China and the other EMEs. A McKinsey online survey of senior executives around the world undertaken in March 2010 revealed that executives in multinational corporations and large businesses reported that they are developing new business models for China (and India) at a significantly higher rate than any other economy (Dye and Stephenson, 2010).

As a large, outward-oriented economy, China influences multilateral trade in a significant manner. It is thereby transforming the nature and volume of international businesses. Likewise on the financial front, China has been the largest creditor country for some time. It became a large creditor economy at an early stage of its growth. It will become an increasingly important entity in the world of international financial. Ma and Haiwen (2009, p. 15) found that the demographic effect due to which China was able to achieve a large creditor position was the "pronounced decline in youth dependency". It is likely remain a creditor economy into 2025 (Kuijs, 2006; Peng, 2008). China's net foreign assets position, measure at market value in 2007, was only a quarter of its current cost position. By the end of the decade gross size of China's international balance sheet is likely to triple, which may turn it into a major financial player (Ma and Haiwen, 2009).

In the post-2000 period, commodity markets saw a remarkable growth as well as prices volatility. Both energy and non-energy commodity prices trended sharply higher. China accounted for the bulk of incremental demand for oil and many base metals and had a decisive impact on them. The fast-growing Chinese economy increased world demand for many commodities. An empirical estimate by Lu and Li (2009) concluded that for 2001–07 period large Chinese consumption was behind global incremental consumption of copper (51 percent), aluminum (56 percent) and iron ore (89 percent). For crude oil this proportion was 33 percent.

7. Role and significance of multinational enterprises in China

As the most visible, active and effectual players in contemporary phase of globalization, MNCs are an important economic entities. There are around 80,000 of them in the world. A recent Boston Consulting Group (BCG) (2010) study fittingly stated that for MNCs that are planning on capturing global advantage, China is a crucial economy. It goes on to say that it may be even more crucial in the future than the MNCs realize. Performance-oriented MNCs could overlook such rapidly growing markets only at their own peril. In this era of globalizing economies, financial markets and businesses, a globally oriented MNC could not disregard China, its resource and market potential. In addition, as they operate in several regional economies and intra-MNC—more correctly intra-subsidiary—trade and production links are common, their China operations help in integrating the region in a market-led manner.

Numerous mature and well-established MNCs have been fine-tuning their China strategy to improve their performance in this important market. With each passing year, as China is learning from its successes and failures, its importance to MNCs is becoming more evident. MNCs need to view China "as a core component of their overarching approach to globalization and not simply as a low-cost country for sourcing, as important as that is in its own right" (Fayol-Song, 2011, p. 457).

With China's growing heft in the world of international business and as its economic and business landscape transformed, its importance for MNCs went on increasing. It became a draw for MNC and foreign firms' operations. For them it is a country of great potential, if enormous complexities. It is not one market but a collection of several markets. These diverse markets are also fast-changing. Also, in 2009 average disposable income in China's richest city was four times higher than that in its poorest city (EIU, 2010). Any simplistic notion of China's market needs to be shunned. In many industrial sectors China is world's largest market. As the impression and views of MNC managements about China changed, hoards of them entered China using entry vehicles like joint ventures (JVs), wholly foreign-owned enterprises (WFOEs) or equity investments. By 2004, 400 of *Fortune* 500 MNCs were represented in China. It can be safely assumed that none of the *Fortune* 500 is missing from China now.

Global players like IBM, Volkswagen, Coca-Cola, 3M and the like were among the early entrants (Park and Vanhonacker, 2007). According to *The World Investment Report 2009* there were 289,661 MNCs and foreign business firms operating in China. For many large MNCs, China is still a small market, but this is expected to change. A survey by the Economic Intelligent Unit (EIU) revealed that in 2010 only 10 MNCs reported that their China revenues were more than 20 percent of their global revenues. For a half of them China accounted for less than 10 percent of their global revenues. Only 8 percent of MNCs reported that China was their biggest market and 17 percent expected that it would be so within five years (EIU, 2011).

When globally valued MNCs like Motorola, Philips and NEC entered China in the 1980s, they were warmly received and were offered lucrative terms for setting up operations. They benefitted from highly concessional corporate tax rates, duty-free imports of capital goods and other inputs. Even during the decade of the 1990s, MNCs and foreign firms were an object of respect and admiration among the customers. This celebratory status phase of MNCs ended in 2000, when China's per caput income climbed to $1,000. Both perception of Chinese consumers and stance of the government about MNCs began to drastically change. The welcome carpet of the pre-2000 was rolled back and they are almost treated as equals of the local business houses. Entry proposals of MNCs began to be strictly scrutinized and judged from the perspective of national economic and business perspectives. Concessional corporate tax rates became a memory of the past. Since 2008, local and foreign firms pay the same tax rates. In terms of employment and environment standards, MNCs are held to the same standards as the local businesses. Equally, consumers are much less awed by MNCs and are far more demanding. They have become less uncritical of the products of MNCs. They increasingly find local firms producing comparable quality products, often at economical prices.

An increase in FDI, foreign transactions, JVs and WFOEs rationally led to a proliferating number of expatriate managers. This trend began weaken somewhat around 2000. The reasons included high turnover, significant failure rate among expatriate managers and lack of appropriate candidates. A trend that slowly emerged was filling up the management positions in MNCs with local Chinese managers. Subject to the availability of local talent, most foreign companies did not plan to increase the proportion of expatriate managers. Attempts to localize management increased in some industries but there were others where few such endeavors were made. However, there were sporadic cases where MNCs were found to trust local talent for higher-level managerial positions (Fayol-Song, 2011; ChinaBiz, 2005).

The Chinese economy, markets and business ambiance were changing fast. China is a mixed economy, with SOEs still playing a significant role. However, by 2000 from the perspectives of the MNCs, China began to look something like an open market with its challenges and opportunities. In the past, stringent regulations and lack of competition were the prime market distorting factors. As regulations were relaxed, market segments and sectors that seemed seriously distorted in the early reform period began to transform and look more normal. As private sector domestic Chinese business firms and foreign firms entered the markets, Chinese markets also grew competitive. They were growing larger every year and in some sectors became the largest in the world in a short time span. As the Chinese middle class grew in size, there was a discernible growth in domestic demand, which made building up businesses not only feasible but also necessary.

During the initial period, China and its markets fed both unbridled and naive optimism for the MNCs as well as skeptical pessimism. The skeptics were not to be dismissed. Not a few MNCs stumbled in China and some will do so in future as well. It is an appropriate reminder that for MNCs, there are risks in China. Naive optimism in this regard needs to be tempered with a wholesome dose of realism on the ground. Operational environment in China was and has remained challenging. That said, the skeptics' view reflects partial reality. Their focus is usually on operational snags, like unmanageable JVs, infringement of intellectual property rights (IPR) and smaller market size than visualized at the time of entry. Some of this is valid essentially because China is still an EME, by no means a mature economy. However, there is a difference; that is, it is not just any EME but the largest and the most important one among them, which is riding the crest of a virtuous cycle of globalization.

Therefore, MNCs must not give too much emphasis on the risks and operational challenges. For the well-established MNCs they are not all-consuming issues any longer. Over the years there has been a marked improvement in the business environment in China. Besides, MNCs are resourceful entities. They usually succeed in resolving issues and work out systems and procedures. For a majority of MNCs in China, the attention of the senior management began shifting to strategic planning and development. For them "China's market has begun to come of age" (EIU, 2004, p. 8). Given the increasing demand, expanding markets and progress in upgrading business environment, MNCs now have more incentives to develop and expand their China operations than they did in the past.

Notwithstanding its unquestionably large allure, a rule of thumb is that for MNCs China was not and has not become an easy place to operate in. Despite improvements, its legal framework still has a lot of snags and can be unpredictable. Corruption is high and remains just below the surface. Business people in China point out that the state does go after the small fry but is leery of targeting corruption in higher ranks (MacFarquhar, 2013). As a one-party rule, its political system has serious imbalances and inconsistencies. In large parts of Western China, establishing marketing and distribution networks is an arduous and costly proposition, to say the least. Filling up managerial ranks with suitably skilled personnel has proved to be challenging for MNCs. Prospects of the so-called China opportunity can only materialize for MNCs if they learn to identify and prevail over China specific problems.

Numerous MNCs serviced China with products created elsewhere but subsequently adapted for the Chinese market. The recent trend is to move R&D closer to the Chinese market not only to get closer to prospective customers but also to the pool of local researchers. Recruiting high-quality R&D talent used to be difficult, but not any more. There has been a wave of creation of R&D centres because MNCs are increasingly eager to provide Chinese consumers with what they want (Waldmeir, 2012).

The global financial and economic crisis (2007–09) and the ongoing sovereign debt crisis in the beleaguered Eurozone drew the attention of the world on the resilience and dynamism of the Chinese economy. Although it decelerated, it continued to record a healthy GDP growth rate in the backdrop of global recession and stagnation. It raised China's global stature, which in turn has induced further changes in the Chinese economic and business environment. MNCs in China count on their Chinese operations more than they did in the past. According to a survey conducted by the EIU (2011), 58 percent of the MNC respondents said that the Government's drive to raise incomes and shift growth towards domestic consumption would have the biggest impact on their China strategy. Almost half (49 percent) of the MNC respondents reported that they had higher expectations from their Chinese operations. Results of this survey show that many MNCs that were merely testing the Chinese waters are deciding to take the plunge. Those MNCs that had left China after poor performance are considering returning. Those that have operated in

China for some time are recalibrating their strategy to seize the opportunity that China offers. These MNCs are noticing the ever-changing world of Chinese business and believe that it would be more challenging to operate in the future. The post-global financial crisis China is more confident. The government, business firms and customers are close to hubristic. Large MNCs with proprietary cutting-edge technology find that the new official environment is increasingly demanding, although the small one can still fly below the radar.

The framework and environment of business in China is in a state of constant and vigorous evolution. In the second decade of the 21st century, it is increasingly becoming obvious that MNCs need to make China more central in their global strategy than it presently is. In an increasingly large number of industries, China has become the competitive battlefield for businesses on which the global leaders, followers and losers are being decided. It will be more so in the future. Some of the industrial sectors in which it is happening are auto parts, consumer electronics, semi-conductors, aviation and power transmission equipment. Under the atypical circumstances when businesses are not competing in the China market, they find that their Chinese and foreign rivals are exploiting the advantages they earned there in the global marketplace. Thus, stakes for MNCs are high. They can no longer treat China as an auxiliary operation on the side and hope for lucrative returns from it and leverage their global performance. Galvin *et al.* (2010, p. 3) contend that MNCs need to commit themselves seriously and build "a second home" in China. The magnitude of MNC commitment should be comparable to that in the home market. They need to set high and measurable targets for important performance indicators for China, which include time spent by boards and senior executives on China operations and strategy, knowledge of fast growing Chinese markets and customers, market shares in China and sourcing volumes. MNCs also need to take their "global best practices across the value chain" to their China operations and adapt them to the local conditions.

China's domestic expenditure on R&D has increased at an accelerating rate since 1995. MNCs played a pivotal role in the globalization of R&D. As it globalized, China and India emerged as global players in attracting R&D investment from the MNCs. The trend of establishing stand-alone R&D laboratories by MNCs in China started in the mid-1990s, with some pioneering MNCs in the information technology (IT) sector starting the first R&D laboratories. Leaders among them were Microsoft, Nortel, Ericsson and Nokia. They were followed by Fujitsu, HP, IBM, Motorola and Sun. This trend accelerated dramatically after 2000, when other MNCs in non-IT industries also began setting up R&D establishments. Biomedical and automobile were the other popular areas. Major global names in the auto industry have R&D units of a substantial size in China. This includes Audi, DaimlerCrysler, GM, Honda, Hyundai, Nissan, Toyota and Volkswagen.

Of the *Fortune* 500, over 400 have R&D centers in China. According to the Ministry of Commerce by 2006, there were approximately 1,000 MNC-established R&D organizations in China (Lundin and Serger, 2007). A study by Zinnov Management Consulting (2011) that analyzed Chinese R&D ecosystem and its opportunities and challenges, concluded that Chinese R&D market was growing at a fast clip and was soon likely to overtake India. China's current MNC R&D market is $7.56 billion, compared to $7.75 billion for India. China's R&D market is currently undergoing a paradigm shift. It is being supported by factors like expansion of secondary cities as R&D locations, rising MNC competition with the domestic firms, maturity and expansion of R&D portfolios, rapid growth in MNC R&D laboratories. Government policies proactively encourage R&D and support MNC R&D centers in China by providing tax benefits and financial incentives. China's R&D ecosystem is maturing, therefore MNCs seem confident about R&D expansion in China. Owing to a rich talent pool in R&D, India did well in attracting MNC investment. However, Chinese R&d centers have now expanded their head count. It currently stands at 56,000 compared to 45,000 in

India. This situation was not feasible five years ago. Market growth and competition from the local businesses have transformed the Chinese R&D markets and MNCs are being forced to revisit their business models. They are being forced to invest more time and resources on innovating their products for the domestic markets and repackage for the markets in the advanced economies.

7.1 Multinationals from China

Ambitious Chinese business firms regard globalization as a strategic priority. In a survey of senior managers in Chinese firms by Dietz *et al.* (2008), nearly 80 percent mentioned that they wanted their companies be become truly global business enterprises in a period of 10 years. Chinese firms in several industries have succeeded in having a large global reach. They include automotive, pharmaceuticals, high technology, energy and basic materials. Almost half of Chinese firms investing abroad look for gaining either intellectual property or a strategic advantage. They try to acquire the former by acquiring firms known for high-technology, product design capabilities, well-known brands and business processes. Notwithstanding their ambitions, the globalization of the Chinese firms has not been rapid. Hesitation came basically from inexperience and a disinclination to adopt business practices followed by firms in the advanced industrial economies.

Although at a slow pace, competitive Chinese business firms have also become serious competitive players in the world marketplace and they have made their presence felt in many areas and products. In mid-2010 PetroChina, the listed arm of the China National Petroleum Corporation (CNPC), an SOE, was ranked as world's second most valuable company by market capitalization by the *Financial Times* (Lucas, 2011). Several Chinese multinationals like Haier, Huawei Technologies, Lenovo, Pearl River Piano, Tsingtao beer, Air China and Bank of China are well known international names. The *Fortune* 500 list of 2001 has only 12 Chinese companies. However, their clout began to grow and a decade later, in 2010 there were 46 Chinese names on the list, of which Sinopec Group was the seventh largest and State Grid the eighth. Although multinationals from the West have shaped and determined the pace and pattern of globalization of business so far, Chinese multinationals and large business firms will soon be making their mark. In the *Fortune 500* list of 2011, there were 61 Chinese companies. With third rank, China is a tad behind Japan.

A word of caution is warranted here. While Chinese MNCs are becoming internationally active and their number is rising, they do not enjoy the status of premier league players in the arena of international business. *Business Week* and Interbrand annually compiles a list of top-100 global brands and there were none from China in 2011 (Shambaugh, 2012). Although in terms of revenues Chinese MNCs have impressive achievements, acquiring the status of a Coca Cola, Intel, Toyota, Disney, or Volkswagen will take Chinese MNCs a while. For the Chinese firms in high-technology and consumer goods areas, brand-building acumen is badly needed. Although endeavors have been made, none of the Chinese companies so far have succeeded in turning Chinese brands into well-regarded global brands. One oft-tried formula of some of the Chinese firms is improving marketing techniques, supporting it by a superior product development strategy and providing value through quality and low costs.

Equally pressing is the need to develop marketing capabilities. In the past large Chinese firms catered for a captive domestic market and therefore they were oblivious of honing marketing skills. Few Chinese large firms have truly global operations and markets. Presently a large number of Chinese companies that seek a genuine MNC status only invest in and operate on some continents. A fully fledged MNC has global production, marketing, distribution, logistics and R&D capabilities. This has not been easy to achieve. Only Haier and Huawei Technologies can be regarded as those having global operations. The three national oil companies, namely, Sinopec, China National Offshore Oil Corporation (CNOOC) and CNPC, can also be added to this short list.

Another problematic issue is the critical shortage of talented managers with international savvy (Shambaugh, 2012). Not having managerial resources with the right know-how is the greatest barrier for Chinese businesses. Managers who have a sound knowledge and understanding of the EU, the USA and other large markets and the aptitude and ability to negotiate with senior executives in these markets are in acute short supply. Pressing limitations on the human resources front are wider. There is little indication that they will be resolved soon. According to a study by the MGI (2005), fewer than 10 percent of Chinese job candidates were found to be suitable to work for an MNC operating in China. Not only the Chinese MNCs but the foreign MNCs operating in China will have problems in finding enough suitable employees in key service and managerial occupations.

8. Summary and conclusions

The objective of this chapter is to present the current state of the Chinese economy, its domestic and external imbalances and its transformations to new growth trajectories. It begins with the discussion of the deep-seated economic problems and distortions in the Chinese economy that periods of heady growth tended to conceal. The following list is not an exhaustive one: persisting flaws in the financial and banking sector; distortions in the factor markets; continuing serious imbalances in the economy; a distorted incentive structure; exceedingly high marginal propensity to save going hand in hand with extraordinarily high investment rates; stark regional imbalances; skewed income distribution between urban and rural populations; environmental degradation; rising "twin surplus"; and a huge buildup of forex reserves. Recognizing these serious problematic issues, the theme of the current 12th Five-Year Plan is rebalancing of the economy. China has pragmatically shifted its growth trajectory before. The 12th Five-Year Plan may well herald another turning point in China's development and be yet another valuable opportunity to shift growth trajectory. A related repositioning in China's growth paradigm is its move to lower economic growth. This shift will affect both the Asian and global economies.

There is an ongoing debate in the academic and media conclaves regarding when China will become the largest global economy, not only in PPP terms but in market prices and exchange rates. The importance of China in the arena of international business has surged. Even in the first decade of the 21st century, there were few businesses in which the so-called "China factor" was not regarded as vital. The scale and speed with which Chinese economy and business corporations are transforming the international economy and business world are unprecedented. Multinational firms and large business firms in the advanced industrial economies see China as a land of promise and opportunities on the one hand and as a serious rival to compete with on the other. Businesses around the world were impressed by the sheer size of China's potential market of more than a billion customers. It is also the fastest growing market for their products.

China has been a high-saving and high-investing economy. Therefore, it was logical for China to adopt a "capital-intensive, industry-led growth model". Although China's growth model has so far served it well, it is no longer ideally suited for future growth. It has ended up creating domestic and global imbalances. At this juncture, it is imperative for it to rebalance its economy. To that end, China needs to switch its growth trajectory. Chinese policy makers recognize that fact and have been trying to do so.

Globalization has had its winners and losers; China is widely regarded as a clear and undisputed winner. In comparison to the other EMEs of comparable size China's pace of economic and financial integration with the global economy was discernibly swifter. It became an archetype of economic and financial globalization. While it eagerly integrated into the global economy and financial markets, China has lately been crafting its own brand of post-American globalization. It has decisively begun to recast the rules, institutions and economic relationships that have been functional in guiding the current wave of globalization. It is beginning to reshape the world economy, presaging a new wave of globalization. A China-led Asian global era is no longer a remote possibility but is in the making.

Notes

1 For the recent progress in regulation and supervision see IMF (2012a).
2 See, for instance, Cristadoro and Marconi (2012).
3 At the present time, in Japan and Korea the consumption share of GDP remains around 55 percent and 48 percent, respectively. In the two relatively consumption-heavy advanced economies, the UK and the USA, it was 67 percent and 71 percent, respectively. In these two economies, the consumption share of GDP is as unbalanced as that in China.
4 China is a signatory of the Kyoto Protocol on reducing greenhouse gases. However, as it is a developing country it is exempted from its restrictions.
5 Premier Wen Jiabao characterized the macro-economic conditions in China in these terms on 15 March 2007. He was addressing reporters at an official press conference after the conclusion of the 10th National People's Congress (NPC), China's parliament, in Beijing. In emphasizing imbalance and instability Premier Wen Jiabao was pointing to an excessively high rate of investment growth and credit extension in the economy, a large proportion of trade in GDP and long persisting imbalance in the balance of payments. According to him China also faced unbalanced development between urban and rural areas, between different regions of the country and between economic expansion and social progress. He also saw poor co-ordination between primary, secondary and tertiary industries. Consumption in the economy was low and investment much too high. Reliance of economic growth was disproportionately high on investment and exports (Reuters, 2007).
6 Only in 1993 China suffered a current account deficit.
7 After reaching its high point 2007, China's current account surplus declined and was reduced to 2.7 percent of GDP in 2011.
8 The top political leadership repeatedly made public statements regarding strengthening domestic consumption and making it a major source of economic growth. Premier Wen Jiabao mentioned it more than once in his important speeches. For instance, he reiterated this strategic shift in his February 2006 speech to the NPC and November 2006 speech to the Central Economic Work Conference.
9 Prasad (2011) provides a detailed account of short- and long-term tasks to be addressed.
10 The fourth annual meeting of the 11th NPC took place during 11–14 March 2011, in Beijing. The NPC is the highest state body and the only legislative house in China.
11 See Figure 2.3, p. 46, Chapter 2, in Subramanian (2011).
12 In 2011 *The Economist* had recomputed this trend and changed the year from 2019 to 2018.
13 This figure is as of December 2011.
14 A large part of these reserves were invested in US private and public securities. They included long-term Treasury debt, long-term agency debt (Freddie Mac and Fannie Mae), long-term US corporate securities and equities, and short-term debt. China's purchase of US treasury securities stood at $1.2 trillion as of June 2011. Largest holder of US securities, China's holdings of total public and private US securities were $1.9 trillion (Morrison and Labonte, 2011). The US Treasury securities finance the federal budget deficits.

References

Andrews, H. and S. Kemper. 2013. "Innovation is Now a Strategic Priority for China." Beijing. *China Daily*. 21 February.

Asian Development Bank (ADB). 2009. *Asian Development Outlook 2009: Rebalancing Asia's Growth*. Hong Kong: Oxford University Press.

Aziz, J. 2006. *Rebalancing China's Economy: What Does Growth Theory Tell Us?* IMF Working Paper No. WP/06/291. Washington, DC: International Monetary Fund.

Bai, C. E., C. T. Hsieh and Y. Qian. 2006. "The Return to Capital in China." *Brookings Papers on Economic Activity*. Vol. 37. No. 2, pp. 61–102.

Bayoumi, T., H. Tong and S. Wei. 2010. "The Chinese Corporate saving Puzzle: A Firm Level Cross-Country Perspective." Washington, DC: International Monetary Fund. Working Paper 10/275.

Benjamin, D., L. Brandt and J. Giles. 2010. *Did Higher Inequality Impede Growth in Rural China?* Policy Research Working Paper 5483. Washington, DC: World Bank.

Blanchard, O. J. and F. Giavazzi. 2006. *Rebalancing Growth in China: A Three-Handed Approach.* Discussion Paper No. PD 5403. London: Center for Economic Policy Research.

Bordo, M. D., A. M., Taylor and J. G. Williamson (eds). 2003. *Globalization in Historical Perspective.* Chicago, IL: University of Chicago Press.

Boston Consulting Group (BCG). 2010. "China and the New Rules of Global Business." Boston, MA.

Bradsher, K. 2012. "China Confronts Mounting Piles of Unsold Goods." *The New York Times."* New York. 23 August, p. 6.

Chaudhury, S. and M. Ravallion. 2007. "Partially Awakened Giants: Uneven Growth in China and India", in L. A. Winters and S. Yusuf (eds). *Dancing with Giants: China, India and the Global Economy.* Washington, DC: World Bank, pp. 175–210.

China Europe International Business School (CEIBS). 2012. "Innovation: China's Next Advantage?" Shanghai. June.

ChinaBiz. 2005. *Localization Continues.* ChinaBiz LT. Available online at chinabiz.com.

Cooks, E. 2011. "GE Targets China Sales Growth." *The Financial Times*, 21 January, p. 13.

Cristadoro, R. and D. Marconi. 2012. "Household Savings in China." *Journal of Chinese Economic and Business Studies.* Vol. 10. No. 3, pp. 275–99.

Das, Dilip K. 2006. *China and India: A Tale of Two Economies.* London and New York: Routledge.

——2008a. *Winners of Globalization.* CSGR Working Paper No. 249/08. University of Warwick: Center for the Study of Globalization and Regionalization. Also available online at www.warwick.ac.uk/fac/soc/csgr/research/workingpapers/2008/24908.pdf [accessed August 2010].

——2008b. "Contemporary Phase of Globalization: Does It Have a Serious Downside?". *Global Economic Review.* Vol. 37. No. 4, pp. 507–26.

——2011. "China in the Domain of International Business." *Human Systems Management.* Vol. 30. No. 1– 2, pp. 71–83.

Davies, K. 2010. "Outward FDI from China and its Policy Context". New York: Columbia University. FDI Profiles. Available online at: www.vcc.columbia.edu/files/vale/documents/China_OFDI_final_Oct_18.pdf.

Dietz, M. C., G. Orr and J. Xing. 2008. "How Chinese Companies Can Succeed Abroad?" *McKinsey Quarterly.* Available online at www.mckinseyquarterly.com/article_print.aspx?L2=21&L3=33&ar=2131.

Dunaway, S. and E. S. Prasad. 2006. "Rebalancing Economic Growth in China: A Commentary." *International Herald Tribune*, 11 January, p. 16.

Dye, R. and E. Stephenson. 2010. "Five Forces Reshaping the Global Economy." *McKinsey Quarterly.* Available online at www.mckinseyquarterly.com/Five_forces_reshaping_the_global_economy_McKinsey_Global_Survey_results_2581

Economic Intelligence Unit (EIU). 2013. *Top of the Heap.* London. 3 April.

——2012. *Retail 2022.* London. November.

——2011. *Multinational Companies and China: What Future?* London. December.

——2010. *Access China.* London.

——2004. *Coming of Age: Multinational Companies in China.* London. June.

The Economist. 2011. "How to Get a Date." 31 December, p. 57.

Fayol-Song, L. 2011. "Reasons behind Management Localization in MNCs in China." *Asia Pacific Business Review.* Vol. 17. No. 4, pp. 455–71.

Feng, W. 2011. "The End of Growth with Equity?" *Asia Pacific Issues.* No. 101. Honolulu, HI: East-West Center. June.

Financial Times. 2011a. "Renminbi Rolls Out." 16 January, p. 1.

——2011b. "Record Leap in China's Forex Reserves Reflects Global Imbalances." 11 January, p. 4.

Fudan University. 2005. *Going Global: Strategy and Change.* School of Management, Shanghai, China.

Galvin, J., J. Hexter and M. Hirt. 2010. "Building a Second Home in China." *McKinsey Quarterly*. Available online at www.mckinseyquarterly.com/Building_a_second_home_in_China_2631.

Garcia-Herrero, A. and D. Santabarbara. 2013. "An Assessment of China's Banking System Reform", in S. Kaji and E. Ogawa (eds). *Who Will Provide the Next Financial Model?* New York: Springer, pp. 147–75.

Ghemawat, P. and T. M. Hout. 2008. "Tomorrow's Global Giants: Not the Usual Suspects." *Harvard Business Review*. Vol. 86. No. 11, November, pp. 80–88.

——2009. "China and India Take on the Multinationals." *The Financial Times*. 12 February, p. 16.

Golley, J. and L. Song. 2011. "China's Rise in a Changing World", in J. Golley and L. Song (eds). *Rising China: Global Challenges and Opportunities*. Canberra: ANU Press, pp. 1–8.

Goodstadt, L. F. 2012. "China's Financial Reforms: Why Dysfunctional Banking Survives." Hong Kong: Hong Kong Institute of Monetary Research. Working Paper No. 02/2012.

Herd, R., C. Pigott and S. Hill. 2010. "China's Financial Sector Reforms." Paris: Organization for Economic Co-operation and Development. Working Paper No. 747. 1 February.

Huang, Y. and B. Wang. 2011. "From the Asian Miracle to an Asian Century?" Paper presented at the Reserve Bank of Australia annual conference in Sydney on 15–16 August.

International Monetary Fund (IMF). 2012a. *Financial Sector Assessment: People's Republic of China.* Washington, DC. March.

——2012b. *World Economic Outlook Update*. Washington, DC. 24 January.

——2012c. *World Economic Outlook Update*. Washington, DC. 16 July.

——2010. *Regional Economic Outlook: Asia Pacific*. Washington, DC. April.

KPMG. 2011. "China's 12th Five-Year Plan: Sustainability." Beijing, China. April.

Kuijs, L. 2006. "How Will China's Saving-Investment Balance Evolve?" Washington, DC: World Bank Policy Research Working Paper No. 3958. 1 July.

Kwan, C. H. 2009. "Growth in Chinese Economy Moving from East to West." Tokyo: Research Institute of Economy, Trade and Industry. Available online at www.rieti.go.jp/en/china/09060501.html?style sheet=print#figure1.

Lardy, N. R. 2012. *Sustaining China's Economic Growth after the Global Financial Crisis*. Washington, DC: Peterson Institute Press.

Lewis, W. A. 1954. "Economic Development with Unlimited Supplies of Labor." *Manchester School of Economic and Social Studies*. Vol. 22, pp. 139–91.

Li, C. and J. Gibson. 2012. "Rising Regional Income Inequality in China: Fact or Artifact?" Hamilton: University of Waikato. Department of Economics. Working Paper No. 09/12. July.

Li, G. and J. Woetzel. 2011. "What China's Five Year Plan Means for Business." *McKinsey Quarterly*. July. Available online at www.mckinseyquarterly.com/What_Chinas_five-year_plan_means_ for_business_2832.

Liu, X. and P. Cheng. 2011. "Is China's Indigenous Innovation Strategy Compatible with Globalization?" Honolulu, HI: East-West Center. Policy Study No. 61.

Lu, F. and Y. Li. 2009. "China's Factor in Recent Global Commodity Price and Shipping Freight Volatility." Beijing: Peking University. China Center for Economic Research. Working paper No. E2009007. 15 December.

Lucas, L. 2011. "China Consumer Goods: Left on the Shelf." *The Financial Times*. London. 4 April, p. 13.

Lundin, N. and S. S. Serger. 2007. "Globalization of R&D and China: Empirical Observations." Stockholm, Sweden: Research Institute of International Economics. IFN Working Paper No. 710.

Ma, G. and Z. Haiwen. 2009. "China's Evolving External Wealth and Rising Creditor Position." Basel, Switzerland. Bank for International Development. BIS Working Paper 286. July.

MacFarquhar, R. 2013. "Tackling Graft Must Come Before the Chinese Dream." *The Financial Times*. London. 12 April, p. 7.

McGregor, J. 2012. "China's Drive for 'Indigenous Innovation'" Washington, DC: US Chamber of Commerce.

McKinsey Global Institute (MGI). 2009. *If You've Got It, Spend It: Unleashing the Chinese Consumer*. San Francisco, CA. August.

——2005. *Addressing China's Looming Talent Shortage*. San Francisco, CA. October.

McMahon, D., L. Wei and A. Galbraith. 2012. "Wen Appeals to Shake Up Bank System." *The Wall Street Journal Asia*. 4 April, p. 1.

Morrison, W. M. and M. Labonte. 2011. "China's Holdings of US Securities: Implications for the US Economy." Washington, DC: Congressional Research Service. CRS Report for the Congress. 26 September.

Needham, J. 1954. *Science and Civilization in China*. Cambridge: Cambridge University Press.

Noble, J. and S. Rabinovitch. 2013. "Fitch Downgrades China." *The Financial Times.* 10 April, p. 1.

Orlik, T. and B. Davis. 2012. "Beijing Diversifies Away from US Dollar." *The Wall Street Journal.* 2 March, p. A1.

Overholt, W. H. 2010. "China in the Financial Crisis: Rising Influence, Rising Challenges." *The Washington Quarterly.* Vol. 33. No. 1, pp. 21–34.

——2005. "China and Globalization." Testimony presented to the US–China Economic and Security Review Commission in Washington, DC. 19 May.

Park, Y. C. 2008. "East Asia's Adjustments to Global Imbalances and Sub-Prime Loan Crisis." Presentation at the distinguished speaker's seminar in Asian Development Bank Institute. 13 March.

Park, S. O. and W. R. Vanhonacker. 2007. "The Challenge for Multinational Corporations in China." *MIT Sloan Management Review.* Vol. 48. No. 4, Summer, pp. W8–W15.

Park, D. and J. S. Park. 2010. *Drivers of Developing Asia's Growth.* Working Paper Series No. 235. Manila: Asian Development Bank. November.

Peng, X. 2008. "Demographic Shift, Population aging and Economic Growth in China: A Computable General Equilibrium Analysis." *Pacific Economic Review.* Vol. 13. No. 5, pp. 680–97.

Pettis, M. 2011. "The Continuous Debate Over China's Economic Transition." Washington, DC: Carnegie Endowment for International Peace. 25 March.

Prasad, E. S. 2009. "Is the Chinese Growth Miracle Built to Last?" *China Economic Review.* Vol. 20. No. 1, pp. 103–23.

——2011a. *Rebalancing Growth in Asia.* Working Paper No. 15169. Cambridge, MA: National Bureau of Economic Research. January.

——2011b. "China's Approach to Economic Development and Industrial Policy." Hearing at the US–China Economic and Security Review Commission, the Government of the United States. Washington, DC, 15 June.

PricewaterhouseCoopers (PwC). 2011. *Global Construction 2020.* London. 3 March.

Ravallion, M. and S. Chen. 2007. "China's (Uneven) Progress Against Poverty." *Journal of Development Economics.* Vol. 82. No. 1, pp. 1–42.

Reuters. 2007. "China's Economic Structure Is Unbalanced: Wen." Available online at www.reuters.com/article/idUSPEK9902420070316. 16 March.

Sender, H. and K. Hille. 2011. "CIC Seeks Funds out of China Reserves." *The Financial Times,* 16 January, p. 13.

Shambaugh, D. 2012. "Are China's Multinational Corporations Really Multinational?" *East Asia Forum.* Vol. 4. No. 2, pp. 7–10.

Song, Z., K. Storesletten and F. Zilibotti. 2011. "Growing Like China." *American Economic Review.* Vol. 101. No. 1, pp. 202–41.

Subramanian, A. 2011. *Eclipse: Living in the Shadow of China's Economic Dominance.* Washington, DC: Peterson Institute for International Economics.

Sun, W., X. Yang and G. Xiao. 2011. "Understanding China's High Investment Rate and FDI Levels." *Journal of International Commerce and Economics.* Vol. 3. No. 1, pp. 157–87.

Waldmeir, P. 2012. "China Offers a Taste of R&D to Come." *The Financial Times.* 13 November, p. 17.

The Wall Street Journal (WSJ). 2012. "Asia Catches a China Chill." 29 May, p. 13.

Wolf, M. 2012. "How to Blow Away China's Gathering Storm-Clouds. "*The Financial Times,* 21 March, p.9.

——2013. "Why China's Economy Might Topple." *The Financial Times,* 2 April, p. 9.

——2011. "Why China Hates Loving the Dollar?" *The Financial Times,* 25 January, p. 14.

World Bank (WB). 2012a. "China Quarterly Update." Beijing: World Bank Mission. April.

——2012b. *East Asia and Pacific Data Monitor.* Washington, DC. October.

World Bank and the Development Research Center (WB/DRC). 2013. *China 2030: Building a Modern, Harmonious and Creative High-Income Society.* Washington, DC.

Yiping, H. 2010. "Dissecting the Chinese Puzzle: Asymmetric Liberalization and Cost Distortion." *Asian Economic Policy Review.* Vol. 5. No. 2, pp. 281–95.

Yongding, Y. 2011. "Rebalancing the Chinese Economy." Seoul, Republic of Korea. Institute for Global Economics. Occasional Paper No. 11–03. October.

Yongjian, L. and X. Jiechang. 2012. "Serving the Nation's Future." *China Daily.* 1 June, p.2.

Zhou, X. 2009. "Some Observations and Analysis on Savings Ratio." Paper presented at the High Level Conference hosted by the Bank Negara, Kuala Lumpur, Malaysia, 10 February.

Zinnov Management Consulting. 2011. "China R&D Globalization Market." New Delhi. Available online at www.1888pressrelease.com/zinnov-globalization/r-and-d-mnc-china/china-r-d-globalization-market-at-usd-7–65-billion-growing-a-pr-309076.html. 08 June.

5

EVOLVING PATTERN OF *DE FACTO* INTEGRATION BETWEEN ASIA AND CHINA

1. Introduction

During the first decade of the 21st century the Chinese economy emerged as an important and energetic locomotive of regional growth. Given its close links with the regional economies, it has a large effect over the economic performance of the regional economies. Trade, foreign direct investment (FDI) and regional and global vertically integrated production networks operated as the principal channels of market-driven or private-sector-led regional integration among the Asian and Chinese economies. The Asian economies were intrinsically driven by the markets forces, which promoted both regional integration and symbiotic growth in the region. If as a result of the ongoing Eurozone crisis and tepid recovery in the USA in 2012, growth and investment rates decline in China, gross domestic product (GDP) growth would be lowered by more than half a percentage point over four quarters in the Asian economies with close regional supply chain links to China, particularly in the Republic of Korea (hereinafter Korea), Malaysia and Taiwan (Teja, 2012).

This chapter suggests that on balance China's rapid GDP growth turned into an opportunity for its Asian neighbors. Certainly, it does not ignore the challenges posed for them by China's vigorous growth. Early in the process of regional growth China was perceived more as a threat to the neighboring Asian economies in the areas of trade and FDI. The principal issue addressed in this chapter is how private business firms and multinational corporations (MNCs) in the region, driven basically by profit maximizing motives, have been interacting with each other and in the process bringing the economies closer together. The eventual outcome is the integration of Asia. As stated above, trade, FDI and vertically integrated production networks effectively and productively promoted inherently *de facto* or market-led regional integration among the Asian and Chinese economies. This mode of economic integration was soft, open and largely uninstitutionalized. It was practical, functional and flexible in nature and followed an incremental path. It was principally motivated by economic and commercial factors.

In this kind of regional integration business firms reach across national boundaries, expand and coordinate trade and investment, creating larger and integrated markets. No formal or officious agreements are required for *de facto* regional integration. Although China joined the vertically integrated regional supply chains somewhat belatedly, it made tremendous contribution of their subsequent robust growth. Its regional trade in parts, components and intermediate goods increased exceedingly rapidly.

Although regional integration in Asia was essentially market-driven, creation of various functional institutions as well as intra-regional fora helped in the progress of regional and sub-regional integration. These institutions covered trade, money and finance and infrastructure. To name the salient ones: the Association of Southeast Asian Nations (ASEAN), ASEAN-Plus-Three (APT), East Asia Summit (EAS), Asian Bond Market Initiative (ABMI), Chiang Mai Initiative (CMI) and its subsequent internationalization (CMIM). CMIM is a regional liquidity support mechanism. In addition, different sub-regions of Asia integrated at a different pace.

As the growth rate of economies and the pace of expansion of their markets in Asia varied, their rate of integration was also diverse. For instance, vertiginous growth in China helped it integrate with the neighboring Asian economies faster. One cannot disagree with the observation that Asian economic integration is "multi-speed and multi-track", although largely market-driven (ADB, 2012, p. 14). It is multi-track because various sub-regions in Asia are integrating at their own pace.

The World Bank's *Doing Business* indicators show that by modifying their regulations smoothing the process of regional integration several Asian economies improved their business environment. The competitiveness of several Asian economies also steadily improved. Sharpening competitiveness generally has a demonstration effect and makes the neighboring economies invest more in physical and human capital and technological upgrades. Asia was not an exception to this rule of thumb. China took a good deal of initiative in proposing, preparing and strengthening the APT[1] framework. This promoted a sense of regional identity and the mindset of seeking regional solutions for regional problems. Significantly, before China became the largest Asian economy, it had begun serving as an important growth driver of the Asian economy. It stimulated regional trade and exerted marked influence over the pattern of regional trade and FDI.

One testimony of Asia's rising global footprint is that business firms in Asia and China have acquired a significant status in the global corporate world. According to the *Forbes* 2012 list of the 2,000 largest business firms, the USA (524) and Japan (258) were the still dominant economies but China (136) and other Asian economies were closing in. For the fifth year in succession, the Asia–Pacific region had the largest number (733) of business corporations on the *Forbes* 2000 list. Japan still has more companies than any other Asia-Pacific economy. Korea boasted of 68 business corporations in the *Forbes* 2000 list. Asia-pacific was the biggest region not only in terms of members but Asian businesses corporations were also top performers in areas like sales growth (up 26 percent), profit growth (up 29 percent) and asset growth (up 19 percent) (DeCarlo, 2012).

1.1 Asian economic integration and the Chinese business communities

Over the last two centuries, a large Chinese Diaspora accumulated in countries around China, in particular in Southeast Asia. It comprises resourceful and dynamic business communities. They are credited with connecting China with the rest of Asia. During the early stages of growth, in the 1980s and 1990s, remittances and investments from the Chinese business communities were a substantial part of the total FDI flowing into China. The initial flows of FDI originated from the overseas Chinese business communities in the neighborly Asian economies. They were needed for China's growth. The Chinese business communities took the risky step of investing into "China's premature market in face of regulatory and political uncertainties". They took the risk of investing in a business environment which was known for "a lack of property law and unclear political systems" (Li and Zhang, 2009, p. 5). The importance of investment by the Chinese Diaspora was high initially, although it declined after the mid-1990s.

Arguably, the most valuable contribution that the capital flows originating from these business communities into China made was the synergy they created between the Asian investors and markets and the rapidly developing Chinese economy. The FDI that came from the other sources was not able to match this. This applied *a fortiori* to the newly established industries in the post-reform period in the coastal provinces of China (Smart and Hsu, 2004). When the production networks developed in the region and expanded rapidly in the post-2000 era, these regional economic and industrial bonds were significantly strengthened. Thus, the Chinese business communities in the surrounding Asian economies became an integrative force in the region.

2. China and the evolving pattern of economic integration in Asia

China and its neighboring Asian economies integrated steadily over the preceding three decades. Largely owing to external factors, China's GDP growth declined from 10.4 percent to 7.8 percent over 2010–12, which adversely affected economic activity in the rest of Asia. It was a direct consequence of the deepening of linkages throughout the region, particularly in the past decade (IMF, 2012a). On balance China's vertiginous economic growth became an opportunity for its Asian neighboring economies, which is not to say that it did not pose challenges for some. The pattern of production that evolved since 1990, involving both China and its Asian neighbors, strongly influenced both investment rates and real wage trends in the region. Both were nudged upwards. This in turn benefitted regional growth, particularly in the North Asian economies. There were times when it was less supportive and advantageous for the Southeast Asian economies. Huang (2012a, p. 13) went so far as saying that China's growth thwarted some of them and that they could not "escape the middle-income trap".[2]

Casual empiricism based on growth data for industry and exports indicated that there were times when China began to exert competitive pressure on its neighboring economies. This occurred both in their domestic markets and those of the rest of the world (ROW). However according to Yusuf and Nabeshima (2010), this competitive pressure thus far has been moderate and was counterbalanced by China's imports from its Asian neighbors, which comprised parts and components, capital goods and raw materials.

Trade, FDI and regional and global production networks are the principal channels through which the Chinese economy has integrated with the neighboring Asian economies in a market-driven manner. In the 1970 and early 1980s Japan overwhelmingly dominated Asian trade. It accounted for almost 60 percent of the regional exports and imports. This scenario morphed as the other Asian economies began liberalizing and improving their trade performance. For successful integration of China with the Asian economies, it is a necessary condition that they liberalize their external sector as well. Significant trade and investment liberalization took place in Indonesia, Korea, Malaysia, the Philippines, Taiwan and Thailand in the mid-1980s. Vietnam embarked on reforms belatedly in the early 1990s. These economies took initiatives in unilateral trade liberalization, which was carried out in a non-discriminatory manner. They also were full participants in the multilateral liberalization measures initiated first by the General Agreement on Tariffs and Trade (GATT) and since 1995 the World Trade Organization (WTO).

Intra-developing economies FDI remained small and was not given a great deal of significance until the early 21st century. This subject was the focus of the *World Investment Report* (WIR) 2006, after which other studies on this issue were launched. Its relevance and significance were also examined in the context of FDI flows from the surrounding Asian economies into China as well as the other way around. Since 2004 intra-developing country FDI increased rapidly. In 2008 its volume reached 16 percent of the total FDI outward stock. Although global FDI flows contracted due to the global financial and economic crisis in 2009, FDI flows originating from the developing economies were affected less adversely. Intra-Asia increase in FDI is a relatively recent phenomenon, which has effectively worked toward integrating the region. This trend successfully advanced China's regional integration with its neighbors as well as general Asian integration.

2.1 Role of intra-regional FDI and trade in integrating Asia

A significant portion of FDI in the Asian economies comes from other Asian economies, which in turn helped in integrating the regional economy (Lipsey and Sjoholm, 2011). As noted earlier (Section 1.1), China received a great deal of FDI from its Asian neighbors in the early stages of its reform program. Although there are data gaps, the WIR 2006 and WIR 2010 made a valiant attempt to make up the lacuna. The WIR 2006 found that approximately half of the FDI inflows in the Asian economies were from the other regional economies, largely from the regional emerging market economies (EMEs). According to this source, around 65 percent of inward stock of FDI in 2004 in Asia was from the other Asian economies. The same source estimated that between 2000 and 2004, average annual intra-Asian FDI flows amounted to $48 billion. The WIR 2010 estimated that of the $875 billion FDI received intra-regionally by Asian economies in 2008, China was the source economy of $307 billion. Furthermore, the four newly industrialized economies (NIEs) of Asia,[3] that were a lucrative source, accounted for $512 billion. China received a great deal of FDI—as much as 65 percent of total receipt—from the NIEs. Owing to increasing labor cost, firms in the NIEs are motivated to invest in China and other Asian economies (Gao, 2005; Kittilaksanawong, 2011). Such a large proportion of intra-regional FDI contributed steadfastly to integration of the real economy.

Taking a balance-of-payments approach, Hattari and Rajan (2009) estimated that 35 percent of FDI flows into the developing Asia during the 1990–2005 period originated intra-regionally. China and Hong Kong, SAR, dominated both as hosts and sources. After WTO accession China became a significant source country investing not only in the region but also outside Asia. China's role in outward FDI flows strengthened after 2004; in 2010 its share amounted for 8.5 percent of the total FDI stemming from the developing countries (Aleksynska and Havrylchyk, 2011). Intra-regional FDI made by Hong Kong, SAR, and Singapore is obscured by the fact that it is often made by business firms from other countries, which are both based in Asia and outside. One general characteristic of intra-Asian FDI is that investing firms tend to prefer locating their affiliate operations in more labor-intensive industries.

Trade among the East and Southeast Asian economies, which includes China, began expanding from the 1980s. It was paltry, less than 1 percent of their total trade, in 1975. It began increasing and reached 10 percent of their total trade in 2001 and 13 percent in 2004.[4] During this period China produced almost half of the regional GDP and a third of total exports. High and sustained GDP growth of the Chinese economy in the decade of the 1980s was the principal driver of intra-regional trade. The Chinese economy had established itself as an outward-oriented economy and by the time it acceded to the WTO it had become trade dependent. The obvious benefit of WTO accession was improvement in access to export markets and reduction in import cost of raw materials and intermediate products. The latter helped China in its production and exports of manufactures. This made Chinese products more competitive in the world markets vis-à-vis exports from the other regions of Asia.

Trade became an important and dynamic channel of regional integration. Also, trade progressively integrated Asian with China (Kim *et al.*, 2011). Intra-regional trade increased steadily since the early 1990s. Formation of APT made a significant contribution to intra-regional trade. China, Japan, Korea and Taiwan displayed a steady level of trade increase and trade interdependence. This group played a major role in Asian's trade and intra-regional trade expansion. By 2011 intra-regional trade in Asia touched 55.5 percent of the total trade. Thus, Asia can be regarded as well-integrated through the trade channel, although it is less than that in the European Union (EU). The extent of integration varied from one sub-region to the other. East Asian economies integrated most through the trade channel, with their intra-subregional trade share reaching 35.4 percent in 2011. For the Southeast Asian sub-region the corresponding proportion was 24.7 percent (ADB, 2012). Trade integration in Asia implies that the continuing economic rebalancing in China will provide opportunities to the Asian neighbors of China. What is pertinent to note is that Asia's integration with the rest of the world through the trade channel has also been intensifying.

2.2 China's trade surpluses and intra-regional trade

Economies in the region tend to be at different stages of economic development. This applies *a fortiori* to industrialization and technological prowess. Therefore trade in Asia is dominated by East Asian economies and China. Dominant products in intra-industry trade in Asia are auto parts, electronics and electrical equipment, furniture and textiles and apparel. Yusuf and Nabeshima (2010) divided Asia into two groups. The first group comprised Hong Kong, SAR, Japan, Korea, Malaysia, the Philippines, Singapore and Thailand. A large proportion of their trade in electronics is intra-industry trade. It had trended upwards until recently. The second group comprised China and Vietnam, whose intra-industry trade was on a decline. As for China, after a rapid increase in intra-industry trade until 1999, it went into reverse gear. As China became the largest exporter of electronics, the import-intensity of its exports declined. Instead of importing parts and components from the neighboring countries, Chinese firms began depending on the local suppliers. They often were foreign-owned firms. China's intra-industry trade in electronics with Japan and Korea increased. These two economies were producers and suppliers of high-technology innovative parts and components as well as production equipment.

Intra-regional trade in Asia steadily increased since 1980. This growth led to an interesting development: the outcome of over two decades of growth in intra-regional trade is that China gradually developed a large trade surplus vis-à-vis the ROW and an equally steady increase in the bilateral trade surpluses of the North Asian economies, namely, Japan, Korea and Taiwan vis-à-vis China. Being technologically more advanced economies, these three countries exported high-technology parts, components, intermediate products which become a part of China's processing trade. These three economies also exported final products and capital goods to China. As the final products are exported to the ROW, particularly the large markets of the EU and the USA, China incurs the wrath of its large importers for increasingly running trade surpluses. The North Asian economies, while running bilateral trade surpluses, were not criticized for them, although they contribute to China's trade surpluses. In case of the Southeast Asian economies these developments occurred differently. Some of them had comparable skill and technology levels to China. In the late 1990s this group of economies had a trade deficit with China which gradually swung into a surplus—although this surplus weakened in the recent years. Thus, China influenced these economies less positively in comparison to the North Asian economies.

Developments in the early 1990s were important and noteworthy in this regard. China began improving its complicated and restrictive trade regime after 1990 and also its export structure began to diversify towards capital- and skill-intensive products. This was the time when China began to emerge as a major player in the global economy. The 1990s were a turning point in that during this period liberalization of trade and FDI accelerated in China and the ASEAN economies. The liberalizing of these two important policy areas together created obvious synergy in the regional economy. In the early 1990s exports of the ASEAN economies to China began picking up in value terms. A significant amount of new ASEAN exports to China were in the category of medium-technology manufactures. More technologically advanced ASEAN economies, like Malaysia, the Philippines, Singapore and Thailand, exported semiconductors and computer components. The other ASEAN economies exported natural resources to China. However, ASEAN-4 essentially exported durable goods to Japan and the NIEs.

In 1995 exports from Japan and the four NIEs to China accounted for 10.6 percent of all exports. This group of five economies is resource-poor. In the case of ASEAN-4 economies this proportion was a mere 3.5 percent (Robertson and Xu, 2010). Therefore, in relative terms the larger ASEAN economies were less integrated with the Chinese economy in 1995 than Japan and the NIEs. As for China's exports to these two groups of Asian economies, Japan and the NIEs accounted for 31 percent of the total exports to the region, while the ASEAN-4 accounted for only 4.2 percent in 1995. China's exports as a fraction of its total multilateral exports were again much higher to Japan and the NIEs (8.4 percent) than to the ASEAN-4 (3.9 percent) economies. These statistics show that in 1995 Japan and the NIEs were far more closely integrated with the Chinese economy than the ASEAN-4 economies. What is noteworthy is that the trade structures of China and the ASEAN-4 economies were identical at this juncture. This state of affairs had changed by the middle of the decade of the 2000s. China, with a market of 1.3 billion consumers, had become the principal engine of growth not only within the region but also for the global economy as a whole (Garnaut and Song, 2006).

By 2006, China had become the fifth largest export market of the ASEAN economies and the third largest source of imports. A direct influence of China on ASEAN economies was giving an impetus to their exports to its large domestic market. In fact as imports and exports of the ASEAN economies are increasingly becoming more China-centric, some scholars have questioned the relevance of ASEAN grouping (Tambunan, 2005 and 2006). Members of ASEAN have larger trade with China than they have with each other. A quantitative examination using highly disaggregated trade data revealed that a lot of changes occurred in intra-industry trade over the 2000–05 period between China and the ASEAN-5 economies. These were the five founding economies of ASEAN for which disaggregated data were available. This demonstrated the unique importance of China for the ASEAN economies, both as a market for exports and source for imports. This empirical study concluded that there was no crowding out of bilateral trade among the five members of ASEAN owing to their increasing trade with China. If anything, increased integration with the Chinese economy resulted in an increase in the intra-ASEAN-5 trade. Thus viewed, while China has influenced and altered trade flows within the ASEAN region, it has not "significantly reorganized trade flows away from intra-ASEAN-5 to that of ASEAN-5-China. There are grounds for suggesting that the ASEAN-5-China trade interaction can be considered an important driver for intra-ASEAN-5 export expansion" (Devadason, 2011, p. 143).

As the ASEAN-China free trade agreement (ACFTA) came in force in January 2010 and tariff were reduced to zero, the two economies integrated further. ACFTA is the third largest in the world after the EU and the North American Free Trade Agreement (NAFTA). In 2011 ASEAN overtook Japan to be China's third largest trading partner after the EU and the USA, with a trade figure of $362.9 billion. It is the largest trading partner of the ASEAN economies. China has a large import demand for farm products, mechanical processing and marine products from the ASEAN economies. It encourages imports from countries that have free trade agreements with it. ASEAN economies have close economic ties with provinces in southern China, the most prosperous region in the country. According to the projections made by the China Council for the Promotion of International Trade, ASEAN-China trade would surpass $500 billion mark in 2015 (King, 2012).

According to the 2010 data published by the Ministry of Commerce of the China, 53.55 percent of China's trade was with its Asian neighbors. China imported more (61.16 percent of its total imports) from them than it exported (47.34 percent of its total exports).[5] The statistical data presented above indicate that since the mid-1990s, trade with China in goods has been increasing for most regional economies. China's trade in goods with the regional economies has increased at a faster rate than that with the rest of the world. Also, while global trade and Asia's trade with the economies outside the region doubled between 2000 and 2011, intra-Asian trade tripled. Furthermore regional trade involving the EMEs of Asia increased even faster. The bulk of that increase was driven by trade in intermediate products (Shinohara, 2012). In 2010 intermediate products accounted for 50 percent of total exports in Asia; of these, 30 percent were traded within the region (ADB, 2012).

However, intra-regional trade in services failed to show comparable dynamism. For deeper regional integration a similar market-driven increase in trade in services, which includes financial services, is needed. Many Asian economies have a high-value-added services sector, which has so far lagged behind manufacturing sector in regional trade. Increased intra-regional trade in services will prove to be beneficial for other sectors domestically and abroad. As barriers to trade and movement of factors of production come down further and the regional integration advances further, regional economies will be able to have stronger links with China and benefit from its dynamism.

The ongoing wave of globalization became another instrument of regional integration in Asia. Globalization enabled latecomer economies like China to integrate regionally and globally through the expansion of production networks. They developed fast over the decade of the 1990s and became extensive throughout Asia, *a fortiori* in East Asia. They involved Asian business firms as well as multinational ones from the EU and the USA. These multinationals changed their operational strategy from exporting to international production. Their newly structured and reorganized businesses in different parts of the global economy enabled them to reduce costs and improve their ability to react to technological advancements. They could meet the requirements of their global markets more swiftly by way of globally integrated production and distribution networks. Many Asian economies, including China, were their preferred locations for setting up such cross-border networks. They were initially intra-firm, but increasingly grew arm's-length inter-firm networks. They made an invaluable contribution to the integration of Asian economies.

2.3 Changing terms-of-trade and shrinking external surplus of China

It appears that China's imports and their prices have been rising faster than those in the export sector. That is, China's terms-of-trade have been suffering from a secular decline (IMF, 2012b).[6] This applies expressly to commodities and capital goods. It seems likely that strong imports are linked to strong domestic investment. There is another related fact to consider. With 10.4 percent share in multilateral exports in 2011, China has reached the level where increasing the market share becomes difficult for a successful outward-oriented economy. Other export-oriented economies like Japan and Korea experienced a waning in their ability to expand market shares during their periods of rapid growth. Given the rapid advancement in the technological level in the economy and the fast-increasing share of high-technology manufactures in its exports, China can increase the level of technology of its export basket, but the pace at which this can be achieved would necessarily be middling.

In China the demand for investment goods rose at a much faster pace than that for consumer goods. The ratio between the two remained at approximately 2:1. Asian economies that exported capital goods to China, namely Japan and Korea, benefitted from the Chinese investment expansion. As regards the future, it may not be sustainable from a domestic perspective. However, should future rebalancing of growth in China be consumption-led, the larger ASEAN economies would be its clear beneficiaries. In comparison to other exporters, they had a comparative advantage in exporting consumer goods to China. This may not be a large or long-lasting benefit for the ASEAN economies because China accounts for merely 2 percent of global consumer goods exports (Shinohara, 2012).

Since the global financial crisis (2007–09) China's once large export-led current account—which includes trade balance, net investment and cash transfers—surplus plummeted sharply. After peaking in 2007 at 10.1 percent of the GDP it declined to 2.7 percent in 2011. This remarkable decline testifies that China is balancing its economy on the external front. In 2011 there was an unexpected surge in imports, which was largely due to Chinese firms restocking raw materials, in particular iron ore and other metals.

One key element of the strategy of rebalancing the domestic economy was boosting domestic demand. With growth in domestic demand and weakening export markets, China's large trade surplus has been shrinking faster and more persistently than anticipated. This fall was essentially caused by decreasing trade balance. If the economy is better balanced than in the past, this would wear away the root of the argument supporting renminbi undervaluation.

China's trade surplus peaked at approximately $300 billion in 2008, and since then it fell continuously and was reduced to $155 billion in 2011. In the first quarter of 2012 it was merely $670 million. Multilateral trade growth in 2012 decelerated to 2.0 percent from 5.2 percent in 2011. In 2012 the trade balance in China will continue to be a drain on the external surplus as well as GDP growth. According to the WTO projections world trade is projected to remain sluggish in 2013 as well, at about 3.3 percent (WTO, 2013). Export growth is expected to suffer a slowdown while imports are likely to be resilient. Projections of China's export growth put it to 9.7 percent in 2012 while import growth to 12 percent. Processing trade is likely to make a significant contribution to reduction in China's trade surplus (WB, 2012).

3. Emergence of Asian production networks and their sequential development

Chronologically, Japan and the four NIEs were the first to participate in production networks and supply chains. Middle-income ASEAN economies followed them. China joined them next. Vietnam was to join them most recently. Asian economies were the precursor in the growth of regional production networks; the celebrated outward-oriented trade policy adopted by this group of economies and the aggressive attraction of FDI enabled them to advance relatively effortlessly in this direction. Industries that form a production network prefer a free-trading environment. Unilateral trade liberalization undertaken by Asian economies proved to be a supportive policy for the growth of production networks and value chains. Expansion production networks in Asia took place rapidly after 1990, its pace picked up further after 2000. By the second decade of the 21st century

Asian production networks, particularly those in the East Asian economies and China, became the most advanced and sophisticated in the world.

The process of vertical fragmentation of production is essentially corporate or private-sector driven. It essentially entails business firms. Production networks are created by business firms in economies having differing degrees of production factor intensities. They engage in an inter-process division of labor. It resulted in dynamic evolution of the intra-regional division of labor in Asia. Trade created by vertically integrated production increased in Asia dramatically in the recent years—particularly in the post-1990 period—and with that cross-border transactions of parts, components, sub-assemblies and intermediate products. With that the imported input content of exports increased (Hummels *et al.*, 2001; Yi, 2003). The regional production networks were the third channel of market-led integration in Asia. Final or finished products produced by networked production in the region have been exported to the large markets like the EU and the USA and the ROW. This is known as the triangle of trade.

This configuration of triangular trade favorably affected its neighboring Asian economies. Over the 2000–10 period the combined trade surplus of Japan, Korea and Taiwan vis-à-vis China jumped from $30 billion to $210 billion (Huang, 2012b). The source of this growth in surplus was an increase in the volume of technology-intensive exports to China. For the most part they comprised parts, components and sub-assemblies. Finished products were fabricated from them in China and exported. Largely due to similarities in resource endowments, this relationship with the ASEAN economies was not so direct. In the post Asian crisis (1997–98) period their trade balance with China shifted from a deficit to a surplus of $20 billion in 2004. Then it started dissipating slowly, so much so that Singapore and Vietnam had a large deficit vis-à-vis China, while the surpluses of the other ASEAN economies declined. In general, Japan and the NIEs benefitted more from China's rapid pace of industrialization and triangular trade pattern. They conspicuously strengthened their position at the high end of the consumer electronics and ICT-related product lines. Production patterns in the ASEAN region were influenced by this triangular pattern of trade and with that investment and labor markets.

Deploying bilateral trade data for 75 countries Ferrarini (2011) measured countries' mutual dependence as suppliers and assemblers of parts and components. His conclusion was that the largest processing trade region in the global economy is the so-called "factory Asia". It is a tightly knit web of production sharing, particularly in electrical machinery and electronics. China and Japan were found to be the most important locales or hubs in these industries. However, in the automotive industry, Japanese firms were the key suppliers of parts, components and intermediate products and countries like Indonesia were the key assembly centers.

While calibrating China's impact on the regional trade, most studies took into account the traditional horizontal trade, which is trade in goods and services that are produced in their entirety in an economy and traded. This important factor has become a determinant of trading pattern in the region. In a very short time, production and trade networks changed the pattern of trade and specialization in the region.

The regional production and trade networks were driven by Asian firms located in Asia as well as affiliates of the USA or EU firms and the subsidiaries of MNCs. The latter category of firms comprised those that moved to Asia because they shifted from export to Asia to international production in Asia. To that end, they methodically and comprehensively reorganized their businesses. Their production facilities were located in several Asian countries in such a manner that they could benefit from diminution in transport and communications costs and eventually profit from slicing of the value chain. This also enabled them to react swiftly to technological advancements and marketing requirements.

Firms from Japan and the NIEs relocated their labor-intensive activities and industries in China. As industrialization in China progressed, many large EU and US firms and MNCs that were operating in the NIEs also moved their facilities to China. Such movements of firms extensively reorganized production pattern in Asia. These trends were instrumental in market-led integration of the Asian economy.

Although China was a latecomer to the phenomenon of regional production networks and vertical fragmentation of trade in Asia, it has succeeded in carving a vitally significant niche in the regional division of labor (Ando and Kimura, 2009). It was instrumental in integrating Asia in a market-led manner. By 2005 the center of gravity of regional networks had shifted to China. The intermediate goods imported by China come through relatively long and complex supply chains. They are characterized by a high degree of fragmentation and sophistication. China succeeded in producing and exporting competitively not only because of its low cost of production but also due to the complexity of its supply chains, which it exploited dexterously. The intermediate goods that it imported from the neighboring Asian economies, sometimes from outside the region, enabled it to effectively enhance its competitiveness (WTO, 2011b). China's trade in parts and components with its neighbors progressively grew large. In the parts and components in the ICT sector, China increased its market share significantly during the 1990s. According to the computations made by Amighini (2005), it ranked among the top three ICT exporters in the world. China has begun to play a pivotal role in regional parts and component trade and with that regional production network in Asia continued to consolidate.

Since the mid-1990s, Japanese firms became major players in production networks in Asia. Recently their network operations in Asia and investment have accelerated. The balance-of-payments statistics proved this.[7] A predominant part of the Japanese investment in regional production networks in Asia went into manufacturing, particularly in the machinery sector (SITC 7 category). The global financial crisis affected Japanese investment adversely, but it recovered fast. The Japanese firms in machinery sector expanded their operations in Asia, and with that their intra-regional trade also intensified. This suggested complementarity between the Japanese and Asian firms. A firm-level analysis demonstrated that fragmentation of production in manufacturing sector enhanced job creation in Japan. This was the result of effectively utilizing the mechanics of production-process-wise division of labor in Asia (Ando and Fukunari, 2011).

It is a well-known fact that growing complementarities of production processes leading to vertical fragmentation of production and trade has turned China into a major assembly center for Asia. The supply chain network of Asia, which is increasingly centered on China, relies intensively on imported inputs from the region. Asia in turn relies on inputs from China. This major development was ignored by some empirical studies that tried to calculate China's impact over the regional economy.[8] This constituted serious negligence because during its reform phase China integrated rapidly into the regional production networks. It does have a great deal of impact on its regional neighbors through the regional production chains or network production. It has come to acquire a unique position as Asia's production platform for export of final goods regionally and even more globally. China's prominent role in Asia's production networks has been methodically examined by Arndt (2008), Athukorala (2010, 2011b), Yeats (2001) and Ng and Yeats (2001).

As China's integration into Asian production networks evolved, China's imports of intermediate products exceeded its exports (Lee *et al.*, 2011). This demonstrated that China was developing as a major world production center. As China's exports of intermediate products also increased steadily, it proved that it was growing into an increasingly important manufacturing base of parts and components. Trade data for China show that SITC 7 (electrical machinery and apparatus) has become the most vital category in trade in parts and components. It accounted for a large proportion of imports and exports of parts and components. China's trade of parts and components displays a high degree of regional concentration. ASEAN, Hong Kong, SAR, Japan and Korea were China's most important regional partners in the region, while the EU and North America were the most important among the extra-regional partners. Exports and imports of intermediate products have different structural characteristics. While regional concentration of this trade is clear, China's parts and component trade volume with the ROW has been growing. Lee *et al.* (2011) also show that the Asian economies engage in a much higher degree of production sharing with China than do the EU and North American economies. China's exports and imports of parts and components with the neighboring Asian economies are larger than that of final products.

3.1 China and the spread of regional production networks

Value chains or production networks operated by multinational corporations (MNCs) have become the backbone of the global economy. Lawrence *et al.* (2012, p. 35) referred to it as the "central nervous system" of the manufacturing sector. Liberalization of the external sector in China in the early 1990s energized expansion of regional and global production networks in China. It gradually emerged as a global center for the assembly of a wide range of manufactured products, many of them high-technology ones. Strategies of the MNCs had a great deal to contribute to this development.

The impact of the spread of regional production networks was the rapid expansion and increase in both FDI and trade between the Asian economies. An influential empirical study concluded that production networks in the region accounted for a large proportion of the trade flows for most member countries. They entailed both intra-firm and arm's-length trade (Ando and Kimura, 2005). The Asian production and distribution networks are idiosyncratic in the following three traits: First, they are enormously significant for the regional economies. Second, they tend to cover a large part of the region and number of countries. Third, over the years they have grown exceedingly sophisticated in terms covering intra- and inter-firm transactions of regional manufacturing firms. No doubt other parts of the global economy also successfully developed such production and distribution networks. The most salient examples are the Mexico–USA networks and Western–Central–Eastern Europe corridor. They are yet to reach the level of sophistication that Asia has been able to achieve (Kimura, 2006).

China was a latecomer, last to be a part of the regional division of labor in Asia. However, it conclusively illustrated how splitting the value-added chain between different countries, at different stages of growth and having different comparative advantage, can drive the process of industrial development, along with regional economic integration (Gaulier *et al.*, 2009). One direct consequence of the expansion of production and distribution networks in Asia was the evolution of a triangular pattern of trade. Japan and the NIEs, that were technologically at a higher strata, exported advanced capital goods, complicated intermediate goods, particularly parts and components, to the relatively less technologically advanced economies like the ASEAN and China. The latter group of economies processed them and got the final products ready for exports to the largest markets in the global economy, the EU and USA. This triangular trade further reinforced regional integration in Asia. Throughout the 2000s, China importance in the regional production networks increased substantially for the neighboring Asian economies.

3.2 China's positioning in the Asian production networks

As China has positioned itself at the center of the production networks in Asia, the trade intensity index of China with the regional economies increased discernibly. This index shows how much

TABLE 5.1 Trade intensity indices, 2000 and 2010

	2000				2010			
	Japan	China	USA	EU-15	Japan	China	USA	EU-15
Japan	–	1.7	1.5	0.4	–	1.9	1.1	0.3
China	2.7	–	1	0.4	1.5	–	1.3	0.5
Hong Kong, SAR	0.9	9.3	1.2	0.4	0.8	5.2	0.8	0.3
South Korea	1.9	2.9	1.1	0.4	1.2	2.5	0.8	0.2
Taiwan	1.8	0.5	3.8	2.4	1.3	2.7	0.8	0.3
Singapore	1.2	1.1	0.9	0.3	0.9	1	0.5	0.3
Indonesia	3.7	1.2	0.7	0.4	3.2	1	0.6	0.3
Malaysia	2.1	0.8	1	0.4	2.1	1.2	0.7	0.3
Philippines	2.4	0.5	1.5	0.5	3	1.1	1.1	0.4
Thailand	2.4	1.1	1.1	0.4	2.1	1.1	0.7	0.3
Vietnam	2.8	2.9	0.3	0.5	2.3	1	1.7	0.5
USA	1.3	0.6	–	0.6	0.9	0.7	–	0.5
EU-15	0.3	0.3	0.5	–	0.2	0.3	0.5	–

Source: JETRO (2011), Table 1–20, p.12
Note: Calculated from export data.

the trade relationship between two countries deviates from the benchmark, which in turn is determined by the overall value of the world trade. A comparison of the trade intensity index for China and its neighboring Asian economies for 2000 and 2010 made by JETRO (2011) shows an increase. Its value is above 1.0 for all the countries (Table 5.1). An index value of more than 1.0 is taken to mean a strong trade linkage between the two countries.

What is noticeable in Table 5.1 is that the trade intensities of Asian economies with the USA declined between 2000 and 2010. China and Vietnam were the only two exceptions, where the index values rose. The trade intensity index of the Asian economies with China in 2010 was 1 or above 1, which indicates a close trade relationship of the Asian economies with China. The NIEs have higher trade intensity with China compared to the ASEAN economies. In 2010 in China's imports from the NIEs intermediate goods accounted for 75.2 percent for Korea, 77.2 percent for Taiwan, 76.4 percent for Singapore and 57.0 percent for Hong Kong. Implying the obvious, that is, these countries are large suppliers of parts and components to China. In 2010, China's exports comprised raw materials (0.9 percent), intermediate goods (40.2 percent) and final goods (58.9 percent). The final goods have a markedly high share in China's exports. These statistics demonstrate that China imports raw materials and intermediate goods from the NIEs and the ASEAN economies, processes them into final finished goods and exports them globally (JETRO, 2011).

3.3 Production networks and enhanced trade in parts and components

Owing to expansion of production networks, global trade in parts, components, sub-assemblies and intermediate products increased fast in recent decades, faster than trade in manufactures. Trade in intermediate goods has become the most dynamic sector of international trade. Over 1998–2009, components and intermediate products exports accounted for 70 percent of the annual export growth in Asia. China accounts for almost 50 percent of all trade flows in imported inputs in Asia, more than double its share in 1995 (IMF, 2011a). These exports have come to have an increasingly wide product coverage. In keeping with this trend, intra-regional trade in components in Asia grew large. In fact, trade in parts, components, sub-assemblies and intermediate products played a more important role in trade expansion in Asia than in any other region of the global economy (Yeats, 2001; Yamashita, 2010). Japan and the NIEs, particularly Korea and Taiwan, have consistently been large exporters of components and intermediate products to China. They account for 80 percent of China's imported components and intermediate products (IMF, 2011a).

Trade in components is a function of demand for final products. Since the early 1990s China's importance as the leading final assembly center in Asia gradually increased. It imported components from the neighboring Asian economies to assemble and export the final products. As China was assembling a variety of manufactured products, the share of parts, components and sub-assemblies in its imports of manufactures grew large. Over the years this process also made Asian economies highly integrated and interdependent in a market-led manner. Many of them also reduced the production of final products because China was doing so. As China exported the final products, it customarily ran a deficit in components trade with the regional trade partners. This production paradigm of the region is essentially controlled by MNCs. As the export volume of China grew, it caused a marked shift in the division of labor in the network production in Asia. The pace of final assembly of products in China accelerated rapidly, *pari passu* the role of the NIEs and ASEAN economies also grew in producing parts, components and subassemblies.

With rising levels of network production, the importance of the Asian economies has increased for the mature industrial economies. As China's integration with the rest of Asia deepened, production fragmentation also intensified. Strengthening bonds of network production between China and the NIEs and ASEAN economies also helped in raising the global status of Asia in the economic and business world (Haddad, 2007; Das, 2011c). Exports of NIEs to China, particularly from Korea and Taiwan, are largely intended for re-exporting after processing in China. For the most part they are not intended for domestic consumption. Consequently components and intermediate products account for the bulk of exports from the NIEs to China (Nicolas, 2009). China accounts for about 50 percent of all intra-regional trade flows in imported inputs in Asia, more than double its share in 1995 (Shinohara, 2012).

The nature of this trade has made China a large recipient of FDI from the other parts of Asia, particularly the NIEs. Since 2000 this trend became stronger. Frequently the largest proportion of annual FDI flows from firms in Asia began to go to China. Also, the destination of a substantial part of exports from the NIEs to China was firms from these very economies exporting to their subsidiaries in China. The subsidiaries' exports from China were targeted to the global markets, primarily the USA and the EU economies.

In several product lines in the SITC 7 category, Asia's export dynamism was primarily driven by vigorous regional production networks. Their active functioning served to closely integrate Asian economies with the global economy. These SITC product lines essentially comprised machinery and transport equipment, particularly information and communication technology (ICT) products and electrical goods. These products fall under SITC 75, 76 and 77 categories.

The global financial crisis (2007–09) had a large impact on Asian trade. Beginning in the last quarter of 2007, Asian economies also began to suffer a severe trade contraction. It was caused by the precipitous deceleration (down to 2.1 percent) in multilateral exports in 2008 and the decline in 2009 (−12.2 percent). The decline in world trade in manufactures was over 20 percent in 2009, although in the last quarter of 2008 it was only 10.4 percent. This decline in world trade was the steepest in seven decades (WTO, 2010). The synchronized pattern of trade contraction in Asia was consistent with the close trading relationship among China and the other Asian economies that regional production networks had engendered. The triangular pattern of trade between Asia, China and the large EU–US markets that had evolved over the last two decades was certainly destabilized and enervated by the global financial crisis, although it was not squelched. As the EU and the US economies begin a normal recovery and resolve the sovereign debt related financial stress, respectively, the triangular trade pattern can potentially resume normalcy. In the post-crisis era, both trade and investment relationships between Asia and China can be expected to deepen further.

3.4 Production networks and the contribution of the Chinese economy

China was not responsible for the market-led creation of regional and global production networks in Asia. They had existed before the emergence of China as a manufacturing powerhouse. With the rise of the Chinese economy a new dimension was added to Asia's standing in global production networks. As proved by the following statistical data, China's trade in components grew at a rapid pace, as its involvement in production networks increased. Between 1992/93 and 2005/06 China's share of world exports of parts and components increased from 1.1 percent to 10.9 percent and its share of world imports of parts and components increased from 2.4 percent to 11.5 percent. Also, components were a larger share of China's imports in 2005/6 (60.4 percent) than they were in exports (34.8 percent). Unlike China, in the other Asian economies percentage shares of components in exports and imports were largely similar (Athukorala and Menon, 2010). The largest concentration of Asian trade in parts and components is currently in electrical machinery and electronics. Also, in the ASEAN Free Trade Area (AFTA) trade in parts and components is more concentrated in electronics.

Trading activity by global production networks rose steadily since the early 1990s. Table 1 in Athukorala (2011b) reveals how production networks in China and Asia enhanced their status in multilateral trade. In global networks production and exports, Asia's share increased from 32.2 percent in 1992/93 to 40.3 percent in 2006/07. This occurred despite a notable decline in Japan's share from 18.4 percent to 9.5 percent over the same period. Apparently the dynamism of Chinese economy was a major driving force for the Asian economy, whose share had increased from 2.1 percent to 14.5 percent during the period under consideration. These statistics show that China's role in Asian production networks was vital. It was responsible for notable synergy in the region.

The world market share of the ASEAN economies in global network production grew faster than the regional average. Singapore was an exception in this regard because its world market share declined. The reason was its changing role from active participation in the production networks to performing an oversight function and product design and capital-intensive tasks in the production process. These functions fall under the services category and are not recorded in merchandise trade.

4. Co-movement of the Renminbi and the Asian Currencies

A lesson of history is that when an economy strengthens in magnitude and rises in significance, its currency becomes a reference point for the other currencies, which track it implicitly or explicitly. In the beginning of the 20th century, the pound sterling reigned supreme. As the century progressed, three currencies rose in status. They were as follows: the dollar in the first half of the century and the mark and the yen in the post-Bretton Woods period (Frankel, 2011). Since 2005, the status of the renminbi has been on the rise.

The influence of the dollar is on the wane in Asia and the EMEs. Influence of the renminbi has been the strongest over the Asian currencies. This opened the probabilities of formation of a renminbi bloc in Asia (Ito, 2012). On several occasions in the 1980s and 1990s China devalued the renminbi, which was seen as an attempt to expand trade and strengthen external competitiveness. Since mid-2010, the renminbi has increasingly achieved the status of a reference currency and displayed a high degree of co-movement. In an influential paper (Subramanian and Kessler, 2012) concluded that the renminbi's influence on the Asian currencies has been on the rise. Seven Asian currencies were found to follow the renminbi more closely than the dollar. When the dollar value changes by 1 percent, these Asian currencies moved in the same direction by 0.38 percent, while with the renminbi the same movement was by 0.53 percent.

Subramanian and Kessler (2012, p. 2) found that more currencies co-move with the renminbi (eight out of 10) in Asia than with the dollar (six out of 10). They also concluded that the currencies of many other economies were experiencing an increase in co-movements of their currencies with the renminbi, in total 34 out of 52 currencies in the sample. A much lesser number of currencies displayed this co-movement with the dollar (14) and the euro (19). By the end of 2012, the renminbi had become "the dominant reference currency" in Asia. Renminbi's influence was not limited to the region. For countries like Chile, Israel, South Africa and Turkey renminbi is a more important reference currency than the dollar.

5. Premonitions of China's threat for the Asian economies

Based on the standard Heckscher–Ohlin theory, one can say that China's opening up and integrating into the regional economy first and then into the global economy caused a shift in effective average factor endowments of the regional and global economies. That is, it altered the relative factor endowments of the individual regional economies as well as global economies, and thereby affected their comparative advantage. It had both regional ramifications and global impact. It was particularly reflected in the trade performance and FDI flows of the regional and global economies. Whether there were negative externalities of China's success for its neighbors became a contentious issue. China's crowding out the exports of its neighbors has been debated fervently in academic and policy conclaves. Likewise, whether China absorbed an increasing proportion of FDI flowing to the region has remained a moot point. For a long time it has remained the most alluring destination for FDI in the global economy.

One source of this concern was the fast-growing exports from China to the USA, the largest market. Between 1990 and 2005 China's share of the US market increased from 3.1 percent to 15 percent. Over this period the shares of Japan and the NIEs declined. The possibility of China crowding out other smaller Asian economies was a larger concern. This was because the trade structure of the economies like the ASEAN-4 was less complementary to that of China. This was responsible for the perception of the so-called China "threat" for the Asian economies. It was intuitively felt that China was developing at the cost of its Asian neighbors and growing prosperous at their expense. Whether China was having a negative effect on their GDP growth is still an open question. This premonition was empirically examined by many analysts. In its public pronouncements the Chinese government tried to emphasize that its rapid growth can benefit its neighbors and create an opportunity for them. It consciously tries to supplant the "China threat" trepidation by a "China opportunity" notion (Ye, 2010).

5.1 China's threat in multilateral trade

Some of the early empirical studies classified exports of Asian economies in different categories to determine the levels of threat from China's burgeoning exports. One of the early studies concluded that the trade performance of the neighboring Asian economies is facing a threat from China's competitive exports in the global marketplace (Lall and Albaladejo, 2004). Another methodology that was deployed to examine the crowding out effect was simulation exercises. Both Ianchovichina and Walmsley (2005) and Ronald-Holst and Weiss (2005) provided evidence of China's rapid trade expansion having a favorable impact on the trade of Japan and the NIEs, particularly improving their terms of trade. Conversely, the relatively less developed ASEAN economies having a similar endowment structure to China faced keen competition from the exports of China. Their terms of trade also worsened. However, Ronald-Holst and Weiss (2005) were dismissive of the proposition that China's successful exports and fast increasing share in multilateral trade were adversely affecting the comparative advantage of the neighboring Asian economies in higher value added goods or skill-intensive activities. The limited theoretical foundations of these empirical exercises made it difficult to come to a final conclusion regarding economic policy responses of the Asian economies.

Haltmaier *et al.* (2007) provided evidence of mixed effect of China's aggressive trade expansion on the Asian economies. They inferred that in general China did not show any proclivity to crowd out exports of the other Asian economies in third-country markets. That being said, those Asian economies whose exports were concentrated in consumer goods sectors were negatively affected. Eichengreen *et al.* (2007), Greenaway *et al.* (2008) and Athukorala (2010) employed more advanced methodologies like Gravity models to examine the effect of China's fast-growing exports on the surrounding Asian economies. Of these three large empirical studies, Eichengreen *et al.* (2007), Greenaway *et al.* (2008) concluded in a positive manner. That is, they found "a relatively small" crowding out effect of China's exports over the exports of the neighboring Asian economies (Greenaway *et al.*, 2008, p. 163). According to their results, this small crowding out effect of China's exports was felt by Asian economies that were exporting consumer goods and not by those that were exporting capital goods. Thus, this effect was more intense over the ASEAN-4 economies but much less so on Japan and the NIEs. They also concluded that China's exports had a positive impact over the exports of high- and middle-income Asian countries.

There were other broad analyses that revealed that the fear of China crowding out the East and Southeast Asian economies from their export markets seems unfounded. For 1969/70 and 2006/07 Athukorala and Hill (2010) computed that the share of East and Southeast Asia including China's exports and imports in total Asian exports increased from 42 percent to 76 percent and in imports from 38 percent to 80 percent. During this period Asia accounted for 40 percent of the total increase in multilateral exports. This reflects strengthening long-term trade performance of the Asian economies in multilateral trade.

Unquestionably China's rise as a large trading economy had a lot to do with its structural transformation. The other Asian economies also increased their global market shares in exports. This includes the NIEs and the larger members of ASEAN. Athukorala (2010) reported that the apprehension concerning China's exports crowding out those from the other Asian economies was highly exaggerated in the policy debate. Viewed in the global context, market share growth of the Asian economies, including that of China, occurred essentially at the expense of the rest of the world, particularly the advanced industrial economies (Athukorala, 2011a). Interestingly, during this period the combined share of the other non-Asian developing countries in global trade also increased, but at a much slower pace than that of the Asian economies.

China and the East and Southeast Asian economies were the major drivers of rapid export growth in Asia. After the 1970s the export structures of this group of Asian economies experienced an intense shift towards manufacturing products. Their share of exports of manufactures in total multilateral trade increased from 12.9 percent in 1969/70 to 36.6 percent in 2006/07. Conversely, during this period, the share of Japan declined from 8.9 percent to 7.8 percent. This reflects greater success of the non-Japan Asia in industrialization and trade in manufactures.

More recent research has concluded that while China succeeded in penetrating markets for traditional labor-intensive manufactured goods at the cost of the high-wage NIEs, it did not have the same effect on the exports of the other low-wage Asian economies (Athukorala, 2010, 2011a; Kong and Kneller, 2012). Also, there was little displacement effect by Chinese exports. China did affect the trade of countries that produced substantial amounts of labor-intensive manufactures that China also produced, although this effect was highly exaggerated (Wood and Mayer, 2011). If anything, China's success in joining in the regional and global production chains or production networks as an important assembly center created opportunities for the other Asian economies to become part of various segments of the value chains in line with their comparative advantage and boost their trade volumes. These studies also concluded that China's exports were complementary to the exports of several Asian economies.

To address some of the weaknesses in the theoretical foundations of the previous models and allow for the trade–growth interaction Robertson and Xu (2010) introduced long-run neo-classical steady state factor accumulation conditions into an open economy growth model. Their simulation model included eleven sectors and three separate regions and was an improvement over such studies in the past. They came up with a strong inference regarding the impact of China's growth over neighboring Asian economies as both substantial and positive. This result applied robustly to Japan and the NIEs. They computed that the impact of China's rapid growth and trade expansion led to a 16 percent growth in both GDP and consumption in a decade in this group of countries. The ASEAN-4 economies also experienced gains of 7 percent to 8 percent in GDP from a decade of Chinese growth. In the post-2000 period, these economies were found to be less complementary with China than Japan and the NIES and were also relatively less integrated with China. The income gains were long-run steady state results, therefore they included increased income from capital deepening. Growth rate in the Asian economies, particularly the ASEAN-4 economies, would have been lower in the absence of a dynamic China next door. Thus viewed, China's robust growth performance augmented the growth performance of its Asian neighbors.

The perception of China as a threat was greater than the reality. It evolved as a major assembly center in the regional and global production networks. This was a significant development because it spawned new opportunities for the neighboring Asian economies to engage in various segments of the value chain, depending upon their respective comparative advantages (Athukorala, 2009).

The nature of the recovery from the Great Recession will influence the global trade pattern and the status of China and the Asian economy. In the advanced industrial economies the recovery obstinately remained tepid. Conversely the recovery and GDP growth rates in China and the other Asian economies have been rapid. Therefore they are likely to dominate global demand in the early part of the second decade. As the large, mature economies have disconcerting levels of structural trade and fiscal deficits, they will need to reduce their imports. They also need to rebalance their macroeconomic structures. This will accentuate the dominance of China and the other Asian economies in the growth of global demand in the foreseeable future.

5.2 China's threat in textiles and apparel

Developing countries' exports of textiles and apparel to the advanced economies were subject to stringent quotas under a special regime outside the GATT. This restrictive regime, christened

Multi-Fiber Arrangement (MFA), was established in 1974 as a short-term measure, but it held sway until the end of 1994. The Agreement on Textiles and Clothing (ATC), which was a transitional instrument, supplanted the MFA on 1 January 1995. The ACT selectively applied tariffs and quotas on textiles and apparel exports of the developing countries. It expired in 2005, freeing multilateral trade in textiles and apparel. The effect of abolition of quotas would be increase in the share of China and the other quota-restricted exporters. China is also a large and competitive exporter. Its exports posed a great competitive threat to the other Asian economies. Several Asian economies are also large and successful exporters of textiles and apparel.

Using the Gravity model, Amann *et al.* (2009) show that China had a mixed effect on the textiles and apparel producers of Asia. Some Asian countries that competed with China in textiles exports lost ground during 1990–2005. However, after the expiration of the ATC in 2005, the EU and the USA reimposed quotas on Chinese textiles exports and the Asian economies honed their comparative advantage. For these two reasons, Asian suppliers continued to remain competitive in the EU and the US markets. Their prices in these two markets remained stable (Lau, 2007). Also, between 1996 and 2008 Chinese apparel exports nearly quintupled to $120 billion. However, this occurred with China lessening its dependence on its traditional export markets while adding new markets to its portfolios. Prominent among them are the central Asian republics and the Russian Federation.

5.3 China's threat in foreign direct investment

Owing to their economic dynamism, Asian economies became progressively significant recipients of FDI from the advanced industrial economies. During the 1980s, a lion's share of these FDI flows went to the NIEs, spreading subsequently to the ASEAN-4 economies in the early 1990s. As the economies in the region developed and industrialized, intra-regional FDI flows also intensified (Gill and Kharas, 2007). Increase in the intra-regional FDI made a significant contribution to industrial upgrading in the regional economies. Additionally, FDI has been a valuable instrument of both regional integration as well as global integration for Asia. In 1992 China recorded an uptick in its FDI receipts, which soon turned into a surge. By the mid-1990s it had become the largest developing country recipient of FDI. As perceptions regarding China's large domestic market became real, it began attracting large amounts of both domestic-market oriented and export-oriented FDI. This augmented domestic Chinese firms' export capabilities through technology and managerial skills transfer and distribution links with global markets.

During the 1960s and 1970s the USA was the principal FDI source economy for Asia and Japan in the 1980s. In the 1990s their shares in total FDI receipts declined. At this juncture, intra-regional FDI was on the rise. The developing country investors, those from Hong Kong, SAR, and Taiwan, accounted for a disproportionately large proportion of FDI in China until the mid-1990s. In the initial years China was known for weak contract laws and suffered from difficulties in the enforcement of contracts. Chinese diaspora communities in Hong Kong, SAR, and Taiwan felt privileged because they had old ties with the Chinese society and businesses and informal means and channels of enforcement of agreements. Therefore, FDI to China from these economies was large. Subsequently the proportion of FDI from these economies declined. An overwhelmingly large proportion, over 80 percent, of FDI flows to Asia originated in the advanced industrial economies (Brandt *et al.*, 2007). However, during the recent period there has been a significant spurt in the intra-regional FDI flows in the region. The principal driver was the active production and trade networks in the region.

China's success in attracting FDI is regarded as excessive. Many of the Asian neighbors realized that its large and growing FDI receipts were depriving them of FDI. The perception among the antagonists was that China was gaining at the expense of its Asian neighbors: China was eating their lunch. This was based on the assumption that FDI was a zero-sum game (Kramer, 2006; Chen, 2010). Some Asian governments, like Korea and Singapore, were strident in expressing their uneasiness on this count.

If this assumption was correct, then for every year in which there was an increase in FDI to China, there should have been a fall in FDI flows in the neighboring Asian economies. Empirical studies failed to establish such a correspondence, however. This assumption was flawed because there were periods when both ASEAN and China recorded higher FDI flows. For instance, one such period was 1989–97, when both shared an increasing FDI trend. In China's case FDI receipts soared from $3.4 billion to $44.0 billion, while for the ASEAN economies it soared from $7.6 billion to $27.0 billion (Das, 2007). These statistical data do not support the assumption that China has benefited at the expense of the other Asian economies.

That China was not pulling FDI at the expense of the other Asian economies can be shown by making a long-term comparison of FDI stock data. A comparison of quinquennial FDI statistics confirms that although China initially affected FDI inflows to the rest of the Asian economies adversely, the negative impact of this did not become a trend. During the 1990–94 quinquennium China's FDI stock averaged $43.9 billion a year, which reached $348.6 billion a year. For the ASEAN economies the corresponding amounts were $8.7 billion and $85 billion. Also, in the other developing Asian economies, the average annual FDI stock increased from $10.8 billion a year in the 1990–94 quinquennium to $55.7 billion a year in 2005–09 quinquennium.[9] Although China became increasingly important and attractive after the WTO accession, the FDI stock of the other Asian economies did not shrink.

Several regression analyses and other empirical exercises were attempted to resolve the issue of China crowding out FDI flows into the Asian economies. Regression analysis by Chantasasavat *et al.* (2005) attempted to estimate the impact of inward FDI flows into China on Hong Kong, SAR, Indonesia, Korea, Malaysia, the Philippines, Singapore, Taiwan and Thailand for data for 1985–2001. Their strategy was to control for all the standard explanatory variables of FDI in the Asian economies. To proxy for China's effect, they chose the level of FDI inflows into China. Their estimates found that the value of coefficient for inward FDI into China was positive and highly significant in all the specifications. They concluded that a 10 percent increase in FDI inflows into China would raise the level of FDI inflows into the eight Asian economies they considered for their study by 2 percent to 3 percent. Thus, the increases in FDI in China did not occur at the expense of the Asian economies but, if anything, they benefited from it. One obvious explanation for this increase was the regional production networks of which China gradually became an integral and active part. As the Asian economies were heavily involved in vertical trade specialization with China, their production processes were interconnected. Therefore, it was logical and feasible that an increase in FDI in China could lead to an increase in FDI in them. This complementarity hypothesis was based on the fact that the factors that made China a more attractive FDI destination also made other Asian economies more attractive destinations.

The same complementarity between China and the surrounding Asian economies was reported by Zhou and Lall (2005). Supporting this premise Ianchovichina and Walmsley (2005) argued that with China liberalizing FDI in flows, the investing MNCs began rationalizing their production processes in Asia, which in turn facilitated and encouraged complementary FDI flows into the Asian economies. Likewise Mercereau (2005) also concluded that China had not diverted FDI inflows from its

Asian neighbors. In his study Singapore and Myanmar (Burma) were the only two exceptions. His results regarding complementarity were similar to those arrived at by Chantasasavat *et al.* (2005).

Eichengreen and Tong (2007) and Wang *et al.* (2007) studied a larger number of Asian economies for estimating the impact of FDI inflows into China and found that owing to complementarities China may have crowded *in* FDI into the Asian economies not crowded *out*. They also explained complementarities by the vertical nature of production fragmentation in Asia. Another large empirical exercise concluded that the changing direction of FDI in Asia could lead to welfare losses in the ASEAN-4 economies "only if the ASEAN-4 economies fail to absorb new foreign technologies quickly and to engage in indigenous technical innovation" (McKibbin and Woo, 2003, p. 22). The ASEAN-4 economies remained technology conscious in the past. There is no reason why they should not continue to be so in the face of China's challenge.

Salike (2010) applied a dynamic panel model to investigate the crowding out effect of Japanese FDI going to Asian economies. He examined this with industry-level data on Japanese FDI. His results show a significant crowding out effect in three of the 12 industrial sectors, which included electronics and the electrical industry. In two industries a complementary effect was found, which included transport. Chemicals did not show any kind of impact. Salike (2010) also inferred that vertically fragmented industries in the region would benefit from China's rise and have a large receipt of FDI. Similarly, Chen's (2010) empirical regression results demonstrated that FDI inflows into China tended to have a statistically significant positive effect on FDI inflows into other Asian economies. The regression results also revealed that *ceteris paribus* marginal effect of the host countries location variables of FDI inflows was far greater than the China effect. The results of these empirical analyses demonstrate that China not only did not receive higher volumes of FDI at the expense of the other Asian economies, but also enabled them to benefit. On the whole, large FDI inflows into China had a significant positive and complementary effect on the Asian economies. It was caused by two factors, first, increased resource demand for a growing China and, second, deepened integration of production networks in China and its Asian neighbors (Chen, 2012).

China's neighbors are regarded as high-performing economies and have earned global accolades for their post-World War II economic dynamism. Many of them created successful niches for themselves in the global economy (Das, 2005). The NIEs did so even before China. Besides, China demonstrated eagerness for regional acceptance and was/is sensitive to allegations of disrupting and dislocating the performance of its neighboring economies. Since 2000, China has endeavored to manage its economic relations with them by proposing free trade agreements of different kinds. This lack of insouciance towards its neighbors' welfare demonstrates China's commitment not only to the lofty ideals of good neighborliness, but also to responsible conduct in the community of nations.

6. Lag in Asia's financial integration

Unlike the rest of the economy, capital and financial markets in China have been awaiting reforms. Capital controls still restrict flows of capital in and out of China. As for Asia, financial integration did not occur at a rapid pace. It was far slower than integration through trade and FDI channels and is still inadequate and lags behind real economy integration (Jang, 2011). One of the reasons behind this is underdeveloped financial infrastructure development. Correlation for real interest rates in the region is either small or even negative. Asian investors show a fairly strong "home bias"; that is, they invest in their respective domestic markets. Alternatively they tend to rush for global financial centers. Consequently, while cross-border equity and bond holdings within the region have been on the rise, Asian economies demonstrate greater financial integration with major extra-regional economies than those within the region.

Owing to growth in intra-regional trade and commitment to greater liberalization and financial market deregulation, capital mobility in Asia increased in the post-1990 period (Lee, 2008). However, greater intra-regional financial flows did not occur. East Asian economies and the Asian EMEs successfully forged stronger links with the global financial markets. Inter-regional financial links appear to be stronger than intra-regional ones. The post-1990 trend in the Asian economies was either to invest financial resources in their domestic markets or move them into the advanced economies, the EU and the USA. Consequently Asian economies, particularly the Asian EMEs grew more financially globalized than they were regionally integrated.

Kim and Lee (2012) estimated that the degree of regional financial integration in Asia is much less than the degree of global financial integration. This has been a long-term trend and did not change even after the Asian crisis (1997–98). An element of surprise here is that while Asia turned into a current account surplus region from a deficit region after the Asian crisis, this long-term trend persisted. Surplus savings of the Asian economies were characteristically invested globally. Although higher yields were available in the region, Asian investors preferred to pay intermediation costs and move their financial capital into the advanced economies. It was essentially invested in the safe US and European assets. Interestingly investors from the advanced economies chose risky but high-yielding Asian assets of their investment. In 2005 portfolio investment in the Asian economies from the other Asian economies was merely 10 percent of the of the regional portfolio holdings (Garcia-Herrero *et al.*, 2009). This went counter to the maxim of geographical proximity being an important determinant of cross-border capital flows. Market liquidity was an important factor that had an effect over the decisions of investors. Lack of liquidity in the Asian financial markets was an important causal factor that sent investors to the major global financial centers (Garcia-Herrero *et al.*, 2009).

The global financial crisis (2007–09), the uncertain US recovery and the ongoing Eurozone sovereign debt crisis rendered global financial markets weak and volatile, which had an impact the Asian investors and policy mandarins. Regional policy co-operation in financial and monetary areas expanded. Multilateralization and enlargement of the CMI was major outcome. Although a strong local bias continued to persist, Asian investors grew more savvy about regions. After 2008 cross-border flows of capital and banks claims increased in Asia. Cross-border equity holdings recorded a sharp increase. Much better growth prospect in the region succeeded in attracting the regional investors' decisions. According to ADB (2012) 23.7 percent of the region's cross-border assets were held in Asian equities and a smaller proportion (7.3 percent) in the Asian debt securities. Although these proportions are far lower than the proportion of intra-regional trade (55.5 percent) in Asia, they have begun to show an increase.

The post crisis environment in the global financial markets has had an understandable impact over the Asian investors. Asian stock markets became more financially integrated because the global markets were unattractive. However, building an integrated capital market in Asia is a work in progress. This applies particularly to banking and fixed income markets. If concerted endeavors are made to develop and deepen the regional financial markets, Asian investors could be drawn to investing in their own region and enhance its financial integration. The ABMI is an appropriate instrument for keeping Asian savings in Asia. In 2012 China, Japan and Korea decided to promote investment by their foreign reserve authorities in one another's government bonds. This would advance financial co-operation in the region.

7. Business and competitive environment in the region

How businesses and economies are run is important for regional integration. Streamlining of domestic business regulations and practices and enforcement of business laws, statutes and procedures are other factors that contribute to businesses and economies flourishing as well as smoothing the progress of integration of regional economies. The *Doing Business* indicators of the World Bank track the business friendliness of government rules. In general this scenario has improved and many countries and regions have been catching up with the advanced economies.

Table 5.1 provides a summary of the *Doing Business* indicators computed in 2012 (WB, 2013). This database annually provides the status of business conditions in each individual economy, that is, the level of efficiency and smoothness with which business can be conducted. Some countries in Asia performed extremely well. Six occur in the top 20. Several Asian economies succeeded in improving their business environment. For instance, China introduced a host of new regulations which brought its business environment closer to internal norms.

Singapore (1) and Hong Kong, SAR (2) were ranked the best in the world. Singapore topped the global ranking for the seventh consecutive year. Korea (8), Malaysia (12), Taiwan (16) and Thailand (18) also enjoyed high rankings. While Japan (24) did not belong in the top-tier rankings, it was a fairly competitive economy. In contrast, Indonesia (128) has a long way to go to improve its business environment. The Philippines (138) was at the bottom in this group of Asian economies. China (91) is marginally better than Vietnam, which was ranked 99. Although they have improved their rankings over the years, they need to focus concerted efforts on the improvement of their business environment. Table 5.2 summarizes import business regulatory practices in selected Asian economies.

As economies grow and transcend from one stage of growth to another, they become more competitive. Macro- and micro-economic policies, business regulations and institutions, *inter alia*, determine the level of competitiveness in such economies. It is obvious that the higher the competitiveness, the greater the productivity of the economy. Competitiveness also determines the rates of return on investment in physical and human capital in an economy. These rates of return are the fundamental drivers of the growth rates of the economy. A competitive economy usually has higher rates of medium- and long-term growth. The notion of competitiveness encompasses both static and dynamic components. A comprehensive index of national competitiveness, which captures both macro- and micro-components, is computed by the World Economic Forum (WEF).

Asia's emergence to economic prominence was accompanied by a remarkable dynamism in terms of escalating competitiveness of several economies. Measured by the global competitiveness index (GCI) many of them have performed well. China, Indonesia and Malaysia need to be particularly mentioned in this regard. Since 2000 they made conspicuous strides in the GCI computed by the World Economic Forum, Switzerland (Table 5.2). Eight Asian economies figured in the top-30 GIC rankings for 2011–12, with Singapore ranked at the second position in the world after Switzerland.

As shown in Table 5.2, Singapore is the most competitive economy in the region. Between 2000 and 2012 its GCI went up from 9 to 2. Japan also performed well during the period under consideration. Although Hong Kong, SAR is not an equal of Singapore, it has also recorded impressive gains. Unlike Taiwan, Korea has not shown a great deal of improvement during the period under consideration. Competitiveness in China steadily improved. It recorded impressive gains. It is the only BRIC country that reinforced its position within the top 30. China continued its steady advance in the rankings, rising to the 26th position in the latest rankings, from 44 in

TABLE 5.2 *Doing Business* Indicators, 2012: Measuring business regulations (rankings out of 185 economies)

	Japan	China	Hong Kong, SAR	Singapore	Korea	Taiwan	Indonesia	Malaysia	Philippines	Thailand	Vietnam
Ranking											
Economy overview	24	91	2	1	8	16	128	12	138	18	99
Starting a business	114	151	6	4	24	16	166	54	161	85	108
Procedures (number)	8	13	3	3	5	3	9	3	16	4	10
Times (days)	23	33	3	3	7	10	47	6	36	29	34
Cost (% of income per caput)	7.5	2.1	1.9	0.6	14.6	2.4	22.7	15.1	18.1	6.7	8.7
Paid-in Min. capital (% of income per caput)	0	85.7	0	0	0	0	42	0	4.8	0	0
Registering property	64	44	60	36	75	32	98	33	122	26	48
Procedures (number)	6	4	5	5	7	3	6	5	8	2	4
Times (days)	14	29	36	21	11	5	22	14	39	2	57
Cost (% of property value)	5.8	3.6	4.0	2.9	5.1	6.2	10.8	3.3	4.8	6.3	0.6
Getting credit	23	70	4	12	12	70	129	1	129	70	40
Strength of legal rights index (0–10)	7	6	10	10	8	5	3	10	4	5	8
Depth of credit information index (0–6)	6	4	5	4	6	5	4	6	3	5	4
Public registry coverage (% of adults)	0	27.7	0	0	0	0	36.0	56.1	0	0	37.8
Private bureau coverage (% of adults)	100	0	89.4	58.3	100	94.1	0	81.8	9	44.1	0
Protecting investors	19	100	3	2	49	32	49	4	128	13	169
Extent of disclosure index	7	10	10	10	7	9	10	10	2	10	6
Extent of director liability index (0–10)	6	1	8	9	4	5	5	9	3	7	1
Ease of shareholder suits index (0–10)	8	4	9	9	7	5	3	7	8	6	2
Strength of investor protection index (0–10)	7	5	9	9.3	6	5.3	6	8.7	4.3	7.7	3

TABLE 5.2 (CONTINUED)

	Japan	China	Hong Kong, SAR	Singapore	Korea	Taiwan	Indonesia	Malaysia	Philippines	Thailand	Vietnam
Paying taxes	127	122	4	5	30	54	131	15	143	96	138
Payments (number per year)	14	7	3	5	10	12	51	13	47	22	32
Time (hours per year)	330	338	78	82	207	221	259	133	193	264	872
Profit tax (%)	26.9	6.2	17.6	6	15.2	12.7	23.6	7.5	21.1	28.1	11.6
Labor tax and contributions (%)	17.4	49.6	5.3	17	13.2	18.6	10.6	15.6	11.3	5.7	22.6
Other taxes (%)	5.7	7.9	0.1	4.6	1.4	3.5	0.1	1.4	14.2	3.8	0.3
Total tax rate (% profit)	50	63.7	23	27.6	29.8	34.8	34.5	24.5	46.6	37.6	34.5
Trading across borders	19	68	2	1	3	23	37	11	53	20	166
Documents to export (number)	3	8	4	4	3	6	4	5	7	5	8
Time to export (days)	10	21	5	5	7	10	17	11	15	14	49
Cost to export (US$ per container)	880	580	575	456	665	655	644	435	585	585	2,590
Documents to import (number)	5	5	4	4	3	6	7	6	8	5	9
Time to import (days)	11	24	5	4	7	10	23	8	14	13	71
Cost to import (US$ per container)	970	615	565	439	695	720	660	420	660	750	2,868
Enforcing contracts	35	19	10	12	2	90	144	33	111	25	80
Procedures (number)	30	37	27	21	33	45	40	29	37	36	30
Times (days)	360	406	306	150	230	510	498	425	842	440	510
Cost (% of claim)	22.2	11.1	21.2	25.8	10.3	17.7	139.4	27.5	26	15	43.7
Closing a business	1	82	17	2	14	15	148	49	165	58	163
Recovery rate (cents on the dollar)	92.8	35.7	81.2	91.3	81.8	81.8	14.2	44.7	4.9	42.4	6.4
Time (years)	0.6	1.7	1.1	0.8	1.5	1.9	5.5	1.5	5.7	2.7	4
Cost (% of estate)	4	22	9	1	4	4	18	15	38	36	38

Source: World Bank, Doing Business Online Database 2013. Washington, DC.

2000. Its score and rank improved every year since 2005. Importantly China always led the BRIC group of large EMEs by a substantial margin. South Africa was the next BRIC economy in the GCI, which was placed 50th. Factors that were considered favorable for China and improved its GCI ranking included its macro-economic situation. It also ranked high in business sophistication and innovation, given its level of development. Corruption and judicial independence were the areas of weakness, which adversely affected China's competitiveness ranking (GCR, 2012). Rankings achieved by Malaysia were superior to those by Thailand. Vietnam has slipped and the Philippines performed poorly in this regard. In a rapidly integrating regional economy, the competitive economies affect the other regional partners by convincing them to invest more in physical and human capital and technology upgradation.

8. China and the ASEAN-Plus-Three (APT) Framework

The Japanese government was not only behind the Asian Monetary Fund (AMF) proposal but was also going to bankroll it. The AMF concept, an independent regional entity, was opposed by China. It was shelved in late 1997. The seed of the APT were sown in December 1997, in the backdrop of the failure of the AMF proposal. This was the period when a sense of regional identity and seeking regional solutions for regional problems was intensifying among the Asian economies. In Kuala Lumpur, Malaysia, an informal meeting of ASEAN leaders took place with the top political leaders of China, Japan and Korea. This was the genesis of the concept of the APT. It was the newest idea in regional economic cooperation and governance. Chinese government supported it with enormous zeal.

As China and Japan were the two economies holding the largest forex reserves in the region, it was logical to come up with the plan of including them and Korea to make an APT grouping.[10] The APT meetings at ministerial and deputy-ministerial level continue to be held. The issues that they cover include regional economy, trade, finance, investment, environment and transportation. This makes APT a significant regional institution. Special working groups have also been formed among the APT government officials. China remained an active participant in the APT meetings. In May 2011 the APT was upgraded. Comprehensive macro-economic policy co-operation in the region was accepted as an issue for the APT meetings. Finance ministers from the APT economies expanded the role of APT by including central bank governors in their meetings so that regional financial co-operation could be strengthened. The central bankers' presence in APT meetings followed the format of the Group of Twenty (G-20). This move would promote discussions on stabilization of the exchange rates of the regional currencies, including that of the renminbi.

In May 2000 during the Ministers of Finance meeting of the APT countries, held in Chiang Mai, Thailand, the CMI was put together. It was the first ever regional agreement involving banking and finance and was made by 13 APT economies. The CMI was an innovative initiative of a network of bilateral swaps intended for mutual assistance among the APT economies at the time of any future crises. Its objective was to address balance of payments and short-term liquidity difficulties of the APT countries. They agreed to draw on each other's dollar reserves to cover sudden outflows of foreign currency. The regional economies agreed to help and support each other through a network of currency swaps. In a future crisis situation they intended to depend less heavily on the IMF or World Bank assistance. Although this issue generated impassioned debate, the CMI was not made a regional alternative of the IMF. Asian economies did not repudiate access to the stand-by facility of the IMF. The expectation was that the CMI will provide emergency dollar liquidity to the APT economies in a currency crisis and serve as a regional crisis prevention and resolution mechanism. It was to be a second or parallel line of defense along with the IMF for the Asian economies.

An important benefit of the CMI was that it enabled regional financial resources to be utilized for meeting the needs of the regional economies in times of financial stress. In the aftermath of the global financial crisis, in May 2010, during the finance ministers' meeting of the APT countries, held in Chiang Mai, extension of CMI as the CMIM was agreed. It became a multilateral currency swap agreement. It was regarded as a step forward and a move towards creation of an AMF, which would be independent of the IMF. Its size of the currency swap was increased to $120 billion. The ratio of contributions was as follows: 80 percent coming from Japan, China and Korea and the balance 20 percent from the ASEAN countries. The CMIM was an important high point. It signaled the maturing of APT co-operation (Grimes, 2011). Under the CMIM, a country could draw up to 20 percent of its quota without being subjected to the IMF conditionality for a maximum period of six months. Any borrowing larger than 20 percent would be tied to the IMF program conditionality (Aizenman *et al.*, 2010; Sussangkarn, 2011).

The significance of a swap line is that it acts to stabilize market concerns in a period when there are deleveraging pressures, which in turn cause pressure on international reserves and exchange rates (Aizenman *et al.*, 2010). Therefore, during the global financial crisis (2007–09), there was a possibility that some Asian central banks might draw on their CMI or CMIM swap lines. This would have made the CMIM more important and demonstrated that the Asian governments were serious about financial co-operation. However, no Asian economies so far drew on their bilateral swap lines. They were protected from the global financial crisis and the sovereign debt crisis (2010–12) of the Eurozone largely by their own sagacious and thoughtful macro-economic and financial policy frameworks as well as their substantive forex accumulations. Given this backdrop, runs on Asian currencies were highly unlikely, if not impossible. Besides, the conservative fiscal policies pursued by them provided them with large fiscal space to maneuver.

However, the global financial crisis did reveal cracks in the evolving, if untested, regional financial institutions in Asia. Although Korea and Singapore were the members of APT and entitled to utilizing the CMI, in the fall of 2008 they turned to the Federal Reserve Board to insure financial stability. Did that mean that the APT economies regarded CMI as inappropriate for their purpose? A defensive argument was that Fed's assistance was sought simply due to operational reasons by the two APT economies. The Bank of Korea needed dollar liquidity for its banking system while the CMI swap lines were denominated in yen-won, renminbi-won and renminbi-yen (Grimes, 2011).

The Eurozone sovereign debt crisis of 2011 escalated the global economic and financial uncertainties in 2012. A taskforce decided that CMIM was regarded as insufficient and that more liquidity was needed for emergencies. In May 2012 CMIM was revised again. The APT Ministers of Finance unanimously decided to double the size of currency swaps to $240 billion. They did not change the ratio of contributions. However, a borrowing country can now draw up to 30 percent of its quota without being subjected to the IMF conditionality for a maximum period of six months. The APT Ministers of Finance also envisioned a longer term role for the CMIM in terms of giving long-term proactive advice to the member economies regarding how to prevent problems.

Although Japan took a great deal of active interest in CMI and CMIM, the strong rivalry between China and Japan for the position of the first director of the APT Macroeconomic Research Office (AMRO) culminated in favor of China in May 2011.[11] AMRO is the CMIM's macro-economic surveillance secretariat. It is designed to have strong professional and analytical expertise and policy experience. The newly established AMRO is a critical component of the emerging regional architecture (Menon, 2012). The region needed an institution with strong professional skills and competence. Although China, Japan and Korea have bankrolled this regional surveillance institution, China's leadership emblematically put it in the position of providing regional public good. At this point the APT Ministers of Finance also decided to double the size of the CMIM to $240 billion.

9. Multinationals' operations and Asia's integration

Over the last two decades, MNE operations in Asia became increasingly significant. Rapidly growing MNE operations played a decisive role in integrating Asian economies in a market-led or *de facto* manner. MNEs are highly resourceful business organizations which can mobilize resources across borders, in different regions of the global economy through vertical and horizontal networks of procurements, production, distribution and marketing. Consequently their operations result in both regional and global integration. Various rounds of multilateral trade negotiations under the sponsorship of the GATT/WTO system successfully liberalized multilateral trade and foreign investment flows. They facilitated MNE operations. They received further support from the ICT revolution as well as steadily declining costs of transportation. They successfully became agents of promoting both regionalization and globalization. Global operations of the so-called *Forbes* Global-2000—the top 2,000 business firms—have expanded at an exceedingly rapid pace since 2000. Their affiliate in different countries account for well over one-third of multilateral trade and their operations led to a significant increase in intra-industry trade (UNCTAD, 2002).

One common trend of MNEs in Asia was that they accounted for larger shares of trade and production in comparison to shares of employment. This reflected their higher productivity levels than their local counterparts. They also exported relatively larger proportions of their output than did their local counterparts (Dunning and Lundan, 2008; Ramstetter, 2012). Large MNEs not only substantially increased intra-subsidiary trade in Asia but also are responsible for the allocation of interconnected regional FDI. Huang and Wang (2011) computed the correlation coefficient to conclude that large MNC presence is related to higher intra-regional FDI flows. As MNEs are financially more stable than other business enterprises, they are usually able to exploit export and investment opportunities better than other enterprises. For instance, during the Asian crisis they were able to exploit the exchange rate variations and decline in asset prices to their advantage.

China and surrounding Asian economies became an important geographical locale for the MNE investment and operations. China's rapid growth made the region more attractive for the MNEs and further dynamism was added to region-wide MNE operations. Expanding MNE operation in the region played a pivotal role in the continued dynamism of Asia and the growth of intra-regional economic interdependence. MNEs are veritable agents of regionalization and globalization through their vast production networks. This dynamic promoted regional and global convergence and integration. Athukorala (2011b) posited that the strong growth of MNC operations and with that production networks indisputably depended on the region's extra-regional trade, which is likely to remain the engine of growth for Asia in the near future.

10. China as an engine for growth in Asia

As China became the largest economy in the region, its impact over the neighboring Asian economies would be logically greater than before. Whether it will be an engine of growth for Asia became a legitimate query. China's market-led economic integration with its neighboring Asian economies has advanced far more than with the other sub-regions of Asia—such as South Asia. Therefore it is rational to expect that imports of the large Chinese economy from these sub-regions—the NIEs and ASEAN—will have a relatively more positive relationship with the output growth in these economies. A vector autoregression (VAR) exercise was conducted by Haltmaier *et al.* (2007) to find the impact of import demand from China and the USA on the Asian economy. The sample countries for this empirical exercise were the four NIEs and the ASEAN-4 economies. Their results showed that external demand played a major role in domestic output fluctuations in the sample economies. Also, import demand from China was found to be as important as that from the USA in explaining the domestic growth fluctuations in the Asian economies. Both the results were still valid when possibility of demand from China was regarded as a derived demand, that is, it was considered to be based on the final demand for the Chinese exports to the USA.

The same VAR model was used by the ADB (2009) for a longer (1990–2008) quarterly data series for a larger group of Asian economies. In view of its large and growing economic weight, India was added to the previous group of sample countries. The most significant result of this empirical exercise was that Chinese import demand was a more important source of GDP fluctuations than the USA in five (Hong Kong, SAR, Indonesia, the Philippines, Taiwan and Thailand) out of nine sample countries. These two empirical exercises did lend support to China-as-an-engine-for-growth hypothesis for Asia. No doubt China's growth engine role varied from economy to economy. There was no uniformity in it. For instance, China's demand did not affect Indian GDP growth but it was hugely important for Singapore. Thus, empirical evidence proves the "China as an engine of growth" hypothesis without a doubt. However, this favorable impact of China "reflects US demand for Asian goods, rather than independent demand from China" (ADB, 2009, p. 46).

The influence of China's rapid growth on the macro-economies and terms of trade (TOT) of the neighboring Asia was estimated with the help of a computable general equilibrium (CGE) model. This empirical study took 11 individual Asian countries and the ROW for assessment (Mai *et al.*, 2010). One significant advantage of using the CGE framework was that it represents detailed structure of the selected economies. Although impact of rapid growth in China on the neighboring Asian economies was found to vary, it was found to lead to a smaller increase in their real gross national product (GNP) than in their real GDP.[12] This difference can be explained by each individual economy's TOT. An improvement in the TOT will cause GNP to increase relative to real GDP, and *vice versa*.

Estimates revealed that ebullient growth in China has both a positive and a negative impact over the TOT of the neighboring Asian economies. Simulations were conducted using MONASH Multi-Country (MMC) model.[13] This model is a global dynamic CGE model of 11 countries and ROW. Simulation results revealed that China's technological convergence and the resulting rapid economic growth would lead to, first, and increase in world prices of energy and primary inputs, second, decrease the world prices of manufactured goods and third, would cause a strong expansion in world trade. The last named effect will cause an increase in the world prices of exports of services, such as transportation and financial services. However, the effects on world prices would have both positive and negative effects on the TOT of the neighboring economies. Whether it will be a positive effect or a negative effect will necessarily depend on each country's economic structure. For a summary of negative and positive TOT effects (see table 24 of Mai *et al.*, 2010).

The simulation exercise also demonstrated that the neighboring Asian economies were quick thinkers and rapid movers. They responded ingeniously and skillfully to the rapid growth in China by expanding their trade and investment links with it. A deepening of production networks was one of the results. This in turn strengthened the positive effects on their TOT. End result was a small improvement in overall improvement on their TOT, which occurred despite the increase in the world price for energy and primary inputs.

The preceding section explained how the structure of Asian trade evolved in the recent past, particularly the sharp growth in China's trade in parts, components and sub-assemblies with the neighboring Asian economies. Apparently, this kind of increasing trade enabled Asian economies to capitalize on regional division of labor and benefit from it. However, it cannot possibly make China a strong source of demand and growth for them. It is open to doubt whether China can become an engine of regional growth and bring about recovery when needed or support long-term growth for the regional economies. The import demand for products for final consumption is more relevant for this purpose.

Recent empirical evidence suggests that import demand for such products from China has been on the rise. The proportion of these products in China's imports from the neighboring Asian economies exceeds that of parts and components (Park and Shin, 2010). This proves that China's role as a consumer has been increasing for its Asian neighbors. This on-going structural transformation in China's imports from the region holds hope that to a limited degree import demand from China could help in offsetting the impact of negative extra-regional shocks such as the global financial crisis of 2007–09. China is growing into an independent source of demand for the Asian economies and therefore a source of future growth. In 2011 it was the "bright spot" of the global economy (Lipsky, 2011). Its GDP growth rate was 9.3 percent. In 2012 it declined marginally to 9.0 percent (Table 5.3, Figures 5.1a and 5.1b). The corresponding statistics for the advanced economies were 1.6 percent and 1.2 percent, respectively (IMF, 2013).[14] Projections for 2013 for Asian are 5.7, while those for advanced economy are 1.2 percent.

As the US economy is recovering rather tepidly from the global economic crisis (2007–09) and soon thereafter the Eurozone was finding it difficult to tame its sovereign debt crisis, the Asian economies, particularly those in East and Southeast Asia are reasonably thinking of the large Chinese market picking up the slack in their exports to these two large markets. Export volumes of the Asian economies from these two sub-regions during the global downturn declined substantially, ranging

TABLE 5.3 Global competitiveness index of selected Asian economies, 2000–12

	2000	2005	2010	2011	2012
Japan	14	10	8	6	9
China	44	48	29	27	26
Hong Kong, SAR	16	14	11	11	11
Singapore	9	5	3	3	2
Korea	27	19	19	22	24
Taiwan	21	8	12	13	13
Indonesia	47	69	54	44	46
Malaysia	30	25	24	26	21
Philippines	46	73	87	85	75
Thailand	40	33	36	38	39
Vietnam	73	74	75	59	65
Total number of countries considered	58	125	131	139	142

Source: World Economic Forum (WEF). *The Global Competitiveness Report 2011–2012* and various earlier issues. Geneva, Switzerland.

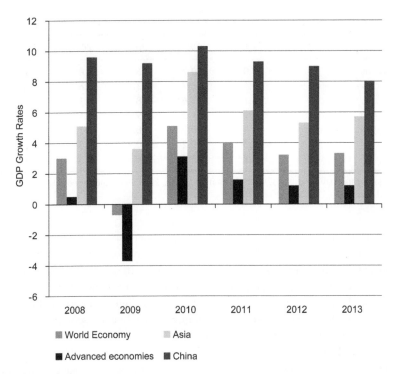

FIGURE 5.1(A) GDP growth rate comparison 2008–12
Source: International Monetary Fund. 2013. World Economic Outlook, 2013, April, and previous Issues.

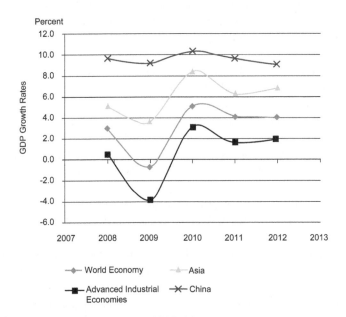

FIGURE 5.1(B) GDP growth rate comparison, 2008–12
Source: International Monetary Fund. 2013. World Economic Outlook, 2013, April, and previous Issues.

TABLE 5.4 GDP growth rate comparison, 2008–13 (year on year) (as a percentage)

	2008	2009	2010	2011	2012	2013P
1. World economy	3.0	−0.7	5.1	4.0	3.2	3.3
2. Advanced economies	0.5	−3.7	3.1	1.6	1.2	1.2
3. Asia	5.1	3.6	8.6	6.1	5.3	5.7
4. Developing Asia	7.9	7.2	9.5	8.1	6.6	7.1
5. Newly industrialized economies	1.8	−0.7	8.4	4.7	4.5	N/A
6. China	9.6	9.2	10.3	9.3	9.0	8.0
7. ASEAN–5	4.7	1.7	6.9	4.5	6.1	5.9

Source: International Monetary Fund. 2013. World Economic Outlook, 2013, April, and previous Issues.
Note: P = projections.

between 10 percent and 50 percent. For most of these Asian economies they recovered fully, in some cases even more than fully, in 2010. This strong recovery portends to the trade links of these Asian economies with China. Trade is an important channel that through which the Chinese economy influences GDP growth in the region. If China works as an engine of growth for the Asian economies, there should be a positive relationship between China's imports and the GDP of the individual neighboring economies. The size of impact that China's imports would have on this individual Asian economy's GDP is an important variable to measure. Also, one needs to find how the size of this variable evolves over the years. If the size of the impact variable is comparable to that of the US imports, then one can say that China is or can be the second engine of growth for Asia.

When this hypothesis was econometrically tested by Park and Shin (2011), they inferred that in the short term China's imports did have an independent and positive impact on its neighbors' GDP growth. For many of them China had a quantitatively comparable impact on the GDP of the Asian economies to exports of the Asian economies to the USA. However, interestingly in the long term, China's positive impact on its neighbors' GDP growth had a close relationship with US demand. It was the US demand for final goods that drove China's demand for parts, components and intermediate goods from the neighboring Asian economies.

The regional economic scenario has evolved in a significant manner in the recent past, in that it has enhanced the regional presence and impact of the Chinese economy. Notable is the declining importance of Japan as a major driver of industrial upgrading and economic growth in Asia. For a short time, the global financial crisis (2007–09) weakened the Asian NIEs and lessened their regional clout. In contrast, China's role in the region expanded. It has been playing a multifaceted role in the ongoing process of industrial restructuring and upgrading in Asia. It became an important source of capital and technology for its neighboring economies. Industrial upgrading that took place in China not only affected its growth trajectory but also that of the regional neighbors. Also, low-end export-oriented manufacturing industries have begun shifting from the coastal regions of China to a number of Asian economies (WIR, 2010).

A related development in this regard is declining incidence of poverty, defined as percentage of population living below $1.25 a day in 2005 PPP, over 1981–2008. Asia made dramatic progress in poverty alleviation. Over the last three decades Asia, particularly China, went through an unprecedented poverty reduction. This means that growth was inclusive. In 1981 Asia suffered from the highest incidence of poverty in the world, with 77.2 percent population living below $1.25 a day. In 1990 this proportion declined sharply to 56.28 percent and in 1999 further to 35.6 percent. In 2008 it was down to 14.3 percent. This achievement is creditable, *a fortiori* in the back drop of two severe financial and economic crises that occurred during this time span. Half the long-term rate of decline in poverty is attributable to one country alone. In China the proportion of the population living below the poverty line during 1981–2008 declined from 84 percent to 13.1 percent. That implies that China accounted for the largest share of the long-term improvement in poverty mitigation; it took 662 million people out of poverty since 1981.[15]

11. Summary and conclusions

This chapter has explored the relationship between China and the surrounding Asian economies. It delved into their *de facto* economic interaction and dynamics. It examined how China is influencing its neighboring Asian economies and attempted to establish whether their economic relationship is synergetic and a market- and institution-led symbiosis. Of the two, the symbiotic relationship has been more market-driven than institution-driven. In following this trend, Asian economies conformed to their past pattern and predilection. That said, the political factors have recently begun reinforcing this trend and their impact is on the rise in the enhancing interaction between Asia and China. This chapter concludes that China has been influencing the pace of economic growth in the rest of Asia for close to two decades. As the 21st century dawned, China began to appear a major driver of regional economic growth.

When the Chinese economy began its resurgence to become the largest regional economy, some of its smaller neighboring Asian economies were on their way to being among the "miracle" economies of the future. As Chinese GDP growth gained momentum, it began influencing its Asian neighbors in a significant manner. The two groups that were affected most due to China's rapid growth were Japan and the NIEs on the one hand and the ASEAN economies on the other. China becoming a regional economic powerhouse was unquestionably a significant and sensitive issue. Although during the pre-reform era China did not have close economic and political relations with its Asian neighbors, during the reform period Chinese political leadership consciously decided to engage and co-operate with the surrounding regional economies.

China adopted an open trade policy stance. It also unilaterally reduced its tariffs rates and non-tariff barriers. Keeping the economy open was instrumental integrating it with its Asian neighbors and in cultivating regional and global interdependence. Developing a close APT grouping and strengthening it was another policy measure that brought China close to the regional economies. The APT network was instrumental in developing a sense of regional identity. This regional framework also made it feasible to seek regional solutions for regional economic and financial problems. It was a functional and valuable regional public good.

International trade and FDI were two of the most important channels that integrated China with its regional neighbors. Trade among the East and Southeast Asian economies, which included China, began increasing in the 1980s. With the passage of time a China "threat" or "fear" perception developed in Asia. It implied that China was crowding out exports of the other Asian economies in the world marketplace. Also, as China became the most attractive FDI destination among the developing countries, it was believed that China was receiving FDI at the expense of the other Asian economies. These concerns were examined by several empirical studies and the conclusion was that they were grossly exaggerated.

Although a latecomer, China adopted vertical fragmentation of production in the region. Soon it came to be an important part of regional production networks. Over the last two decades, Asian economies became highly active and successful in innovative regional co-operation through production networks. Owing to rapid expansion, intra-regional trade in parts, components, sub-assemblies and intermediate products has increased swiftly in recent decades. Regional and global production networks in Asia existed before the emergence of China as a hub, or central assembly platform. However, with the rise of the Chinese economy a new dimension has been added to Asia's standing within global production networks. Trading activity by global production networks rose steadily since the early 1990s. Production networks in Asia and China have also successfully enhanced their status in international trade. In that context the dynamism of the Chinese economy has assisted the Asian economies. Thus, evidence abounds that the rapid growth of China added to the dynamism of the surrounding Asian economies and the two have now developed a market-driven symbiotic relationship. China serves as an engine for regional growth.

Notes

1 ASEAN-Plus-Three (APT) comprises the 10 members of ASEAN, plus China, Japan and Korea.
2 Malaysia and Thailand provide two good examples of the growth slowdown that characterizes a middle-income trap. Many such middle-income countries failed to move up the value chain and resume rapid growth by breaking into fast-growing markets for knowledge and innovation-based services.
3 They are Hong Kong, SAR, Korea (Republic of), Singapore and Taiwan.
4 The source of these statistical data is Coxhead (2007).
5 Source of these data is the Ministry of Commerce (MOFCOM), of the China. Available online at http://english.mofcom.gov.cn/static/column/statistic/lanmubb.ASEAN.html/1. Accessed on 15 April 2012.
6 There is little surprise in secular terms-of-trade decline of China. As explained in box 1.3 (IMF, 2012b), comparable trends were observed in the other rapidly growing Asian economies as well. It is borne out by the history of development of Japan and the four NIEs. They also recorded similar and lasting terms-of-trade deterioration as they gained significant global export shares.
7 See Figure 1 in Ando and Fukunari (2011).
8 See Gill and Kharas (2007) in which the two authors delve into regional integration through accelerating trade, financial flows and technological linkages.
9 The source of these statistical data is Table 2.3.1 in ADB (2011), p. 66.
10 At the end of September 2012 China's forex reserves were $3.29 trillion and Japan's $1.28 trillion. Korea was the seventh largest forex holder in the region with $316.8 billion.
11 Although Japan had a strong young candidate in Yoichi Nemoto, the hard-fought diplomatic battle ended in favor of Wei Benhua. A compromise was reached between China and Japan. Wei Benhua will be the first director of AMRO.
12 See the First row in Mai et al. (2010), Table 23, p. 115.
13 Description of MONASH Multi-Country (MMC) model is not necessary here, but those interested can refer to Mai (2004).
14 See IMF (2013), Table 1, p. 2.
15 The source of these data is the World Bank, PovertyNet. Available online at www.povertynet.org.

References

Aizenman, J., Y. Jinjarak and D. Park. 2010. "International Reserves and Swap Lines: Substitutes or Compliments?" Cambridge, MA: National Bureau of Economic Research. Working Paper No. 15804. March.

Aleksynska, M. and O. Havrylchyk. 2011. "FDI from the South: The Role of Institutional Distance and Natural Resources." Paris: Centre d'Études Prospectives et d'Informations Internationales. Working Paper No. 2011–05. March.

Amann, E., B. Lau and F. Nixson. 2009. "Did China Hurt the Textiles and Clothing Exports of Other Asian Countries?" *Oxford Development Studies*. Vol. 37. No. 4. pp. 333–62.

Amighini, A. 2005. "China in International Fragmentation of Production: Evidence from the ICT Industry." *European Journal of Comparative Economics*. Vol. 2. No. 2, pp. 203–19.

Ando, M. and K. Fukunari. 2011. "Globalizing Corporate Activities in East Asia and Impact on Domestic Operations." Tokyo: Research Institute of Economy, Trade and Industry. Discussion Paper No. 11-E-034. March.

Ando, M. and F. Kimura. 2009. "Fragmentation in East Asia: Further evidence." Tokyo: Economic Research Institute for ASEAN and East Asia. ERICA Discussion Paper Series No. 2009–20. October.

Ando, A. and F. Kimura. 2005. "The Formation of International Production and Distribution Networks in East Asia", in T. Ito and A. Rose (eds.) *International Trade*. Chicago, IL: University of Chicago Press, pp. 177–213.

Arndt, S. W. 2008. "Production Networks and the Open Economy." *Singapore Economic Review*. Vol. 53. No. 3, pp. 509–21.

Asian Development Bank (ADB). 2012. *Asian Economic Integration Monitor*. Manila, the Philippines. July.

——2011. *Asian Development Outlook 2011*. Manila, Philippines. April.

——2009. *Asian Development Outlook 2009 Update*. Manila, Philippines. September.

Athukorala, P. C. 2010. "The Rise of China and East Asian Export Performance", in P. C. Athukorala (ed.). *The Rise of Asia*. London and New York: Routledge, pp. 267–91.

——2011a. *Asian Trade Flows: Trends, Patterns and Projections*. Working Paper No. 2011/05, March. Australian National University, Crawford School of Economics and Government, Canberra.

——2011b. "Production Networks and Trade Patterns in East Asia." *Asian Economic Papers*. Vol. 10. No. 1, pp. 65–95.

——2009. "The Rise of China and East Asian Export Performance." *The World Economy*. Vol. 32. No. 2, pp. 234–66.

Athukorala, P. C. and H. Hill. 2010. "Asian Trade and Investment", in P. C. Athukorala (ed.). *The Rise of Asia*. London and New York: Routledge, pp. 11–57.

Athukorala, P. C. and J. Menon. 2010. *Global Production Sharing, Trade Patterns and Determinants of Trade Flows*. Working Paper No. 2010/06. July. Australian National University, Crawford School of Economics and Government, Canberra.

Brandt, L., T. G. Rawski and X. Zhu. 2007. "International Dimension of China's Long-Term Boom", in W. W. Keller and T. G. Rawski (eds). *China's Rise and Balance of Influence in Asia*. Pittsburgh, PA: Pittsburgh University Press, pp. 14–46.

Breslin, S. 2009. "Understanding China's Regional Rise: Interpretations, Identities and Implications." *International Affairs*. Vol. 85. No. 4, pp. 817–35.

Buiter, W. H. and E. Rahbari. 2011. "Global Growth Generators: Moving beyond Emerging Markets and BRICs." *Policy Insight*. No. 55. London: Center for Economic Policy Research. April.

Chantasasavat, B., K. C. Fung, H. Lizaka and A. Siu. 2005. "The Giant Sucking Sound: Is China Diverting Foreign Direct Investment from Other Asian Economies?" *Asian Economic Papers*. Vol. 3. No. 3, pp. 122–40.

Chen, C. 2012. *Foreign Direct Investment in China*. Cheltenham: Edward Elgar.

——2010. "Asian Foreign Direct Investment and the 'China Effect'", in R. Garnaut, J. Golley and L. Song (eds). *China: The Next Twenty Years of Reform and Development*. Australian National University Press, pp. 221–37.

Coxhead, I. 2007. "A New Resource Curse? Impact of China's Boom on Comparative Advantage and Resource Dependence in Southeast Asia." *World Development*. Vol. 35. No. 7, pp. 1109–19.

Das, Dilip K. 1992. *The Yen Appreciation and the International Economy*, London: Macmillan Press, and New York: New York University Press.

——2005. *Asian Economy and Finance: A Post-Crisis Perspective*. New York: Springer Publications.

——2007. "Foreign Direct Investment in China: Its Impact on the Neighboring Asian Economies." *Asian Business and Management*. Vol. 6. No. 3, pp. 285–302.

——2008a. *The Chinese Economic Renaissance: Apocalypse or Cornucopia*. Basingstoke: Palgrave Macmillan.

——2008b. *The Chinese Economy: Making a Global Niche*. Working Paper No. 239. March. Centre for the Study of Globalization and Regionalization, University of Warwick, Coventry.

——2011a. *Asian Economy: Spearheading the Recovery from the Global Financial Crisis*. London and New York: Routledge.

——2011b. "China: Epitome of an Emerging Market." *Journal of Emerging Knowledge on Emerging Markets*. 2011. Vol. 3. No. 1, pp. 57–81.

——2011c. "China in the Domain of International Business", in M. Warner (ed.). *Management in China*. Amsterdam: IOS Press, pp. 71–84.

——2012. "The Eurozone Financial Crisis and the Resilience of Asia's Economies." Daejeon, Korea. SolBridge International School of Business. Institute of Asian Business. Research Paper No. 2012–02. 15 April.

DeCarlo, S. 2012. "The World's Biggest Companies." *Forbes*. April.

Devadason, E. S. 2011. "Reorganization of Intra-ASEAN-5 Trade Flows: The China Factor." *Asian Economic Journal*. Vol. 25. No. 2, pp. 129–49.

Eichengreen, B. S. and H. Tong. 2007. "Is China's FDI Coming at the Expense of Other Countries?" *Journal of Japanese and International Economics*. Vol. 21. No. 1, pp. 153–72.

Dunning, J. H. and S. M. Lundan. 2008. *Multinational Enterprises and the Global Economy*. 2nd edition. Cheltenham: Edward Elgar.

Eichengreen, B. S., Y. Rhee and H. Tong. 2007. "China and the Exports of Other Asian Countries." *Review of World Economics*. Vol. 143. No. 2, pp. 201–26.

Ferrarini, B. 2011. "Mapping Vertical Trade." Manila: Asian Development Bank. Working Paper No. 263. June.

Findlay, R. and K. H. O'Rourke. 2007. *Power and Plenty: Trade, War and the World Economy in the Second Millennium*. Princeton, NJ: Princeton University Press.

Frankel, J. 2011. "Historical Precedents for Internationalization of the RMB." Washington, DC: Council on Foreign Relations. November.

Gao, T. 2005. "Foreign Direct Investment from Developing Asia." *Economic Letters*. Vol. 86. No. 1, pp. 29–35.

Garnaut, R. and L. Song. 2006. *The Turning Point in China's Economic Development*. Canberra: Asia Pacific Press.

Gaulier, G., F. Lemoine and D. Unal-Kesencu. 2009. "China's Integration in East Asia: Production Sharing." Paris: Centre d'études Prospectives et d'Informations Internationales. Working Paper No. 2005–9. June.

Garcia-Herrero, A., P. Wooldridge and D. Y. Yang. 2009. "Why Don't Asians Invest in Asia? The Determinants of Cross-Border Portfolio Holdings." *Asian Economic Papers*. Vol. 8. No. 3, pp. 228–46.

Gill, I. and H. J. Kharas. 2007. *An East Asian Renaissance*. Washington, DC: World Bank.

Gilman, D. B. 2010. "The New Geography of Global Innovation." New York: Global Markets Institute. 20 September.

Global Competitiveness Report 2011–2012 (GCR). 2012. Geneva. Switzerland. World Economic Forum.

Global Competitiveness Report 2010–2011 (GCR). 2011. Geneva, Switzerland: World Economic Forum.

Greenaway, D., A. Mahabir and C. Milner. 2008. "Has China Displaced Other Asian Countries' Exports?" *China Economic Review*. Vol. 19. No. 1, pp. 152–69.

Grimes, W. W. 2011. "The Asian Monetary Fund Reborn?" *Asia Policy*. Vol. 11. No. 1, pp. 79–104.

Haddad, M. 2007. *Trade Integration in East Asia: The Role of China and Production Networks*. Policy Research Working Paper No. 4160. March. Washington, DC: World Bank.

Haltmaier, J., S. Ahmad, B. Coulibaly, R. Knippenberg, S. Leduc, M. Marazzi and A. Wilson. 2007. "The Role of China in Asia: Engine, Conduit or Steamroller?" *International Finance*. Washington, DC: Board of Governors of the Federal Reserve System. Discussion Paper No. 904. September.

Hattari, R. and R. S. Rajan. 2009. "Understanding Bilateral FDI Flows in Developing Asia." *Asia Pacific Economic Literature*. Vol. 23. No. 2, pp. 73–93.

Huang, Y. 2012a. "In the Middle Kingdom's Shadow." *The Wall Street Journal*. 27 March, p. 13.

——2012b. "China's Economic Rise: Opportunities or Threat for East Asia?" *East Asia Forum*. 20 May. Available online at www.eastasiaforum.org/2012/05/20/chinas-economic-rise-opportunity-or-threat-for-east-asia.

Huang, Y. and X. Wang. 2011. "Does Financial Repression Inhibit or Facilitate Economic Growth? A Case Study of Chinese Reform Experience." *Oxford Bulletin of Economics and Statistics*, Vol. 73. No. 4, pp. 833–855.

Hummels, D., J. Ishii and K. M. Yi. 2001. "The Nature and Growth of Vertical Specialization in World Trade." *Journal of International Economics*. Vol. 54. No. 1, pp. 75–96.

Ianchovichina, E. and T. Walmsley. 2005. "Impact of China's WTO Accession on East Asia." *Contemporary Economic Policy*. Vol. 23. No. 2, pp. 261–77.

International Monetary Fund (IMF). 2013. "World Economic Outlook." Washington, DC. April.

——2012a. "World Economic Outlook." Washington, DC. October.

——2012b. "World Economic Outlook." Washington, DC. April.

——2011a. "Regional Economic Outlook: Asia and Pacific." Washington, DC. April.

——2011b. "World Economic Outlook." Washington, DC. September.

Ito, T. 2012. "The Internationalization of the RMB." CGS/IIGG Working Paper. The Council on Foreign Relations. November.

Jang, H. B. 2011. "Financial Integration and Cooperation in East Asia." Tokyo: Institute for Monetary and Economic Studies. Bank of Japan. Discussion Paper No. 2011-E5. February.

Japan External Trade Organization (JETRO). 2011. *JETRO Global Trade and Investment Report*. Tokyo, Japan.

Kharas, H. J. 2010. "The Emerging Middle Class in Developing Countries." Paris: Organization for Economic Co-operation and Development. The Development Center. Working Paper No. 285. January.

Kim, S. and J. W. Lee. 2012. "Real and Financial Integration in East Asia." *Review of International Economics*. Vol. 20. No. 2, pp. 332–49.

Kim, S., J. H. Lee and C. Y. Park. 2011. "Emerging Asia: Decoupling or Recoupling." *The World Economy*. Vol. 34. No. 1, pp. 23–53.

Kimura, F. 2006. "International Production and Distribution Networks in East Asia: Eight Facts." *Asian Economic Policy Review*. Vol. 1. No. 2, pp. 326–44.

King, M. 2012. "Major Growth Forecast for ASEAN-China Trade." *The Journal of Commerce Online*. Available online at www.joc.com/global-trade/major-growth-forecast-asean-china-trade. Posted on 24 April.

Kittilaksanawong, W. 2011. "FDI in High-Tech Firms from Newly Industrialized Economies in Emerging Markets." *African Journal of Business Management*. Vol. 5. No. 4, pp. 1146–57.

Kong, Y. F. and R. Kneller. 2012. "China's Export Expansion: A Threat to Its Asian Neighbors?" Paper presented at the conference on *Trade, Investment and Production Networks in Asia* at the University of Nottingham, Kuala Lumpur campus. Malaysia, 15–16 February.

Kramer, C. 2006. "Asia's Investment Puzzle." *Finance and Development*. Vol. 43. No. 2, pp. 38–46.

Lall, S. and M. Albaladejo. 2004. "China's Competitive Performance: A Threat to East Asian Manufacturing Exports?" *World Development*. Vol. 39. No. 9, pp. 1441–66.

Lau, B. K. F. 2007. "The Post-ATC Scenario for Asian Exporters." Paper presented at the 85th Textile Institute World Conference held in Colombo, Sri Lanka, 1–3 March.

Lawrence, R. Z., M. Drzeniek and S. Doherty. 2012. *The Global Enabling Trade Report 2012*. Geneva: World Economic Forum.

Lee, H. H., D. Park and J. Wang. 2011. "The Role of People's Republic of China in International Fragmentation of Production Networks." Manila, the Philippines: Asian Development Bank. Working Paper No. 87. September.

Lee, J. H. 2008. "Patterns and Determinants of Cross-border Financial Asset Holdings in East Asia." Manila, Philippines: Asian Development Bank. Working Paper, No. 13. February.

Li, X. and S. Zhang. 2011. "The Rise of China in East Asian Regional Integration." *The IUP Journal of International Relations*. Vol. 4. No. 3, pp. 29–49.

Li, X. and S. Zhang. 2009. "China and Regional Integration in East Asia." Aalborg: Aalborg University. Center for Comparative Integration Studies. Working Paper No. 9.

Lipsey, R. E. and F. Sjoholm. 2011. "South-South FDI and Development in East Asia." *Asian Development Review*. Vol. 28. No. 2, pp. 11–31.

Lipsky, J. 2011. "Remarks by John Lipsky at the Conclusion of Article IV Mission to China." Beijing. 9 June. Available online at www.imf.org/external/np/speeches/2011/062011.htm.

Mai, Y. 2004. "The Monash Multi-Country Model." CoPS Working Paper No. G-150. Melbourne: MONASH University. Center of Policy Studies.

Mai, Y., P. Adams, P. Dixon and J. Menon. 2010. "The Growth Locomotive of the People's Republic of China." *Asian Development Review*. Vol. 27. No. 2, pp. 82–121.

McKibbin, W. J. and W. T. Woo. 2003. "The Consequences of China's WTO Accession on Its Neighbors," *Asian Economic Papers*. Vol. 12. No. 2, pp. 1–38.

Menon, R. 2012. "Regional Safety Nets to Complement Global Safety Nets." Paper presented at the opening ceremony of the AMRO, Monetary Authority of Singapore, Singapore, 31 January.

Mercereau, B. 2005. *FDI Flows to Asia: Did the Dragon Crowd out the Tigers?* Working Paper No. WP/05/189. Washington, DC: International Monetary Fund.

Ming, Z. and P. J. Williamson. 2007. *Dragon at Your Door*. Boston, MA: Harvard Business School Press.

Ministry of Commerce (MOC). 2010. *Statistical Bulletin of China's Outward Foreign Direct Investment 2009*. Beijing: Government of the People's Republic of China.

Neumann, F. and T. Arora. 2011. "Chart of the Week: Can Asia Save the World?" Hong Kong: HSBC Global Research. 26 August.

Ng, F. and A. Yeats. 2001. "Production Sharing in East Asia: Who Does What for Whom?" in L. K. Cheng (ed.). *Global Production and Trade in East Asia*. Boston, MA: Kluwer Academic, pp. 63–109.

Nicita, A. and M. Olarreaga. 2006. *Trade, Production and Protection, 1976–2004.* Washington, DC: World Bank.

Nicolas, F. 2009. "The Changing Economic Relations between China and Korea." *Journal of Korean Economy.* Vol. 10. No. 3, pp. 341–65.

Park, C. S. 2011."China's Innovation Capability is Catching Korea's." *Weekly Insight.* Seoul: Samsung Economic Research Institute, pp. 9–13. 25 July.

Park, D. and K. Shin. 2011. "People's Republic of China as an Engine of Growth for Developing Asia?" *Asian Economic Papers.* Vol. 10. No. 2, pp. 120–43.

——2010. "Can Trade with the People's Republic of China be an Engine of Growth for Developing Asia?" *Asian Development Review.* Vol. 27. No. 1, pp. 160–81.

Pei, M. 2011. "China's Cultural Devotion." *The Wall Street Journal Asia.* 9 November, p. 15.

Ramstetter, E. D. 2012. "Foreign Multinationals in Asia's Large Developing Economies." Japan: Kyushu University. Graduate School of Economics. Working Paper No. 2012–06. March.

Robertson, P. E. and J. Y. Xu. 2010. *In China's Wake: Has Asia Gained From China's Growth?* Discussion Paper No. 10.15. June. University of Western Australia, Adelaide.

Ronald-Holst, D. and J. Weiss. 2005. "People's Republic of China and its Neighbors: Evidence on Regional Trade and Investment Effect." *Asia-Pacific Economic Literature.* Vol. 19. No. 2, pp. 18–35.

Salidjanova, N. 2011. "Going Out: An Overview of China's Outward Foreign Direct Investment." Washington, DC: US-China Economic & Security Review Commission. Research Report. 30 March.

Salike, N. 2010. "Investigation of the 'China Effect' on Crowding Out of Japanese FDI: An Industry Level Analysis." *China Economic Review.* Vol. 21. No. 3, pp. 582–97.

Shambaugh, D. 2005. "The Rise of China and Asia's New Dynamics", in D. Shambaugh (ed.). *Power Shift: China and Asia's New Dynamics.* Berkeley, CA: University of California Press, pp. 1–18.

Shinohara, N. 2012. "Global and Regional Economic Outlook and Role of Integration in Asia." Paper presented at Chulalongkorn University, Bangkok, Thailand, 27 March.

——2010. "Leading the Global Recovery: Policy Challenges Facing Asia." Paper presented at the Singapore National University, Singapore, 9 June.

Siow, M. W. 2010. "Chinese Domestic Debates on Soft Power and Public Diplomacy." *East-West Center Asia Pacific Bulletin.* No. 86, 7 December.

Smart, A. and J. Y. Hsu. 2004. "The Chinese Diaspora, Foreign Investment and Economic Development in China." *The Review of International Affairs.* Vol. 3. No. 4, pp. 544–66.

Stiglitz, J. E. 2002. *Globalization and its Discontents.* New York and London: W .W. Norton.

Subramanian, A. and M. Kessler. 2012. "The Renminbi Bloc is Here: Asia Down, Rest of the World to Go?" Washington, DC: Peterson Institute of International Economics. Working Paper No. 12–19. October.

Sussangkarn, C. 2011. "Chiang Mai Initiative Multilateralization: Origin, Development and Outlook." *Asian Economic Policy Review.* Vol. 6. No. 2, pp. 203–20.

Tambunan, T. 2005. "Is ASEAN Still Relevant in the Era of the ASEAN-China FTA?" Paper presented at the Asia-pacific Economic Association conference in Seattle, WA, 29–30 July.

Tambunan, T. 2006. "The Likely Impact of the ASEAN Plus China on Intra-ASEAN Trade." Paper presented at the conference held on *WTO, China and the ASEAN Economies,* in Beijing, 24–25 June.

Tang, S. and Y. Zhang. 2006. "China's Regional Strategy", in D. Shambaug (ed.). *Power Shift: China and Asia's New Dynamics.* Los Angeles, CA: University of California Press, pp. 48–68.

Teja, R. 2012. "IMF: 2012 Spillover Report." Washington, DC: International Monetary Fund. 9 July.

United Nations Conference on Trade and Development. 2010. *World Investment Report 2010.* Geneva and New York.

——2002. *World Investment Report 2002.* Geneva and New York.

United Nations Economic and Social Commission for Asia and Pacific (UNESCAP). 2011. *Asia-Pacific Trade and Investment Report 2011.* New York.

Wang, C., Y. Wei and X. Liu. 2007. "Does China Rival its Neighboring Economies for Inward FDI?" *Transnational Corporations.* Vol. 16. No. 3, pp. 35–60.

Wood, A. and J. Mayer. 2011. "Has China De-Industrialized other Developing Countries?" *Review of World Economics.* Vol. 147. No. 2, pp. 325–50.

World Bank (WB), 2012. "China Quarterly Update." Beijing: World Bank Mission. April.

——2011. "East Asia and Pacific Economic Update." Washington, DC, March.

——2013. *Doing Business Online Database 2011.* Washington, DC.

——2010. *World Development Indicators 2010.* Washington, DC.

World Investment Report (WIR). 2006. Geneva and New York. United Nations Conference on Trade and Development.

——2010. Geneva and New York. United Nations Conference on Trade and Development.

World Trade Organization (WTO). 2013. "Trade to Remain Subdued in 2013." Geneva, Switzerland. Press Release No. 688. 10 April.

——2012. "Trade Growth to Slow in 2012 after Strong Deceleration in 2011." Press Release. Press/658. Geneva, Switzerland. 12 April.

——2011a. *International Trade Statistics 2010*. Geneva. Switzerland.

——2011b. "Trade Patterns and Global Value Chains in East Asia." Geneva, Switzerland. July.

——2010. "International Trade Statistics." Press Release PRESS/598. Geneva, Switzerland. 26 March.

Yamashita, N. 2010. *International Fragmentation of Production*. Cheltenham: Edward Elgar.

Ye, S. 2010. "China's Regional Policy in East Asia and its Characteristics." Nottingham: University of Nottingham. China Policy Institute. Discussion Paper No. 66. October.

Yeats, A. J. 2001. "Just How Big is Global Production Sharing?" in S. W. Arndt and H. Kierzkowski (eds). *Fragmentation: New Production Pattern in the World Economy*. Oxford: Oxford University Press, pp. 63–109.

Yi, K. M. 2003. "Can Vertical Specialization Explain the Growth of World Trade?" *Journal of Political Economy*. Vol. 111. No. 1, pp. 52–102.

Yiwei, W. 2008. "Public Diplomacy and the Rise of Chinese Soft Power." *Annals of the American Academy of Political and Social Sciences*. Vol. 616. No. 1, pp. 257–73.

Yusuf, S. and K. Nabeshima. 2010. *Changing the Industrial Geography in Asia*. Washington, DC: World Bank.

Zheng, B. 2005. "China's 'Peaceful Rise' to Great Power Status." *Foreign Affairs*. Vol. 84. No. 5, pp. 18–24.

Zhengyi, W. 2004. "Conceptualizing Economic Security and Governance: China Confronts Globalization," *The Pacific Review*. Vol. 17. No. 4, pp. 523–45.

Zhou, Y. and S. Lall. 2005. "The Impact of China's FDI Surge on FDI in South-East Asia: Panel Data Analysis for 1986–2001." *Transnational Corporations*. Vol. 14. No. 1, pp. 41–65.

6

FROM MARKET-LED TO INSTITUTION-LED REGIONAL INTEGRATION IN ASIA

Introduction

In Chapter 5 we saw that regional integration in Asia evolved in an intrinsically *de facto* or market-led manner. This mode of regional integration brought China and its regional neighbors together in a soft and uninstitutionalized way. In comparison to the other economically prominent regions of the global economy, Asia is widely considered to be under-institutionalized. That said, there has been a marked transformation in Asia's regional architecture in a short span of a decade-and-a-half. The genesis of policy-led or formal regionalism, also termed *de jure* economic integration, was the creation of the Association of Southeast Asian Nations (ASEAN). This is a top-down approach of regional integration, which results from the endeavors of political leadership and national governments. Recent progress in *de jure* integration has been strengthening market-driven economic integration in Asia. It is preparing ground for establishing formal architecture for regional economic integration in the medium term.

Although ASEAN is the oldest institution of regional co-operation in Asia, the launch of Asian regionalism was not only slow but also did not progress consistently for a long period. The Bangkok Declaration was signed in 1967 between the five founding members of ASEAN, namely, Indonesia, Malaysia, the Philippines, Singapore and Thailand. At the time of its inception, none of the founding principles of ASEAN were economic in nature. It was a loosely founded political organization, whose primary purpose was to promote regional peace and stability in a sub-region that had a history of volatility. It is Asia's only multipurpose regional organization and remained dormant until the Bali Summit in 1976 (Ariff, 2011).

Further poorly visualized and somewhat *maladroit* attempts were made to build a formal regional community of nations, but they produced few tangible results of value and utility. From the perspective of regional integration, the Asian economy underwent a great many alterations but a genuine economic community of Asian economies has remained a work in progress. The region is not only far from forming a European Union (EU)-like community of nations but even the outlines of regional architecture are nebulous and ill-defined. Candidly assessed, a monetary union, or an Asian single market, or an Asian Economic Community are not a few short years away. However, although little tangible progress has been made in this direction, this is not to deny that some semblance of regional architecture has evolved and that it is supporting the integration of the real side of the Asian economy. It needs to be clarified that the oft-used term regional architecture implies "institutions, mechanics and arrangements that together provide necessary functions for regional cooperation" in the areas of trade, economic development and finance (Hu, 2009, p. 4).

The objective of this chapter is to examine the real sector- or trade-related regional integration in Asia. Its principal focus is the post-Asian crisis (1997–98) growth in Asian regionalism and the main associated issues. Crises and external shocks have the potential to reshape or bring about new institutional orders. The discussion deals with this issue through institutional and theoretical investigation, supported by insightful data analysis. Real sector or trade-related regional integration could plausibly be the beginning of the natural sequencing of future monetary, financial and economic integration. This was the trajectory of progression in the EU. How this process unfolds would have notable implications for and impact on the region. Given the rising importance of Asia and the ongoing shift in the global center of gravity, it would also be of global significance.

1.1 Defining regionalism

In forming a preferential trade agreement two or more economies begin by significantly reducing or eliminating trade barriers among them. Terms like "preferential trade agreement" or "regional trade agreement" are used to denote an exception from the non-discriminatory principle of the General Agreement on Tariffs and Trade (GATT)/World Trade Organization (WTO) system, or the most-favored-nation (MFN) clause, enshrined in Article I. Trade policy discrimination, permitted under Article XXIV of the GATT[1] and Article V of the General Agreement in Trade in Services (GATS),[2] is the central principle behind the formation of preferential trade agreements. Free trade agreements (FTAs)[3] are also allowed under the Enabling Clause of the GATT for special treatment for the developing countries. Trade policy discrimination was adopted under the GATT in 1979 and it enabled developed countries to give differential and favorable treatment to developing countries. As a rule of thumb, agreements notified under the Enabling Clause tend to be less comprehensive than agreements notified under GATT Article XXIV.

There can be a whole range of discriminatory preferential agreements between countries, ranging from minimal agreements that simply exchange partial tariff preferences to full-blown FTAs that go way beyond agreements on tariff reductions. Different types of trade agreements can be demarcated in three different stages of progressive integration. The familiar Balassa (1961) classification in this regard is as follows: (1) An FTA or preferential trading arrangement (PTA) comprises the first stage of shallow integration. An FTA is the principal and commonly used instrument of formal regional integration. In a basic and simple form an FTA is a legal treaty between the governments of the signatory countries to reduce or eliminate trade barriers, usually in a phased manner. However, in an FTA the member countries determine and keep their own levels of trade barriers vis-à-vis the non-member countries.

The deep integration measures are: (2) A customs union (CU), which differs from an FTA in that it adopts common trade barriers or external tariff structure vis-à-vis the non-member economies. (3) The next stage is a common or single market. It is essentially a CU with deeper integration between member economies, entailing liberalized movement of factors of production between the members. A monetary union comes next when the countries have a common currency and to an extent they also have common economic policies. The last stage is an economic union. This taxonomy presents a sequenced pattern towards closer and deeper integration. Analysts usually focus on FTAs or CUs while analyzing trade blocs. Two types of effects of forming an FTA are generally estimated, the first is the trade effects and the second the welfare effects. FTA is often used as a generic term. To clarify, an FTA can also be bilateral.

The present era of regionalism began with the Treaty Establishing the European Economic Community (EEC), signed in Rome in 1957. Over the years regional agreements evolved considerably and in their present form can be really complex, having an enormous impact over the national and regional economies. Conceptually and physically regional integration progresses in stages from an FTA to a customs union (usually between two neighboring countries or within sub-regions), then a deeper common market and further on to an economic and monetary union, encompassing multifaceted financial and fiscal issues. Asia is no different. An acknowledged late-comer to regionalism, Asia's regional architecture may well pass through these stylized stages. Conventionally FTAs aimed at liberalizing trade in goods by eliminating tariffs, but in recent years FTAs frequently go beyond this mark. Their addresses issues related to behind-the-border protection and includes tariff-equivalent non-tariff barriers (NTBs), trade in services, investment, intellectual-property rights (IPR), competition policy, government procurement and dispute settlement. Since 2000 this trend in what is known as "deep" or "WTO-Plus" regional integration has intensified.

1.2 On-going policy debate

During the 1990s, efforts towards regional community building were made under the auspices of an Asia-Pacific Economic Cooperation (APEC) forum, but trade and economic liberalization under APEC petered out without making much headway by the end of the decade. Since then endeavors to build a regionally integrated economic community shifted to Asia, particularly the Northeast and Southeast. After the mid-1990s, particularly following the Asian crisis, driven by a shared sense of purpose several earnest attempts were made to build an Asian regional architecture that would have an Asian identity, character and disposition. In the post-crisis period more regional or preferential trade agreements were signed in Asia than in any other region. Plans to consolidate the myriad existing free trade agreements and negotiate a region-wide free trade zone are often debated. Also, an Asia-Pacific initiative picked up momentum in 2011. It was in the form of the Trans-Pacific Partnership (TPP).

Commissioning of the East Asian Vision Group (EAVG) in 2000 was a defining moment in this regard. Leaders of ASEAN-Plus-Three (APT)[4] countries took initiative to establish the EAVG. In their report in October 2001 the EAVG recommended formation of "a *bona fide* regional community" making collective efforts towards not only economic progress and prosperity but also peace. The EAVG advocated that the Asian governments "work towards building an 'East Asian Community' ... " (EAVG, 2001, p. 2). During the first decade of the 21st century, myriad small and large attempts were made to integrate regionally by mostly individual and occasionally sub-groups of Asian economies. These approaches were largely multipronged. During the second decade they reached a critical juncture to start carving their regional institutional architecture for the future. If the Asian countries stay the course, they have a long way to go in conceptualizing and implementing a functional regional architecture.

The first initiatives that the Asian economies took were to integrate globally. As this chapter elucidates, in the post-2000 period trade policy took a discernible regional turn and regional initiatives became predominant. For deep-seated economic and political reasons, regionalism supplanted the multilateral initiatives in trade liberalization. Discrimination against multilateral trade had a distorting effect on it. In accordance with this new proclivity, the regional economic structure in Asia began altering. The pace of change gradually accelerated. Asian economies have been mutually integrating, first in a market-driven manner and then in a policy-driven, formal manner, with the regional governments taking the initiative.

For the Asian economies, in order to maintain and stabilize their dynamic gross domestic product (GDP) growth at this juncture, collective action toward regional economic co-operation and *de jure* regionalism would be appropriate. As the Asian economies took the initiative to integrate globally, their relatively recent advances towards a shared vision of regional co-operation need not be seen as turning away from their wish for global integration. It would be pragmatic as well as reasonable for them to ensure that, as far as possible, their emerging regionalism should be complementary to globalism and multilateral initiatives, not a substitute for it.

Also, since the turn of the century China played a steadfast role in the growth of both market-led and formal regionalism. As the regional economic structure began to grow in a China-centric manner, the recent growth of Asian regionalism also became partially China-centric. More accurately China led the path of regional integration, *a fortiori* in the post-Asian crisis period (Gill and Kharas, 2009). It was a severe crisis. Virtually all Asian currencies depreciated sharply, some losing almost 50 percent of their value by January 1998. The economic, social and political fallout of the crisis was distressingly huge. Since the crisis formal regionalism made material progress in Asia. In the medium- or long-term this process will result in significant geo-economic and geo-political transformation of Asia. Rapid clip regional economic growth, particularly China's vertiginous growth, catalyzed the process of regional integration. A growing number of trade agreements and progress in regional integration resulted in a decline in trade costs in Asia relative to the other regions of the global economy (Pomfret and Sourdin, 2009).

The policy debate on the future of economic agreements in Asia became progressively lively and energetic. The present surfeit of reciprocal or bilateral trade agreements (BTAs), and FTAs in the region is seen by some analysts as having a low utility in increasing trade and welfare in the region. Both trade theory and computable general equilibrium (CGE) analysis suggest that larger number of participating economies in an FTA result in greater benefits. Towards the end of the last decade, scholarly attention was focused more on the possible creation of an Asia-wide consolidated economic co-operation agreement. In addition, subsequent APEC summits kept on moving towards building on the existing regional cooperation frameworks and following up on the concept of a Free Trade Area of the Asia-Pacific (FTAAP). There are others who point to the difficulties in arriving at a consensus on a region-wide agreement (Chia, 2010). The process of expansion of the TPP is presently underway. It is the latest model of this kind.

2. Deepening market-led integration in the Asian economies

Japan-led Asian production networks were behind the creation of a vibrant market-led regionalism. As noted above, this bottom-up process progressed essentially through the market-driven forces of trade, foreign direct investment (FDI) and financial flows, which were the result of the normal business activities of the large Asian business firms and MNEs. Between the decades of the 1970s and 1990s this process picked up considerable momentum. These decades are known for the rapid growth in trade in goods and services as well as for FDI expansion, both globally and regionally. It had occurred as a result of multilateral and unilateral trade liberalization, dismantling of trade barriers, financial market deregulation, capital account liberalization and other similar measures. MNCs had a noteworthy and well-defined role to play in the regionalization of Asia. During this period, regional organizations were led by business groups. Participation by countries was voluntary and based on mutual self-interest. There were few rules. Consultation and freely exchanging information was the modus operandi.

The notion or strategy to lock "national economies into the neo-liberal global economy via regionalization" was at the heart of many Asian economies integrating together (Breslin, 2010, p. 714). This process of regionalization was markedly different, in fact contrary, from the EU-like integration of the economies. While national economies were integrating but they did so in the absence of regional institutions promoting it. Thus viewed, *de facto* (deepening intra-regional trade and investment linkages) regional integration in Asia started long before *de jure*. It bears mentioning here that these were the decades when globalization progressed impressively and that regionalization comprises an essential facet of globalization (Das, 2009). Two factors were essentially spurring regional economic integration: first, there was the growth dynamics of the integrating Asian economies; and second, it was a normal outcome of economic globalization. It was in harmony with the contemporary trends of regionalization and globalization that had commenced in the early 1980s (Das, 2009).

During this period, non-state actors and market forces were the principal drivers of regional integration. They were building a community of mutually collaborating nations in business. Countries and business enterprises tend to seek market-driven economic integration because they aspire for larger markets for their products so that they can exploit economies of scale and scope. Having enlarged markets also makes it feasible for them to diversify their production and benefit from specialization. In addition, product differentiation increases intra-regional trade. As they grow and move up technologically, larger business firms, expand their trade, and in the process they enhance integration, both regional and global.

As the Asian economies are situated in a contiguous geographical area and many of them share geographical borders, close economic linkages among them were natural and developed relatively fast. Asia is regarded as a region where market-led regionalization advanced rapidly and successfully. Consequently by the late 1990s, Asian economies were more integrated than many other regions of the global economy (Panitchpakdi, 2011). The apparent exceptions were the EU and North American Free Trade Area (NAFTA). Asian economies not only increased intra-regional trade, they became biased towards it and towards regional trade partners since the mid-1980s (Petri, 2006).

Owing to successful development of vertically integrated production networks in the region (as discussed in detail in Section 3), Asian economies not only increased intra-regional trade in parts and components but also in finished products. This indicated the growing importance of the intra-regional markets as an increasing source of demand for their exports. WTO (2011) statistics demonstrated that compared to the other regions of the global economy, intra-regional trade progressed more rapidly in Asia. In 2010, 52.6 percent of Asian trade was intra-regional. It was merely 37 percent in 1980 and declined to 33 percent during the early 1980s. Also, according to the latest availability of data, the intra-regional trade level for Asia was much higher in comparison to those in Africa (12.3 percent) and Latin America (25.6 percent). These statistical data demonstrate that intra-regional trade in Asia is not only higher in comparison to its historical norms but it is also higher than the other two developing regions. For North America (48.7 percent), a developed industrialized region, the corresponding figure is lower than that for Asia. For obvious reasons, only intra-region trade in Europe (71.0 percent) is more than that in Asia. The EU is not only a pioneer but also the most mature of the intra-regional groupings in the global economy.[5]

As a part of their economic reforms and restructuring programs, Asian economies followed neoliberal economic policies, in that they liberalized their trade regimes and adopted proactive FDI policies. Consequently, the region enjoyed a large market-driven expansion of trade and FDI. Liberalization of FDI occurred under both regional and global production frameworks. Asian economies exhibited an obvious preference for multilateral non-discriminatory trade liberalization over the discriminatory variety, which is an innate feature of *de jure* regionalism. Their belief in the time-tested multilateral liberalization was strong and continued to be so. To this end, they adopted policies of sweeping reduction of both tariffs and NTBs.[6] This liberalization and deregulation was an integral part of their comprehensive structural reform policies, which is regarded as one of their strategic economic characteristics.

These liberalization measures were not only taken under the auspices of the erstwhile GATT but also unilaterally. During the 1980s and 1990s there were several spurts of unilateral liberalization in the Asian economies. It was partly encouraged by the successful culmination of the Uruguay Round (1986–94) of multilateral trade negotiations (MTNs). The expectation was that this structural transformation on the lines of neoclassical economic principles would strengthen the market forces and stimulate economic growth in the Asian economies. Liberalization, economic reforms and macroeconomic restructuring were instrumental in turning Asian economies into a successful, outward-oriented group of economies. This structural transformation was immensely significant in that it made it possible for them to allow FDI inflows in order to develop their manufacturing sector, which in turn became a driver of their export-led growth. It became a much-acclaimed characteristic of the Asian economies. In the post-1980 period, the long-term growth rate of Asian exports was twice that of global export growth.

The region has sustained one of the highest real GDP growth rates in the global economy, which *inter alia* facilitated and gave momentum to its market-led regional integration. In addition, the outward-oriented policy framework was a crucial instrument, which enabled the Asian economies to integrate in a market-led manner. A large body of literature exists that clarifies how this policy stance was instrumental in Asia's economic dynamism and market-driven expansion of trade and FDI inflows. In particular, intra-regional and multilateral trade of the Asian economies, predominantly in light manufacturing, grew at a remarkable pace. Asian economies earned fond sobriquets like the "global factory" or "factory Asia".

2.1 Role and operation of private-sector enterprises and MNCs

The operation of market forces succeeded in creating a successful web of transnational linkages across the regional economies. The dominant driving force behind regionalization was the profit-maximizing behavior of business firms, corporations and MNCs. The micro-economic decision-making of non-state actors, like the large business firms, particularly MNCs, played an active role in Asia's regional integration. MNCs were an important driver of economic integration through trade and FDI activities. They played a major role in international trade, FDI and expansion creation of production networks and supply chains. The first MNCs to play a positive role were those from Japan. MNCs customarily looked for cost-effective locations for their production networks. Asia provided them with a variety of such locales. Operations of MNCs in the region contributed in a meaningful manner to market-led integration in Asia (Das, 2005a).

Particular mention should be made of the Plaza Accord in 1985 and the ensuing yen appreciation. Cost-conscious MNCs from Japan sought to relocate production to Asian economies to rein in high costs (Chapter 2, Section 1.1). These moves were motivated by MNCs seeking market efficiency. In the initial stages, Japanese vertical FDI played a particularly important role in the development and spread of production networks in Asia. The Japanese MNCs were followed by MNCs from advanced economies and the last to come were the MNCs from the newly industrialized economies (NIEs) and emerging-market economies (EMEs). Efficiency-seeking FDI of MNCs as well as their procurement and sales patterns was conducive in advancing market-led integration of the Asian economies (Das, 1992).

Asian industrial production and exports gradually shifted from labor-intensive to capital- and technology-intensive. *Pari passu* brisk technological up-gradation of the economies played a crucial role in the rapid growth of the Asian economies. They acquired high technology through legal channels, using normal modes like licensing and inward FDI. The latter were particularly conducive to large technology transfer (Petri, 2011). Asian economies also used informal channels like reverse engineering for technology acquisition. By learning, importing, adopting and absorbing modern industrial technologies numerous domestic Asian firms were able to improve production engineering skills. It made them a part of the fast expanding global industrial activity (Mathews and Cho, 2000; Wignaraja, 2008).

By enhancing their technological capabilities and skillfully utilizing the regional production networks many Asian firms became local suppliers to large MNCs and in the process grew closely integrated into their regional and global operations. Some domestic Asian firms went a step ahead and even began to successfully compete with the MNCs. By making necessary investments in research and development (R&D) they significantly enhanced their technological and innovative capabilities. It had turned them into leading firms in production networks and supply chain operations in the region. They grew important in their own right. The eventual outcome was steady and rapid-clip industrialization of Asia and business firm-led regional integration. Many manufacturing Asian firms produced advanced technological products—some even at the cutting edge of technology.

Yet another factor that contributed to private sector-led regional integration was the recent fall in transport and communication costs. It had the same effect as increase in productivity, or increase in the exploitation of comparative advantage. Falling trade barriers in the region, discussed above, were also helpful in enhancing regional integration. Strengthening and expansion of regional and global value chains in Asia can be explained by differences in the stages of economic growth and comparative advantage among the regional economies. The latter occurred owing to differences in endowments of labor, capital and technological know-how. They gave them an edge in different steps in production processes.

2.2 Unique role of the electronics industry in Asia's market-led integration

The electronics and information and communication technology (ICT) industry has developed into a major industrial sector in Asia. It became an important driver of growth and development and in its present state it has spread virtually all over the region. This modern industrial sector has been a "trailblazer and test bed" for Asian regionalism (Ernst, 2006, p. 161). It not only dominated trade and investment in the region but also shows a high degree of regional and global integration. Since the 1970s, this sector benefitted from the initiatives taken by the Japanese firms and MNCs. They used to be a rich source of capital, technology, components and machinery as well as strategic management models. Over the years, this situation has changed and cards were reshuffled.

Asia appropriately and lucratively exploited differences in factor endowments and locational advantage; consequently the output value of electronic and ICT products in the region is huge. By 2004 China had become the largest exporter of ICT products, surpassing the USA, Japan and the EU. The five leading exporters in this industry are China, the Republic of Korea (hereinafter Korea), Malaysia, Singapore and Taiwan. Governments in these countries aggressively supported the growth and development of this industry. By participating in regional and global networked production, Asian ICT firms were able to access leading-edge technology and best practice management techniques. They created new opportunities for them (Ernst, 2008).

As the domestic markets in the Asian economies were small, they needed to access the larger global markets. This industry has created millions of jobs in Asia and supported construction of essential infrastructure. The electronics industry evolved more rapidly in the 1990s in the region than in the 1980s. With its growth, its competitiveness in several Asian economies markedly improved. It became geared to production for exports. The region now accounts for a large proportion of multilateral trade in several electronics sectors. In 2010 Asia accounted for 32.9 percent of total world exports in office and telecom equipment, more than Europe (13.0 percent) and North America (13.6 percent).[7]

Another characteristic development of the 1990s was that trade, including intra-regional trade, in electronics within the region accelerated at a strikingly rapid pace. This trade had been increasing since the early 1980s. Increases in intra-regional trade and investment in the electronics industry mirrored the broader process of market- and firm-led regionalization discussed above. Both the swift evolution and acceleration in trade have been interpreted in terms of the well-known "flying geese" and "product cycle" paradigms. That is, Japan playing the role of the leading innovative economy, followed by the NIEs. They in turn were followed by the other Asian economies that were on the lower rungs of comparative advantage.

This industry covered several sectors, including electronic parts and components as well as finished computers and other products. Electronics firms in Japan, Korea, Taiwan and affiliates of MNCs in the ASEAN-4 countries manufacture technology-intensive intermediate goods and exported them to other parts of Asia, where relatively lower-skilled labor force could assemble them into finished products. Increases in regional trade in electronic goods reflected this mode of production. According to the trade statistics compiled by Thorbecke and Salike (2011), in 2009 33 percent of imports of ASEAN-4 from the NIEs came under the category of electronic goods. Also, 60 percent of exports of the ASEAN-4 economies to China fell under this category.

Two outstanding characteristics of this industry are as follows: first, both the industry and market in Asia are huge; and second, they play an active and leading role in integrating the Asian economy. The evolutionary trend in Asia is described by the hard disk drive (HDD) industry below. Parts and components are traded between countries and then final assembled products flow to the global markets, particularly the EU and the USA. These parts and components are, *inter alia*, inputs into computers and other final electronic products. Thorbecke and Salike (2011) contended that trade in category known as "electronic parts and components" is the largest category traded within the region. Also, the category termed "components and office equipment" is the largest category of traded items from Asia to the rest of the global economy.

During the 1980s the volume of trade in electronic parts and components from the NIEs was equally divided between the other NIEs and the ASEAN-4 economies. This pattern of trade changed in the 1990s because the NIEs lost their locational advantage in assembling the final products. One of the reasons was rising wages in this sub-group of economies. This caused NIEs trade in parts and components with the ASEAN-4 economies to rise, while that to the other NIEs, or intra-NIE trade, to significantly diminish. Transformation in this trading pattern continued in the 2000s, when there was a strong surge in imports of electronic parts and components from the NIEs to China. These imports of electronic inputs into China soon surpassed those into ASEAN-4. As regards the evolving trend in exports of final assembled computers and other electronic products to various regions of the global economy, Japan was in the lead during the 1980s, the ASEAN-4 in the 1990s and in the 2000s China became the largest exporter. Strong growth performance in electronic parts and components and final goods in the region went hand in hand with creation of intricate production networks. Intra-trade, arm's-length transactions and outsourcing were the *modus operandi* of these production networks.

An archetypal example of the efficient and successful operation of regional value chain is production and intra-regional trade in HDDs. It operated in the following sequential manner: affiliates of Japanese MNCs in the electronics industry manufactured parts and components in the Philippines and shipped them to Thailand to produce HDDs. They were in turn exported to China to assemble computers, which were exported from there to the rest of the world (Hiratsuka, 2010a). In numerous electronic product lines value chains of this kind mushroomed all over the region.

In the second decade of the 21st century this trend is changing. The middle class in Asia, particularly in the EMEs, is growing in size at a rapid pace. Also, urbanization is progressing briskly. As a result, Asian consumers are buying more and more of the electronic products produced in the region. As the regional catch-up picks up momentum, demand from domestic consumers of electronic goods in the region will rise and the electronics industry in Asia will grow less export-reliant. In addition, several Asian economies are latecomers to the digital era. This status will enable the region to leapfrog several developmental stages (EIU, 2011).

3 A *de facto* region-wide preferential trading area

One of the many economically consequential developments in the Asian economy was market-led or private-sector-driven regionalization. It progressed far in a *de facto* manner during the preceding four decades. An early instrument of *de facto* integration was the free trade zones (FTZ) and export-processing zones (EPZs) which were established by the Asian economies. The pioneer in this regard was the Taiwan's Kaohsiung FTZ, established in 1966. These FTZs and EPZs worked as a considerable pull factor for pro-trade FDI, which was made by both business firms and multinational enterprises (MNEs) from within the region as well as those from the advanced economies. The MNEs and other manufacturers that operated in these FTZs and EPZs innovatively and profitably utilized them for their production and trade. They used their FTZ and EPZ operations for trade with the other similar zones in the region as well as outside the region. While operating in and trading from these FTZs and EPZs they enjoyed virtual free trade privileges. After the Plaza Accord in 1985, MNEs and large businesses enterprises from Japan and NIEs rushed to invest in the FTZs and EPZs in China and the ASEAN economies (Section 2). This pro-trade foreign direct investment (FDI) soon became a driving force of *de facto* integration in the region.

Another channel of *de facto* regional integration was the tariff regime in the region. In the tariff regime of a country, "bound" tariff rate is lower than the "applied" tariff rate. The difference between the two is termed the "binding overhang" (Pelc, 2009). The WITS/TRAIN data base of the WTO reveals that a new trend emerged in Asia in this regard. Binding overhang in Asian economies displays a pattern. When trading with each other Asian economies allow lower tariffs. They did not extend these tariff concessions to economies outside the region. This implies that they have formed a *de facto* preferential trading area (PTA), before or without negotiating a region-wide trade agreement. This trend has particularly been observed in intra-regional trade in manufactured products. The result was creation of a *de facto* PTA in trade in manufactured products in Asia. This was a somewhat lesser known addition to the regional institutional architecture. It decisively adds to regional integration and cohesion.[8]

Thus, Asian economies are "liberalized vis-à-vis their neighbors above and beyond their legal requirement" (Hale, 2011, p. 210). This trend has materialized largely owing to the demands made by MNEs that operate vertically integrated production networks in the region and moved parts and components from one regional economy to the other. Thus impetus for this *de facto* regional PTA formation was essentially bottom-up rather than top-down. It was the economic interests of the MNEs that promoted bottom-up regional integration. Therefore as production fragmentation accelerates in Asia this genre of regional integration is likely to deepen and inter-industry relations will be strengthened further. Industrial sector and output in one Asian economy will be influenced by what is transpiring in the other Asian economies. This mechanism is termed as "spatial linkage". Such linkages are strong in several industries, in particular electronics and automobile.

After a detailed study of tariff structures, Hale (2011) identified the following three unambiguous patterns. First, Asian economies displayed binding overhang in their relationship with the other Asian economies, albeit for non-agricultural products binding overhang was never larger with countries outside the region than those within the region. Second, when members of FTAs, Asian economies did not exhibit binding overhang with countries within or outside the region. Third, they did not exhibit binding overhang under MFN rates with economies outside the region, but fairly high binding overhang with countries within the region.

4. Expansion of production networks and deeper regional integration

As alluded to in the preceding section, regional integration through trade was enhanced by recent changes in industrial organization and the spread of vertically integrated production networks, which became a global phenomenon. Geographical fragmentation of production is responsible for the creation of a new trade veracity and private-sector-led regional integration. It intuitively enhances productive efficiency of the regional economy. Krugman (1998) pointed out that both FDI and trade respond to the complex forces of economic geography. There are factors that promote their geographical concentration or oppose it. MNCs have been the major players and decision-makers in this area. They significantly influenced the trade and investment flows in a geographical region. The MNCs are consequential global economic entities and their operations not only affect economies but also have an influence on their macroeconomic policy making.

There is nothing new about the phenomenon of vertical fragmentation of production and the resulting expansion of trade in intermediate goods. It dates back to the 1960s, when intra-industrial specialization in Asia increased due to the NIEs climbing up of the industrial development ladder. The role of vertical fragmentation of production increased during the 1980s, albeit it is widely perceived that its magnitude and impact grew substantially since 1990.[9] Since the early 1990s, production networks brought about a notable expansion of trade in intermediate inputs in Asia (Hiratsuka and Uchida, 2010). Production networks expanded because, *inter alia*, East and Southeast Asian economies succeeded in reducing frictions and costs of trade, rendering them more appealing as production and investment platforms for the MNCs.

The policy measures that Asian economies took to achieve the advantageous results from regional and international production networks included investment in transport infrastructure, formation of special purpose economic and export zones, having bonded industrial warehouses, instituting duty-drawback schemes, reducing or eliminating "behind-the-border" obstacles to trade and other parallel of measures. These policy measures enabled business firms and MNCs to take advantage of economies of scale and scope, which made their operations more efficient, productive and lucrative. They were essentially driven by sheer commercial pragmatism, the economic forces and profit motives.

Falling trade barriers in the region provided further incentives for vertically integrated production fragmentation (Grossman and Rossi-Hansberg, 2008). This decline resulted in an increase in trade, which in turn promoted vertical specialization and production fragmentation (Hummels *et al.*, 2001). These developments were behind recent disproportionate rise in trade in intermediate goods in Asia in comparison to overall multilateral trade increase. Owing to these policy measures adopted by the Asian economies, MNCs from the advanced industrial economies and those from the NIEs and EMEs were particularly attracted towards them. The eventual effect was a burgeoning vertical intra-industry trade.

Theoretical understanding of the formation of production networks is imparted by both the fragmentation theory and the concept of new economic geography. They are located across countries depending upon comparative advantage of each location (Section 2). Differences in factor endowments were particularly important in explaining expansion of production networks in Asia (Hiratsuka, 2010b). These differences tended to generate opportunities for MNCs and large business firms to locate fragmented production processes in different locations, enabling them to reap advantages of locations. They in turn are reflected in the bottom lines of their balance sheets. Production networks proliferated faster in Asia than in the other regions of the global economy. Their expansion has largely been regional (Athukorala, 2010; Athukorala and Menon, 2010). One direct effect of the expansion of production networks was increase in trade in intermediate inputs, which recorded hefty increases in Asia. Spread and deepening of production networks and supply chain operations spawned positive welfare effects in several regional economies.

Production networks in Asia were created in myriad of industries. Several large industrial sector like automobile, machinery, chemicals and electronics and ICT have the most sophisticated production networks in Asia. Intra-regional trade in parts and components in these and other industries went on increasing. These production networks have significantly deepened over the preceding two decades. Using data for trade in parts and components, Ng and Yeats (1999) assessed the magnitude of production sharing in Asia. They showed that that production sharing in Asia went on deepening over the years. Although production networks *per se* and the resulting trade in intermediate products were an instrument of market-led regionalization, they also supported the trend towards pro-liferation of *de jure* regionalism (Section 2). As, with the passage of time, these vigorous networks progressively became more advanced and sophisticated, they created an increasing need for trade and investment liberalization. By the second decade of the 21st century, they progressed to the point in which Asia began to look like a regional factory.

As regards the classification of trade in parts and components, if it is taken at a disaggregated level, trade in parts and components and the finished products in same production chains or industries should be classified as inter-industry trade. However, if they are considered at an aggre-gated level, the classification will necessarily be different. They will need to be classified in the same category and therefore regional trade in them is treated as vertical intra-industry trade (Wakasugi, 2007). Vertically integrated production networks in Asia have been dynamic. Their configuration underwent manifest transformation. For instance, their hub was first located in Japan, but subsequently with remarkably rapid expansion of the industrial sector in China it shifted to China. Rapid expansion of production networks and regional supply chains necessitated deeper regional integration to facilitate their growth, particularly in the economies like Japan, China and the four NIEs. The larger economies of the ASEAN bloc also became intertwined in the production networks. Viet Nam was to join them last.

To promote MNC-led production networks, the large ASEAN economies, particularly Malaysia and Thailand, as well as the other Asian economies made pointed and piecemeal policy reforms. Their objective was to attract and facilitate FDI from MNCs and other large foreign investors so that they can get started with the intricate production fragmentation processes and networked production. To this end they encouraged MNCs to make policy suggestions and proactively sought their advice. They sincerely acted on the individual pieces of advice that they received from them. Policy makers in these economies energetically tried to find the sources and causes of glitches and problems in establishing production networks and adopted measures to smooth them down. This process had started in the latter half of the 1980s in the large ASEAN economies. With some time lag the smaller ones also followed this process.

The expansion and deepening of production networks and value chains, as it happened in Asia, should logically lead to increased interdependence among the regional economies, and therefore to a proliferation of BTAs, FTAs, regional trade agreements (RTAs) and economic partnership agreements (EPA). When regional integration occurs owing to the deepening of production networks, it is sure to enhance trade volumes in the region and generate positive welfare effects. When economies in a region develop trade relations through expansion of production chains, those ties continue and survive for long periods. They break down only when the final products that they produce lose their importance. Given the sunk costs in fragmented production, the network-forming firms tend to assign high importance and value to the sustainability of their trade links and endeavor to preserve them. Therefore when cross-border transactions in intermediate goods between firms are based on special relationships, the intra-firm relations and trade last for a longer duration. This pattern of trade distinguishes itself from the normal import–export of final products. The relation-specific trade has also tended to be more stable and resilient in Asia (Obashi, 2010a). An empirical examination of trade relations in production chains in machine parts and components industry in Asia revealed that trade relations among the Asian economies had much higher probability of continuance compared to those in finished products (Obashi, 2010b). In addition, Asian economies were found to engage in longer-lasting trade relationships in parts and components with each other than they did with the non-regional economies.

4.1 Active business lobbyists

It was expected that by facilitating trade and investment wider and deeper FTA-led regionalism would make regional value chains more profitable. This is a highly suitable strategy for a region like Asia that has low MFN tariffs. In the vertically integrated production or value chains profitability was dependent upon the cost of moving parts and components across borders as well as time taken in such movements. Therefore business lobbies in the Asian countries supported the ongoing government-led regionalism endeavors and pressured for more trade facilitation and investment liberalization.

Thus viewed, production networks and supply chain operations were an important motivation for the expansion of Asian regionalism. Vertically integrated production and value chains enhanced economic interdependence among the Asian economies. Some (like Pomfret, 2011) even went so far as arguing that Asian regionalism is rooted in regional production networks. Empirical studies have demonstrated that the expansion of intra-industry trade, in particular that driven by vertical specialization, leads to synchronization in business cycles in the Asian economies (Calderon *et al.*, 2007). This kind of intra-industry trade is a major factor responsible for generating higher co-movement of output among the Asian economies (Shin and Wang, 2004).

The most germane point in this context is that the impact of expansion of vertically integrated production network related trade can lead to higher probability of creation of deeper regional integration among countries in a region. In order for the production networks in two or more regional economies to operate efficiently, certain national standards, regulations and other policies need to be harmonized. This in turn creates an expected demand for regional integration from business firms for harmonization of standards, regulations and other policies. This kind of policy harmonization subsequently becomes an instrument of deeper regional integration. Thus, increasing volume of trade in parts and components and intermediate goods has a direct correlation with regional integration (Antras and Staiger, 2008, 2012; Lawrence, 1996). It became a force for *de facto* economic integration in Asia.

Development of production networks grew in tandem with the trend in vertical FDI, which was initiated by Japanese MNCs and followed by those from NICs. The so-called complex vertical FDI theory is of recent evolution. Hayakawa and Matsuura (2009, 2011) illustrated the applicability of this theory for Asia. They provide empirical validity for how Japanese MNCs established their operations in different Asian economies having different factor prices and succeeded in reaping lucrative benefits from production networks. By linking vertical FDI and intra-industry trade with the MNCs' operations in the region one can assess the contribution made by them to regional integration in Asia. Such an empirical estimate was made for one important industry, electrical machinery, by Fukao *et al.* (2003).

An augmented gravity equation was estimated by Orefice and Rocha (2011) to investigate the relationship between higher levels of production networks related trade and deeper agreements. For their investigation they took WTO data for 96 FTAs for 1958–2010. Of these, 52 FTA covered ASEAN, China, India and Japan. The results show that higher levels of trade in production networks increased the probability of signing deeper regional integration agreements by 6 percentage points. This positive effect of production networks related trade on deep regional integration was essentially driven by Asian FTAs. The same empirical study found another link between production network trade and deep regional integration. It calculated that signing a deeper integration agreement increases trade in production networks between member countries by almost 35 percentage points. UNESCAP (2011) also emphasized a positive link between FTAs and production networks-related trade in East Asia.

4.2 Upgrading FTA regulations for strengthening production networks

Operation of production networks can be further strengthened in the region by improving, upgrading and fine-tuning the BTA and FTA regulations. Owing to variations in definition, rules of origin (ROOs) have become a technical issue, often regarded as incomprehensible by some (Lazaro and Medulla, 2006). While forming regional agreements Asian economies did not co-ordinate, which led to inconsistency in their ROOs, resulting in high information and transaction costs for the business firms in the partner countries. Inconsistent ROOs can create problems and impede or slow flow of goods and services, introducing uncertainties in the conduct of trade as well as functioning of the production networks. In the present BTAs and FTAs, ROOs is a policy area that has a pressing need for upgrading. If they are better designed than they were in the past, the production network trade in intermediate inputs will be made easier and more efficient. It can be done and was done in changes in ROOs made by AFTA in the 1990s and 2000s. What is needed is the harmonization of ROOs. When ROOs are harmonized, the negative "noodle-bowl effect" is ameliorated. Asian firms that have large regional trade and MNCs have opined in surveys that ROOs in the region need to be harmonized (JETRO, 2007).

Another area where BTAs and FTAs can refine their regulations and support the production networks is by introducing less restrictive cumulation rules. These rules determine how inputs from preferential trading partner countries can be used in producing products that are finally exported. There are three types of rules in this regard: bilateral cumulation, diagonal cumulation and full cumulation. Of these three the first one has the least duty-free access, while the second and third have higher duty-free access. For the smooth functioning of production networks, full cumulation could facilitate more fragmentation of production processes among the members of an FTA. This in turn would increase both intra-FTA-trade and economic integration (Manchin and Pelkmans-Balaoing, 2007). Full cumulation is not very common but is applied by in AFTA and in the EU's Cotonou Agreement.

Likewise, in principle the tolerance or *de minimis* rule reduces the burden of the ROOs for those business firms that use non-originating inputs. These rules determine a percentage of non-originating inputs in producing products without affecting the origin status of the final product. The EU allows 10 percent of non-originating inputs in most of its preferential agreements. Agreeing on reasonable tolerance or *de minimis* rules contributes to easier network production.

5. From market-led to institution-led integration: Why a strategic switch?

Having begun and advanced in a market-led manner, regional integration in Asia was subsequently overtaken by institutional arrangements and agreements, which was the result of inter-governmental initiatives. Therefore it is termed as government- or policy-led regionalism. In so doing the Asian policy mandarins broke from their past trend. Several static and dynamic factors, discussed below, were responsible for Asia's shift from the market-led regional integration to institution-led regionalism, which is formal and policy-induced in character.

In the early 1990s, efforts towards institution-led regional integration made lethargic progress in Asia. At the time of the birth of the WTO in 1995, regionalism in Asia had a conspicuously low profile. Asia was perceived as institutionally underdeveloped. Although there was substantial intra-regional trade, governments agreeing on coverage of tariff reduction and NTBs was found to be difficult among the Asian economies. Such disagreements were obvious even during the negotiations for the ASEAN-China FTA (ACFTA) which was finalized in 2002, where China was exceedingly eager to have the FTA.

Unlike other regions in the global economy, Asia had ignored FTA-led regionalism. Until recently, formation of FTAs and plurilateral regional trade agreement (RTAs) was not a part of Asia's dynamic growth story. There is little element of surprise here. Although Asian economies were successful outward-oriented economies, they displayed little interest in forming intra-regional FTAs in the past because their trade was essentially with the large markets outside the region. Intra-regional trade in Asia was weak and ineffectual before the mid-1980s. It was the yen appreciation of 1985 that gave it a large impetus (Section 2.1). Intra-regional trade and investment began increasing in the 1990s. By the mid-1990s intra-trade reached 50 percent of the total trade, compared to 33 percent in the early 1980s (Section 2).

The institution-led regionalism endeavors in Europe were essentially politically oriented. Resolute initiatives of the governments in European economies integrated them. Their integration progressed in stages. The European economies were advancing towards a so-called Single Market objective in the early 1990s. Their Single European Act had come in to force in 1987. Within seven years this Act sought to abolish all physical, technical and tax-related barriers to free movement of goods within the European community. In 1999 the euro became the currency of eleven of the EU-15 economies. This was the beginning of the final stage of Economic and Monetary Union. The EU is globally most advanced regional cooperation plan. Although some market-driven regionalization had occurred in North America, it was also moving toward the goal of institution-led regionalism in the late 1980s. NAFTA came into being in 1994.[10] Negotiations for the Free Trade Area of the Americas (FTAA) began in 1994. The FTAA is to be a comprehensive hemisphere-wide agreement between 34 countries of North and South America. The last Summit of the Americas was held in 2005 at Mar del Plata, Argentina. It ended without an agreement.

Regionalism was becoming a global trend in the 1990s. The creation of enormous RTAs and numerous FTAs (including BTAs) in other parts of the global economy created the impetus to do the same in Asia. Policy makers in Asia feared being marginalized (Das, 2004). Europe and the Americas were regionalizing, in the process creating giant trading blocs. Asian leaders did not think it wise to leave the global rule-setting and governance to them and play a second fiddle in global governance, or the global economic and financial affairs. It was rational and normal for the Asian economies to want to benefit from regionalism in a similar manner to those that other large trading blocs were benefitting. As the EU and the NAFTA began expanding their network of FTAs globally and promoting their growth, the Asian economies found that they were being excluded from some markets.

5.1 Driver of the proliferation of FTAs: Failure of multilateral liberalization

Failure of multilateral trade liberalization caused frustration among the flourishing trading countries and provided the direct impetus to the proliferation of FTAs and EPAs. This is not an Asia-specific factor but is applied to economies globally. Recent proliferation of FTAs and EPAs was the consequence of the policy-makers' reaction to the disarray during the Uruguay Round, its repeated failures and resurrections. It took twice the length of time for which it was originally scheduled to be completed in. An increase in the membership of the GATT, a sizeable divergence in the interest of members and intransigence shown by large trading economies and groups thereof were some of the reasons behind the discomfiture during the Uruguay Round. Although it concluded successfully, the disparities and disagreements did not. In 1999 an utterly confused, hapless and ignominious failure of the ministerial conference of the WTO occurred in Seattle. During this ministerial conference the decision to launch a new round of MTNs was meant to be taken. It was shelved. This failure had a large impact over the multilateral trading system. Its past achievements began to be underrated and doubts were raised openly about its capability to deliver (Das, 2001).

Furthermore, the Doha Round of MTN was launched in late 2001. It was an extraordinary round of MTNs in many ways. The most conspicuous part was that it was to address the issues affecting the developing countries and their special needs (Das, 2005b). By this time many Asian developing economies as well as those in other regions had emerged as trading economies of significance. The Doha Round was christened the Doha Development Agenda (DDA) because it was intended to promote trade-led growth in the low-income developing countries. Three of the key areas of negotiations in the Doha Round were agriculture, non-agricultural market access (NAMA) and trade in services. In short, the advanced economies were to reduce heavy subsidies to their agricultural trade and the developing ones were to reduce tariffs on industrial goods imports and liberalize trade in services.

The Doha Round proved to be egregiously problem-prone and progressed dismally. As a result of the limited mandates and explicitly mercantilist mindsets of the large and important negotiators, participating countries could not even decide on the modalities of negotiations. The round failed to take off in a substantive manner. The negotiating positions of developing and industrial countries on several substantive issues remained far apart. Owing to deep dissentions among WTO members it had to be suspended after the failure of a meeting of Group-of-Six (G-6) members (Australia, Brazil, the EU, India, Japan and the USA) Ministers of Trade in mid-2006. This exemplified the grossly disappointing failure of multilateralism.

Although the mercantilist mindset of the participants has been frequently blamed for the consistently tardy progress of negotiations during the DDA, there was more to this situation than just the mindset (Das, 2008). Multilateral trade liberalization had become progressively ineffectual and difficult. Forming FTAs (or BTAs) with like-minded countries to liberalize trade and investment further was a logical option. Negotiators from the like-minded countries can readily and easily make more progress on a wider range of issues than they can in a diverse and complex WTO environment. The number of these agreements began to grow fast globally. In 1990 this number was merely 70. In January 2012 the total number notified to the WTO was 319. Of these, 174 were FTAs and 15 were CUs notified under the GATT Article XXIV, while 35 were notified under the Enabling Clause. A total of 95 were notified under the GATS Article V. Additionally, the coverage of these FTAs has been widening. Other than dismantling tariff barriers, they include disciplines such as the movement of capital, investment, intellectual property rights, competition policy, trade in services and technical barriers to trade.

5.2 Expansion of regionalism: Quantitative review

As BTA and FTA formation picked up globally, the Asian economies followed suit. To overcome this disadvantage they also decided to form BTAs and FTAs themselves. They did so with enormous zest and élan and Asia is now home to a large number of FTAs in a short period. In 1980 there were only two FTAs in Asia, one of which was in effect and the other was signed (Table 6.1). This was Asia's period of aloofness from regionalism and therefore the number of FTAs in the region did not increase much. The cumulative number of FTAs in Asia in 1991 was eight, in 1997 it was 44 and in 2000 it was 55.

Launched in October 2006, the Asian Regional Integration Center (www.aric.adb.org) of the Asian Development Bank (ADB), provides comprehensive information and maintains statistical data for both intra- and extra-regional BTAs and FTAs of the Asian economies. Singapore has earned the distinction of being the most proactive in this regard with 35 total FTAs, of which 21 were concluded (Tables 6.1 and 6.2; Figure 6.1). It not only has the largest network of BTAs in Asia but their geographical coverage is the widest. Singapore is the most developed member country of the ASEAN trading bloc and is a founding member of the ASEAN Free Trade Area (AFTA), the oldest (1992) FTA in Asia.

Tables 6.1 and 6.2 are based on ARIC data. Together they present a brief and clear spectacle of quantitative evolution of regionalism in Asia. By the middle of the last decade (2005) the number of FTAs in Asia had soared to 169, of which 56 were in effect and 24 signed. Five years later in 2010, they had increased to 238, 92 in effect and 27 signed. This was a 40 percent increase in short span of five years. This decade (2000–10) saw a phenomenal rise in regionalization in Asia. A four-and-a-half-fold increase in the total number of FTAs in a decade can be described as explosive. FTA-led regionalism in Asia is now a substantial phenomenon. In 2011, the number of FTAs in effect increased to 104, albeit their total number did not change very much. It needs to be clarified that the number of FTAs reported in Table 6.1 and plotted in Figure 6.1 are both, intra- and extra-regional FTAs. They include both bilateral and plurilateral FTAs. In 2013 their total number was 257, of which 109 were in effect. There is another database called the APTIAD,[11] which puts trade agreements at bilateral or plurilateral or regional levels that were operational as of March 2012 at 128. Of these, 58 are FTAs covering only trade in goods, and another 41 cover trade in goods and services. The remaining agreements are partial scope agreements.

TABLE 6.1 FTAs by status (cumulative)

Year	Proposed	Under negotiation		Concluded		Total
		Framework agreement signed/under negotiation	Under negotiation	Signed	In effect	
1975	0	0	0	1	0	1
1980	0	0	0	1	1	2
1991	1	0	0	2	5	8
1997	2	0	0	21	25	44
2000	3	0	6	16	30	55
2005	43	18	28	24	56	169
2006	48	18	37	20	69	192
2007	46	18	42	23	75	204
2008	46	16	42	22	85	213
2009	53	16	45	22	91	227
2010	57	17	47	23	97	241
2011	60	17	47	23	104	251
2012	50	14	61	24	108	257
2013	50	14	61	23	109	257

Source: Author's compilation from Asian Development Bank, 2013. *Asian Regional Integration Center website.* Manila, Philippines.

TABLE 6.2 FTA status by country, 2013

Country	Proposed	Under negotiation		Concluded		Total
		Framework agreement signed/under negotiation	Under negotiation	Signed	In effect	
China	8	2	3	1	11	25
Hong Kong, SAR	1	1	0	0	2	4
Indonesia	6	1	2	1	7	17
Japan	7	0	3	1	11	22
Korea	12	2	5	3	6	28
Malaysia	3	2	6	2	9	22
Philippines	4	0	1	0	7	12
Singapore	4	1	9	3	18	35
Taiwan	1	1	1	0	5	8
Vietnam	4	1	2	0	7	14

Source: Author's compilation from Asian Development Bank, 2013. *Asian Regional Integration Center website.* Manila, Philippines. Available online at www.aric.adb.org.

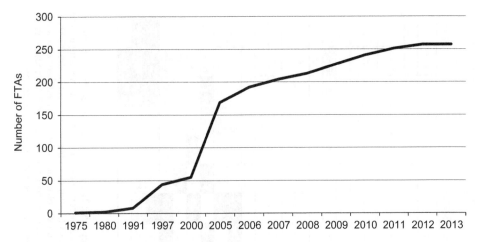

FIGURE 6.1 Total number of FTAs
Source: Author's compilation from Asian Development Bank, 2013. Asian Regional Integration Center website. Manila, The Philippines.

It should, however, be noted that the BTAs and FTAs struck by the Asian economies were not all intra-regional. BTAs and FTAs negotiated during the current period revealed a high degree of extra-regionalism. As a generalization it can be stated that for every one intra-regional FTA, Asian economies negotiated three outside the region.

China and Japan, the two largest regional economies in that order, were latecomers to the regionalization scenario, but both of them became proactive in the BTA and FTA formation during the last decade. Several other regional economies had shown a lot of enthusiasm in adhering to regionalism and forming BTAs and FTAs. Singapore displayed the most active with a total of 35 FTAs, of which 21 were in effect. Korea took the next place with 28 FTAs, of which only nine were concluded. China came next with 25 FTAs, of which 12 were concluded. In this tally Japan and Malaysia were next with 22 FTAs and Indonesia 17, with eight concluded. Among the smaller economies, Viet Nam made healthy progress with a total of 14 FTAs (Table 6.2).

Asia and the Asia-Pacific region combined together now have networks of FTAs, including BTAs. This somewhat intricate picture is portrayed in Figure 6.2. It includes plurilateral FTAs, like the ongoing endeavors to form a Trans Pacific Partnership (TPP).

5.3 Impact of the Asian crisis

Recent economic history of Asian economies is known for their being competitive rather than co-operative, but first the Asian crisis (1997–98) proved to be a defining moment for the Asian economies. It changed the priorities of Asian governments. As the Asian institutions performed poorly during the Asian crisis, it left the regional economies looking highly vulnerable (Section 1.2). This crisis revealed the inadequacy of regional institutions and a perception among the regional leaders that they need to be developed, changed or supplemented. It also inculcated and strengthened a sense of regional identity in Asia. A concept of finding regional solutions for regional economic and financial problems was born and policy measures to realize this objective were encouraged and adopted by the political leadership. In myriad ways this mindset provided a critical impetus to

	Japan	Korea	China	ASEAN	Brunei	Indonesia	Malaysia	Philippines	Singapore	Thailand	Vietnam	CLM	India	Australia	New Zealand	USA	Canada	Mexico	Colombia	Peru	Chile	EU	EFTA	Switzerland
Japan		○ (suspen	△	◎: 2008 -	◎: 2008	◎: 2008	◎: 2006	◎: 2008	◎: 2002	◎: 2007	◎: 2009		◎:2011	○			△	◎: 2005		◎	◎: 2007			◎: 2009
Korea	○ (suspen		△	◎: 2007 -		△			◎: 2006		△		◎: 2010	○	○	◎	○	○	○	◎: 2011	◎: 2004	◎: 2011	◎: 2006	
China	△	△		◎: 2005 -					◎: 2009				△	○	◎: 2008					◎: 2010	◎: 2006			○
ASEAN	◎: 2008 -	◎: 2007 -	◎: 2005 -	◎: 1973-		(1992)	(1992)	(1992)	(1992)	(1992)	(1995)	(LM:1997/C:1999)	◎: 2010 -	◎: 2010 -	◎: 2010 -									
Brunei	◎: 2008			(1992)		(1992)	(1992)	(1992)	(1992)	(1992)	(1995)	(LM:1997/C:1999)		○	◎	○				○	◎: 2006			
Indonesia	◎: 2008	△		(1992)	(1992)		(1992)	(1992)	(1992)	(1992)	(1995)	(LM:1997/C:1999)	△	○								△	○	
Malaysia	◎: 2006			(1992)	(1992)			(1992)	(1992)	(1992)	(1995)	(LM:1997/C:1999)	◎	○	◎:2010	○				○	◎	○		
Philippines	◎: 2008			(1992)	(1992)	(1992)	(1992)		(1992)	(1992)	(1995)	(LM:1997/C:1999)				△								
Singapore	◎: 2002	◎: 2006	◎: 2009	(1992)	(1992)	(1992)	(1992)	(1992)		(1992)	(1995)	(LM:1997/C:1999)	◎: 2005	◎: 2003	◎: 2001	◎: 2004	○	○		◎: 2009	◎: 2006	○	◎: 2003	
Thailand	◎: 2007			(1992)	(1992)	(1992)	(1992)	(1992)	(1992)		(1995)	(LM:1997/C:1999)	△	◎: 2005	◎: 2005	○				○	△		○	
Vietnam	◎: 2009	△		(1995)	(1995)	(1995)	(1995)	(1995)	(1995)	(1995)		(LM:1997/C:1999)		○	○	○				○	○		△	
CLM				(LM:1997/C:1999)	(LM:1997/C:1999)	(LM:1997/C:1999)	(LM:1997/C:1999)	(LM:1997/C:1999)	(LM:1997/C:1999)	(LM:1997/C:1999)	(LM:1997/C:1999)													
India	◎: 2011	◎: 2010	△	◎: 2010 -		△	◎		◎: 2005	△				○	○		○				◎: 2007	○	△	
Australia	○	○	○	◎: 2010 -	○	○	○		◎: 2003	◎: 2005	○		○		◎:1983	◎: 2005				○	◎: 2009			
New Zealand		○	◎: 2008	◎: 2010 -	◎: 2006		◎: 2010		◎: 2001	◎: 2005	○		○	◎:1983		○				○	◎: 2006			
USA		◎			○		○	△	◎: 2004	○	○			◎: 2005	○		◎: 1989	◎: 1994	◎	◎: 2009	◎: 2004			△
Canada	△	○							○				○			◎: 1989		◎: 1994	◎	◎: 2009	◎: 1997	○	◎: 2009	
Mexico	◎: 2005	○							○							◎: 1994	◎: 1994		◎: 1995	○	◎: 1999	◎: 2000	◎: 2011	
Colombia		○														◎	◎	◎: 1995		◎: 1969	◎: 2009	○	◎: 2011	
Peru	◎	◎: 2011	◎: 2010		○		○		◎: 2009	○	○			○	○	◎: 2009	◎: 2009	○	◎: 1969		◎: 2009	○	◎: 2011	
Chile	◎: 2007	◎: 2004	◎: 2006		◎: 2006		◎		◎: 2006	△	○		◎: 2007	◎: 2009	◎: 2006	◎: 2004	◎	◎: 1999	◎: 2009	◎: 2009		◎: 2003	◎: 2004	
EU		◎: 2011				△	○		○				○				○	◎: 2000	○	○	◎: 2003	◎: 1958	◎: 1994	◎: 1973
EFTA		◎: 2006				○			◎: 2003	○	△		△				◎: 2009	◎: 2001	◎: 2011	◎: 2011	◎: 2004	◎: 1994	◎: 1960	(1960)
Switzerland	◎: 2009		○													△						◎: 1973	(1960)	

FIGURE 6.2 Current FTA network in Asia (as of August 2011)

Notes: ◎: signed or being effective. ○: under negotiation or agreed to negotiate. △: feasibility study or preparatory talks. The year indicates when the concerned FTA was in force. "-" after the year means that some ASEAN countries are under the corresponding FTAs in force and other countries follow later. Black shading indicates FTAs signed before or in the 1990s, dark grey indicates FTAs in the first half of the 2000s, and light grey indicates FTAs signed in the second half of the 2000s. For some FTAs, their status in this table is based on the agreement of trade in goods negotiations may be still ongoing over other areas such as investment and services even if the agreements are identified as those signed or being effective here. The year in parenthesis shows the year for the corresponding ASEAN country to be a member of ASEAN/AFTA. Countries with grey shading are current participants in TPP negotiations. Sources: Websites of trade ministries in each country

Source: Courtesy of Fuku Kimura, Faculty of Economics, Keio University, Toyko, Japan.

regionalism. The true beginning of institution-driven formal regionalism in Asia took place in the late 1990s. The Asian crisis was a defining moment in its development. This could be called the real initiation of an FTA *zeitgeist* in Asia. Second, the twin crises that hit the global economy in 2007 had an identical impact.

The political environment in the 1990s in Asia was honing for building up networks of bilateral plurilateral agreements. The reason was that this was the post-Cold War period and there was a thaw in the political relations among countries in Asia, particularly between China and its immediate Asian neighbors. The mutual suspicion and distrust of the past was receding. Not only were Asian economies more willing to enter into bilateral and multilateral agreements than previously, but also those economies outside the region.

5.4 Contagion of regionalism and bilateralism in Asia

One characteristic of FTAs is that they are contagious. This trend is borne out by what ensued in Asia. On the eve of the Asian crisis in 1997, there were 43 FTAs in total Asia, 20 in effect and 21 signed (Table 6.1). The Asian crisis was a problematic confluence of currency and banking crises that made Asian policy makers realize the value of regional economic co-operation. The crisis transformed the regional architecture of Asia. Pomfret (2011) regarded Asian regionalism as economic regionalism that was largely crisis driven. In 2005 the cumulative number of FTAs in Asia jumped to 170. Of these, 51 FTAs were in effect and 28 signed. The rate of increase in the number of FTAs increased further and in 2011 their number reached 238. Of these 93 were in effect, 27 signed and good numbers under negotiation and proposed (Table 6.1; Figure 6.1). Strategic initiatives like regional economic surveillance, regional liquidity support facility and determination to develop an Asian bond market were born of the crisis.

Many FTAs in Asia were BTAs. The mushrooming of bilateralism was a global phenomenon. These BTAs were customized to reflect the specific interests of the participating countries. There was a concern that this tide of bilateralism would sweep away multilateralism, or at least pose a serious threat to it. Asian economies took to bilateralism in the late 1990s. Economies that took the lead in regionalism were the relatively better-off economies of Asia. Singapore, Japan, China, Korea and Thailand were the most energetic in forming BTAs and FTAs. In 1995 there were only three BTAs in the region that were notified to the WTO, but by 2005 their number vaulted to 27. These five economies dominate the number of concluded agreements. The poorer economies (like Cambodia, Lao PDR and Viet Nam) depended on their ASEAN membership for concluding BTAs and FTAs with the largest economies of the region. Apparently the poorer economies are also the weaker economies in terms of institutional development. They were not ready and could ill-afford long-drawn-out negotiations.

The post-Asian-crisis period was the era of financial co-operation. The ASEAN-Plus-Three (APT) Ministers of Finance became purposefully and tenaciously active. This core group included ASEAN, China, Japan and Korea. The crisis motivated a lot of other material changes in the Asian economic policy and structure. One of them was virtual abandonment of their wish to liberalize unilaterally. Asian economies made a short-term retreat from trade liberalization. Apparently after the Asian crisis policy makers considered adoption of regionalism as a necessary source of stability and economic revitalization. Asian economies faced several common challenges and regionalism could become an instrument of addressing them. The Asian economies switched their commitment from their customary multilateralism to regionalism.

Since the Asian crisis, regional economic integration progressed through intra-regional trade, FDI and financial and macro-economic interdependence in the Asian economies. During the post-Asian crisis period efforts to regionally integrate in a government-led manner became vigorous, resulting in a profuse proliferation of FTAs in Asia—even some RTAs (Table 6.1, Figure 6.1). One of the responses to the crisis of the Asian economies was to try to create a regional economic community, or at least an Asian FTA. Expectation was that a close-knit community of Asian economies will be able to cope with an Asian-crisis-like situation better and sustain each other in their hour of need. While they were not taking steps to form an EU-like centralized institution, a core group of concurring and compatible Asian economies was ready during the crisis period to cooperate and collaborate to form some kind of stable Asian institutional grouping.

At the turn of the century, pace of movement towards regionalism increased further. Asian FTAs grew both intra-regionally and inter-regionally and the growth rate was faster than in the past (Table 6.1). At this juncture (2000), China, Japan, Korea, Mongolia and Taiwan were the only countries whose faith in multilateralism had not wavered. However, situation began to change drastically after this time point. In the first decade of the twenty-first century BTAs proliferated globally at a far more rapid rate than in the past. In keeping with this global trend, a large number of BTAs and a small number of FTAs were signed in Asia as well (Table 6.1). Their number soared at an extraordinary pace. Asia is now regarded as "the vanguard of a new wave of regional and bilateral trade agreements" (Pomfret, 2009, p. 1). In the late 1990s Japan, Korea, Singapore and New Zealand took lead in entering into BTAs and by 2000 Australia, China, Thailand and the USA also joined in this trend.

In the aftermath of the Asian crisis, the need for financial co-operation and monetary integration was felt not only by the crisis-affected economies but also by the entire Asian region. Asian governments realized that financial cooperation can be planned and implemented more efficaciously if the region is a close, cohesive financial unit. It would enable regional governments to plan defensive financial strategies for a possible period of financial distress. The proposal of the Chiang Mai Initiative (CMI) was made by all the regional economies, small and large, in May 2000. It was the first ever regional agreement involving banking and finance. Having a regional framework as its home was considered necessary for schemes like the CMI to function and develop further. It is widely considered as the most successful regional integration effort involving the 13 APT economies. During the global financial crisis (2007–09) the Asian economies did not feel the need to utilize CMI because their national reserves were more than adequate to fend off the crisis (Das, 2011).

The CMI was the first formal regional agreement in the area of finance, albeit informal agreements like Executives' Meeting of East Asia-Pacific Central Banks (EMEAP) had existed since 1991. The EMEAP is a co-operative organization of 11 central banks in the Asia-Pacific region.[12] Its primary objective is to strengthen the co-operative relationship between the member central banks. The EMEAP launched the Asian Bond Market Initiative (ABMI), which was endorsed by the finance ministers of APT countries in 2003. The ABMI had a logical, timely and desirable goal of mobilizing regional financial resources for fulfilling region's needs, but the value of bonds issued so far has remained small. Assessing candidly, CMI and ABMI have so far made minor contributions to regional monetary integration. The same can be stated regarding the Chiang Mai Initiative Multilateralization (CNIM). In early 2009 the Ministers of Finance of APT countries decided to multilateralize the swap arrangements under CMI. It would allow a country with balance-of-payments (BOP) problems to access the entire pool of $120 billion (Pomfret, 2009). Endeavors towards strong regional financial integration have not been made in the region and it still remains meager. Asia is not regarded as financially integrated region.

As the first decade ended, most small Asian economies and *a fortiori* the large ones had accepted regionalism as a policy instrument for pursuing regional and global trade expansion and economic integration. This applies particularly to China, Japan and Korea. In this context, Korea's success in forming FTAs with the EU (2010) and the USA (2011) is particularly striking. In 2012 Korea was making overtures to negotiate a BTA with China (Das, 2012). For all appearances FTA-led regionalism has found a home in Asia. In 2012 it could be justly stated that after the EU, regionalism is most advanced in Asia.

5.5 Impact of the twin financial crises

First, the global financial crises originating in the USA (2007–09) and then the sovereign debt crisis in the Eurozone caused economic stress globally.[13] Global recovery weakened after 2010, when the global GDP growth rate was 5.2 percent. It plummeted to 3.8 percent in 2011. In early 2012 Europe continued to be the epicenter of economic threat and the outlook for the EU was uncertain. There were apprehensions of global recovery stalling and the IMF (2012) reduced the projected growth rate of the global economy by 0.7 percent, to 3.3 percent for 2012.[14] The twin financial crises had a significant impact over the Asian economies, particularly the EMEs and the NIEs as well as on their on-going economic integration process. In early 2012 the IMF (2012) revised the projected growth rate for the Asian economies downward. The largest cut (by 1.2 percent) was made in the projected growth rate of the Asian NIEs. Their 2012 output growth prospects were reduced to 3.3 percent.

In a depressed or recessionary climate concerns regarding protectionism impulsively rise, policy makers grow defensive and prospects of regional trade policy liberalization and integration logically decline, if not evaporate. This line of thinking does not seem illogical at all. In periods of economic distress public support for trade liberalization suffers a setback. Often the primary concerns of the sluggish or stagnating economies are to make domestic economic adjustments for defending inefficient and non-competitive sectors. This ambiance goes counter to any movement towards regionalism and the trade policies become polarized. Solis (2011, p. 312) goes as far as saying that "policy makers may be pressed to renege on intra-regional trade liberalization commitments on all fronts". The impulse or momentum to negotiate FTAs and BTAs during these periods can be totally dissipated. For instance, negotiations for the China-Korea FTA were going to be launched in 2008, but the global financial crisis disrupted their schedule and made everything seem unimportant (Das, 2012).

In the backdrop of what transpired in Asia, it is difficult to unquestioningly accept the above line of logic that the recessionary and crisis environment obstructs trade liberalization and region-alism. We cannot ignore the stark reality that the Asian crisis (1997–98) turned out to be a true stimulus to intra-Asia regionalism. For the Asian economies difficult times increased the appeal of bilateral and regional negotiations. Insulation from crises in other parts of the globe—as in the case of the twin financial crises—can be achieved by integrating regionally and thereby protecting the domestic and regional economies from external shocks. Participation in FTAs may be seen as a more practical method of sheltering inefficient industrial sectors. One meaningful outcome of the global financial crisis and the Eurozone sovereign debt crisis in Asia was the desire to expand intra-regional trade and have larger and deeper regional markets to rely on. This was seen as an effective defensive strategy to minimize external financial contagion in difficult economic times.

The theoretical proposition in this regard is that financial crises have a catalytic effect in promoting economic and financial regionalism as well as institutional innovation and integration

(Calder and Ye, 2004; MacIntyre *et al.,* 2008; Chin and Stubbs, 2011). The post-Asian financial crisis-like developments are more common than uncommon. During the decade following the Asian financial crisis Asian economies gradually financially liberalized and cooperated on financial issues of mutual interest. Asian economies responded to the twin financial crises by pushing ahead more earnestly with regional cooperation and integration (Arner and Schou-Zibell, 2010 and Chin, 2012). This was their method of dealing with the exogenous pressures. To this end, they attempted to institute fundamental structural, financial and monetary reforms in a co-ordinated manner. They paid particular attention to regional trade and financial co-operation. The CMI was expanded into the CMIM in 2010.

As the export-oriented growth in the Asian economies was excessively reliant on two of the largest global markets, the EU and the USA, they found themselves truly vulnerable in the times of crises and recession. During and after the crises, they needed to rebalance their growth strategies towards domestic and regional demands. The Obama Administration made it clear in 2010 that the days of treating the USA as the "importer of last resort"[15] have receded into the past.[16] Also, in this context, the advent of China as a global economic power, a large market and the largest regional economy that was also interested in advancing regional integration agenda was of large significance. In the post-2007 period, China's endeavors in this direction intensified. These regional integration measures contributed to reshaping economic globalization.

Even before the twin crises precipitated, Asia's role in mitigating global imbalances was being debated in the policy conclaves. In the aftermath of the global financial crisis Asian economies, particularly the EMEs and the NIEs, suffered from a brief recession. The so-called Great Recession not only caused this short and in the case of the NIEs deep recession, but it also demonstrated that it could be a source of vulnerability in the region. This motivated calls for a fundamental restructuring of demand, that is for relying more on the domestic and regional demand to countervail the excessive reliance on extra-regional markets. This was an apparent case of a global crisis promoting regionalist tendencies. Furthermore, the export-led model served the Asian economies well in the past. In the post-crises period Asian economies will need to restructure. They not only needed to alter their past pattern of emphases on domestic and external components of demand but also shift from export-led to domestic consumption-led growth. Such a transformation in the regional EMEs, like China, was under way.

This large and crucial shift in turn would require a significant industrial reorganization, both domestically and regionally. In the absence of the adoption of major strategic modifications in the Asian EMEs, imperative policy objectives like sustainable regional growth and the stabilization of the global economy will be difficult to attain. A rebalancing economic growth in Asia would be in the direct interest of the regional economy as well as important to the stability of global economy. The reason is that according to Prasad (2011) the feedback loop between the real economy and financial sector has become short. Also, in the short term the old global demand leaders, the EU and the USA, will not be able play their customary role. Therefore the dynamic Asian economies will be expected to, first integrate regionally more than they did in the past, and second take over the roles that the demand leaders of the past played during the pre-crises period.

Taking on this new regional role will not be easy for the Asian EMEs. The reason is that an important part of the Asian exports, particularly those from the EMEs and the NIEs, are specifically manufactured for their export markets in the advanced economies. They are customized to the need of the markets. Domestic demand for those products is either limited or nonexistent. Likewise a good part of physical capital and infrastructure in the Asian economies was created for the manufactured products intended for exports, not for domestic consumption. In addition, several industries are known to have excess capacity, particularly in China. Therefore a slowdown in import demand in the EU and the USA could become an onerous problem for the region (Prasad, 2011). All medium and large Asian economies are linked through supply chains to the regional production networks and are suppliers of parts, components and sub-assemblies so that final products for export can be manufactured. A slowdown in Asian exports will exacerbate their problems. These parts and components again have little utility in the domestic markets of the producing economies. The imminent deceleration in Asian exports will require reconfiguration and consolidation of the regional production networks, which will need to be downsized initially. This in turn will limit the opportunities and scope for benefitting from the regional division of labor.

The twin crises have been causing a change in global and regional macro-economic structures. Ongoing regional integration in Asia will need to adjust to it. Asian economies will need to restructure their domestic industrial sector in such a manner that the final goods for domestic consumption can be produced in lieu of exportables. This is evidently a viable option. However, it would necessarily entail creative destruction. Even if factor endowments allow such restructuring, it is a high cost option. If the Asian economies succeed in moving away from their present structure of vertically integrated production networks and trade and if they even partially return to horizontal specialization and classical pattern of production and trade in final goods, it will be helpful for the changing global economic structure. This will eventually lead to restoration of the traditional "flying geese" pattern of trade and production in Asia (Akyuz, 2011).

6. Characteristic features of Asian integration

Regional integration, as it progressed since 2000, has several notable characteristics. The first one is that FTAs and EPAs tend to be area-based and function-based (Okamoto, 2011). Function-based integration entails liberalization of trade in goods and services, in investment, in government procurement and in movement of skilled or unskilled labor. It also covers protection of IPR. However this coverage of FTAs is not uniform across the region and all FTAs and EPAs vary according to the preferences of the partners. In addition, efforts to co-operate in areas like finance, structural reforms, energy and food security and environmental protection were also made. They were not taken up under FTAs, but under different frameworks. Secondly, both bilateral and multilateral integration worked simultaneously in the region. Thirdly, although it did not happen frequently, extra-regional partners also participated in the regional integration process.

Thus, Asian integration process is a "flexible", "inclusive" and "multi-layered" process (Okamoto, 2011, p. 311). First of all, one of the reasons behind flexibility and inclusivity is the pragmatic search for gains by the partners from the integration process. Second, an important lesson of the Asian crisis for the Asian governments was to regain the confidence of markets in their economic governance. Having restored it, they thought they needed to keep it so that domestic economies can be run in a stable manner. This reason applied more to the ASEAN economies than to the other Asian economies. The ASEAN governments endeavored to strengthen their economic governance and to enhance their investment environment. Their regional integration efforts were, *inter alia*, directed towards this objective. Third, notwithstanding the increase in intra-regional trade and investment, for the Asian economies FTAs with the extra-regional partners are still important. The EU and the USA are still large trading partners of many Asian economies. Korea entered into FTAs with the EU and the USA before it finalized one with China, its largest trading partner. Fourth, flexibility and inclusiveness also helped in balancing country influences.

7. Summary and conclusions

The principal thematic strand of this chapter is Asia's market-driven region integration and its subsequent turn towards institution-led or policy-oriented regionalism. In adopting the latter, Asian economies are justly regarded as slowpokes but there were good reasons behind it. Asian economies were able to sustain one of the highest real GDP growth rates in the global economy, which, *inter alia*, facilitated and gave momentum to its market-driven regional integration. This process of market-led regional integration had started in a low-key manner since the 1970s, but it picked up momentum since the Plaza Accord in 1985. This was a bottom-up process of regionalization. This integration was driven by trade, FDI and financial flows, which was the result of normal business activities of Asian business firms. MNCs played an active role in this kind of regionalization, so did the operations of the medium and large private sector businesses in this *de facto* process of regionalization.

Asian economies actively began entering into FTAs and BTAs with each other and with extra-regional economies. The cumulative number of FTAs in Asia in 1991 was eight, in 1997 it was 43 and in 2000 54. By the middle of the last decade (2005) the number of FTAs in Asia had soared to 170, of which 51 were in effect and 28 signed. Five years later in 2010, they increased to 238, 92 in effect and 27 signed. This was a 40 percent increase in short span of five years. This decade (2000–10) saw a phenomenal rise in regionalization in Asia. A four-and-a-half-fold increase in the total number of FTAs in a decade can be unhesitatingly described as explosive. FTA-led regionalism in Asia is now a substantial phenomenon. In 2011 the number of FTAs in effect increased to 93, although their total number did not change. It needs to be clarified that the number of FTAs reported in table 6.1 and plotted in Figure 6.1 are both, intra- and extra-regional FTAs. They include both bilateral and plurilateral FTAs.

The Asian economy has become recognized for vertically integrated production networks and supply chains. In several major industrial sectors like automobile, machinery, chemicals and electronics and ICT there are most sophisticated production networks in Asia. These production networks have significantly deepened over the preceding two decades and motivated market-led integration of Asia. When economies in a region develop trade relations through the expansion of production chains or value chains, those ties continue and survive for long periods. They break down only when the final products that they produce lose their importance. Vertically integrated production-network-related trade was a significant phenomenon. It led to a higher probability of the creation of deeper regional integration among countries in a region. In order for the production networks in two or more regional economies to operate efficiently, certain national standards, regulations and other policies need to be harmonized. This in turn creates an expected demand for regional integration from business firms for harmonization of standards, regulations and other policies. This kind of policy harmonization subsequently becomes an instrument of deeper regional integration.

A large number of FTAs in Asia were BTAs. Mushrooming bilateralism became a global phenomenon. They were customized to meet the needs of the participating economies. Asian economies that took lead in bilateralism were generally the better off economies. China, Japan, Korea, Singapore and Thailand were the most prominent in BTA formation. Also, the APT group of economies became purposefully and evidently active.

Although it began in a market-led manner, regional integration in Asia was subsequently overtaken by institutional arrangements and agreements, which were the result of inter-governmental initiatives. Therefore it is termed as government- or policy-led regionalism. In so doing the Asian policy mandarins broke from their past trend. Several static and dynamic factors were responsible for Asia's shift from the market-led regional integration to institution-led regionalism, which is formal and policy-induced in character. Although in the early 1990s institutional-led regionalism progressed in Asia lethargically, but by the end of the decade several strong forces began to drive it and it soon began to proliferate. This chapter provides quantitative details of agreements at bilateral and plurilateral or regional levels. The Asian crisis was a watershed point in this regard. The post-Asian crisis period became the FTA *zeitgeist* in Asia. After that the twin crises that struck the global economy after 2007 proved to be another stimulus to the proliferation of institution-led regionalism in Asia. The three crises caused a significant change in regional and global macro-economic structures. They particularly had a discernible impact over the Asian institution-led regionalism.

Notes

1 The original GATT text (GATT 1947) is still in effect under the WTO framework, subject to the modifications of GATT 1994.
2 Although in the original articles of agreement of the GATT there were clear rules regarding the formation of PTAs, they were fairly imprecise, incomplete and were never seriously enforced.
3 They are also called regional trade agreements (RTA) or preferential trade agreements (PTAs). The GATT Article XXIV uses the term FTA in reference to a "free trade area".
4 The ASEAN-Plus-Three (APT) economies comprise the 10 members of the ASEAN bloc, plus China, Japan and Korea.
5 See WTO (2011) Table 1.4, p. 21.
6 A statistical proof is provided in WB (2000).
7 See WTO (2011), Table II. p. 40.
8 See also Searight (2009).
9 See Feenstra and Henson, 1996; Feenstra, 1998; Jones *et al.*, 2005; Kimura and Ando, 2005. See also Kimura and Obashi (2011) for a lucid and succinct account of the growth of production networks in Asia.
10 The agreement was initially pursued by governments in the USA and Canada supportive of free trade, led by Canadian Prime Minister Brian Mulroney, US President George H. W. Bush, and the Mexican President Carlos Salinas de Gortari. The three-nation NAFTA was signed on 17 December 1992, pending its ratification by the legislatures of the three countries. It came in effect in January 1994.
11 Asia-Pacific Trade and Investment Agreements Database (APTIAD) can be accessed online at www. unescap.org/tid/aptiad.
12 The 11 central banks are the Reserve Bank of Australia, the People's Bank of China, the Hong Kong Monetary Authority, Bank Indonesia, Bank of Japan, Bank of Korea, Bank Negara Malaysia, the Reserve Bank of New Zealand, Bangko Sentral ng Pilipinas, the Monetary Authority of Singapore and Bank of Thailand.
13 The European sovereign debt crisis began in Greece in May 2010. Greece requested assistance from the EU and the International Monetary Fund (IMF). A substantial size aid package (€110 billion or $145 billion) was announced in May. The twin objectives of this package were to rescue Greece from defaulting on its debt obligations and to stall the contagion from spreading to Portugal, Spain, Ireland and Italy. In late 2010 the crisis took a turn for the worse.
14 See IMF (2012) Table 2, p. 2 .
15 This phrase was coined and used by Larry Summers in an interview with the *Financial Times* on 11 July 2009. It was published under the heading, "Lunch with the FT" on 11 July 2009. It is available online at www.ft.com/intl/cms/s/0/6ac06592–96ce0–11de-af56–00144feabdc0.html#axzz1mEWr4YNV.
16 Speaking in Yokohama in Japan on 13 November 2010, on the sidelines of the APEC summit, President Barack Obama said: "Going forward, no nation should assume that their path to prosperity is simply paved with exports to America." Available ononline at www.bbc.co.uk/news/world-asia-pacific-11748433?print=true. In an apparent reference to China and Japan he also said that countries with a large surplus must take steps to boost domestic demand.

References

Akyuz, Y. 2011. "The Global Economic Crisis and Trade and Growth Prospects in East Asia." Manila, the Philippines: Asian Development Bank. Working paper Series No. 242. January.

Antras, P. and R. W. Staiger. 2012. "Offshoring and the Role of Trade Agreements." *American Economic Review.* Vol. 102. No. 7, pp. 3140–83.

——2008. "Offshoring and the Role of Trade Agreements." London: Center for Economic Policy Research. Working Paper No. 6966.

Ariff, M. 2011. "Comments on Politics of Association of Southeast Asian Nations Economic Cooperation." *Asian Economic Policy Review.* Vol. 6. No. 1, pp. 39–40.

Arner, D. and L. Schou-Zibell. 2010. "Responding to the Global Financial and Economic Crisis: Meeting the Challenge in Asia." Manila, the Philippines: Asian Development Bank. Working Paper No. 60. October.

Balassa, B. 1961. *The Theory of Economic Integration.* London: Allen & Unwin.

Breslin, S. 2010. "Comparative Theory, China and the Future of East Asian Regionalism." *Review of International Studies.* Vol. 36. No. 3, pp. 709–29.

Calder, K. and M. Ye. 2004. "Regionalism and Critical Junctures." *Journal of East Asian Studies.* Spring. Vol. 4. No. 2, pp. 191–226.

Calderon, C., A. Chong and E. Stein. 2007. "Trade Intensity and Business Cycle Synchronization: Are Developing Countries Any Different?" *Journal of International Economics.* Vol. 71. No. 1, pp. 2–21.

Chia, S. Y. 2010. "Regional Trade Policy Cooperation and Architecture in East Asia." Tokyo: Asian Development Bank Institute. Working Paper Series No. 191. October.

Chin, G. 2012. "Responding to the Global Financial Crisis: The Evolution of Asian Regionalism." Manila, the Philippines: Asian Development Bank. Working Paper No. 343. January.

Das, Dilip K. 2012. "Regional Implications of China-Korea FTA." *The Korea Times.* 27 January, p. 7.

——2011. *Asian Economy: Spearheading the Recovery from the Global Financial Crisis.* London and New York: Routledge.

——2009. *The Two Faces of Globalization: Munificent and Malevolent.* Northampton, MA, and Cheltenham: Edward Elgar.

——2008. "Suspension of the Doha Round of Multilateral Trade Negotiations." *Estey Journal of International Law and Trade Policy.* Vol. 9. No. 1, pp. 51–73.

——2005a. "Market-Driven Regionalization in Asia." *Global Economic Journal.* Vol. 5. No. 2, Article 2. Available online at www.bepress.com/gej/vol5/iss3/2.

——2005b. *The Doha Round of Multilateral Trade Negotiations: Arduous Issues and Strategic Responses.* Basingstoke: Palgrave Macmillan.

——2004. *Regionalism in Global Trade: Turning Kaleidoscope.* Northampton, MA, and Cheltenham, UK: Edward Elgar Publishing

——2001. *The Global Trading System at Crossroads: A Post-Seattle Perspective.* London and New York: Routledge.

——1992. *The Yen Appreciation and the International Economy.* London: Macmillan Press; and New York: The New York University Press.

East Asia Vision Group (EAVG). 2001. "Towards An East Asian Community." Jakarta, Indonesia. The ASEAN Secretariat. Available online at www.mofa.go.jp/region/asia-paci/report2001.pdf.

Economic Intelligence Unit (EIU). 2011. *Rising Consumption, Rising Influence: How Asian Consumers will Reshape the Global Electronics Industry.* London.

Ernst, D. 2008. "Innovation Offshoring and Asia's Electronics Industry." *International Journal of Technological Learning, Innovation and Development.* Vol. 1. No. 4, pp. 551–76.

——2006. "Searching for a New Role in East Asian Regionalization", in P. J. Katzenstein and T. Shiraishi (eds). *Remaking East Asia: Beyond Americanization and Japanization.* NY: Cornell University Press, pp. 161–87.

Feenstra, R. C. 1998. "Integration of Trade and Disintegration of Production." *Journal of Economic Perspective.* Vol. 12. No. 1, pp. 31–50.

Feenstra, R. C. and G. H. Henson. 1996. "Globalization, Outsourcing and Wage Inequality." *American Economic Review.* Vol. 86. No. 2, pp. 240–45.

Fukao, K., H. Ishido and K. Ito. 2003. "Vertical Intra-Industry Trade and Foreign Direct Investment in East Asia." *Journal of Japanese and International Economies.* Vol. 17. No. 4, pp. 468–506.

Gill, I. and H. J. Kharas. 2009. "Gravity and Friction in Growing East Asia." *Oxford Review of Economic Policy.* Vol. 25. No. 2, pp. 190–204.

Grossman, G. M. and E. Rossi-Hansberg. 2008. "Trading Tasks: A Simple Theory of Offshoring." *American Economic Review*. Vol. 95. No. 5, pp. 1978–97.

Hayakawa, K. and T. Matsuura. 2011. "Complex vertical FDI and firm heterogeneity: Evidence from East Asia." *Journal of the Japanese and International Economies*. Vol. 25. No. 3, pp. 273–89.

——2009. "Complex Vertical FDI and Firm Heterogeneity: Evidence from East Asia." Tokyo: Institute of Developing Economies, Japan External Trade Organization (JETRO). IDE Discussion Papers No. 211.

Hiratsuka, D. 2010a. "Production Networks in Asia: A Case Study of Hard Disk Drive Industry." Paper presented at the *Comparative Analysis of Production Networks in Asia, and Europe*. Organized by the Vienna Institute for International Economic Studies, Vienna, 15–16 July.

——2010b. "Characteristics and Determinants of East Asia's Trade Patterns", in D. Hiratsuka Y. Uchida (eds). *Input Trade Production Networks in East Asia*. Cheltenham: Edward Elgar, pp. 62–83.

Hiratsuka, D. and Y. Uchida. 2010. *Input Trade and Production Networks in East Asia*. Cheltenham and Northampton, MA: Edward Elgar.

Hu, R. W. 2009. "Building Asia Pacific Regional Architecture." Washington, DC: The Brookings Institutions Press. July.

Hummels, D., J. Ishii and K. M. Yi. 2001. "The Nature and Growth of Vertical Specialization in World Trade." *Journal of International Economics*. Vol. 54. No. 1, pp. 75–96.

International Monetary Fund (IMF). 2012. *World Economic Outlook: Update*. Washington, DC. 24 January.

Japan External Trade Organization (JETRO). 2007. "2006 Survey of Japanese Firms." Tokyo, Japan.

Jones, R., H. Kierzkowski and L. Chen. 2005. "What Does Evidence Tell Us about Fragmentation and Outsourcing?" *International Review of Economics and Finance*. Vol. 14. No. 3, pp. 305–16.

Kimura, F. and M. Ando. 2005. "Two-Dimensional Fragmentation in East Asia: Conceptual Framework and Empirics." *International Review of Economics and Finance*. Vol. 14. No. 2, pp. 317–44.

Kimura, F. and A. Obashi. 2011. "Production Networks in east Asia: What We Know So Far." Tokyo: Asian Development Bank Institute. Discussion Paper No. 320.

Krugman, P. 1998. "What's New about the New Economic Geography?" *Oxford Review of Economic Policy*. Vol. 14. No. 2, pp. 7–17.

Lazaro, D. C. and E. M. Medulla. 2006. "Rules of Origin: Evolving Best Practives for RTAs." Manila, the Philippines. The Philippines Institute for Development Studies. Discussion Paper No. 2006–01.

Lawrence, R. Z. 1996. *Regionalism, Multilateralism, and Deeper Integration*. Washington, DC: The Brookings Institution Press.

MacIntyre, A., T. J. Pempel and J. Ravenhill (eds). 2008. *Crisis as Catalyst: Asia's Dynamic Political Economy*. Ithaca, NY: Cornell University Press.

Mathews, J. A. and D. S. Cho. 2000. *Tiger Technology: The Creation of a Semi-Conductor Industry in East Asia*. Cambridge: Cambridge University Press.

Manchin, M. and A. O. Pelkmans-Balaoing. 2006. "Rules of Origin and the Web of East Asian Free Trade Agreements." Washington, DC: World Bank. Policy Research Working paper No. 4273.

Ng, F. and A. J. Yeats. 1999. "Production Sharing in East Asia." Washington, DC: World Bank. Policy Research Working Paper No. 2197.

Obashi, A. 2010a. "Stability of Production Networks in East Asia: Duration and Survival of Trade." *Japan and World Economy*. Vol. 22. No. 1, pp. 21–30.

——2010b. "Stability of International Production Networks: Is East Asia Special?" *International Journal of Business and Developmental Studies*. Vol. 2. No. 1, pp. 63–94.

Okamoto, J. 2011. "Institutional Building for Economic Integration in Asia", in M. Fujita, I. Kuroiwa and S. Kumagai (eds). *The Economics of East Asian Integration*. Tokyo: Institute of Developing Economies, pp. 287–319.

Orefice, G. and N. Rocha. 2011. "Deep Integration and Production Networks: An Empirical Analysis." Geneva, Switzerland. World Trade Organization. Staff Working Paper No. 2011-11. July.

Panitchpakdi, S. 2011. "East Asia in the World: Prospects and Challenges." Geneva and New York: United Nations Conference on Trade and Development. 24 February.

Petri, P. A. 2011. "The Determinants of Bilateral FDI: Is Asia Different?" *Journal of Asian Economics*. Vol. 23. No.1, pp. 201–9.

——2006. "Is East Asia Becoming More Interdependent?" *Journal of Asian Economics*. Vol. 17, No. 3, pp. 381–94.

Pomfret, R. 2011. *Regionalism in East Asia: Why has it Flourished Since 2000?* Singapore: World Scientific.

——2009. "Regionalism in the Asia-Pacific Region," Adelaide: University of Adelaide. School of Economics. Research Paper No. 2009–31. July.

Pomfret, R. and P. Sourdin. 2009. "Have Asian Trade Agreements Reduced Trade Costs?" *Journal of Asian Economics.* Vol. 20. No. 3, pp. 255–68.

Prasad, E. S. 2011. "Rebalancing Growth in Asia." *International Finance.* Vol. 14. No. 1, pp. 27–66.

Shin, K. and Y. Wang. 2004. "Trade Integration and Business Cycle Co-movements: The Case of Korea with Other Asian Countries." *Japan and the World Economy.* Vol. 16. No. 2, pp. 213–30.

Solis, M. 2011. "Global Economic Crisis: Boom or Burst for East Asian Trade Integration?" *The Pacific Review.* Vol. 24. No. 3, pp. 311–36.

Thorbecke, W. and N. Salike. 2011. "Understanding Foreign Direct Investment in East Asia." Manila, the Philippines and Tokyo, Japan. ADBI Working Paper Series, No. 290. June.

United Nations Economic and Social Commission for Asia and the Pacific. (UNESCAP). 2011. *Fighting Irrelevance: The Role of Regional Trade Agreements in International Production Networks in Asia.* New York.

Wakasugi, R. 2007. "Vertical Intra-Industry Trade and Integration in East Asia." *Asian Economic Papers.* Vol. 6. No. 1, 26–39.

Wignaraja, G. 2008. "FDI and Innovation as Drivers of Export Behavior." Maastricht, Netherlands. UNU-MERIT. Working Paper Series 2008–61.

World Bank (WB). 2000. *East Asia: Recovery and Beyond.* Washington, DC.

World Trade Organization (WTO). 2011. *International Trade Statistics 2011.* Geneva, Switzerland.

7

MATURING REGIONAL ECONOMIC ARCHITECTURE IN ASIA

1. Introduction

This chapter essentially delves into the progress of institution-led or formal (*de jure*) regionalism in Asia. After pursuing multilateral or non-discriminatory liberalization, Asian economies turned energetically toward institution-led or discriminatory regionalism. It gradually became a strong regional trend. This was a major tactical shift in their trade and regional integration strategy. This chapter traces the evolution of Asia's economic architecture. It demonstrates how in a short span of a decade-and-a-half the region underwent a sea change in this regard. This trend largely materialized in the post-2000 period. Its growth during the 21st century is the first focus of this chapter.

China is the largest trader and the hub of production networks in Asia. As an economic driving force it was expected to play an active role in the expansion of institutionalized regionalism in Asia. Although a China-centric economic structure has been emerging in Asia, the *de jure* regionalism in Asia is far from China-centric. Other Asian emerging-market and newly industrialized economies (NIEs) also negotiated and signed free trade agreements (FTAs) or regional trade agreements (RTAs).[1] Arguably the most notable characteristic of its evolution was that the Association of Southeast Asian Nations (ASEAN) bloc became the locus of Asian regionalism. Quantitatively regional economies succeeded in entering an impressive array of agreements of different kind. A variety of regional integration agreements proliferated fast; so much so that after a decade these agreements needed consolidation. Recent endeavors in the direction of consolidation and various plausible alternatives have been discussed in this chapter.

2. Asian regionalism: Vintage 21st century

The conduct of multilateral trade has undergone a discernible transformation during the first decade of the 21st century, and *pari passu* so has the nature of regionalism. Contemporary regionalism is different from that in the 20th century and in turn it has influenced multilateral trade. The 21st-century regionalism is not principally and primarily about preferential market access, which was the case with the 20th-century regionalism. This transformation was aided by two important factors: First, the advances in the information and communication technology and second vertical specialization of trade and expansion of supply chains discussed in detail in the previous chapter (Section 2.3). Together they have created a "trade–investment–services nexus" (Baldwin, 2011, p. 1), which in turn gave Asia an appearance of a regional factory. This nexus has become highly relevant for the contemporary international commerce. Therefore contemporary regionalism is more concerned about supporting it than simply emphasizing market access.

The trade–investment–services nexus evolved because multilateral trade was no longer merely confined to goods. The nexus came into being sequentially in a rational and somewhat intricate manner. The process worked as follows. First, trade expanded to trade in goods and services, and it combined with cross-border investment in production facilities. To that technology transfer and use of high-technology infrastructure for co-ordinating dispersed production activities were added. Trading activity was no longer simple. The next development was trade in parts, components and sub-assemblies, which increased progressively and became a high proportion of total trade in several Asian economies. The relevant services needed for the 21st-century trading practices include telecommunications, the Internet, express package delivery, air cargo facilities, trade finance, customs clearance services and the other business services. This new dimension as well as technique and mode of trading have affected the evolving makeup of FTAs or RTAs.

The evolution of trade on the above-mentioned lines in the 21st century made trade more complex than in the past and it needed to be governed by a different set of equally intricate rules. The novelty of 21st-century regionalism is that it is not so much about the conventional preferential market access in the FTA partner economies, but about the policy framework that supports the trade–investment–service nexus and keeps it proficiently operating. This implies that the 21st-century regionalism is driven by different politico-economic forces from those that drove the 20th century.

Unlike the FTAs or RTAs of the 21st century, the older ones were simpler and shallower in their composition, frequently dealing merely with phased tariffs slashing and the rules of origin (ROOs). The agreements of the present period need to respond to the needs of business firms that either produce part of their product in the neighboring countries or have a quasi-permanent relationship with suppliers in the neighboring countries. By making their operations international, business firms are exposing themselves, their capital, technological prowess, marketing knowhow to international risks. According to Baldwin (2011) this mode of operations entails hazards for tangible and intangible property rights. Such threats work as the new kind of trade barriers.

2.1 Stylized features of the growth of FTAs

Unlike the bilateral trade agreements (BTAs) and FTAs of the earlier period, the ones that are being formed in the present period need to take these barriers into account. Another requirement of the current period is co-ordination in production facilities in two or more neighboring countries in such a way that customers receive quality goods at competitive prices. This would call for a well thought-out business plan on trade in parts, components and intermediate goods as well as a range of commercial services. To be effective, applicable and functional the 21st-century BTAs and FTAs need to ensure that their operations facilitate the new mode of conducting businesses, in turn making them more efficient and profitable. An increasing number of the 21st-century FTAs have been so negotiated that they respond to the emerging needs of the time and therefore they tend to be different and deeper compared to the ones that were negotiated in the past.

Given the new business and economic environment and changing industrial structure, let us first examine the idiosyncratic features of FTAs in Asia. The first one is that they differ widely in terms of design, objective, intent, scope and purpose. They vary from the narrow FTAs, which are focused only on trade in goods and therefore trade liberalization attempted by them is minimal, to those that are more comprehensive and entail the deep liberalization and regulatory co-operation and harmonization characteristically needed by a contemporary FTA. Some FTAs still emphasize economic objectives more, while others are basically inclined towards political objectives. This wide diversity in FTAs is essentially attributed to the level of economic development of the FTA forming countries, the development strategy followed and the basic motivation for entering into a trade agreement (Capling and Ravenhill, 2011).

The second one is the concern of the potential partner economies at the time of FTA formation with regard to coming to an agreement with the least discord, keeping the negotiations cost-effective and completing negotiations proficiently in a small number of negotiation rounds, and in a reasonable time. This concern led to formulation of a large number of BTAs in Asia that could be negotiated relatively faster. A general reason behind the proliferation of FTAs is that negotiating plurilateral RTAs is always a complex and time-consuming process. The partners may also have to settle intricate and controversial issues on which accord may take a long while. There have been cases when after prolonged negations an agreement eluded. In 2000 Asian economies were a part of 46 FTAs, eight of which were plurilateral RTAs. In 2010 this numbers shot up to 180, of these 58 were plurilateral.

2.2 Limitations originating from the rapid growth in regionalism

Asian economies formed a good number of BTAs and FTAs, and many of them were of the shallow variety. Consequently, they remained limited and uneven in their impact (Mercurio, 2011). Policy makers in Asia did so despite being fully cognizant of the fact that many agreements that covered mere border trade measures and were made between two partners have a limited payoff in terms of increasing trade. Also, welfare implications of such BTAs were not high. Nevertheless, the emphasis on BTAs in Asia continued to be high. A multiplicity of BTAs promoting formal regional integration evolved as a characteristic feature and an accepted mode for progressing towards regionalism. For instance, when the ASEAN-Plus-Three (APT) ministers of finance met in the aftermath of the Asian crisis to establish the framework of currency swaps, the agreement was for the region. However, the swaps themselves were to be negotiated bilaterally.

An excessive degree of importance was placed on market access for goods in the Asian FTAs. The low level of ambition and motivation in designing them was another drawback of Asian BTAs and FTAs. In many cases liberalization rates are low, which limits integration of the member economies. The Asian agreements also suffer from a significant range of exclusions, which also limits the payoff from forming a BTA or an FTA. In addition, the persisting non-tariff barriers (NTBs) go a long way in reducing the impact of regional integration. Impediments like these tend to restrict the coverage, depth and scope of Asian BTAs and FTAs. Mercurio (2011, p. 121) asserted that they simply are not "broad enough to have a meaningful impact on the business community or broader economy".

Another much-debated characteristic of the Asian FTAs is that majority of them tend to be of the hub-and-spoke variety. Many BTAs and FTAs overlap. They create the problem of what Bhagwati *et al.* (1998) termed the "noodle bowl" or "spaghetti bowl" syndrome. As there is a profusion of bilateral agreements in Asia, it tends to exacerbate the "noodle bowl" effect. This effect is caused by overlapping or criss-crossing of BTAs and FTAs. Overlapping agreements, no matter what kind, create a complicated web that in turn become a serious operational snag. The overlapping agreements are usually inconsistent with respect to tariff phasing-out schedules, exclusions, standards and rules dealing with antidumping and other mutually agreed regulations. Their conflicting provisions could generate complex patterns of discrimination and exclusion in the region.

This effect results in inefficiency and high costs owing to multiple ROOs. They pose a severe burden on business firms, eventually increasing the cost of doing business and rendering BTAs welfare-reducing. Such a "noodle bowl" or "spaghetti bowl" effect may well spawn a greater distortion in the multilateral trading system (Bhagwati, 2008; Menon, 2009). There are many other problems that the "noodle bowl" effect can potentially create. For instance, it can encourage protectionism.

2.3 GATT/WTO paradigm

FTAs following the General Agreement on Tariffs and Trade (GATT)/World Trade Organization (WTO) paradigm were regarded as narrow in scope because their essential focus was on the border liberalization measures, which implies phased reduction or elimination of tariffs. They were usually limited to trade in goods, or sometimes extended to services. It was not appreciated that a mere reduction in tariffs could not be helpful in providing a level field to the firms of two or more trade partner economies. In general the agreements made by China and ASEAN are of this kind. They are low in ambition and narrow in coverage. For the most part they were limited to trade in goods and infrequently trade in services was included. With a few exceptions, they followed the GATT/WTO paradigm. Their detailed features are elaborated in the following paragraph.

Characteristically Japan and the Republic of Korea (hereinafter Korea) are known for making relatively more comprehensive agreements, which did not stay confined to the GATT/WTO Paradigm. The agreements in which the USA is a partner are the most comprehensive of all in terms of their coverage. Not only their coverage is wide but also they have the largest WTO-Plus provisions, including labor and environmental standards. As a rule, BTAs and FTAs in the Asia-Pacific region are more comprehensive in compared to those within Asia. Australia and New Zealand follow the US model, but fewer WTO-Plus provisions than the USA. Close scrutiny of FTAs negotiated since 2000 in Asia makes it obvious that Asian policy mandarins were not fixated on matching their efforts with those of the European Union (EU) and were not advancing towards a common market and deeper economic integration.

2.4 WTO-Plus FTAs

The realization of Asian policy makers regarding WTO-Plus FTA being more functional, result-oriented and potentially more rewarding was somewhat late to dawn. Therefore they turned belatedly towards the WTO-Plus kind of BTAs and FTAs. The USA became a trend setter in this regard. The blueprint and norms followed by the USA had a demonstration effect. Therefore many Asian BTAs and FTAs that were negotiated during recent years went beyond the GATT/WTO model. Asian economies that negotiated agreements during recent years preferred to enter into what became known as the "new age" or "WTO-Plus" FTAs, which had rationally wider scope and therefore comprehensive ramifications for the FTA partners. They eventually led to higher welfare gains.

The behind-the-border issues that come under WTO-Plus agreements include NTBs, FDI regulations, trade in services, mobility of labor, IPRs and the like. Competition policy is yet another area that needs to be settled in such a manner that the firms in FTA partner economies are able to fairly compete with countries that negotiated a FTA. The WTO-Plus agreements commonly include the four Singapore issues as well.[2] This kind of coverage can potentially create new business opportunities for the firms in the FTA partner economies (Freund and Ornelas, 2010). The eventual impact is deeper integration among the regional economies.

Three ASEAN-Plus-One agreements, with China, Japan and Korea, are WTO-Plus. It is indicated by their formal names and by their comprehensive scope.[3] Conversely, China preferred to have limited scope FTA agreements that cover merely trade in goods and services. However, this has lately changed and the more recent agreements made by China have the WTO-Plus elements in it. Of late, other Asian economies have also changed their approach and they began favoring the WTO-Plus agreements rather than the narrowly limited ones. Indonesia, Korea, Malaysia, the Philippines and Vietnam all have recently turned towards the WTO-Plus kind of agreements.[4]

Numerous large multinational corporations (MNCs), which made Asia their home, played a significant role in making Asia more conscious of the WTO-Plus FTAs. They were absolutely *au point* in hypothesizing that a policy environment of free trade and investment in neighboring Asian economies would benefit them by making it efficient for them to operate in Asia. It would be more lucrative, effectual and efficacious for the MNCs to operate in the Asia if Asian agreements are negotiated WTO-Plus. As more and more economies in Asia are linked through the WTO-Plus kind of BTAs and FTAs, deepening their regionalism, MNCs' production networks could be expanded and deepened. Furthermore, investment liberalization under this kind of FTAs could be more welfare enhancing for the region. Thus, the gains are mutual.

2.5 Underutilization of FTAs

Theoretically it is a valid belief that FTAs unify a region and usher in free trade in the unified region. Whether it really happens in regional trade is open to question. Mercurio (2011) compiled and compared the utilization rates from multiple surveys. A survey of Japanese firms all over Asia reported that 31.8 percent of them in Singapore made use of the provisions of the ASEAN agreement. This was the highest use of reported. Only 5.0 percent Japanese firms in Malaysia reported using the ASEAN agreement. Low utilization rates imply that the increase in intra-trade was not the direct result of trade agreements.

The Asian utilization rates compare unfavorably to those of other FTAs like NAFTA. The US firms importing from Canada reported 54 percent utilization and those exporting to Canada reported 50 percent utilization. Mexican firms exporting to the USA reported 62 percent utilization. The reason why these rates are not still higher is that a large number of tariff lines receive duty-free treatment under the most-favored-nation (MFN) clause. Therefore 45 percent of Canadian exports to the USA and 37 per percent from Mexico enter the US markets free of any tariffs. Therefore these exports did not need any preferential treatment engendered by NAFTA.

Hiratsuka *et al.* (2009) investigated Japanese MNCs and large firms' behavior while dealing with Asian FTAs. Their study included the affiliates of the Japanese MNCs that operated in Asia. Their conclusion regarding utilization of FTA was negative, that is, the Japanese MNCs or large firms had not only inadequate knowledge regarding the current FTAs in Asia but also they infrequently utilized by them. A JETRO (2009) survey of Japanese MNCs corroborated this conclusion regarding the underutilization. It put the finger on the rationale behind underutilization of FTAs. Japanese MNCs found that the difference between preferential tariff rates under the FTA and the MFN tariff rates was so minuscule that it was not worth their while to utilize the former. Besides, the duty drawback system managed to recover their tariff payments. The JETRO (2009) survey did not mention lack of knowledge of FTAs or complexities in their operations as the reasons behind underutilization.

A large quantitiy of micro-data generated by the JETRO (2009) survey was utilized by other analysts. Hiratsuka *et al.* (2009) used these micro-data to analyze further the pattern of FTA utilization by the Japanese MNCs and affiliates. One generalized conclusion they arrived at was that the smaller the affiliate or business firm, the less likely was its utilization of FTAs in exporting its goods and services. Be it noted that a smaller firm also had less diversified sources of procurement. Additionally, complications created by overlapping FTAs in Asia owing to the "noodle bowl" effect could well deter firms from utilizing them. However, based on a large firm-level survey in Japan, Korea, the Philippines, Singapore and Thailand, Kawai and Wignaraja (2009) inferred that business firms did not see these complications as serious and therefore the overlapping FTAs were not deterrents in the utilization of FTAs. For sure more facilitation in dealing with FTA operations was considered necessary.

Recent country-level and industry-level studies indicated businesses not utilizing those preferential arrangements adequately (Kawai and Wignaraja, 2011). Share of export value benefitting from the preferential arrangements remained low. This is a good measure of FTA utilization. Inadequate utilization remained the biggest problematic issue for the Asian BTAs and FTAs. One reason for underutilization of Asian FTAs was low trade volumes between the BTA or FTA partners. FTA partners of Japan often reported low utilization due to this reason. A primary survey of 841 of exporting firms conducted in 2007–08 in six Asian economies by the Asian Development Bank (ADB) showed that the Chinese (45.1 percent) and Japanese firms (29.0) were the highest users of FTA preferences, while those from Korea (20.8 percent), the Philippines (20.0 percent), Thailand (24.9 percent) and Singapore (17.3 percent) made low use of the FTA preferences. Insufficiency of information regarding the FTA and its provisions was given as the most frequent reason behind underutilization of FTAs. Low preference rates was the second most frequent answer. The ADB survey also indicated that 25 percent of the Asian business firms did intend to utilize the FTA preferences more in future. They have plans in place to achieve this objective.[5]

As regards industry-wise FTA utilization, available data reveal that firms trading in food, electronics, textiles and garment industries are low users of FTA, while those in machinery and automotive industries use them relatively more. Also, a larger proportion of firms in the latter industries try to make use of the FTA preferences. Approximately half of the firms in the machinery sector and a third in the automotive sector made use of the FTA preferences. In the textile and garment sector this proportion did not rise above one-third, while in the food and electronics it was the lowest. Only one-fifth of the total number of firms reported utilizing FTA preferences. This pattern of industry-wise utilization confirms the fact that more protected industries with higher margins of preference tend to use FTAs more than other firms which are in industries that are less protected and face lower margins of preference.

A greater proportion of Chinese firms was able to use FTAs because of the rapid ascendance of China and its firms in the global economy as well as the fast build up of production networks in important industrial sectors like automotive and electronics. Similarly better utilization by Japanese firms was essentially due to a sophisticated industrial structure in Japan, which is based on large MNC activities. These MNCs function as anchors for production networks in the region. The Japanese business firms and MNCs also enjoy the benefit of private sector industry associations as well as public trade support institutions. In contrast to these, the Korean firms' utilization of FTAs was much lower because Korea began negotiating FTAs late, in 2004. Also, its initial FTAs were made with smaller economies like Chile and Singapore. In Korean FTAs, the margins of preference were also low.

An array of firm-level factors adversely affected utilization of FTAs. For one, firm size was found to have a decisive impact over the use or non-use of an FTA. Kawai and Wignaraja (2011) inferred that larger firms and MNCs were greater users of FTAs than the smaller ones. This corroborated the conclusions reached by Hiratsuka *et al.* (2009). This pattern of FTA use can be explained by the fact that there are fixed costs of using FTAs. First, acquiring knowledge regarding the FTA provisions, then adapting production patterns and business plans according to the complex tariff schedules and obtaining certificates of origin are all processes that require financial and human resources. Large business firms and MNCs are able to cope with these requirements much better than the small firms.

In the ADB survey the complex set of ROOs was noted as being a deterrent. It caused delays and high administrative costs. It is generally acknowledged that complexities relating to ROOs are a challenging characteristic of Asian FTAs. ROOs are mutually agreed regulations that determine the country of origin of a product for the purpose of trade. In their ROOs partner countries determine and record the proportion of non-originating input in a product in order for it to qualify for preferential access under a FTA. In addition, a "cumulative zone" is determined in the ROO, which specifies the countries whose products can be considered to have originating status for the purpose of the agreement.

Opinions regarding the ROO related problems in Asia vary. There are some who believe that the ROO in Asia are complicated and have high administrative costs. However consensus on this issue is missing and Chia (2010) argued the opposite. According to this view, Asian ROOs are not only orderly and logical but they have created a foundation for a strong regional trading system. The survey referred to above in this section also provided some information on this issue (Kawai and Wignaraja, 2011). Owing to the "noodle bowl" of overlapping FTAs in Asia, multiple ROOs do impose some burden on firms. Only 20 percent of firms reported the significant cost of multiple ROOs. As regards the countrywide perception, in the ADB survey highest (38 percent) negative experiences were reported by Singaporean firms. Chinese firms were on the other extreme, with only 6 percent firms reporting negative experiences of the ROOs. As regards the firm-wise experiences, the larger firms had higher levels of complaints regarding the multiple ROOs than small and medium-sized companies. The number of concluded agreements in the region increases is sure to increase with time, the ROOs may become increasingly problematic for the trading firms. Therefore administrative efforts to rationalize ROOs are needed to mitigate the negative effects of the "noodle bowl".

2.6 Persistent challenging issues and inadequacies

Notwithstanding the fact that regionalism in Asia was adopted late and became operational relatively recently, it is facing several challenges. As decision-making in most Asian FTAs is based on forming a consensus, substantial and bold decisions are usually not attempted. Agreements in summits and conventions can be obtained easily if the agendas are kept lightweight. In addition, members' commitments are frequently non-binding and voluntary. When international secretariats were created, the powers delegated to bureaucracies were limited and closely scrutinized by the member governments. There was little institutional independence for these secretariats (Haggard, 2011).

As initially Asian FTAs were excessively focused on market access and did not engage in negotiating comprehensive and deep FTAs, lowering or eliminating tariff barriers was their customary beginning. Gradually comprehension and knowledge developed, the negotiation process matured and advanced towards the so-called behind-the-border issues. NTBs, trade in services, investment, IPRs, competition policy, government procurement and dispute settlement fell under this category. Although these issues have become increasingly important in multilateral trade and relationships between important trade partners, they made limited progress in the Asian FTA. This is a serious blemish of the Asian FTAs. The reason is that under the sponsorship of the GATT/WTO system, tariffs incessantly came down to a low level over the last six decades. The FTA negotiating countries need to know that benefits of an FTA now have to come through the behind-the-border measures, not from lowering or eliminating the tariffs.

Although recently negotiated agreements do go beyond the liberalization of trade in goods only, Mercurio (2011) contended that the tariff line coverage of most agreements was not large. Lack of comprehensiveness of Asian FTAs is a widespread problem. This means that the condition stipulated by Article XXIV of the GATT is not met by the Asian FTAs. Article XXIV is the basis of all the FTAs and emphasizes that trade barriers be eliminated on "substantially all trade". It does not consent to exclusion of any sector of a FTA forming economy. Majority of agreements also have a long list of "sensitive" products, excluding them from the coverage. When they are not excluded, the tariff reductions are only meager. Often these sensitive products are those that are principal export items of the FTA partner economy. The inadequacy of coverage led to just criticism by the UNCTAD/ JETRO (2008) study that regarded Asian FTAs as not being genuine free trade agreements.

Furthermore, the liberalization commitments in the majority of the Asian FTAs are usually shallow. There are too many exclusions and NTBs watering down their effectiveness and utility, and they fail to enhance trade. Owing to these limitations, the coverage and scope of FTAs becomes narrow, not very useful from the perspectives of regional trading firms. This discourages the intended beneficiaries and they ignore the FTAs in effect and their utilization rate suffers. The FTAs have limited utility for the exporters and importers or the broader partner economies in general.

Asian FTAs have also been criticized for the uneven coverage in their trade in goods. In the majority of them agriculture is not covered significantly and sufficiently. As the farm lobby in most Asian countries has a lot of political clout, it has frequently succeeded in pressurizing negotiating governments and keeping trade in agricultural products out of the agreements. This is another feature that goes counter to the grain of Article XXIV of the GATT/WTO and Article V of the General Agreement on Trade in Services (GATS). The WTO failed to prevent the proliferation of low-quality trade agreements. Trade in agricultural products needs to be gradually liberalized and its coverage in future Asian FTAs needs to increase. By advancing in stages this coverage should be made comprehensive.

Although exhaustive country-wise information on the scope of Asian FTAs is sparse, inadequacy of data and information has been a matter of question. In general the Asian FTAs are an unusual mix of simple and limited ones, coexisting with a small number of comprehensive, mature and intricate ones. That being said, on balance a large number of Asian FTAs lack WTO-Plus orientation. The fact that many of them are not what is called "new age" FTAs is regarded as their persisting weakness. Apparently they were slow in keeping up with the global trend in this regard.

Considering FTAs for individual Asian economies, each one of them curiously has both, narrow FTA-s that deal only with trade in goods, or trade in goods and services trade and the more in-depth WTO-Plus agreements. Two countries are exceptions to this generalization. First, Japan has all its agreements following the WTO-Plus format. Second, Singapore has the largest number of its agreements falling in the WTO-Plus category. An overwhelming majority of its BTAs and FTAs follow the WTO-Plus format. Korea and Malaysia also displayed an increasing propensity to form WTO-Plus kinds of FTAs.

3. The role and participation of China in *de jure* regional integration in Asia

During the 1990s China's relationship with its Southeast Asian neighbors was much more conciliatory and assuaging than that with the Northeastern ones. This was partly owing to the fact that the latter group did not reciprocate China's regionalist intentions and overtures. The regional role of an ascendant economy like China was bound to increase. It gradually became proactive in *de jure* regionalism in Asia. China signed FTAs with ASEAN and Singapore, has closer economic and partnership agreements (CEPA) with Hong Kong, SAR and Macau and economic co-operation framework agreement (ECFA) with Taiwan. In academic debate there are proponents and opponents of China-centric Asian regionalism. Ye (2011) divided China's regionalism into three temporal phases: 1978–89; 1990–97; and 1998 and thereafter. In each one of the three phases scope and depth of China's regional involvement differed, albeit they remained consistent with its economic prowess and degree of openness.

During the first period (1978–89) the market-led or *de facto* regional integration in Asia progressed in a vibrant manner. However, China remained wary and aloof because the leadership did not regard it as good for China's on-going reforms and restructuring. During the second period (1990–97) China's interest in regionalism increased. The Tiananmen Square episode had turned China into a pariah for the advanced economies of the West. Strong condemnation from them made the Chinese leaders concerned (Hu, 1996). They considered the possibility of international isolation, both economic and political. Western countries imposed economic sanctions on China. Therefore, China worked hard at improving relations with its Asian neighbors. A somewhat muted denunciation from its regional neighbors encouraged China to turn towards them. The Asian regionalism of the second period was dominated by the doctrine of "open regionalism", which originated in the Asia-Pacific economies like Australia, New Zealand and the USA. The concepts advocated by the Asia-Pacific Economic Cooperation (APEC) forum exemplified open regionalism.

In the early 1990s, China's political leadership began to recalibrate its relations with its neighbors. China's overtures in regionalism began in the early 1990s, with its approach to the ASEAN bloc in 1991 and membership in APEC forum. APEC includes members from outside the region. Although China was not a founding member of APEC, it joined in 1991. At this point China was not as confident regarding its role in Asian regionalism as China appears at present. Essentially as a result of its rapid gross domestic product (GDP) growth, its relationship with its southern neighbors developed rapidly. China's joining APEC was an admirably logical economic decision because this region dominated both China's trade (80 percent) and foreign direct investment (FDI, 90 percent) in 1990 (Ye, 2011). It was also a turning point for China. During this period the limited and weak Asian economic co-operation was continuing under the APEC framework. By the end of this period, the APEC ran out of steam in its trade liberalization endeavors. China did not take any leadership positions; it followed the "open regionalism" banner of APEC.

China was more of a latecomer to regionalism than the other Asian economies. Under the leadership of Deng Xiaoping, its regional and global policies had an economic orientation. According to Yuzhu (2011) the fundamental Chinese strategic premise in this regard was economy-centered. In adopting regionalism, Chinese policy mandarins tried to identify primarily economic costs and benefits. Their simple logic was that if an FTA is formed, it should economically benefit the partners. Economic gains, reflected in real GDP growth rates and welfare gains, have continued to be the principal target of regional economic cooperation for China. Yuzhu (2011, p. 199) noted that by "establishing FTAs or other arrangements, China seeks to develop or foster stable markets that can help diversify its export destinations on the one hand, and exploit more material resources on the other". Both of these objectives became more important for growth in the third period (from 1998 onwards). As widely recognized, Asian regional cooperation and regionalism and China's association, participation and contribution to it grew more intense after this critical juncture. China suddenly became more active in regionalism after the Asian crisis and took a great deal of initiative in the Chiang Mai Initiative (CMI) and its subsequent expansion into Chiang Mai Initiative Multilateralized (CMIM). China's regional image improved during the Asian crisis (1997–8) when it decided not to devalue its currency. Both the regional leaders and the Group-of-Seven (G-7) countries respected China's responsible and clairvoyant gesture.

Since the WTO accession in 2001, China turned to regionalism more energetically and became an engine of institutional regionalism in Asia. In collaboration with its neighbors to the east and south, it actively began carving a new regional order. It is difficult to put behind that China's relationship with its neighbors until the recent past was that of mistrust and hostility. Many of them did not have diplomatic ties with China until the early 1990s. China regarded many of them as close US allies and therefore its relationship with them was that of distrust and suspicion.

ASEAN and China first developed bilateral economic ties, which subsequently grew. China's concept of regionalism and its ambitions in this realm changed since the formation of the ASEAN-China FTA (ACFTA). It was christened the Framework Agreement on Comprehensive Economic Co-operation. ACFTA was the initiative of Premier Zhu Rongji, who proposed it in 2000. Although official efforts began in 2001, the so-called framework agreement of ACFTA was signed in 2002. At the time of signing China considered it a major diplomatic triumph (Ravenhill, 2008). The two partners developed an economic, political and legal framework for their comprehensive co-operation. China was more self-assured in negotiating this FTA than that it could possibly be with Japan or Korea. The reason was that it had greater similarities with the ASEAN economies. Tariffs between the five founding members of ASEAN and Brunei (or the so-called ASEAN-6) and China had been declining since 2005.

On 1 January 2010, when ACFTA came into effect, it was one of the world's largest FTAs. The ACFTA encompassed a population of 1.9 billion, had a combined GDP of $6.6 trillion and total trade volume of $4.3 trillion in 2010. By population ACFTA is the largest FTA and by value the third largest in the world. Four of the ASEAN members (Singapore, Malaysia, Indonesia and the Philippines) were China's major trading partners even before the ACFTA came in force. China's trade with the ASEAN was robust in 2010. In 2011 it surpassed Japan to be China's third largest trading partner, after the EU and the USA. Zero tariffs and preferential trade policies as well as vertically integrated trade and cross-border supply chains contributed to this fast-paced rise in ASEAN–China trade. Owing to geographical proximity, the Southern and Western provinces of China benefitted relatively more and integrated with the ASEAN economies across the border.

In 2010 a zero-tariff began to apply for 90 percent of all trade between China and the ASEAN-6. This covered around 7,000 traded items. By 2015, tariffs on the "highly sensitive" products will be cut to no more than 50 percent. China and many of the ASEAN-6 countries specialize in low-cost manufactured products. As the trade structure between them is competitive rather than complementary, they are facing implementation problems. In the medium term, both consumers and producers in the ASEAN-6 will benefit from less expensive imports from China. Businesses in this sub-group of economies will pay less for the intermediate inputs imported from China without tariffs. The fastgrowing middle class in China will also create markets for goods and services that can be exported from the ASEAN-6 countries. However, there is a downside. The ASEAN-6 economies should expect short-term disadvantages in their labor-intensive industries being displaced by Chinese exports in the third-country markets. This category of industries would include textiles, garments, footwear, toys and foodstuff processing. Some capital-intensive production, like steel and machinery, will also be adversely affected (Thangavelu, 2010).

Southwestern provinces of China, namely Guangxi, Yunnan, Chongqing and Sichuan, were particularly interested in entering into the ACFTA because of their geographical proximity to the

ASEAN countries. The provincial governments persuaded the central government to negotiate an FTA with their neighbor. Logistics costs for products produced for export from these provinces are higher than those from the coastal cities, which reduces the competitiveness of their exportables. This was an incentive to trade with the neighboring ASEAN economies. The construction of highways in the southwest provinces was evidence of the government's intention to reduce logistics costs in the region. As the ACFTA came into effect, business firms in the southern provinces of China began exploring trade opportunities with the adjoining ASEAN economies.

ACFTA has recently deepened more than it was. This has happened despite the apparent formidable competitiveness of the Chinese economy. This was owing to the long-term perspective taken by the ASEAN decision-makers. They saw the potential of the large China market and gave precedence to the interests of their exporters over the possible loss of those who feared Chinese competition—an astute and spirited policy measure indeed. In addition, they seem to have taken a futurist perspective. In the medium term, China is slated to be not only an inevitable regional power but also a global one. Integrating with it and thereby reaping the benefits from its ascendance is a pragmatic, functional and sagacious strategy. Closer economic relations would be mutually beneficial economically both for ASEAN and China. Escalating trade, investment and financial ties can not only become an additional source of economic growth but also would stimulate the process of economic integration. The final outcome would be welfare gains for both partners.

China is important to its Asian neighbors because, *inter alia*, it is a large and growing market for their products. Other Asian economies successfully found their niches in Chinese markets and increased their share of China's imports (Krumm and Kharas, 2004). Since the early 1990s, many medium-sized and large Asian economies managed to increase markedly China's share in their exports. Gradually China's imports became a key factor supporting sustained growth for Japan, Korea and Taiwan. Besides, China's growing market holds great potential for their future. By 2005, China had become the largest regional importer. According to an estimate, by 2020 China's trade may significantly exceed that of Japan and equal that of the USA. At that time, China may rely on its Asian neighbors for half of its imports, if not more (Zhang, 2006).

As the triangular trade pattern evolved, China maintained large trade deficits with its Asian neighbors and surpluses vis-à-vis the EU and the USA. The global financial crisis and the Eurozone sovereign debt crisis steadily reduced the magnitude of China's trade surpluses. The trade surplus was 7.3 percent of GDP in 2007, and in 2011 it shriveled to 2.1 percent. Once the global economy recovers from these crises, China's trade surpluses is likely to return, albeit it seems unlikely that will reach the pre-crises levels. Various simulation exercises support this inference (see, for example, Roland-Holst *et al.*, 2003). China will recycle its trade surpluses regionally. China is uniquely integrated with its neighbors through, *inter alia*, vertically integrated production networks. This distinctive relationship is also likely to strengthen and mature with the passage of time.

China showed continuous and proactive interest in the ASEAN-Plus-One BTAs, as well as the APT framework. Its interest and involvement in the establishment of the APT in Kuala Lumpur, Malaysia, in 1997 brought to China the goodwill of its Asian neighbors, particularly the ASEAN. The ACFTA is expected to catalyze these China-related or China-centric FTAs, in particular the APT and ASEAN-Plus-Six (APS).[6] The latter is also known as the Comprehensive Economic Partnership of East Asia (CEPEA). Australia, New Zealand and India were the last three countries to form BTAs with ASEAN. They were invited for the first time in the ASEAN Summit of December 2005 in Kuala Lumpur. Recently these six economies took steps to deepen their relationship. Under these co-operation frameworks top political leaders of China and ASEAN met annually. China also signed numerous bilateral agreements with several economies both intra-regionally and extra-regionally. More efforts were ongoing in 2011. APS or CEPEA is a vision, or a possible future blueprint, of a wider future Asia-Oceania market. Although it is far from being a reality, if it does materialize, it will provide prospects of forming an EU-like economic community in the Asia-Oceania region. Simulation using dynamic Global Trade Analysis Project (GTAP) model (version 7.1), Itakura (2013) showed that APS leads to the largest positive impact on real GDP for most of the ASEAN economies. In late 2012 APS countries agreed to launch a new FTA negotiation called the Regional Comprehensive Economic Partnership (RCEP). All the current FTAs have not been able to achieve full trade and investment liberalization in the region. There is a lot of room for the RCEP to strengthen ASEAN and Asian production base as well as trade and investment. Several ASEAN-Plus-One FTAs have been causing the noodle-bowl problem and have been impeding the utilization of FTAs, which makes an RCEP essential (Fukunaga and Isono, 2013).

From the Chinese perspective, if something extraordinary had happened it was the Asian crisis, which radically changed the situation in favor of China. It also styled its future regional role. Regional debate on the economic rise of China and the so-called China threat to the neighboring economies was heating up in the mid-1990s. While the Asian crisis affected several Asian economies and the region adversely, it did not harm the Chinese economy much. This made China loom larger in the post-Asian crisis period. The neighboring Asian economies agreeably found China playing a congenial and assuaging role, promoting Asian co-operation. This logically made China important to its Asian neighbors. Following its principle of economic regionalism, China began actively engaging with the Asian economies making bilateral and plurilateral agreements.

China emerged as an important player in the Asian production networks stretched across the region. This increased involvement was not only in terms of increased trade value but also a large number of exported products. Its regional diversity is reflected in the degree of its participation in the intra-regional production networks. As factor prices widely differ across the regions, they affect the comparative advantage of each region. The inadequate mobility of the factors of production is another reason behind the marked regional diversity in China. Also, the high cost of services is crucial in explaining the differences between the coastal and inland provinces. However, these regional differences are diminishing. The latecomer provinces are gradually catching up with those that were in the lead.

Using comparable general equilibrium (CGE) model, Estrada et al. (2012) quantitatively assessed which FTA arrangement, existing or potential, would benefit the members more. Four FTAs were taken into consideration in this CGE study, China-ASEAN, China-Japan, China-Korea and the APT. Output and welfare effects were computed for all the four. Results show that member countries would benefit most from the APT, which is the largest Asian FTA. This result is in accordance with the trade theory, which posits that the larger the FTA the greater the benefits in terms of welfare and output gains. As for the bilateral FTAs, the results show that China will benefit more from the ACFTA than from the other two FTAs, between China and Japan and China and Korea. This quantitative exercise demonstrates that ACFTA should have greater policy significance for the members. China's income level is closer to many ASEAN members and its trade structure is more complementary with many of them than with the other two potential FTA partners, Japan and Korea. Furthermore, an analysis of the pre-FTA trade structure reveals that China's net trade position with ASEAN is more favorable than its position with Japan or Korea.

4. Growing regional dynamism of the ASEAN bloc

After delays and dormancy the ASEAN members began endeavors to integrate not only economically but also politically and socially. It is a sub-regional inter-governmental arrangement. The ASEAN bloc is a fairly successful case of sub-regional merger, after two not-so-successful attempts at co-operation and integration. The first attempt took place in 1961 between Malaysia, the Philippines and Thailand, and called the Association of Southeast Asia (ASA). The second one took place in 1962 between Malaysia, the Philippines and Indonesia in 1962. It was christened MAPHINDO. Although ASEAN started as a political and strategic grouping, its activities shifted in economic direction in the 1970s with agreements on joint industrial projects. Economic co-operation increased in the second half of the 1980s and 1990s (Severino, 2011; Chia, 2011; Ito *et al.*, 2011). It followed a gradual approach to building regional cooperation and legally binding institutionalized agreements.

The member countries of ASEAN are characterized by very high diversity in a number of respects, particularly stages of growth. Although not all, several of the ASEAN economies are highly open economies. They also have locational, infrastructure and logistics advantages. Singapore is the richest (2011 per caput GDP equalled $46,241) economy in the sub-region as well as in Asia. As it is one of the most open economies in the world and has an outstanding business infrastructure and efficient government, Singapore is the headquarters or regional headquarters of many MNCs.

The total GDP of ASEAN was $1.86 trillion in 2010, with Indonesia being the largest member economy. According to the International Monetary Fund (IMF) projections its GDP will be $3.8 trillion by 2017 with a population of 660 million. This would make ASEAN per caput income $5,782 in 2017.[7] Intra-ASEAN competition in the region is sure to rise as the better-off economies like Singapore and Thailand strengthen their position and rising economies (like Indonesia, Malaysia and the Philippines) try to catch up with them. As this sub-region still has a good supply of low-wage labor-force it is highly competitive in labor-intensive products. It has surpassed China in this area. Many large manufacturers have been moving from China to ASEAN economies because of rapid wage inflation in China. Japanese textiles and apparel moving to Vietnam is a good example of this industrial dynamics. Several ASEAN members have built up foreign currency reserves and signed currency swap arrangements with other countries, which has strengthened their financial systems. The group was able to withstand the global financial crisis (2007–09) resiliently. Leading global MNCs have been increasing their presence in ASEAN. While China is the fastest growing market for the MNCs operating in Asia, ASEAN is the second fastest growing market (ECN, 2013). This group of economies displayed surprising resilience in the face of a relatively soft global economy.

Capital-intensive industrial sectors, like electronics and autos, have also transferred from the other parts of Asia to ASEAN economies like Indonesia and Thailand. Their reasons for moving are risk diversification and market entry. To draw such industrial sectors the more open ASEAN economies has been trying to enhance business-friendly environment. Some of them, like Singapore and Thailand, have made excellent progress in this regard, although many like Indonesia still lag. The ASEAN economies continuously refine their incentive structures for attracting large global companies. One important area in which the ASEAN economies suffer is industrial infrastructure. They are behind China in transportation facilities and energy supply. Also, in parts and component supply they are no match for China. A KOTRA survey, conducted in 2012, demonstrated that the Korean manufacturers operating in Vietnam could procure 10 percent or less of their parts and component needs locally (Kim, 2013).

4.1 ASEAN bloc as the nucleus of regional integration

The ASEAN strategy to regionalize was slow and deliberate. It moved towards regional co-operation gradually and entered into more legally binding and institutionalized agreements. By the early

1990s, these economies had begun adopting market-driven and export-led policy framework and also signed an FTA (in 1992) of their own. The basic objective of the ASEAN Free Trade Area (AFTA) was to reduce transactions costs associated with intra-regional integration. Initially AFTA merely covered trade in manufactures and was to come in force in 15 years. Originally it also defined trade liberalization loosely, implying 0 percent to 5 percent tariffs, in lieu of no tariffs. It blends well with the flexible and informal approach that characterized ASEAN since its inception. The zero-tariff objective will take time to achieve. Although its membership is not open, it does practice "open regionalism".

However, the pace of implementation of AFTA was subsequently accelerated and the scope was broadened. It came in effect in the beginning of 2004 for the five founding members and Brunei Darussalam, the so-called ASEAN-6. As agriculture was a sensitive area for them, they provisionally put several agricultural and food products on exclusion list from time to time. An important development in this regard was that AFTA also became a part of numerous BTAs and FTAs made by the ASEAN bloc. *Prima facie*, AFTA is a plurilateral agreement but it was so designed that each member was to maintain its own tariff schedule with its own list of exclusions. This model made AFTA look like a web of separate bilateral agreements among its 10 members.

AFTA was negotiated as an FTA made under the 1979 Enabling Clause of the GATT. Therefore, it was not obliged to follow all the disciplining measures that the WTO imposed. The principal criticism was regarding not complying with "substantially all" the trade liberalization within 10 years, as prescribed by Article XXIV 5(c) of the WTO. One saving grace is that the liberalization coverage under the Common Effective Preferential Tariff (CEPT) is high. The CEPT specifies a gradual tariff reduction schedule for the member countries. ASEAN also recently harmonized traded commodity classification, which was a useful achievement.

From January 2010, ASEAN-6 eliminated intra-ASEAN import tariffs on 99.65 of their tariff lines. In addition, the remaining four members reduced their tariffs to 0 percent to 5 percent on 98.86 of their tariff lines. This implies that trade in goods in the ASEAN region is almost tariff-free. This was followed by liberalization of trade in services in 1995 under the aegis of ASEAN Framework Agreement on Services (AFAS) and liberalization of investment flows in 1998 under the aegis of ASEAN Investment Area (AIA) initiative. The AIA was the first agreement to promote ASEAN as a single investment area and increase regional co-operation on investment issues. It also provided guarantees of national treatment and transparency in investment relations to investors. AIA covered a wide range of industries and "one-stop investment centers" were also started under the AIA. Together they enabled ASEAN economies to make significant strides in investment co-operation. In two important areas of regional policy, namely trade and investment, the ASEAN bloc has emerged as the *de facto* fulcrum of Asian co-operation arrangements (see below).

In addition these economies have gradually integrated with each other. Share of intra-trade among the ASEAN economies nearly doubled over the last two decades. In 2009 it was a quarter of the sub-region's total trade. For Singapore this share was the highest (36 percent), which reflects its importance as a port and trans-shipment point. Trade and FDI within the sub-region and with the neighboring Asian economies have been mutually reinforcing. Consequently business cycles in the ASEAN economies have been growing increasingly synchronized. It is partly caused by intensifying economic linkages through trade and investment flows among this sub-group of economies (Tanaka, 2009). Three of the new members of ASEAN, namely Cambodia, Laos and Viet nam, recorded higher GDP growth rates since the 1990s (Menon, 2012). It was essentially driven by trade, investment and other market reforms. It succeeded in reducing income disparities between these members and the original ASEAN-6. Although the development divide has narrowed, huge gaps persist.

Of particular relevance in this regard was the forging of a series of ASEAN-Plus-One agreements, which were BTAs. The APT were the first three. They were followed by an ASEAN-Plus-One agreement with India. Most recently Australia and New Zealand also entered into similar ASEAN-Plus-One agreements. ASEAN has ASEAN-Plus-One agreements, or BTAs, with all the important regional economies. The surge in these AEAN-Plus-One agreements is considered a case of what is known as the domino effect (Ravenhill, 2010). Negotiations for two more ASEAN-Plus-One agreements, with Russia and the USA, are to be launched. The regional economies are linked together through multiple BTAs. Both financial and trade regionalism processes are driven by them. When this network of BTAs comes into force, it would create some semblance of an economically integrated Asia-Pacific region (Breslin, 2010).

So many ASEAN-Plus-One agreements turned ASEAN into a hub. That is, the ASEAN members were acting collectively as a group. This is termed a "hub-and-spoke" arrangement. ASEAN-China FTA (ACFTA) and ASEAN-Korea FTA (AKFTA) apply comparable tariff reduction schemes to the CEPT, while ASEAN-Japan FTA (AJFTA) adopted higher standards in tariff reduction. Not only is APT an important intra-regional regional grouping, but a combination or amalgamation of these three BTAs can also serve as a modality of a broader Asian FTA.

In this "hub-and-spokes" arrangement it is implicit that while connected to the hub, the spokes are separate. Therefore bilateral distortions can be phased out between the hub and spokes, whereas they will not be phased out between the spoke economies. To that extent trade and welfare gains from this "hub-and-spoke" arrangement will be limited. Thus, unco-ordinated bilateralism can amount to sacrificing welfare gain.

4.2 ASEAN as the locus of Pan-Asian integration

As described above, developments during the last decade prove that the ASEAN bloc is fast developing into a possible locus of a prospective pan-Asian institution-led integration. Three significant regional economic initiatives taken by ASEAN are Asian Regional Forum (ARF), the East Asia Summit (EAS) and the APT are of considerable regional significance. In addition, it has formed trade and economic alliances with several large Asian as well as Oceania[8] economies. The ASEAN-Japan Comprehensive Economic Partnership (AJCEP) came into effect onr 1 Decembe 2008. It was followed by the ASEAN-Australia-New Zealand Free Trade Area (AANZFTA), which came in effect on 27 February 2009. Next, the ASEAN-China Free Trade Area (ACFTA), the ASEAN-India Free Trade Area (AIFTA) and the ASEAN-Korea Free Trade Area (AKFTA) came into effect as of 1 January 2010. Thus, ASEAN has emerged as both *de jure* and *de facto* hub of economic integration in the region.

This inventory of completed FTAs by the ASEAN bloc is highly impressive and made it an imperious regional grouping. These five FTAs have prepared the ground for an East, Southeast and South Asian integration, which is an invaluable accomplishment. Furthermore, the network of BTAs and FTAs of individual members in these five FTAs is sure to weave these economies and sub-regions closely. Therefore, it is reasonable to expect that the ASEAN bloc together with its five FTAs can potentially develop into a comprehensive regional partnership. It can facilitate the free pan-Asian flow of goods, services, factors of production, technology and ideas. It can also smooth the operation of vertically integrated production networks.

The attraction of the ASEAN bloc as the primary platform for regional co-operation and integration is due to the fact that some of its member economies are resource rich, have low wages and are presently enjoying a demographic dividend. Indonesia, Malaysia, Thailand and Myanmar come under this category. They cautiously and consciously try to exploit their comparative advantages. They utilized these advantages to be competitive economies and also took measures like strengthening their legal systems and promoting social stability. Over the years, several of the ASEAN economies also took the initiative to introduce a series of policies and regulations that are conducive to attracting investment and creating a business-friendly macroeconomic environment (Das, 2007).

Many MNCs operating in Asia do not consider it wise to invest too much in China and regard it as a safe bet to diversify in the region. Besides, wages and other factor costs in China have been on the rise. This applies particularly to the coastal provinces of China. These factors make the ASEAN economies an appealing alternative to China. The next logical step for the ASEAN bloc is liberalizing investment regulations, unification of ROOs and the harmonization of product and technical standards to facilitate ASEAN-wide trade and investment flows. They successfully took some of these policy measures. For instance, they proactively liberalized investment regulations in 2010 and benefitted by attracting larger FDI flows than those in the past (UNCTAD, 2011).

4.3 The ASEAN-Plus-Three initiative

The formation of the APT was a constructive and functional measure, having meaningful consequences for regional integration. Proposed by China, the APT provides the primary institutional framework for Asian economic integration. The members met for the first time in Kuala Lumpur in 1997. The APT initiative gained unprecedented momentum in the wake of the Asian crisis. The creation of the APT in 1998 was a first step towards financial and monetary co-operation in Asia. The APT economies became actively involved in various regional initiatives. Given the dynamism and significance of the three economies in the region, this could as well be named Three-Plus-ASEAN.

The three governments, China, Japan and Korea, led the initiative that worked as an unassailable stimulus to regionalism. Japan and Korea had a tradition of commitment to multilateralism. They radically altered their stance on trade policy to move towards formal regionalism. China began overtures on the ACFTA (or Framework Agreement on Comprehensive Economic Cooperation) with ASEAN in 2001. In the aftermath of the Asian Crisis, the political leaders in the APT economies were cognizant of the fact that there was a compelling need for economic, monetary and financial cooperation and created a regional economic architecture, which in turn stimulated camaraderie and team spirit in regional trade and investment.

The regional importance and significance of the APT continued to increase. It now works as a region-wide umbrella for devising new integration measures. The APT members developed a Cooperation Work Plan (2007–17) and adopted it in the November 2007 APT Summit in Singapore. This document deals with opportunities and challenges faced by APT cooperation and provides strategic guidelines for future APT cooperation. The guidelines to implement the Cooperation Work Plan (2007–17) were endorsed in the 13th Director-General meeting in July 2009 in Seoul, Korea. Over the years the APT has developed slowly into an important mechanism for strengthening and deepening co-operation and support teamwork among Asian economies in economic, financial and other related areas. However some Asian economies were concerned about the negative impact on their sensitive sectors, which slowed the progress in the implementation of the APT.

To support the CMIM, the APT countries agreed to establish an independent regional surveillance unit in April 2010. It was christened the APT Macroeconomic Research Office (AMRO). Furthermore, the APT Finance Ministers and Central Bank Governors met in May 2012 in Manila,

Philippiness. As this meeting took place in the backdrop of the Eurozone sovereign debt crisis, the members agreed on strengthening CMIM, including doubling its total size to $240 billion. They also increased the IMF de-linked portion to 30 percent, introduced crisis prevention function and enhanced the ABMI by adopting the New Roadmap+. The New Roadmap+ was proposed by Korea and covered directions to further develop the Asian bond markets. One negative aspect of CMIM is that the pledged amount of $240 is too small to stave off any potential crisis. This amount is close to 5 percent of the forex reserves of the APT countries. The CMIM was never activated. Whether it is ready for activation is an open question.

4.4 ASEAN–China synergy

From the mid-1990s China began cultivating its political and economic relationship with the ASEAN countries. It did not allow the old territorial disputes and rivalry to overshadow the new relationship of economic cooperation (Ye, 2011). China's importance as an ascendant economic power for ASEAN is enormous. A good deal of private-sector-led integration between the large ASEAN economies and China took place during the last decade. It intensified particularly since the Asian crisis. Although the Chinese economy had a lot of similarities with the larger members of ASEAN and the two did not have a great deal of natural economic complementarities, trade between China and ASEAN increased six-fold during the decade of the 2000s. Reciprocal FDI also rose exceedingly fast. However, it needs to be pointed out that in comparison to ASEAN China's trade and FDI are much larger with Japan and the NIEs and their rate of expansion also remained much higher during the period under consideration. Also, the ASEAN markets were relatively less important for China.

Yet, China regarded it as a priority to have an FTA with the ASEAN bloc than with Japan or the NIEs. One reason for prioritizing ASEAN in trade and economic ties was China's national interests. Securing a source of raw material and energy supplies and expanding its market of manufactured goods could well be the first motivation. A second important reason for China taking early and earnest steps and more positive approach to cultivate good-neighborly relations with the ASEAN bloc was its eagerness to be seen by its neighbors as peaceful and trustworthy, which could ease up the evolving China-as-a-threat assertion. It had caused economic security concerns among the smaller neighbors of China. Its acceptance of the so-called "ASEAN-Way" could well be for the same reason.

While negotiating the ACFTA, the Chinese negotiators took a yielding, flexible and mature stance, to ensure that the negotiations were perceived as successful. They put forth a slogan, "giving six, taking four" and also came up with the "early harvest" programs. One such scheme was agricultural trade liberalization, which counteracted the hesitancy of some of the ASEAN countries in entering into the ACFTA. Also, under the early harvest scheme the ASEAN-6 got early access to the large Chinese market. Negotiations on the ACFTA progressed well and they were effectively reinforced during the last decade. The ACFTA soon became "entrenched within the institutional layout of the region" (Chin and Stubbs, 2011, p. 279).

The ASEAN economies became upstream suppliers of intermediate goods to China. With that their trade surplus with China increased. The trade relationship in intermediate goods evolved as follows: for each dollar worth of increase in intermediate goods export to China, ASEAN countries imported $0.60 worth of intermediate goods from China. Conversely, these economies have become net importers of consumer goods from China. For each dollar worth of consumer goods exported to China, ASEAN economies imported almost $4 worth of consumer goods from

China (IMF, 2011). Consequently China has had a trade deficit vis-à-vis the ASEAN economies for some time.

As China became the assembly hub of network production, it imported parts, components and intermediate goods from Japan, Korea and Taiwan, which are three of the most industrialized economies of Asia. The final products which were assembled in China were then exported to North America and the Eurozone economies. Thus, China's exports became dependent on economic climate in these advanced industrial economies. Regression analysis shows that this result holds for the electronics sector but not for the machinery sector. Owing to the global financial and economic crisis, China's exports of electronics products to the advanced economies fell by 50 percent, which led to a simultaneous fall in China's imports from Japan, Korea and Taiwan by 60 percent (Zinabou, 2011).

Over the last two centuries Chinese Diaspora spread into the ASEAN economies. While ethnic Chinese account for less than 5 percent of the population, their investment is a much larger part of the total capital invested in the ASEAN countries. According to Kim (2013), in 2011 the total market capitalization of 72 ethnic Chinese businesses was $411 billion, which was 20 percent of the aggregate market capitalization in these countries. The large ethnic Chinese business firms in ASEAN are quite influential in their respective countries. They have been historically strong in real estate, finance and commodities. These commodity traders from the ASEAN economies met China's large commodity import needs. Through *guanxi*, large and medium-sized ethnic Chinese businesses in the ASEAN countries were able to establish business ties with their counterparts in China.

4.5 ASEAN-led progress towards institution building

The Asian vision of an institutionalized regional community is different from that of the EU. So is the process of advancing towards this objective. Unlike the EU-type exceedingly institutionalized community, Asian economies prefer soft regionalism, which Hu (1996, p. 7) called "the ASEAN Way". This implies a relatively easy-going neighborly relationship among countries, which ultimately promotes economic cooperation. It is a consensus-based institution. The modality and operational code of this relationship is determined by the ASEAN Way. One characteristic of this process is that member states engage with each other at their own level of comfort. This was responsible for creating a unique intra-regional economic dialogue between the members of ASEAN, China, Japan and the four NIEs. In the post-Asian crisis period ASEAN-led efforts became more substantive than in the past.

The "ASEAN Way" has had several notable successes. One of its important achievements is that it has made it possible for the small states to lead the big ones. In this case the ASEAN states are the small states, whereas China and Japan are the big ones. Conversely, in the EU or NAFTA, the big states are accepted as the natural leaders and they throw their weight around. They believe that they are the natural leaders. In the incessant APT dialogue, the small ASEAN states succeeded in motivating China and Japan to participate in an ASEAN-led institution building. They came up with novel ideas and initiatives and determined the direction and path to take.

The small ASEAN members together showed the way and persuaded the larger economies to work in the interest of the region and abandon their narrow national goals. ASEAN kept both China and Japan informed about the small states' plans of regional prosperity and stability, and engaged them in achieving their goals as common regional goals. As the origin of the majority of initiatives was ASEAN, the response from China and Japan was promptly favorable. Without the ASEAN Way, mutual rivalry, mistrust and circumspection between China and Japan would have stalled negotiations towards institutionalized regionalism and progress towards any regional objectives.

The ASEAN culture naturally determined the idiosyncratic traits of the "ASEAN Way" of intra-regional economic diplomacy. The code of conduct is based on consultation and mutual respect. The ASEAN culture totally refrains from coercion of any kind and emphasizes consensus building. Some analysts believe that the "ASEAN Way" is the Malay cultural approach of handling serious situations and the Malay manner of interaction with people. It emphasizes a non-confrontational attitude and mandates a sincere readiness to appreciate the viewpoints of others. Patience and perseverance are regarded as highly valued attributes (Vermonte, 2005).

4.6 Forming the ASEAN Economic Community

After a prolonged period of sluggish growth performance and policy-induced isolation, both China and India adopted market-oriented reforms and economic restructuring, which in turn resulted in rapid and sustained GDP growth in these two economies. It led to the approbation of their achievements as well as causing a wave of anxiety about the rise of power and wealth outside the advanced economies. Their ascent was changing both regional and global economic structures. When the economic status of the two regional giants began to rise, the ASEAN members reacted to this consequential regional development (Das, 2006 and 2012). Geographically situated between these two rapidly growing EMEs, ASEAN members saw both opportunities and threats. If they felt a competitive threat coming largely from China, they saw trading and other economic opportunities as well. The challenge for the ASEAN group was to initiate a policy and institutional environment that could enhance the complementation and competition of each member economy.

A plan for the ASEAN Economic Community (AEC) was broadly conceived in early 2002 during the ASEAN Summit in Phnom Penh, Combodia. A decision to create an AEC was taken during the ASEAN Summit in October 2003, when the Bali Accord II was signed. The AFAS and AIA formed the basis of the AEC. This was a momentous development for the ASEAN group, which had moved slowly in the past. The AEC concept was to create a single unified market and production base for ASEAN. This decision underscored a need to establish a comprehensive integrated market. The AEC is an innovative initiative that can help maintain economic dynamism in the region. The sagacious vision of the ASEAN leaders was to create a competitive sub-regional economy that would also be globally integrated and competitive. Global integration was high on the priority of "The AEC Blueprint (see below)". Among other imperatives, the ASEAN economies needed to improve their investment regime, their trading environment, transport and logistics infrastructure and communications networks. There are constraints to cross-border trading in the ASEAN bloc. These measures would go a long way in reinforcing their supply side capabilities. In some ways, the AEC concept was similar to that of the EU. It was a hybrid FTA-Plus arrangement, with some elements of a common market but not common external tariffs.

This group of countries is not only not homogeneous but their economic performance is also dissimilar. Indonesia is the largest economy of the sub-region. The AEC covers a population of 574 million and several rapidly growing economies. Many of the ASEAN economies are outward oriented and open to trade and investment. Their combined trade to GDP ratio was 131 percent in 2010, for Singapore it was 421 percent. At this point their combined GDP was $1.856 trillion and the long-term average growth rate was 5 percent (1990–2010). The region is benefitting from competitive courting by economic giants like the EU and the USA as well as the two largest regional economies, China and Japan (Chachavalpongpun, 2010). Establishing an AEC will take much hard work and face technical and political obstacles. In economics market size matters but ASEAN has so far failed to integrate into a single market or economic entity. The growth prospects of the middle class in economies like Indonesia, Malaysia and Thailand have not been fully realized.

In January 2007 the ASEAN members agreed to sign the AEC agreement. According to the plan, by 2015 there would be a free flow of goods, services, investment and skilled labor among the ASEAN economies (Ito *et al.*, 2011). The Action plan for the implementation of the AEC was published in late 2007 and was christened "The ASEAN Blueprint". The ASEAN Charter was accordingly ratified by members in December 2008. This was an ambitious initiative by the 10 ASEAN members. A successful development of AEC would go a long way in addressing obstacles to seamless trading in goods and services in the ASEAN region.

The overarching objective of the AEC is to reduce transaction costs in the sub-region by economically integrating and making it more attractive for FDI and the operations of MNCs. This has been the primary objective for the ASEAN policy makers. In a globalizing economy FDI inflows have become of paramount importance. They are a source of non-debt-creating capital, foreign exchange and technology. They also provide easy access to larger foreign markets. In addition, they tend to strengthen institutions in the developing economies, particularly the financial sector (Prasad *et al.*, 2006).

Another important objective of AEC is to create a market for the free movement of goods and services as well as capital and skilled labor. The formation of the AEC would call for more endeavors in terms of policy harmonization among the ASEAN economies, which in turn would require the willingness to cede sovereignty. This was a sensitive issue, something the ASEAN member states never considered seriously in the past. The belief of the ASEAN leaders was that the MNCs would see AEC as a profit-enhancing proposition, be drawn by the economic diversity of the integrated sub-region and choose to invest in and locate their vertically integrated production networks in it. This policy environment would eventually facilitate the emergence from the ASEAN sub-region. This strategy is in keeping with the outward-oriented regionalism, from which Asia has benefitted. It needs to be recalled that the past economic co-operation endeavors of this nature by ASEAN were somewhat disappointing. One of the reasons behind the failure was that they were top-down initiatives, in which the local business communities did not take an interest.

For estimating the economic effects of the comprehensive AEC project, Petri *et al.*, (2010) used a computable general equilibrium (CGE) model. Implications of reduction of trade barriers and liberalizing the trade in goods are clear and can be quantified easily, but the effects of liberalization of trade in services and investment is relatively difficult to quantify. The same can be said about the effects of movement of skilled labor and co-operation in the capital markets. This study was based on a comprehensive model. One of its principal conclusions was that the value of AEC for the ASEAN economies was large. Their welfare would rise by 5.3 percent, that is much more than the welfare gains from AFTA. Integration with the global economy would further increase the welfare gains to 11.6 percent. More than half of these gains would stem from the FTA formation with the large economies of East Asia and the remaining gains from the FTAs with the EU and the USA.

Using a dynamic CGE model, Lee and Plummer (2011) also estimated the potential effects of the AEC on the economic welfare, trade flows and sectoral output of the member economies of the AEC. This empirical exercise was less comprehensive than the one noted above. According to its results, elimination of trade barriers resulted in maximum welfare gains for Singapore, while Malaysia, the Philippines and Thailand are expected to realize welfare gains of 1 percent or more.

However, estimates show that the remaining ASEAN members are likely to incur welfare losses. As noted above, one of the objectives of the AEC is to reduce transaction costs. The impact of trade costs reduction is direct and the result is trade-creation in the sub-region. When reduction in trade costs owing to AEC creation is taken into account, the magnitude of welfare gains for the ASEAN members increases substantially. Lower administrative costs and trade barriers also result in generating more intra-ASEAN trade. As expected, this empirical exercise predicted a huge increase in intra-ASEAN trade. An intra-ASEAN average trade increase of 54 percent was estimated. Imports from the non-ASEAN countries were found to contract by 6.1 percent. This study also showed a large increase in the FDI stock for the individual ASEAN economies, ranging between 28 percent and 63 percent.

The AEC concept is a decade old. At this stage it must be more ambitious and needs to seek integration at more than mere trade level. Integration of financial markets, standards and compliance are some of the other significant areas where they need to step up efforts to come closer and try to seamlessly integrate. To this end, appropriate institutional architecture needs to be developed. An active and strong ASEAN Secretariat with trans-ASEAN jurisdiction and authority would go a long way in moving this country group towards becoming a single economic entity. To achieve this broader objective, ASEAN member states will need to change their mindset and give priority to the sub-regional interests over individual national interests.

5. Trilateral FTA: A critical missing link

So far there is no trilateral FTA (TFTA) between China, Japan and Korea (CJK), although over the years the three economies have broached different possibilities and approaches. Largely because of the size and openness of their economies, China, Japan and Korea make their presence felt in any regional arrangement and agreement. Business corporations in these three economies increasingly became integrated, particularly since 2000. Their bilateral trade and other non-state-led economic exchanges grew at a swift pace. Their integration was further reinforced by production networks and related trade, which in turn accelerated intra-firm trade.

Trade among the CJK group of countries expanded rapidly over the preceding two decades. The share of intra-group trade between them expanded from 12.3 percent to 24.1 percent between 1990 and 2004, although it fell to 21.5 during the Asian financial crisis period (1997–98) percent. By 2010, it recovered somewhat to 22.5 percent. Over the same period (1990–2010) the share of intra-trade of NAFTA expanded from 37.2 percent to 40.5 percent while in case of the EU-15 it contracted from 64.5 percent to 56.3 percent. In comparison to the EU-15 and NAFTA, the share of CJK is evidently much lower, albeit its rate of increase was much faster. Over the same period Japan's intra-regional trade dependency on China and Korea recorded a steep rise, from 9.1 percent to 26.9 percent. Similarly Korea's dependency on China and Japan soared from 21.9 percent to 34.5 percent. However China's trade dependency with the other two rose from 15.0 percent to 27.6 percent between 1990 and 1996, but thereafter recorded a slow decline reaching 16.9 percent in 2010. This was owing to China's rising trade with the EU and the USA. A fall in China's dependency on the other two explains the weakening of intra-CJK trade in the recent years.[9]

China is a major investment destination for both Japan and Korea. It received substantial FDI from the Japanese and Korean firms in high- and medium-technology manufacturing industries. This provided an opportunity for China to develop its manufacturing sector and raise domestic technological standards, rendering its manufacturing industries more competitive. Japanese and Korean firms benefitted because China provided them with an opportunity to restructure their operations. Also, these firms were able to improve their competitiveness in the global market place. This was essentially a market-driven phenomenon, undertaken by business firms in the three countries to continue to be profitable and competitive. This rational, symbiotic and complementary structural relationship between the three economies is likely to continue and benefit them in the future.

During the Manila Summit in 1999, the leaders of the three countries launched a joint research project on "Strengthening the Economic Cooperation among China Japan Korea". The three nations had their first Trade Ministers' Talk on this issue in 2002. A joint feasibility study was submitted on a TFTA to the Trilateral Summit Meeting in 2003. This research focused on the impact of the TFTA on the macro-economies of the three countries. It computed gains for all the three potential partners and came to favorable conclusions for them. Yet, since then policy priorities, emphases and interests among the three possible partners varied and there was little tangible progress. Academic scholars in the three countries continued to research on the TFTA and its benefits. FTAs are basically premised on political decisions. Weakness in political will to take concrete steps was evident in the three countries. It seems that due to historical factors mutual trust between the three economies is still absent.

In 2004–06 the three economies conducted joint research on the "Sectoral Implications of a CJK FTA", which covered agricultural sector, fisheries and principal manufacturing sectors and services trade. Another trilateral feasibility study was launched in 2009 by a larger group of academics and business community members and trade bureaucrats. It took time to publicize its results and finalize its recommendations because the three potential members had sensitive issues to settle. Korea expressed concerned about trade in agriculture, fisheries and forestry sectors where China has comparative advantage. China was alarmed about high-technology industries like semiconductors, smart phones and services sector as well as medium-technology industries like shipbuilding and steel, where Japan and Korea have strong comparative advantage. Similarly Japan is concerned about both China and Korea having a comparative advantage in several industrial sectors. Opening trade in them will injure the domestic Japanese industries. The joint study was completed in December 2011, albeit the report was not made public but was to be released in early 2012.

Since 2008, four tripartite CJK summits took place and a fourth one in May 2011 in Tokyo. These summits provided a platform for co-ordinating responses to immediate regional issues and concerns. The first summit was held in the background of the global financial crisis. Although delays, discord and disagreements persisted and progress towards forming a TFTA was glacial, these three economies have become closely economically intertwined over the preceding two decades. Absence of an FTA did not impede or slow their economic and business interactions and integration. Trade and investment among them increased at a rapid pace. Yet, there is an apparent need to build political trust between the three potential partners if TFTA has to be born and emerge as a serious and influential entity (Byun, 2011).

Although a rapidly changing global economic environment, prolonged global financial crisis andstagnating EU and US markets may succeed in spurring on this process in starting trilateral negotiations, they cannot be completed in a short while. The three economies need to start negotiations on a TFTA without delay. Even after TFTA negotiations are completed, ratification takes time. A joint statement of the Joint Study Committee, which met in Pyeongchang, Korea, on 16 December 2011, issued joint recommendations for the three governments to decide on how to proceed with a TFTA, to announce an appropriate course of action and time frame of for the negotiations. At their annual trilateral summit in Beijing in May 2012 the top political leaders agreed to launch negotiations for the TFTA before the end of that year.

When completed, this TFTA will be the third largest in the world and the largest in Asia. These three economies have large GDPs and trade volumes. In 2010 their combined GDP was $12.2 trillion and trade volume $5.3 trillion. Although these statistics are smaller than the corresponding figures for the EU and NAFTA, they were not far below their levels. China, Japan and Korea accounted for 22.3 percent of the global population, 17.6 percent of the world GDP and 47 percent of the forex reserves. Their active interact with each other went on increasingly progressively. During the last decade Korea's trade volume with China outgrew that with the USA and Japan. China is Korea's largest export market and the largest source of its imports.

Results of a Trilateral Joint Research (TJR, 2008) project that quantified the economic impact of a CJK FTA by deploying a computable general equilibrium (CGE) model for 2003, 2005 and 2007, respectively, indicated the same direction and similar magnitude of economic effects. It demonstrated that the CJK FTA would be a win–win strategy to reap macro-economic benefits for the members. The simulation results indicated that the FTA will bring about large benefits to all the three CJK economies. It found that China's GDP will rise by 0.4 percent, Japan by 0.3 percent and Korea by 2.8 percent. No doubt to maximize benefits of the CJK FTA will call for industrial adjustments and cause labor dislocation in the damaged sectors. However, the TFTA can be carefully designed to reduce social costs of labor displacement by adopting mitigating measures, including sectoral exclusion and grace periods.

China has been the most actively interested in the TFTA negotiations, while Japan the most passive. Korea took the middle ground, although according to estimates made by the Ministry of Finance in Korea, it is likely to be the largest beneficiary of the TFTA. The results of this study show that Korea will see its GDP rise by 2.6 percent, while China GDP gains will be by 0.6 percent and Japan by 0.2 percent (KITA, 2010). The reason for larger benefits of the FTA going to Korea is that it relies on trade much more than China and Japan. Trade between them is more focused on intermediate goods. They need to enlarge their market for final goods.

6. Consolidation for Pan-Asia regional economic integration

The age-old neo-classical principle is that the larger the region, or the coverage in terms of the number of economies, the higher the welfare gains from regional integration. These gains are of both static and dynamic kind. Static gains are associated with reallocation of resources, that is, productive resources moving to sectors in which a country enjoys comparative advantage. The dynamic gains originate from the learning effect and additional capital accumulation. Trade creation or trade volume effect is another channel of welfare gains from regional economic integration. As regional integration directly increases comparative advantage-based trade, which leads to production moving from higher-to lower-cost production locations.

A larger integrated region covering many Asian economies necessarily implies that trade in goods and services will be higher in volume. Also, regional firms will have access to more skills and technology. Additionally, a larger integrated region integrates more markets resulting in a bigger final market size. This is an important variable because larger market in turn offers opportunities to business firms for greater specialization. Equally important are the scale and scope opportunities provided by the larger market size, which benefit firms from all the integrating partner economies. If a large number of economies come together in a pan-Asian RTA, the MNC operations in the region are sure to become easier, more productive and more profitable. This will necessarily include investments made by MNCs as well as technology transfer between firms and economies. Both are an important component of a dynamic regional economy.

Chia (2010) proposed that there are more benefits from expanding regional co-operation in Asia and consolidating the existing BTAs and FTAs. As markets grow larger and integrate and in the process lower or eliminate barriers to trade and investment, they provide incentives to both domestic and foreign investors to increase investment in productive resources, manufacturing activities, services and infrastructure development. The direct result is that the regional economies come closer together and become more closely connected. Furthermore, a larger pan-Asia RTA will not only increase the static and dynamic benefits of regional integration, but also reduce geopolitical regional tensions. Regional integration between the ASEAN economies is a testimony to this fact. In addition, it is axiomatic that a pan-regional integration is certain to give Asia a greater influence in various international fora and increase the regional clout as well as allow a greater say in the institutions of global economic governance, like the Bretton Woods twins and the WTO. This process would increase both Asia's global clout and contribution to global economic and business decision-making process.

A larger RTA entailing many regional economies will limit, or eliminate, the so-called "spaghetti bowl" or "noodle bowl" problem created by overlapping BTAs and FTAs. A pan-regional RTA can also eliminate multiple ROOs without much difficulty. Next step for the RTA members could be creating compatibility in product and technical standards. Although these measures will be time consuming, they will go a long way in avoiding market fragmentation in Asia. As seen in Section 4, the consequence of the explosive post-2000 regional integration scenario is a surfeit of bilateral and multilateral agreements. As multiplicity and overlapping FTAs have a cost, thoughts of consolidation are normal, even necessary.

6.1 Geometry of regionalism: A favorable BTA and FTA configuration for Asia

With the rapid proliferation of BTAs in Asia, empirical literature on the welfare implication of formal regional integration has been expanding. Such empirical studies are essential for bringing to the fore the costs entailed in the proliferation of BTAs and FTAs. Now that the FTA-led regionalism has expanded at a rapid pace in Asia and is believed to be here to stay, the next relevant question is how to shape it further. Several analysts took into consideration the present range of BTAs and FTAs and proposed consolidation of regionalism on varying lines.[10] Four broad alternative strategies to which empirical studies have frequently paid attention are as follows:

1) The ASEAN Free Trade Area (AFTA).
2) ASEAN+One BTAs, the so-called "hub-and-spoke" approach. According to this approach three BTAs of essence can coexist in a parallel manner, that is ASEAN+China, ASEAN+Japan and ASEAN+Korea, or the APT.
3) ASEAN coexisting together with a China-Japan-Korea FTA, which is yet to come in existence. These two may compete or collaborate.
4) Expansion of the ASEAN to an APS grouping, in which the first three are China, Japan and Korea. To these, three more ASEAN+1 are added, which cover India and Oceania (Australia and New Zealand).

Static and dynamic CGE analysis is another powerful analytical tool. The CGE empirical studies not only can quantify the income effects but also have a great deal of practical use. Kawai and Wignaraja (2007, p. 17) noted that "CGE studies can help in framing negotiation positions with FTA partners, indicate implementation schedules for trade and liberalization and suggest the need for appropriate structural reforms to mitigate adverse impacts". That said, they are not without their limitations. This analytical tool was used by Park (2006) and Lee and van der Mensbrugghe (2007), respectively, to evaluate quantitatively the impact of the above-mentioned RTA strategies. They concluded that the APT is the most productive and lucrative RTA strategy for the region. According to their conclusions this regional integration strategy would not have the detrimental effect of overlapping. Two more recent empirical studies that used a Gravity model regression analysis concluded that the consolidated Asian RTAs would have a trade-creating effect on the region, but they would not have a trade-diverting effect over the non-members from outside the region or even support global free trade (Lee and Park, 2005; Lee and Shin, 2006).

A CGE analysis was conducted by the Asian Development Bank (ADB) that used a variant of the Global Trade Analysis Project (GTAP) model (Kawai and Wignaraja, 2007). For the purpose of this empirical study, the dataset used was GTAP version 6.3, which had the advantage of including detailed national input-output, trade and final demand structures. This model was characterized by an input-output structure based on regional and national input-output tables. The notable conclusion of this study was that regionalism in the form of APT and APS offered the largest gains to the world income compared to the alternative strategies. Computations revealed that of the two, APS offered larger gains than APT. In the former case they were $214 billion, while in the latter $260 billion. The APT grouping minimized the negative effect arising from the "noodle bowl" phenomenon. This analysis expanded its recommendation to creation of an APS. The APT and APS were found to have dissimilar impacts on individual economies and sub-regions. As regards the influence on the non-participants, computations demonstrated that APT and APS had rather a small impact. For a range of economies there were losses, but these were small. This category included South Asian economies, the Oceania, Central Asian economies and the USA. In contrast, there were small gains for the EU, Canada, Mexico and Sub-Saharan Africa. The largest regional economies have their preferences; for instance, China has been shown to prefer the APT, whereas Japan has favored APS.

By applying CGE model analysis, Park (2006) concluded that the static effect of an East Asian RTA between China, Japan and Korea will be positive on welfare of the member economies and that of the world economy. Also, it inferred that there will be an increase in non-discriminatory free trade by setting off a domino effect in Asia. In a more recent study, Park (2009) further supported the old results by applying the traditional multi-country, multi-sector, static CGE model simulation. However, Park (2009) was a little ambivalent. It concluded that both APT and the CJK FTA were sustainable and desirable for the regional and global economies. There was no clear choice between the two.

6.2 Consolidation of BTAs and FTAs

Other than the partial consolidation of BTAs as APT and APS on the lines indicated above, a full regional consolidation can also be considered. Consolidation of gains of regional integration can be captured either through a co-operative multilateral approach or through non-discriminatory regional agreements or open regionalism. When economies in a larger region form a large multilateral RTA, the preexisting smaller BTAs can be consolidated as a solitary RTA. This makes the pre-existing BTAs and FTAs redundant. This was found to have happened when the EU and NAFTA were formed. For instance, the Canada-US BTA that preceded NAFTA, was superseded by the formation of NAFTA.

A large, region-wide RTA consolidates the smaller BTAs in the region by framing the rules of the RTA in such a manner that the previous BTAs can be accommodated. Pan-Asian regionalism and the optimal size of the RTA in the region have recently begun to generate a good deal of deliberations and weighing up. The reason is that the most welfare-enhancing way of shaping regional integration in Asia is the formation of a Pan-Asian RTA. No doubt it will need a great deal of political will, skill and coordination. If a region-wide RTA can be formed, myriad BTAs can be absorbed in it. This strategy can gradually eliminate the intra-regional BTAs completely. It also has the potential of deepening the regional integration for the economies involved.

This kind of regional consolidation would not be an easy and smooth process but may face several operational and technical difficulties. Its implementation may well be arduous and time-consuming. As the BTAs are highly heterogeneous, differing provisions of the BTAs in the region have different tariff rates phasing out schedules, different treatment of quantitative restrictions (QRs), different sector exemptions and ROOs. It would be really difficult to merge them into one large RTA. Under these circumstances, region-wide consolidation will necessarily imply an RTA with the "lowest common denominator" (Menon, 2009, p. 14). If a successful BTA in Asia, that started off with superior provisions, is consolidated in this manner, both BTA partner economies would suffer. Given a choice they would prefer to continue to operate under their original BTA, which provided entry to higher proportion of their exports into the partner economy.

6.3 Multilateralization of preferences

Multilateralization of preferences could work as a practical and constructive manner of consolidation of the existing BTAs and FTAs. This is a proposal to first equalize preferences across BTAs and then offer them to the non-BTA trade partners on a MFN basis, in a non-discriminatory manner. Such a move to multilateralize in turn can also remedy the problematic and welfare-reducing noodle bowl effect. There are two principal avenues of achieving this objective. First, through expansion of the geographical scope of an FTA and inclusion of new member economies in the preexisting agreements. The second approach could be by substituting the existing agreements with new agreements, which further extend to new members. There is no *a priori* method of determining which one of the two methods is superior.

The assessment in this regard would have to be based on the premises of the preexisting architecture of the preferential arrangements. It would also depend on the economic and political policies of the member countries that drive them towards rationalizing the multiple overlapping agreements (Baldwin, 2006; Baldwin and Low, 2009). One of the large benefits of multilateralization is to bring down the administrative burden for the governments and eliminate trade distortions, both for the national economy and multilateral trade. This is not a mere theoretical concept; it has been tried and tested. There was a proposal to multilateralize the AFTA accord and apply it to APEC.

7. The Trans-Pacific Partnership: A state-of-the-art agreement?

Although conceived earlier (in 2003), the Trans-Pacific Partnership (TPP) Agreement, or the Pacific-4 (P4) agreement, between Brunei, Chile, New Zealand and Singapore, entered into force in 2006. Since its establishment, P4 was intended as a model avant-garde agreement, open to other economies. To attract more Asia-Pacific members, it provided a platform for negotiations. As Asia is regarded as an important region by the USA, in 2008 the USA announced its willingness to join the P4. Australia, Peru and Vietnam followed suit. Negotiations for the expanded agreement began in March 2010. During the third round in Brunei in October 2010, Malaysia also decided to join in.

These nine countries are APEC members and the grouping is trans-Atlantic. They belong to four different regions: Asia, Oceania, Latin America and North America. The TPP is a newly emerging track of agreements in the Asia-Pacific region, which can help consolidate the multiplicity of FTAs and resolve the current "noodle bowl" malaise. As these economies are like-minded and open, the probabilities of success of TPP are high. China is a considerable trade partner of the TPP economies. It is a net exporter of manufactures to them and net importer of agricultural products. Although 23 percent of China's total trade was with the TPP economies in 2011, TPP negotiations did not include China. China was paying close attention to progress in TPP negotiations. A valid question in this regard is that given the regional significance of China, could the TPP succeed without it?

In terms of issues covered, the TPP is an ambitious agreement. An all-important objective of the TPP is to develop a premium, 21st-century, comprehensive, trans-regional FTA. In its comprehensiveness it embraces provisions on market access for trade in goods and related rules, trade in services, intellectual property, government procurement, competition policy, dispute settlement including investor-state dispute settlement, data flows and supply chain management. Baldwin (2013, p. 2) described it as a "mega-regional" comparable to the EU–Canada and EU–Japan FTAs. If the negotiations succeed then the rules of supply chain trade will be harmonized plurilaterally by the end of the decade. When the TPP is finalized, it is expected to be ahead of its time. The USTR (2011) describes it as "the most credible pathway to Asia-Pacific regional economic integration". The intended objective of the TPP is to deepen economic ties between the nine diverse economies of the Asia-Pacific region. These countries are endeavoring to go beyond the WTO charter and conclude a state-of-the-art agreement that will address the contemporary needs of trading economies in the areas of trade and investment.

Members expect the TPP agreement to deal with the issues of modern trade, the kind that received little attention in the past. They believe that this could eventually pave the way for the formation of a broader free trade area for the wider Asia-Pacific region. The large coverage of the TPP will, *inter alia*, include regulatory coherence, transparency, competitiveness-related issues, economic development and deeper production and supply chain linkages. Initiative for inclusion of these issues was taken by the USA, with strong support from Australia and New Zealand. These proposed cross-cutting regulations will shape the behind-the-border regulatory barriers under the TPP. It is the inclusion of these regulatory issues that became the basis of calling the TPP a 21st-century FTA.

One challenging issue is that the nine member countries are part of other BTAs and FTAs as well. This complicated the ongoing negotiations. For the present this issue was resolved by permitting a somewhat untidy hybrid approach. The members have a choice to continue with the existing FTA or to make a new offer on a bilateral or multilateral basis (Barfield, 2011). A noteworthy point is that the negotiations of the TPP took place when the multilateral trade negotiations failed to progress, the US economy was recovering was anemic and the Eurozone sovereign debt crisis was unresolved.

By liberalizing trade in goods and services, raising FDI flows as well as promoting closer links across a range of economic policy and regulatory issues, the TPP is to be made into a deep-integration agreement. This is one of the strategic objectives of the TPP. During the Asia-Pacific Economic Cooperation (APEC) Forum in November 2011, the leaders from the nine countries endorsed a report from their trade ministers. This report defined the broad contour of a nine-member TPP agreement. The TPP will remove 11,000 tariff lines. It is also designed as a template for future agreements entailing the other APEC members. In 2012 Canada, Japan and Mexico announced their intentions to be the members of TPP in future.

The immediate impact of the TPP cannot be large. The reason is that the partner economies are both open and small. The USA is the only exception to this generalization. Besides, many TPP members are parts of existing BTAs and FTAs. In addition, the USA has FTA agreements with four of the TPP members. The ability of the TPP members to liberalize further is limited. This is not to imply that the TPP does not have utility and value. It could be useful first, in mitigating effect of the tangle of FTAs with different rules and second in achieving greater regulatory coherence by promoting greater integration in such a way that it supports multilateral trading system. It can be an instrument of "multilateralizing regionalism" in the Asia-Pacific region. Furthermore, it could help salvage the region from its present "noodle bowl" and a flood of ROOs (Barfield, 2011).

The US decision to be included in the TPP has given it an added significance and created notable dynamics. Notwithstanding its recent fiscal difficulties and international financial predicament, it is still the largest economy and one of the top traders in the world. Its membership of the TPP will work as a catalyst for the other APEC economies to join in. If this comes to pass, TPP may well prove to be a seed for a larger free trade area, like a Free Trade Area of the Asia-Pacific (FTAAP). It will enable the USA to enhance its economic and strategic linkages with the dynamic Asian region. As the USA becomes a part of the integrating Asian economy, it will be mutually beneficial for the two and create synergy of its own (Fergusson and Vaughn, 2011). CGE model analysis indicates that the FTAAP has a great potential for improving welfare of participating APEC countries and will contribute to economic growth of Asia (Kim *et al.*, 2013).

The TPP could possibly take assistance from the WTO framework. If it is made as a "plurilateral" agreement under the enforceable WTO regulations, it could proceed more smoothly and accomplish more for the Asia-Pacific region as well as the global economy. The new framework of rules can benefit the members only when it can be enforced. Two such agreements have been signed under the WTO. The first one was on government procurement and the second on information technology (Bacchus, 2011).

Although negotiations were to be completed by October 2013, the progress was slow. During the 16th round of the negotiations held in March 2013 in Singapore, little progress was made. Negotiations among 11 Asia-Pacific countries were bogged down in traditional trade issues, namely, agriculture and textiles. The 18th round was held in Malaysia in July 2013, when Japan joined the negotiations. Its late entry may complicate negotiations and delay the agreement further. The 12 Pacific Rim nations cover 40 percent of the global GDP.

A quantitative analysis of TPP conducted by Petri *et al.* (2011) reported benefit for all the members, essentially because this agreement calls for deep liberalization. Their simulations for the 2010–25 period emphasized that the benefits would be initially small, but will enlarge as TPP expands. In the early stages the TPP will benefit small, low-income, economies like Vietnam more. Subsequently, it will benefit relatively larger economies like Korea and Japan. Only in the final stages will benefits accrue to large economies like the USA. The largest source of gains for the TPP members will be from trade creation. The reason is that various groups of TPP economies have the traits of being natural trading blocs that are based on efficient specialization. One piece of good news from this simulation exercise is that it found the adjustment cost for the member countries to be manageable. This applies even to the short term, when economies experience the greatest impact of integration and therefore adjustment costs are steep. These are indubitably encouraging results.

8. Summary and conclusions

The objective of this chapter is to examine the evolution of Asia's regional architecture, which developed at an exceedingly fast clip. Government-led or formal regionalism was a major tactical shift in the regional trade and integration strategy. At the turn of the century multilateral trade liberalization took the backseat and regional liberalization became increasingly prominent. A China-centric regional economic structure began to evolve in Asia. China also took a great deal of initiative in the post-2000 evolution of regionalism and influenced it significantly. China showed continuous and proactive interest in the development of ASEAN-Plus-One BTAs, particularly the APT fora.

At the end of the first decade of the 21st century, most small Asian economies and even more the large ones had accepted regionalism as a policy instrument for pursuing regional and global trade expansion and economic integration. This applies particularly to China, Japan and Korea.

The mode and conduct multilateral trade has been significantly transformed during the first decade of the 21st century, Asia could not possibly remain immune from it. Importance of regionalism in the multilateral trade has been on the rise. Also, trade–investment–services nexus were formed and grew increasingly important. It combined with cross-border investment in production facilities. The next development was trade in parts, components and sub-assemblies, which increased progressively and became a high proportion of total trade in several Asian economies. These new dimensions of trade affected formation of FTAs. The 21st-century BTAs and FTAs were different from the older ones, which were shallower in their composition, frequently dealing merely with phased tariffs.

As business firms now manufacture parts of their products across the border, the BTAs, FTAs and RTAs of the contemporary period need to take into account the new kind of trade barriers that have been created owing to the changing mode of trade. The contemporary regional agreements need to be so designed as to facilitate the new modes of conducting business and trade. As regionalism grew in Asia, Asian economies formed a good number of BTAs and FTAs, many of them were of shallow variety. Consequently they remained limited and uneven in their impact. This policy error was made despite being cognizant of the fact that agreements that covered mere border trade measures and were made between two partners have a limited payoff in terms of increasing trade. Also, many of the FTAs are of the "hub-and-spoke variety" and overlap each other. This leads to operational inefficiency. Numerous Asian agreements followed the GATT/WTO paradigm and focused more on border measures in liberalization. These entered into by ASEAN and China characteristically come in this category. As opposed to them, the ones formulated by Japan and Korea are known for being more comprehensive. They did not stay restricted to the GATT/WTO paradigm.

That the WTO-Plus FTAs are more functional and result-oriented was understood somewhat late in Asia. This explains the delay in turning toward them. An important trend setter in this regard was the USA. The blueprint and norms followed by the USA had a demonstration effect. Therefore many Asian BTAs and FTAs that were negotiated during the recent years went beyond the GATT/WTO model. Asian economies that negotiated agreements during the recent years preferred to enter into what became known as the "new age" or "WTO-Plus" FTAs, which had rationally wider scope and therefore comprehensive ramifications for the FTA partners. The behind-the-border issues were covered well under the WTO-Plus FTAs. With the spread of this trend the three ASEAN-Plus-One agreements, negotiated with China, Japan and Korea, were

WTO-Plus. The MNCs, that have been playing active roles in Asia, made Asian countries conscious of the added value of the WTO-Plus FTAs.

Numerous surveys reveal that the utilization rates of the FTAs in Asia are usually low. They compare unfavorably to that of NAFTA. This implies that the increasing intra-regional trade in Asia was not the direct result of progress in regionalism. Recent country-level and industry-level studies have indicated several clear and cogent reasons behind the underutilization of FTAs in the region.

BTAs and FTAs in Asia have several shortcomings that often rendered them lightweight and insubstantial. Many of them stem from their initiation and negotiations. As market access was frequently their goal, they did not consider it necessary to engage in negotiating comprehensive and deep FTAs. Also, tariff line coverage in most FTAs was not large. Many of them have long lists of "sensitive" products. Liberalization commitments in many of them are shallow and do not go far. They are also uneven in their coverage of trade in goods. For instance, in many of them the agricultural sector is inadequately covered. This is one characteristic that goes counter to the grain of Article XXIV of the GATT/WTO and Article V of the GATS. There is also a dearth of statistical data regarding the Asian FTAs.

Although China was a latecomer to regionalism, it sought to develop FTAs with the regional partners to foster stable markets as well as diversify export destinations. China suddenly became more active in regionalism after the Asian crisis. Since its WTO accession it turned to it more energetically. It even took the lead in promoting institutional regionalism. ASEAN and China first developed bilateral ties, which further developed into ACFTA. China subsequently developed FTAs with several regional economies. China is important to its neighbors because it is a large and growing market.

After long delays, the members of ASEAN began to integrate economically. By the late 1990s it became obvious that the ASEAN bloc is a fairly successful case of sub-regional integration. AFTA came into being in 1992. Although it took off to an indifferent start, its scope was subsequently broadened and it came in effect in 2004. Regionalism picked up momentum in the post-2000 period. Since the turn of the century a China-centric economic structure of the regional economy began to evolve, with that formal regionalism progressed in Asia. A surfeit of reciprocal or bilateral trade agreements and FTAs were negotiated in Asia after 2000, which was seen by some as having low utility in increasing trade and welfare in the region.

One of the most important developments was the formation of ASEAN-Plus-Three agreements, with China, Japan and Korea. All three were BTAs. Subsequently more such BTAs followed with India and Oceania (Australia and New Zealand). ASEAN became a hub of Asian regionalism. When this network of BTAs comes into force it will create some semblance of an economically integrated Asia-Pacific region. By 2010, many of these BTAs had come in effect. Since this juncture sub-regional integration in the areas of trade and investment intensified further. Similar BTAs with Russia and the USA were in the early stages of conceptualization.

With expansion in hub-and spokes BTAs, ASEAN became an imperious sub-regional grouping. Developments during the last decade prove that ASEAN bloc is fast developing into a locus of a prospective pan-Asian institution-led integration. It has formed trade and economic alliances with several large Asian as well as Oceania economies. Many important BTAs in which ASEAN was the hub had come in effect by January 2010. These five regional agreements put down the ground work for an East, Southeast and South Asian integration. For advancing towards the goal of regionalization, it is undoubtedly a valuable achievement. Various sub-regions of Asia would be woven closely by this network of BTAs.

The formation of the APT was a constructive and functional measure, having meaningful consequences for regional integration. This inter-governmental initiative worked as a real stimulus to regionalism. The regional significance of the APT continued to increase and it became a regional umbrella establishment for integration initiatives. China's importance as an ascendant economic power was high for the ASEAN bloc. A great deal of private-sector-led integration between China and the large ASEAN economies took place during the last decade. Their trade relationship, particularly in intermediate goods, evolved at a fast pace.

The ASEAN economies had a unique manner of operating in their endeavors to regionalize. Their so-called "ASEAN Way" implied a relatively easy-going neighborly relationship among the member countries. Member states engage with each other at their own level of comfort. It enabled the regional economies to discuss, negotiate and reach common goals. It also succeeded in making it possible for small states to lead the large ones. When the two regional giants, China and India, sustained a period of rapid growth, this sub-group of economies launched a plan for creating an ASEAN Economic Community.

The missing TFTA between China, Japan and Korea is something that is greatly needed for completing the regional integration arrangement. In spite of being bilaterally linked to the ASEAN bloc, so far there is no TFTA between the CJK economies. Over the years the three economies have broached different possibilities and approaches for integrating, but they failed to come to a mutually agreed arrangement. Since 2008, four tripartite CJK summits took place and a fourth one in 2011 in Tokyo. These summits provided a platform for co-ordinating responses to immediate regional issues and concerns. China has been the most actively interested in the TFTA negotiations, while Japan has been the most passive. Korea took the middle ground, although it is likely to be the largest beneficiary of the TFTA.

A larger integrated region covering many Asian economies implies a higher volume of trade. There are benefits from consolidating the existing BTAs and FTAs in Asia. As markets grow larger and integrate and in the process lower or eliminate barriers to trade and investment, they provide incentives to both domestic and foreign investors to increase investment in productive resources, manufacturing activities, services and infrastructure development. The direct result is that regional economies are brought closer together and become more deeply connected. Several modes of consolidation have thus been suggested and discussed in this chapter.

Notes

1 These two terms are often used interchangeably.
2 The four so-called Singapore issues are investment, competition policy and transparency in government procurement. The fourth issue is simplification of trade procedures, an issue sometimes referred to as "trade facilitation".
3 Their formal names are as follows: (1) ASEAN–China Framework Agreement and Comprehensive Economic Cooperation; and (2) ASEAN–Japan Framework Agreement and Comprehensive Economic Partnership and ASEAN–Korea Comprehensive Economic Partnership.
4 This section draws on Kawai and Wignaraja (2010).
5 Kawai and Wignaraja (2011), Chapter 2, extensively reposts and analyzes the ADB survey results. See pp. 33–73 for details. A total of 841 firms were surveyed in six Asian economies.
6 The ASEAN-Plus-Six (APS) economies comprise the 10 members of the ASEAN bloc, plus Australia, China, India, Japan, Korea and New Zealand. It is also referred to as the ASEAN+3+3.
7 Cited in Kim (2013).
8 Oceania is the term that is used to denote Australia, New Zealand and the proximate Pacific islands.
9 The source of statistical data here is Lee (2011).
10 For example, see Baldwin (2004), Lee and van der Mensbrugghe (2007), McKibbin et al. (2004), Kawai and Wignaraja (2007, 2008), Park (2009) and Urata and Kiyota (2003).

References

Bacchus, J. 2011. "Marry the TPP to the WTO." *The Wall Street Journal*. 14 November, p. 13.

Baldwin, R. 2011. "Twenty-First Century Regionalism." London: Center for Economic Policy Research. *Policy Insight*. No. 56. May.

——2013. "The WTO and Global Supply Chain." *East Asia Forum*. 24 February. Available online at www.eastasiaforum.org.

——2006. "Multilateralizing Regionalism: Spaghetti Bowls as Building Blocs on the Path to Global Free Trade." *The World Economy*. Vol. 29. No. 11, pp. 1451–518.

——2004. "The Spoke Trap: Hub and Spoke Bilateralism in East Asia." Seoul: Korea Institute for International Economic Policy. Research Series No. 04–02.

Baldwin, R. and P. Low. 2009. "Introduction", in R. Baldwin and P. Low. (eds). *Multilateralizing Regionalism*. Cambridge: Cambridge University Press.

Barfield, C. 2011. "The Trans-Pacific Partnership: A Model for Twenty-First Century Agreements." *International Economic Outlook,* No. 2. Washington, DC: American Enterprise Institute. Available online at www.lachamber.com/clientuploads/Global_Programs/TPP%20White%20Paper.pdf.

Bhagwati, J. N. 2008. *Termite in the Trading System: How Preferential Agreements Undermine Free Trade*. Oxford: Oxford University Press.

Bhagwati, J. N., D. Greenaway and A. Panagariya. 1998. "Trading Preferentially: Theory and Policy." *The Economic Journal*. Vol. 108, pp. 1128–48.

Breslin, S. 2010. "Comparative Theory, China and the Future of East Asian Regionalism." *Review of International Studies*. Vol. 36. No. 3, pp. 709–29.

Byun, S. W. 2011. "The China-South Korea-Japan Triangle: The Shape of Things to Come." *Asia-Pacific Bulletin*. Hondulu, HI: East-West Center.

Capling, A. and J. Ravenhill. 2011. "Multilateral Regionalism: What Role for the Trans-Pacific Partnership?" *The Pacific Review*. Vol. 24. No. 5, pp. 553–75.

Chachavalpongpun, P. 2010. "How the US Plays into the East Asia Summit for ASEAN." *East Asia Forum*. 17 August. Available online at www.eastasiaforum.org.

Chia, S. Y. 2010. "Regional Trade Policy Cooperation and Architecture in East Asia." Tokyo: Asian Development Bank Institute. Working Paper Series No. 191. October.

——2011. "Association of Southeast Asian Nations Economic Integration: Developments and Challenges." *Asian Economic Policy Review*. Vol. 6. No. 1, pp. 43–63.

Chin, G. and R. Stubbs. 2011. "China, Regional Institution-Building." *Review of International Political Economy*. Vol. 18. No. 3, pp. 277–98.

Das, Dilip. K. 2006. *China and India: A Tale of Two Economies*. London and New York: Routledge.

——2007. "Shifting Paradigm of Regional Integration in Asia." Coventry: Warwick University. Center for the Study of Globalization and Regionalization. CSGR Working Paper No. 230/07. June.

——2012. "Growth Paradigms of China and India: A Conventional Framework of Growth Analysis", in X. Huang (ed.). *China, India and the End of Development Model*. Basingstoke: Palgrave Macmillan, pp. 32–50.

The Economist Corporate Network (ECN). 2013. *Investing in an Accelerating Asia?* London. February.

Estrada, G., D. Park, I. Park and S. Park. 2012. "The PRC's Free Trade Agreements with ASEAN, Japan and the Republic of Korea." Manila, the Philippines: Asian Development Bank. Working Paper No. 92. January.

Fergusson, I. F. and B. Vaughn. 2011. "The Trans-Pacific Partnership Agreement." Washington, DC: Congressional Research Service. 12 December.

Freund, C. and E. Ornelas. 2010. "Regional Trade Agreements." Washington, DC: World Bank. World Bank Policy Research Working Paper No. 5314.

Fukunaga, Y. and I. Isono. 2013. "Taking ASEAN+1 FTAs Towards the RCEP." Jakarta, Indonesia. Economic Research Institute for ASEAN, Discussion Paper No. 2013–02. January.

Haggard, S. 2011. "The Organizational Architecture of Asia-pacific: Insights from the New Institutions." Manila, the Philippines: Asian Development Bank. Working Paper No. 71. January.

Hale, T. 2011. "The De Facto Preferential Trade Agreement in East Asia." *Review of International Political Economy*. Vol. 18. No. 3, pp. 299–327.

Hiratsuka, D. 2010b. "Characteristics and Determinants of East Asia's Trade Patterns", in Hiratsuka, D. and Y. Uchida (eds). *Input Trade Production Networks in East Asia*. Cheltenham: Edward Elgar, pp. 62–83.

Hiratsuka, D., H. Sato and I. Isono. 2009. "Impacts of Free Trade Agreements on BusinessActivity in Asia." Tokyo, Japan. ADB Institute. Working Paper No. 143.

Hu, W. 1996. "China and Asian Regionalism: Challenge and Policy Choice." *Journal of Contemporary China*. Vol. 5. No. 11, pp. 43–56.

International Monetary Fund (IMF). 2011. *World Economic Outlook*. Washington, DC. April.

Itakura, K. 2013. "Impact of Liberalization and Improved Connectivity in ASEAN." Jakarta, Indonesia. Economic Research Institute for ASEAN, Discussion Paper No. 2013–01. January.

Ito, T., A. Kojima, C. McKenzie and S. Urata. 2011. ASEAN Economy: Diversity, Disparities and Dynamics." *Asian Economic Policy Review*. Vol. 6. No. 1, pp. 1–21.

Japan External Trade Organization (JETRO). 2009. "Survey of Japanese Affiliated Firms in Asia and Oceania." Tokyo, Japan.

Kawai, M. and G. Wignaraja. 2011. *Asia's Free Trade Agreements*. Cheltenham: Edward Elgar.

——2010. "Asian FTAs: Trends, Prospects and Challenges." Manila, the Philippines: Asian Development Bank. Working Paper Series No. 226. October.

——2009. "The Asian 'Noodle Bowl': Is it Serious for Business?" Tokyo, Japan: ADB Institute. Working paper No. 136.

——2008. "Regionalism as an Engine of Multilateralism: A Case for a Single East Asian FTA." Manila, the Philippines: Asian Development Bank. Working Paper Series No. 14. February.

——2007. "ASEAN+3 or ASEAN+6: Which Way Forward?" Tokyo: Asian Development Bank Institute. Discussion Paper No. 77.

Kim, K. H. 2013. "Potential of ASEAN Economy Revisited." *SERI World*. Samsung Economic Research Institute. 18 February, pp. 9–13.

Kim, S., I. Park and S. Park. 2013. "A Free Trade Area of the Asia Pacific: Is it Desirable?" *Journal of East Asian Economic Integration*. Vol. 17. No. 1, pp. 3–25.

Korea International Trade Association (KITA). 2010. "Korea is the Biggest Beneficiary of Northeast Asian FTA." Seoul, Korea. 20 December. Available online at global.kita.net/news/01/read.jsp?seq=3605.

Krumm, K. and H. J. Kharas. 2004. *East Asia Integrates: Trade Policy Agenda for Shared Growth*. Washington, DC: World Bank.

Lee, C. J. 2011. "Prospects for a China-Japan-Korea FTA", in *Financing for Regional Economic Development*. Published by The Korea Institute for International Economic Policy, Seoul, Korea, pp. 38–65.

Lee, H. and M. G. Plummer. 2011. "Assessing the Impact of the ASEAN Economic Community." Osaka. Osaka School of International Public Policy. Discussion Paper No. 2011-E-002. 23 March.

Lee, J. H. and I. Park. 2005. "Free Trade Areas in East Asia: Discriminatory or Nondiscriminatory?" *The World Economy*. Vol. 28. No. 1, pp. 21–48.

Lee, J. W. and K. Shin. 2006. "Does Regionalism Lead to More Global Trade Integration in East Asia?" *The North American Journal of Economic and Finance*. Vol. 17. No. 2, pp. 283–301.

Lee, H. and D. van der Mensbrugghe. 2007. "Regional Integration, Sectoral Adjustments and Natural Groupings in East Asia." Osaka: Osaka School of International Public Policy. Discussion Paper No. DP-2007-E-008.

McKibbin, W. J., J. W. Lee and I. Cheong. 2004. "A Dynamic Analysis of a Korea-Japan Free Trade Area: Simulations with the G-Cubed Asia-Pacific Model." *International Economic Journal*. Vol. 18. No. 1, pp. 3–32.

Menon, J. 2012. "Narrowing the Development Divide in ASEAN." Manila, the Philippines: Asian Development Bank. Working Paper No. 100. July.

——2009. "Dealing with the Proliferation of Bilateral Trade Agreements." *The World Economy*. Vol. 32, No. 10, pp. 1381–407.

Mercurio, B. 2011. "Bilateral and Regional Trade Agreements in Asia: A Skeptic's View", in R. Buckley, R. Hu and D. Arner (eds). *East Asian Economic Integration: Law, Trade and Finance*. Northampton, MA and Cheltenham: Edward Elgar, pp. 120–44.

Park, I. 2009. "Regional Trade Agreements in East Asia: Will They Be Sustainable?" *Asian Economic Journal*. Vol. 23. No. 2, pp. 169–94.

——2006. "East Asian Regional Trade Agreements: Do they Promote Global Free Trade." *Pacific Economic Review*. Vol. 11. No. 4, pp. 547–68.

Pelc, K. J. 2009. "The Cost of wiggle-Room: On the Use of Flexibility in International Trade Agreements." Washington, DC: Georgetown University, Doctoral Dissertation. 7 August.

Petri, P. A., M. G. Plummer and F. Zhai. 2011. "The Trans-Pacific Partnership and Asia-Pacific Integration." Honolulu, HI: East-West Center. Working Paper No. 119. 24 October.

———2010. "The Economics of the ASEAN Economic Community." 15 September. (Unpublished manuscript). Washington, DC: ASEAN Studies Center. American University. Available online at www.american.edu/sis/aseanstudiescenter/upload/Brandeis_WP13.pdf.

Prasad, E., M. A. Kose, K. S. Rogoff and S. J. Wei. 2006. "Financial Globalization: A Reappraisal." Cambridge, MA: National Bureau of Economic Research. NBER Working Paper. 12484.

Ravenhill, J. 2010. "The 'New East Asian Regionalism': A Political Domino Effect." *Review of International Political Economy*. Vol. 17. No. 2, pp. 1–31.

———2008. "The New Trade Bilateralism in East Asia", in K. E. Calder and F. Fukuyama (eds). *East Asian Multilateralism: Prospects for Regional Stability*. Baltimore, MD: Johns Hopkins University Press, pp. 78–108.

Roland-Holst, D., I. Aziz and L.G. Liu. 2003. "Regionalism and Globalism: East and Southeast Asian Trade Relations in the Wake of China's WTO Accession." Tokyo, Japan. ADB Institute. Research Paper No. 20. January.

Searight, A. 2009. "Emerging Economic Architecture in Asia: Opening or Insulating", in M. Green and B. Gill (eds). *Asia's New Multilateralism*. New York: Columbia University Press, pp. 132–63.

Severino, R. C. 2011. "Politics of Association of Southeast Asian Nations Economic Cooperation." *Asian Economic Policy Review*. Vol. 6. No. 1, pp. 22–38.

Tanaka, K. 2009. "Regional Integration in Southeast Asia." *Policy Insight*. No. 90. Paris: OECD Development Centre. February.

Thangavelu, S. 2010. "Will ASEAN Benefit From the ASEAN–China Free Trade Agreement?" *East Asian Forum*. 1 September. Available online at www.eastasiaforum.org/2010/01/27/will-asean-benefit-from-the-asean-china-fta.

Trilateral Joint Research (TJR). 2008. "Joint Research and Policy Recommendations on the Possible Roadmap of a Free Trade Agreement between China, Japan and Korea." Tokyo: Japan. December. Available online at www.nira.or.jp/pdf/0805report-E.pdf.

United Nations Conference on Trade and Development (UNCTAD). 2011. *World Investment Report, 2011*. Geneva and New York.

United Nations Conference on Trade and Development/Japan External Trade organization (UNCTAD/JETRO). 2008. "South-South Trade in Asia." Geneva and New York.

United States Trade Representative (USTR). 2011. "Engagement with the Trans-Pacific Partnership to Increase Exports." Washington, DC. Available online at www.ustr.gov/about-us/press-office/fact-sheets/2011/february/engagement-trans-pacific-partnership-increase-export. February.

Urata, S. and K. Kiyota. 2003. "The Impact of an East Asia FTA on Foreign Trade in East Asia" Cambridge, MA: National Bureau of Economic Research. Working Paper Series 10173.

Vermonte, P. J. 2005. "China-ASEAN Strategic Relations", in J. K. Chin and N. Thomas (eds). *China and ASEAN: Changing Political Strategic Ties*. Hong Kong: Center of Asian Studies, University of Hong Kong, pp. 85–105.

Ye, M. 2011. "The Rise of China and East Asian Regionalism", in M. Beeson and R. Stubb (eds). *The Handbook of Asian Regionalism*. London and New York: Routledge, pp. 120–45.

Yuzhu, W. 2011. "China, Economic Regionalism and East Asian Integration." *Japanese Journal of Political Science*. Vol. 12. No. 2, pp. 195–211.

Zhang, Y. 2006. "China and East Asian Economic Integration and Cooperation." *Journal of Economic Development*. Vol. 31. No. 2, pp. 169–85.

Zinabou, G. 2011. "East Asian Value Chain and the Global Financial Crisis." Toronto, Canada. Foreign Affairs and International Trade Office, Government of Canada. ASP No. 8.

BIBLIOGRAPHY

Aitken, B. and A. E. Harrison. 1999. "Do Domestic Firms Benefit from Direct Foreign Investment?" *The American Economic Review*. Vol. 89, No. 3, pp. 605–18.

Aizenman, J., Y. Jinjarak and D. Park. 2010. "International Reserves and Swap Lines: Substitutes or Compliments?" Cambridge, MA: National Bureau of Economic Research. Working Paper No. 15804. March.

Akyuz, Y. 2011. "The Global Economic Crisis and Trade and Growth Prospects in East Asia." Manila, Philippines. Asian Development Bank. Working paper Series No. 242. January.

Aleksynska, M. and O. Havrylchyk. 2011. "FDI from the South: The Role of Institutional Distance and Natural Resources." Paris: Centre d'Etudes Prospectives et d'Informations Internationales. Working Paper No. 2011–05. March.

Amann, E., B. Lau and F. Nixson. 2009. "Did China Hurt the Textiles and Clothing Exports of Other Asian Countries?" *Oxford Development Studies*. Vol. 37, No. 4, pp. 333–62.

Ambler, T., M. Witzel and C. Xi. 2009. *Doing Business in China*. 3rd edition. London and New York: Routledge.

Amighini, A. 2005. "China in International Fragmentation of Production: Evidence from the ICT Industry." *European Journal of Comparative Economics*. Vol. 2, No. 2, pp. 203–19.

Amiti, M. and C. Freund. 2010. "An Anatomy of China's Export Growth", in R. C. Feenstra and S. J. Wei (eds). *China's Growing Role in World Trade*. Chicago, IL: University of Chicago Press, pp. 35–62.

Anderlini, J. 2012. "China's Growth Model Running Out of Steam." *Financial Times*. London. 5 March, p. 9.

Anderlini, J. and G. Parker. 2011. "China Fund Targets Big Projects in the West." *Financial Times*. London. 28 November, p. 1.

Ando, M. and K. Fukunari. 2011. "Globalizing Corporate Activities in East Asia and Impact on Domestic Operations." Tokyo: Research Institute of Economy, Trade and Industry. Discussion Paper No. 11-E-034. March.

Ando, M. and F. Kimura. 2009. "Fragmentation in East Asia: Further evidence." Tokyo: Economic Research Institute for ASEAN and East Asia. ERICA Discussion Paper Series No. 2009–20. October.

——2005. "The Formation of International Production and Distribution Networks in East Asia", in T. Ito and A. Rose (eds). *International Trade*. Chicago, IL: University of Chicago Press, pp. 177–213.

Andrews, H. and S. Kemper. 2013. "Innovation is Now a Strategic Priority for China." Beijing: *China Daily*. 21 February.

Antras, P. and R. W. Staiger. 2012. "Offshoring and the Role of Trade Agreements." *American Economic Review*. Vol. 102, No. 7, pp. 3140–83.

——2008. "Offshoring and the Role of Trade Agreements." London: Center for Economic Policy Research. Working Paper No. 6966.

Arayama, Y. and K. Miyoshi. 2004. "Regional Diversity and Sources of Economic Growth in China." *The World Economy*. Vol. 27, No. 7, pp. 1583–1607.

Ariff, M. 2011. "Comments on Politics of Association of Southeast Asian Nations Economic Cooperation." *Asian Economic Policy Review*. Vol. 6, No. 1, pp. 39–40.

Arndt, S. W. 2008. "Production Networks and the Open Economy." *Singapore Economic Review*. Vol. 53, No. 3, pp. 509–21.

Arner, D. and L. Schou-Zibell. 2010. "Responding to the Global Financial and Economic Crisis: Meeting the Challenge in Asia." Manila, Philippines: Asian Development Bank. Working Paper No. 60. October.

Arrighi, G. 2007. *Adam Smith in Beijing: Lineages of the Twenty-First Century*. London: Verso.

Asian Development Bank (ADB). 2013. *Asian Economic Integration Monitor*. Manila, Philippines. March.

——2012. *Asian Economic Integration Monitor*. Manila, Philippines. July.

——2011. *Asian Development Outlook 2011*. Manila, Philippines. April.

——2010. *Institutions for Regional Integration*. Manila, Philippines. April.

——2009. *Asian Development Outlook 2009: Rebalancing Asia's Growth*. Hong Kong: Oxford University Press.

——2009. *Asian Development Outlook 2009 Update*. Manila, Philippines. September.

Athukorala, P. C. 2009. "The Rise of China and East Asian Export Performance." *The World Economy*. Vol. 32, No. 2, pp. 234–66.

——2010. "The Rise of China and East Asian Export Performance", in P. C. Athukorala (ed.). *The Rise of Asia*. London and New York: Routledge, pp. 267–91.

——2011a. *Asian Trade Flows: Trends, Patterns and Projections*. Working Paper No. 2011/05. March. Australian National University, Crawford School of Economics and Government, Canberra.

——2011b. "Production Networks and Trade Patterns in East Asia." *Asian Economic Papers*. Vol. 10, No. 1, pp. 65–95.

Athukorala, P. C. and H. Hill. 2010. "Asian Trade and Investment", in P. C. Athukorala (ed.). *The Rise of Asia*. London and New York: Routledge, pp. 11–57.

Athukorala, P. C. and J. Menon. 2010. *Global Production Sharing, Trade Patterns and Determinants of Trade Flows*. Working Paper No. 2010/06. July. Australian National University, Crawford School of Economics and Government, Canberra.

A. T. Kearney. 2012. *Cautious Investors Feed a Tentative recovery. A.T.Kearney FDI Confidence Index*. Vienna, VA: Global Business Policy Council.

——2010. *Investing in a Rebound: The 2010 A.T.Kearney FDI Confidence Index*. Vienna, VA: Global Business Policy Council.

Aziz, J. 2006. *Rebalancing China's Economy: What Does Growth Theory Tell Us?* IMF Working Paper No. WP/06/291. Washington, DC: International Monetary Fund.

Bacchus, J. 2011. "Marry the TPP to the WTO." *The Wall Street Journal*. 14 November, p. 13.

Baek, S. W. 2005. "Does China Follow "the East Asian Development Model"?" *Journal of Contemporary Asia*. Vol. 35, No. 4, pp. 485–98.

Bai, C. E., C. T. Hsieh and Y. Qian. 2006. "The Return to Capital in China." *Brookings Papers on Economic Activity*. Vol. 37, No. 2, pp. 61–102.

Balassa, B. 1961. *The Theory of Economic Integration*. London: Allen & Unwin.

Baldwin, R. 2011. "Twenty-First Century Regionalism." London: Center for Economic Policy Research. *Policy Insight*. No. 56. May.

——2013. "The WTO and Global Supply Chain." *East Asia Forum*. February 24. Available online at www.eastasiaforum.org [accessed December 2012].

——2006. "Multilateralizing Regionalism: Spaghetti Bowls as Building Blocs on the Path to Global Free Trade." *The World Economy*. Vol. 29, No. 11, pp. 1451–1518.

——2004. "The Spoke Trap: Hub and Spoke Bilateralism in East Asia." Seoul: Korea Institute for International Economic Policy. Research Series No. 04–02.

Baldwin, R. and P. Low. 2009. "Introduction", in R. Baldwin and P. Low. (eds). *Multilateralizing Regionalism*. Cambridge: Cambridge University Press.

Barfield, C. 2011. "The Trans-Pacific Partnership: A Model for Twenty-First Century Agreements." *International Economic Outlook*. No. 2. Washington, DC: American Enterprise Institute. Available online at www.lachamber.com/clientuploads/Global_Programs/TPP%20White%20Paper.pdf [accessed December 2012].

Barton, D. 2013. "Asia's Titans Play the Long Game." *Global Brief*. 5 March. Available online at globalbrief.ca/blog/2013/03/05/asia%E2%80%99s-titans-play-the-long-game [accessed December 2012].

Battelle. 2010. "*2011 Global R&D Funding Forecast*." R&D Magazine. Vol. 28. Available online at www.battelle.org/aboutus/rd/2011.pdf [accessed December 2012].

Baumol, W. J., R. E. Litan and C. J. Schramm. 2007. "Sustaining Entrepreneurial Capitalism." *Capitalism and Society*. The Berkeley Electronic Press. Vol. 2, No. 2, Article 1.

Bayoumi, T., H. Tong and S. Wei. 2010. "The Chinese Corporate saving Puzzle: A Firm Level Cross-Country Perspective." Washington, DC: International Monetary Fund. Working Paper 10/275.

Benjamin, D., L. Brandt and J. Giles. 2010. *Did Higher Inequality Impede Growth in Rural China?* Policy Research Working Paper 5483. Washington, DC: World Bank.

Bernanke, B. S. 2006. "The Chinese Economy: Progress and Challenges." Paper presented at the Chinese Academy of Social Sciences, Beijing, 15 December.

——2000. "Japanese Monetary Policy: A Case of Self-Induced Paralysis", in R. Mikitani and A. S. Posen (eds). *Japan's Financial Crisis*. Washington, DC: Institute of International Economics, pp. 149–66.

Bhagwati, J. N. 2008. *Termite in the Trading System: How Preferential Agreements Undermine Free Trade*. Oxford: Oxford University Press.

Bhagwati, J. N., D. Greenaway and A. Panagariya. 1998. "Trading Preferentially: Theory and Policy." *The Economic Journal*. Vol. 108, pp. 1128–48.

Blanchard, O. J. and F. Giavazzi. 2006. *Rebalancing Growth in China: A Three-Handed Approach*. Discussion Paper No. PD 5403. London: Center for Economic Policy Research.

Bloomberg Businessweek (BB). "China Tops India as Asian Economy Best Placed for Growth." 27 May. Available online at www.businessweek.com/news/2011–05–27/china-tops-india-as-asian-economy-best-placed-for-growth.html [accessed December 2012].

Boltho, A. and M. Weber. 2009. "Did China follow the East Asian Development Model?" *The European Journal of Comparative Economics*. Vol. 6, No. 2, pp. 267–86.

Bordo, M. D., A. M., Taylor and J. G. Williamson (eds). 2003. *Globalization in Historical Perspective*. Chicago, IL: University of Chicago Press.

Borensztein, E. and D. J. Ostry. 1996. "Accounting for China's Growth Performance." *American Economic Review*. Vol. 86, No. 6, pp. 224–28.

Boston Consulting Group (BCG). 2013. "Maintaining Momentum in a Complex World: Global Wealth 2013." Boston, MA. May.

Bosworth, B. and S. M. Collins. 2008. "Accounting for Growth: Comparing China and India." *Journal of Economic Perspectives*. Vol. 22, No. 1, pp. 45–66.

Brandt, L. and T. G. Rawski. 2008. "China's Great Economic Transformation", in L. Brandt and T. G. Rawski (eds). *China's Great Economic Transformation*. Cambridge: Cambridge University Press, pp. 1–34.

Brandt, L., T. G. Rawski and X. Zhu. 2007. "International Dimension of China's Long-Term Boom," in W. W. Keller and T. G. Rawski (eds). *China's Rise and Balance of Influence in Asia*. Pittsburgh, PA: Pittsburgh University Press, pp. 14–46.

Bradsher, K. 2012. "China Confronts Mounting Piles of Unsold Goods." *The New York Times*. New York. 23 August, p. 6.

Branstetter, L. and N. Lardy. 2008. "China's Embrace of Globalization", in L. Brandt and T. G. Rawski (eds). *China's Great Economic Transformation*. Cambridge: Cambridge University Press, pp. 633–82.

Breslin, S. 2010. "Comparative Theory, China and the Future of East Asian Regionalism." *Review of International Studies*. Vol. 36, No. 3, pp. 709–29.

——2009. "Understanding China's Regional Rise: Interpretations, Identities and Implications." *International Affairs*. Vol. 85, No. 4, pp. 817–35.

Buckley, P. J., J. Clegg and C. Wang. 2010a. "Inward FDI and Host Country Productivity", in P. J. Buckley (ed.). *Foreign Direct Investment, China and the World Economy*. Basingstokes: Palgrave Macmillan, pp. 216–38.

——2002. "The Impact of Inward FDI on the Performance of Chinese Manufacturing Firms." *Journal of International Business Studies*. Vol. 33, No. 4, pp. 637–55.

Buckley, P. J., J. Clegg, A. Cross and H. Tan. 2010b. "China's Inward Foreign Direct Investment Success", in P. J. Buckley (ed.). *Foreign Direct Investment, China and the World Economy"* Basingstoke: Palgrave Macmillan, pp. 239–69.

Buiter, W. H. and E. Rahbari. 2011. "Global Growth Generators: Moving Beyond Emerging Markets and BRICs." *Policy Insight, No.* 55. London: Center for Economic Policy Research. April.

Byun, S. W. 2011. "The China-South Korea-Japan Triangle: The Shape of Things to Come." *Asia-Pacific Bulletin*. Honolulu, HI: East-West Center.

Calder, K. and M. Ye. 2004. "Regionalism and Critical Junctures." *Journal of East Asian Studies*. Spring. Vol. 4, No. 2, pp. 191–226.

Calderon, C., A. Chong and E. Stein. 2007. "Trade Intensity and Business Cycle Synchronization: Are Developing Countries Any Different?" *Journal of International Economics*. Vol. 71, No. 1, pp. 2–21.

Capling, A. and J. Ravenhill. 2011. "Multilateral Regionalism: What Role for the Trans-Pacific Partnership?" *The Pacific Review*. Vol. 24, No. 5, pp. 553–75.

Ceglowski, J. and S. Golub. 2007. "Just How Low Are China's Labor Costs?" *The World Economy*. Vol. 30, No. 4, pp. 597–617.

Chachavalpongpun, P. 2010. "How the US Plays into the East Asia Summit for ASEAN." *East Asia Forum*. 17 August. Available online at www.eastasiaforum.org.

Chadha, R. and P. Husband. 2007. *The Cult of the Luxury Brand*. Hong Kong: NB Publishing.

Chantasasavat, B., K. C. Fung, H. Lizaka and A. Siu. 2005. "The Giant Sucking Sound: Is China Diverting Foreign Direct Investment from Other Asian Economies?" *Asian Economic Papers*. Vol. 3, No. 3, pp. 122–40.

Chaudhury, S. and M. Ravallion. 2007. "Partially Awakened Giants: Uneven Growth in China and India", in L. A. Winters and S. Yusuf (eds). *Dancing with Giants: China, India and the Global Economy*. Washington, DC: World Bank, pp. 175–210.

Chen, C. 2012. *Foreign Direct Investment in China*. Cheltenham: Edward Elgar.

——2010. "Asian Foreign Direct Investment and the 'China Effect'", in R. Garnaut, J. Golley and L. Song (eds). *China: The Next Twenty Years of Reform and Development*. The Australian National University Press, pp. 221–37.

Chen, S., G. H. Jefferson and J. Zhang. 2011. "Structural Change, Productivity Growth and Industrial Transformation in China." *China Economic Review*. Vol. 22, No. 1, pp. 133–50.

Chen, Y. 2001. "Evidence of the Effects of Openness Policy on TFP and Its Components: The Case of Chinese Provinces." Paper presented at the Third International Conference on the Chinese Economy in Clermont-Ferrand, France, 21 May.

Chenery, H., S. Robinson and Syrquin, M. 1986. *Industrialization and Growth: A Comparative Study*. New York: Oxford University Press.

Chia, S. Y. 2011. "Association of Southeast Asian Nations Economic Integration: Developments and Challenges. *Asian Economic Policy Review*. Vol. 6, No. 1, pp. 43–63.

——2010. "Regional Trade Policy Cooperation and Architecture in East Asia." Tokyo: Asian Development Bank Institute. Working Paper Series No. 191. October.

Chin, G. 2012. "Responding to the Global Financial Crisis: The Evolution of Asian Regionalism." Manila: Asian Development Bank. Working Paper No. 343. January.

Chin, G. and R. Stubbs. 2011. "China, Regional Institution-Building." *Review of International Political Economy*. Vol. 18, No. 3, pp. 277–98.

ChinaBiz. 2005. *Localization Continues*. ChinaBiz LT. Available online at chinabiz.com.

China Europe International Business School (CEIBS). 2012. "Innovation: China's Next Advantage?" Shanghai. June.

Chow, G. 1993. "Capital Formation and Economic Growth in China." *Quarterly Journal of Economics*. Vol. 108, No. 4, pp. 809–42.

Cimoli, M., G. Dosi and J. E. Stiglitz (eds). 2009. *Industrial Policy and Development: The Political Economy of Capabilities Accumulation*. New York: Oxford University Press.

Cliff, R., C. J. R. Ohlandt and D. Yang. 2011. *Ready for Takeoff: China's Advancing Aerospace Industry*. Santa Monica, CA: RAND Corporation.

Coase, R. and Wang, N. 2012. *How China Became Capitalist*. Basingstoke, UK: Palgrave Macmillan.

Cooks, E. 2011. "GE Targets China Sales Growth." *Financial Times*, 21 January, p. 13.

The Conference Board (CB). 2012. *Global Economic Outlook 2012*. New York. March.

Coxhead, I. 2007. "A New Resource Curse? Impact of China's Boom on Comparative Advantage and Resource Dependence in Southeast Asia." *World Development*. Vol. 35, No. 7, pp. 1109–19.

Cristadoro, R. and D. Marconi. 2012. "Household Savings in China." *Journal of Chinese Economic and Business Studies*. Vol. 10, No. 3, pp. 275–99.

Dahlman, C. J. 2010. "Global Challenges from the Rapid Rise of China." Oxford: Oxford University. Department of International Development. RMD Working Paper Series No. 41. 13 July.

Daily Telegraph. 2011. "Rolls-Royce Sets Record Car Sales in 2010." 11 January.

Das, Dilip K. 1992. *The Yen Appreciation and the International Economy*. London: Macmillan Press, and New York: New York University Press.

——1993. *Market-led Integration in the Asia-Pacific Region*. Fontainebleau: Euro-Asia Centre. European Institute of Business Administration (INSEAD), Research Series, No. 24. April. pp. 45.

——2001. *The Global Trading System at Crossroads: A Post-Seattle Perspective*. London and New York. Routledge.

——2004. *Regionalism in Global Trade: Turning Kaleidoscope*. Northampton, MA, and Cheltenham: Edward Elgar.

——2005. *Asian Economy and Finance: A Post-Crisis Perspective*. New York: Springer Publications.

——2005. "Market-Driven Regionalization in Asia." *Global Economy Journal*. Vol. 5, Issue 3, Article 2. The Berkeley Electronic Press. Berkeley, CA. Available online at www.bepress.com/cgi/viewcontent. cgi?article=1082&context=gej [accessed December 2012].

——2005. *The Doha Round of Multilateral Trade Negotiations: Arduous Issues and Strategic Responses*. Basingstoke: Palgrave Macmillan.

——2006. *China and India: A Tale of Two Economies*. London and New York: Routledge.

——2007. "Shifting Paradigm of Regional Integration in Asia." Coventry: Warwick University. Center for the Study of Globalization and Regionalization. CSGR Working Paper No. 230/07. June.

——2007. "Foreign Direct Investment in China: Its Impact on the Neighboring Asian Economies." *Asian Business and Management*. Vol. 6, No. 3, pp. 285–302.

——2008. "Suspension of the Doha Round of Multilateral Trade Negotiations." *Estey Journal of International Law and Trade Policy*. Vol. 9, No. 1, pp. 51–73.

——2008. *The Chinese Economic Renaissance: Apocalypse or Cornucopia*. Basingstoke: Palgrave Macmillan.

——2008. *The Chinese Economy: Making a Global Niche*. Working Paper No. 239. March. University of Warwick: Centre for the Study of Globalization and Regionalization.

——2008. *Winners of Globalization*. CSGR Working Paper No. 249/08. University of Warwick: Center for the Study of Globalization and Regionalization. Available online at www.warwick.ac.uk/fac/soc/csgr/research/workingpapers/2008/24908.pdf [accessed August 2010].

——2008. "Contemporary Phase of Globalization: Does It Have a Serious Downside?" *Global Economic Review*. Vol. 37, No. 4, pp. 507–26.

——2009. *The Two Faces of Globalization: Munificent and Malevolent*. Northampton, MA, and Cheltenham: Edward Elgar.

——2011. "China: Epitome of an Emerging Market." *Journal of Emerging Knowledge on Emerging Markets*. Vol. 3, No. 1, pp. 57–81.

——2011. *Asian Economy: Spearheading the Recovery from the Global Financial Crisis*. London and New York: Routledge.

——2011. "China in the Domain of International Business." *Human Systems Management*. Vol. 30, No. 1, pp. 71–83.

——2012. "The Eurozone Financial Crisis and the Resilience of Asia's Economies." Daejeon, Korea. SolBridge International School of Business. Institute of Asian Business. Research Paper No. 2012–02. 15 April.

——2012. "Regional Implications of China-Korea FTA." *The Korea Times*. 27 January, p. 7.

——2012. "Growth Paradigms of China and India: A Conventional Framework of Growth Analysis", in X. Huang (ed.). *China, India and the End of Development Model*. Basingstoke: Palgrave Macmillan, pp. 32–50.

Dean, J. M., K. C. Fung and Z. Wang. 2007. *Measuring the Vertical Specialization in Chinese Trade*. Working Paper No. 2007/01/A. January. Washington, DC: US International Trade Commission.

Davies, K. 2010. "Outward FDI from China and its Policy Context." New York: Columbia University. FDI Profiles. Available on the Internet at: www.vcc.columbia.edu/files/vale/documents/China_OFDI_final_Oct_18.pdf [accessed December 2012].

DeCarlo, S. 2012. "The World's Biggest Companies." *Forbes*. April.

Dekle, R. and G. Vandenbroucke. 2006. "A Quantitative Analysis of China's Structural Transformation." *Proceedings*. Federal Reserve Bank of San Francisco. June.

Denning, L. 2011. "US and China Play the Blame Game." *The Wall Street Journal Asia*. 12 April, p. 30.

Devadason, E. S. 2011. "Reorganization of Intra-ASEAN-5 Trade Flows: The China Factor." *Asian Economic Journal*. Vol. 25, No. 2, pp. 129–49.

Dietz, M. C., G. Orr and J. Xing. 2008. "How Chinese Companies Can Succeed Abroad?" *McKinsey Quarterly*. Available online at www.mckinseyquarterly.com/article_print.aspx?L2=21&L3=33&ar=2131.

Dobbs, R. and S. Sankhe. 2010. "Comparing Urbanization in China and India." *McKinsey Quarterly*. July.

Drucker, P. 1977. "The Rise of Production Sharing." *The Wall Street Journal*. 15 March. p. 8.

Du, L., A. Harrison and G. H. Jefferson. 2012. "Testing for Horizontal and Vertical Foreign Investment Spillovers in China, 1998–2007." *Journal of Asian Economics.* Vol. 23, No. 3. pp. 234–43, June 2012.

Dunaway, S. and E. S. Prasad. 2006. "Rebalancing Economic Growth in China: A Commentary." *International Herald Tribune.* 11 January, p. 16.

Dunning, J. H. and S. M. Lundan. 2008. *Multinational Enterprises and the Global Economy.* 2nd edition. Cheltenham: Edward Elgar.

Dye, R. and E. Stephenson. 2010. "Five Forces Reshaping the Global Economy." *McKinsey Quarterly.* Available online at www.mckinseyquarterly.com/Five_forces_reshaping_the_global_economy_McKinsey_Global_Survey_results_2581 [accessed December 2012].

East Asia Vision Group (EAVG). 2001. "Towards An East Asian Community." Jakarta, Indonesia: The ASEAN Secretariat. Available online at www.mofa.go.jp/region/asia-paci/report2001.pdf [accessed December 2012].

The Economist. 2013. "The Alibaba Phenomenon." 23 March, p. 13.

——2012. "Manufacturing: The End of Cheap China." 10 March, p. 45.

——2011. "How to Get a Date." 31 December, p. 57.

——2011. "How to Get a Date." 31 December, p. 57.

——2011. "Rising Power, Anxious State." Special Report. 25 June.

——2011. "Capitalism Confined." 3 September, pp. 62–4.

——2011. "Bamboo Capitalism." 12 March, p. 11.

——2010. "The World's Biggest Economy: Dating Game." 16 December, p. 40.

——2010. "Jim O'Neill Looks at the Global Economy of 2036." 22 November, p. 64.

——2010. "The Next China." 31 July, pp. 46–48.

The Economist Corporate Network (ECN). 2013. *Investing in an Accelerating Asia?* London. February.

The Economic Intelligence Unit (EIU). 2013. "Top of the Heap." London. 3 April.

——2012. "Supersized Cities: China's 13 Megalopolis." London.

——2012. "Asia Competition Barometer." London. January.

——2012. "China in Focus: Spreading the Wealth." London. February.

——2012. "Retail 2022." London. November.

——2011. *Rising Consumption, Rising Influence: How Asian Consumers will Reshape the Global Electronics Industry.* London.

——2011. "Heavy Duty: China's Next Wave of Exports." London. October.

——2011. "Multinational Companies and China: What Future?" London. December.

——2010. *Access China.* London.

——2004. "Coming of Age: Multinational Companies in China." London. June.

Easterly, W. and R. Levine. 2001. "It's Not Factor Accumulation: Stylized Facts and Growth Models." *World Bank Economic Review.* Vol. 15, No. 2, pp. 177–219.

Egger, P. and M. Pfaffermayer. 2001. "A Note on Labor Productivity and Foreign Inward Direct Investment." *Applied Economic Letters.* No. 8, pp. 229–32.

Eichengreen, B., Y. C. Park and C. Wyplosz. 2008. "Introduction", in B. Eichengreen, Y. C. Park and C. Wyplosz (eds). *China, Asia and the New World Economy.* Oxford: Oxford University Press, pp. xv–xxii.

Eichengreen, B. S., Y. Rhee and H. Tong. 2007. "China and the Export of Other Asian Countries." *Review of World Economics.* Vol. 143, No. 2, pp. 201–26.

Eichengreen, B. S. and H. Tong. 2007. "Is China's FDI Coming at the Expense of Other Countries?" *Journal of Japanese and International Economics.* Vol. 21, No. 1, pp. 153–72.

Ernst, D. 2011. "China's Innovation Policy Is a Wake-up Call for America." *Asia Pacific Issues,* No. 100. Honolulu, HI: East-West Center. May.

Ernst, D. and B. Naughton. 2008. "China's Emerging Industrial Economy", in C. McNally (ed.). *China's Emergent Industrial Economy: Capitalism in the Dragon's Lair.* London and New York: Routledge, pp. 39–59.

Ernst, D. 2008. "Innovation Offshoring and Asia's Electronics Industry." *International Journal of Technological Learning, Innovation and Development.* Vol. 1, No. 4, pp. 551–76.

Ernst, D. 2006. "Searching for a New Role in East Asian Regionalization", in P. J. Katzenstein and T. Shiraishi (eds). *Remaking East Asia: Beyond Americanization and Japanization.* Ithaca NY: Cornell University Press, pp. 161–87.

Estevadeordal, A. and A. M. Taylor. 2008. "Is the Washington Consensus Dead? Growth, Openness and the Great Liberalization." Cambridge, MA: National Bureau of Economic Research. Working Paper No. 14264. August.

Estrada, G., D. Park, I. Park and S. Park. 2012. "The PRC's Free Trade Agreements with ASEAN, Japan and the Republic of Korea." Manila, Philippines: Asian Development Bank. Working Paper No. 92. January.

Fardoust, S., J. Y. Lin and X. Luo. 2012. "Demystifying China's Fiscal Stimulus." Washington, DC: World Bank. Policy Research Working Paper No. 6221. October.

Farrell, D., U. A. Gersch and E. Stephenson. 2006. "The Value of China's Emerging Middle Class." *McKinsey Quarterly*. Available online at www.mckinseyquarterly.com/The_value_of_Chinas_emerging_middle_class_1798 [accessed December 2012].

Farrell, D., S. Lund and F. Morin. 2006. "How Financial System Reform Could Benefit China." *The McKinsey Quarterly*, pp. 92–105.

Fayol-Song, L. 2011. "Reasons behind Management Localization in MNCs in China." *Asia Pacific Business Review*. Vol. 17, No. 4, pp. 455–71.

Feenstra, R. C. 2010. *Offshoring in the Global Economy*. Cambridge, MA: MIT Press.

——998. "Integration of Trade and Disintegration of Production." *Journal of Economic Perspective*. Vol. 12, No. 1, pp. 31–50.

Feenstra, R. C. and S. J. Wei. 2010. "Introduction", in R. C. Feenstra and S. J. Wei (eds). *China's Growing Role in World Trade*. Chicago, IL : University of Chicago Press, pp. 1–31.

Feenstra, R. C. and G. H. Henson. 1996. "Globalization, Outsourcing and Wage Inequality." *American Economic Review*. Vol. 86, No. 2, pp. 240–45.

Feng, W. 2011. "The End of Growth with Equity?" *Asia Pacific Issues, No.* 101. Honolulu, HI: East-West Center. June.

Fergusson, I. F. and B. Vaughn. 2011. "The Trans-Pacific Partnership Agreement." Washington, DC: Congressional Research Service. 12 December.

Ferrarini, B. 2011. "Mapping Vertical Trade." Manila, Philippines: Asian Development Bank. Working Paper No. 263. June.

Financial Times. 2011a. "Renminbi Rolls Out." 16 January, p. 1.

——2011b. "Record Leap in China's Forex Reserves Reflects Global Imbalances." 11 January, p. 4.

Findley, R. 1978. "Relative Backwardness, Direct Foreign investment and Transfer of Technology." *Quarterly Journal of Economics*. Vol. 92, No. 1, pp. 1–16.

Findlay, R. and K. H. O'Rourke. 2007. *Power and Plenty: Trade, War and the World Economy in the Second Millennium*. Princeton, NJ: Princeton University Press.

Frangos, A. 2011. "China Boosts Export Edge." *The Wall Street Journal Asia*. 11 July, p. 1.

Freund, C. and E. Ornelas. 2010. "Regional Trade Agreements." Washington, DC: World Bank. World Bank Policy Research Working Paper No. 5314.

Friedman, V. 2011. "Britain's Global Brander." London. *Financial Times*. 23 April/ss24. p. 7.

Fudan University. 2005. *Going Global: Strategy and Change*. School of Management, Shanghai, China.

Fukao, K., H. Ishido and K. Ito. 2003. "Vertical Intra-Industry Trade and Foreign Direct Investment in East Asia." *Journal of Japanese and International Economies*. Vol. 17, No. 4, pp. 468–506.

Fukunaga, Y. and I. Isono. 2013. "Taking ASEAN+1 FTAs Towards the RCEP." Jakarta, Indonesia. Economic Research Institute for ASEAN, Discussion Paper No. 2013–02. January.

Gallup. 2011. *World Affairs*. February. Available online at www.gallup.com/poll/146099/China-Surges-Americans-Views-Top-World-Economy.aspx?version=print [accessed December 2012].

Garcia-Herrero, A. and D. Santabarbara. 2013. "An Assessment of China's Banking System Reform", in S. Kaji and E. Ogawa (eds). *Who Will Provide the Next Financial Model?* New York: Springer, pp. 147–75.

Garcia-Herrero, A., P. Wooldridge and D. Y. Yang. 2009. "Why Don't Asians Invest in Asia? The Determinants of Cross-Border Portfolio Holdings." *Asian Economic Papers*. Vol. 8, No. 3, pp. 228–46.

Gang, X. 2011. "Boosting the Private Sector." *The China Daily*, 12 February, p. 5.

Gao, T. 2005. "Foreign Direct Investment from Developing Asia." *Economic Letters*. Vol. 86, No. 1, pp. 29–35.

Garnaut, R. and L. Song. 2006. *The Turning Point in China's Economic Development*. Canberra: Asia Pacific Press.

Gaulier, G., F. Lemoine and D. Unal-Kesencu. 2009. "China's Integration in East Asia: Production Sha ing." Paris: Centre d'Etudes Prospectives et d'Informations Internationales. Working Paper No. 2005–9. June.

——2007. "China's Emergence and Reorganization of Trade Flows in Asia." *China Economic Review*. Vol. 18, No. 2, pp. 209–43.

Ghemawat, P. and T. M. Hout. 2008. "Tomorrow's Global Giants: Not the Usual Suspects." *Harvard Business Review.* Vol. 86, No. 11. November, pp. 80–8.

Gill, I. and H. J. Kharas. 2009. "Gravity and Friction in Growing East Asia." *Oxford Review of Economic Policy.* Vol. 25, No. 2, pp. 190–204.

——2007. *An East Asian Renaissance.* Washington, DC: World Bank.

Gilman, D. B. 2010. "The New Geography of Global Innovation." New York: Global Markets Institute. 20 September.

Global Competitiveness Report 2011–2012 (GCR). 2012. Geneva, Switzerland: World Economic Forum.

Global Competitiveness Report 2010–2011 (GCR). 2011. Geneva, Switzerland: World Economic Forum.

Global Wind Energy Council (GWEC). *Global Wind Energy Outlook 2010.* Brussels. October

Golley, J. and L. Song. 2011. "China's Rise in a Changing World", in J. Golley and L. Song (eds). *Rising China: Global Challenges and Opportunities.* Canberra: The ANU Press, pp. 1–8.

Goodstadt, L. F. 2012. "China's Financial Reforms: Why Dysfunctional Banking Survives." Hong Kong: Hong Kong Institute of Monetary Research. Working Paper No. 02/2012.

Greenaway, D., A. Mahabir and C. Milner. 2008. "Has China Displaced Other Asian Countries' Exports?" *China Economic Review.* Vol. 19, No. 1, pp. 152–69.

Greenspan, A. 2000. "Global Challenges." Paper presented at the conference on *Financial Crises* by the Council on Foreign Relations, New York, 12 July. Available online at www.federalreserve.gov/boarddocs/speeches/2000/20000712.htm [accessed December 2012].

Grimes, W. W. 2011. "The Asian Monetary Fund Reborn?" *Asia Policy.* Vol. 11, No. 1, pp. 79–104.

Grossman, G. M. and E. Rossi-Hansberg. 2008. "Trading Tasks: A Simple Theory of Offshoring." *American Economic Review.* Vol. 95, No. 5, pp. 1978–97.

Haddad, M. 2007. *Trade Integration in East Asia: The Role of China and Production Networks.* Policy Research Working Paper No. 4160. March. Washington, DC: World Bank.

Haggard, S. 2011. "The Organizational Architecture of Asia-pacific: Insights from the New Institutions." Manila, Philippines. Asian Development Bank. Working Paper No. 71. January.

Hale, G. and C. Long. 2011. "What are the Sources of Financing for Chinese Firms?" in Y. W. Cheung (ed.). *The Evolving Role of Asia in Global Finance.* Bingley: Emerald Group Ltd, pp. 313–39.

Hale, G., C. Long and H. Miura. 2010. *Where to Find Productivity Spillovers from FDI in China?* Working Paper No. 14/2010. Hong Kong: Hong Kong Institute for Monetary Research. June.

Hale, T. 2011. "The De Facto Preferential Trade Agreement in East Asia." *Review of International Political Economy.* Vol. 18, No. 3, pp. 299–327.

Haltmaier, J., S. Ahmad, B. Coulibaly, R. Knippenberg, S. Leduc, M. Marazzi and A. Wilson. 2007. "The Role of China in Asia: Engine, Conduit or Steamroller?" *International Finance.* Washington, DC: Board of Governors of the Federal Reserve System. Discussion Paper No. 904. September.

Hanson, G. H., R. J. Mataloni and M. J. Slaughter. 2001. "Expansion Strategies of US Multinational Firms", in S. M. Collins and D. Rodrik (eds). *Brookings Trade Forum.* Washington, DC: Brookings Institution Press, pp. 120–48.

Harris, R. G. and P. E. Robertson. 2009. "Trade, Wage and Skill Accumulation in the Emerging Giants." Adelaide: University of Western Australia. Discussion Paper No. 09–19.

Hattari, R. and R. S. Rajan. 2009. "Understanding Bilateral FDI Flows in Developing Asia." *Asia Pacific Economic Literature.* Vol. 23, No. 2, pp. 73–93.

Hayakawa, K. and T. Matsuura. 2011. "Complex vertical FDI and firm heterogeneity: Evidence from East Asia." Journal of the Japanese and International Economies. Vol. 25, No. 3, pp. 273–89.

——2009. "Complex Vertical FDI and Firm Heterogeneity: Evidence from East Asia." Tokyo: Institute of Developing Economies, Japan External Trade Organization (JETRO). IDE Discussion Papers No. 211.

Henderson, J. 2008. "China and Global Development: Towards a Global-Asian Era?" *Contemporary Politics.* Vol. 14, No. 4, pp. 375–92.

Henry, P. B. 2007. "Capital Account Liberalization: Theory, Evidence and Speculation." *Journal of Economic Literature.* Vol. 45, No. 4, pp. 887–935.

Herd, R., C. Pigott and S. Hill. 2010. "China's Financial Sector Reforms." Paris: Organization for Economic Co-operation and Development. Working Paper No. 747. 1 February.

Heytens, P. and H. Zebregs. 2003. "How Fast Can China Grow?" in W. Tseng and M. Rodlauer (eds). *China Competing in the World Economy.* Washington, DC: International Monetary Fund, pp. 8–29.

——2010. "Production Networks in Asia: A Case Study of Hard Disk Drive Industry." Paper presented at the *Comparative Analysis of Production Networks in Asia, and Europe.* Organized by the Vienna Institute for International Economic Studies, Vienna, 15–16 July.

Hiratsuka, D. and Y. Uchida. 2010. *Input Trade and Production Networks in East Asia.* Cheltenham and Northampton, MA: Edward Elgar.

Hiratsuka, D., H. Sato and I. Isono. 2009. "Impacts of Free Trade Agreements on Business Activity in Asia." Tokyo, Japan: ADB Institute. Working Paper No. 143.

Hong, E. and L. Sun. 2006. "Dynamics of Internationalization and Outward Investment." *The China Quarterly.* No. 187, pp. 610–34.

Horn, J., V. Singer and J. Woetzel. 2010. "A True Picture of China's Export Machine." *McKinsey Quarterly.* September. Available online at www.portugalglobal.pt/PT/PortugalNews/EdicaoAicepPortugalGlobal/Documents/China041010.pdf [accessed December 2012]

Hout, T. M. and P. Ghemawat. 2010. "China Vs the World: Whose Technology Is It?" *Harvard Business Review.* Vol. 88, No. 12, pp. 95–103.

Hsieh, C. T. and P. J. Klenow. 2009. "Misallocation and Manufacturing TFP in China and India." *Quarterly Journal of Economics.* Vol. 124, No. 4, pp. 1403–48.

Hu, A. 2011. *China in 2020: A New Type of Superpower.* Washington, DC: Brookings Institution Press.

Hu, R. W. 2009. "Building Asia Pacific Regional Architecture." Washington, DC: Brookings Institutions. July.

Hu, W. 1996. "China and Asian Regionalism: Challenge and Policy Choice." *Journal of Contemporary China.* Vol. 5, No. 11, pp. 43–56.

Hu, Z. and M. S. Khan. 1997. "Why is China Growing so fast?" Washington, DC: International Monetary Fund. Economic Issues Paper No. 8. April.

Huang, Y. 2012. "Time for China to Give Up Financial Repression." *Financial Times.* 2 May, p. 9.

——2012. "In the Middle Kingdom's Shadow." *The Wall Street Journal.* March 27. p. 13.

——2012. "China's Economic Rise: Opportunities or Threat for East Asia?" *East Asia Forum.* 20 May. Available online at www.eastasiaforum.org/2012/05/20/chinas-economic-rise-opportunity-or-threat-for-east-asia.

Huang, Y. and B. Wang. 2011. "From the Asian Miracle to an Asian Century?" Paper presented at the Reserve Bank of Australia annual conference in Sydney. 15–16 August.

Huang, Y. and X. Wang 2011. "Does Financial Repression Inhibit or Facilitate Economic Growth? A Case Study of Chinese Reform Experience." *Oxford Bulletin of Economics and Statistics*, Vol. 73, No. 4, pp. 833–55.

Hummels, D., J. Ishii and K. M. Yi. 2001. "The Nature and Growth of Vertical Specialization in World Trade." *Journal of International Economics.* Vol. 54, No. 1, pp. 75–96.

Ianchovichina, E. and T. Walmsley. 2005. "Impact of China's WTO Accession on East Asia." *Contemporary Economic Policy.* Vol. 23, No. 2, pp. 261–77.

Ikenson, D. J. 2006. "China: Mega-Threat or Quiet Dragon." Paper presented at the American Institute of International Steel conference in Chicago, IL: 6 March, Available online at www.cato.org/pub_display.php?pub_id=10912 [accessed December 2012].

International Monetary Fund (IMF). 2013. *World Economic Outlook.* Washington, DC: April.

——2012. *World Economic Outlook Update.* Washington, DC. 24 January.

——2012. *World Economic Outlook Update.* Washington, DC. 16 July.

——2012. *World Economic Outlook.* Washington, DC. April.

——2012. *World Economic Outlook.* Washington, DC. October.

——2012. *Financial Sector Assessment: People's Republic of China.* Washington, DC. March.

——2011. *World Economic Outlook.* Washington, DC. April.

——2011. *Changing Pattern of Global Trade.* Washington, DC. 15 June.

——2011. *World Economic Outlook.* Washington, DC. April.

——2011. *Regional Economic Outlook: Asia and Pacific.* Washington, DC: April.

——2011. *World Economic Outlook.* Washington, DC. September.

——2010. *Regional Economic Outlook: Asia Pacific.* Washington, DC. April.

——2005. *World Economic Outlook.* Washington, DC. April.

Itakura, K. 2013. "Impact of Liberalization and Improved Connectivity in ASEAN." Jakarta, Indonesia. Economic Research Institute for ASEAN, Discussion Paper No. 2013–01. January.

Ito, T. 2012. "The Internationalization of the RMB." CGS/IIGG Working Paper. The Council on Foreign Relations. November.

Ito, T., A. Kojima, C. McKenzie and S. Urata. 2011. "ASEAN Economy: Diversity, Disparities and Dynamics." *Asian Economic Policy Review.* Vol. 6, No. 1, pp. 1–21.

——2011. "Developments in Asian Finance." *Asian Economic Policy Review.* Vol. 6, No. 1, pp. 157–75.

Jang, H. B. 2011. "Financial Integration and Cooperation in East Asia." Tokyo: Institute for Monetary and Economic Studies. Bank of Japan. Discussion Paper No. 2011-E5. February.

Japan External Trade Organization (JETRO). 2011. *JETRO Global Trade and Investment Report*. Tokyo, Japan.

——2009. "Survey of Japanese Affiliated Firms in Asia and Oceania." Tokyo, Japan.

——2007. "2006 Survey of Japanese Firms." Tokyo, Japan.

Jefferson, G. H. 2008. "How Has China's Economic Emergence Contributed to the Field of Economics?" *Comparative Economic Studies*. Vol. 50, No. 1, pp. 167–209.

Jensen, B. 2012. *Catching Up: Learning from the Best School Systems in East Asia*. Carlton Grattan Institute.

Johnson, R. C. and G. Noguera. 2012. "Proximity and Production Fragmentation." *American Economic Review*. Vol. 102, No. 3, pp. 407–11.

Jones, R., H. Kierzkowski and L. Chen. 2005. "What Does Evidence Tell Us about Fragmentation and Outsourcing?" *International Review of Economics and Finance*. Vol. 14, No. 3, pp. 305–16.

Kassel, J. 2012. "Asia's Lust for Labels Tempts Brands to Tap the Markets." *Financial Times*. 31 May, p. 5.

——2010. "Asian FTAs: Trends, Prospects and Challenges." Manila, Philippines. Asian Development Bank. Working Paper Series No. 226. October.

——2009. "The Asian 'Noodle Bowl': Is it Serious for Business?" Tokyo, Japan. ADB Institute. Working Paper No. 136.

——2008. "Regionalism as an Engine of Multilateralism: A Case for a Single East Asian FTA." Manila, Philippines: Asian Development Bank. Working Paper Series No. 14. February.

——2007. "ASEAN+3 or ASEAN+6: Which Way Forward?" Tokyo: Asian Development Bank Institute. Discussion Paper No. 77.

Kharas, H. J. 2010. "The Emerging Middle Class in Developing Countries." Paris: Organization for Economic Co-operation and Development. The Development Center. Working Paper No. 285. January.

Kim, K. H. 2013. "Potential of ASEAN Economy Revisited." *SERI World*. Samsung Economic Research Institute. 18 February, pp. 9–13.

Kim, S. and J. W. Lee. 2012. "Real and Financial Integration in East Asia." *Review of International Economics*. Vol. 20, No. 2, pp. 332–49.

Kim, S., J. W. Lee and C. Y. Park. 2011. "Emerging Asia: Decoupling or Recoupling." *The World Economy*. Vol. 34, No. 1, pp. 23–53.

——2010. "The Ties that Bind Asia, Europe and the United States." Manila, Philippines: Asian Development Bank. Working Paper No. 192. October.

Kim, S., I. Park and S. Park. 2013. "A Free Trade Area of the Asia Pacific: Is it Desirable?" *Journal of East Asian Economic Integration*. Vol. 17, No. 1, pp. 3–25.

Kimura, F. 2006. "International Production and Distribution Networks in East Asia: Eight Facts." *Asian Economic Policy Review*. Vol. 1, No. 2, pp. 326–44.

Kimura, F. and M. Ando. 2005. "Two-Dimensional Fragmentation in East Asia: Conceptual Framework and Empirics." *International Review of Economics and Finance*. Vol. 14, No. 2, pp. 317–44.

Kimura, F. and A. Obashi. 2011. "Production Networks in east Asia: What We Know So Far." Tokyo: Asian Development Bank Institute. Discussion Paper No. 320.

King, M. 2012. "Major Growth Forecast for ASEAN-China Trade." *The Journal of Commerce Online*. Available online at www.joc.com/global-trade/major-growth-forecast-asean-china-trade. Posted on 24 April.

Kittilaksanawong, W. 2011. "FDI in High-Tech Firms from Newly-Industrialized Economies in Emerging Markets." *African Journal of Business Management*. Vol. 5, No. 4, pp. 1146–57.

Kohli, H. S., A. Sharma and A. Sood. 2011. *Asia 2050: Realizing the Asian Century*. New Delhi: Sage Publications India.

Kong, Y. F. and R. Kneller. 2012. "China's Export Expansion: A Threat to Its Asian Neighbors?" Paper presented at the conference on *Trade, Investment and Production Networks in Asia* at the University of Nottingham, Kuala Lumpur campus, Malaysia. 15–16 February.

Koopman, R. and Z. Wang. 2008. "How Much Chinese Exports Is Really Made in China? Assessing Domestic Value-Added." Cambridge, MA: National Bureau of Economic Research. Working Paper No. 14109.

Kopytoff, V. G. 2011. "China Overtakes US in PC Shipment." *The New York Times*. 23 August, p. 9.

Korea International Trade Association (KITA). 2010. "Korea Is the Biggest Beneficiary of Northeast Asian FTA." Seoul, Korea. 20 December. Available online at global.kita.net/news/01/read.jsp?seq=3605 [accessed December 2012].

Koresnikov-Jessop, S. 2010. "Swiss Makers Reward the Chinese Market." *The New York Times*. 17 March, p. 16.

KPMG. 2011. "China's 12th Five Year Plan: Sustainability." April. Beijing, China.

——2011. "Product Sourcing in Asia Pacific." Beijing, China. 4 October. Available online at www.kpmg. com/Global/en/IssuesAndInsights/ArticlesPublications/Documents/product-sourcing-asia-pacific.pdf [accessed December 2012]

——2010. "Refined Strategies: Luxury Extends its Reach across China." Beijing, China. 13 August. Available online at www.kpmg.com/Ca/en/IssuesAndInsights/ArticlesPublications/Documents/Refined%20 Strategies%20-%20Luxury%20extends%20its%20reach%20across%20China.pdf [accessed December 2012].

Kramer, C. 2006. "Asia's Investment Puzzle." *Finance and Development.* Vol. 43, No. 2, pp. 38–46.

Krugman, P. 1998. "What's New about the New Economic Geography?" *Oxford Review of Economic Policy.* Vol. 14, No. 2, pp. 7–17.

——1995. "Growing World Trade: Causes and Consequences." *Brookings Paper on Economic Activity.* 25th Anniversary Issue, pp. 327–77.

——1994. "The Myth of Asia's Miracle?" *Foreign Affairs.* Vol. 73, No. 1, pp. 62–78.

Krumm, K. and H. J. Kharas. 2004. *East Asia Integrates: Trade Policy Agenda for Shared Growth.* Washington, DC: World Bank.

Kuijs, L. 2006. "How Will China's Saving-Investment Balance Evolve?" Washington, DC: World Bank Policy Research Working Paper No. 3958. 1 July.

Kuijs, L. and T. Wang. 2006. "China's Pattern of Growth: Moving to Sustainability and Reducing Inequality." *China and World Economy.* Vol. 14, No. 1, pp. 1–14.

Kuznets, S. 1979. "Growth and Structural Shifts", in W. Galenson (ed.). *Economic Growth and Structural Change in Taiwan.* London: Cornell University Press, pp. 115–31.

Kwan, C. H. 2009. "Growth in Chinese Economy Moving from East to West." Tokyo: Research Institute of Economy, Trade and Industry. Available online at www.rieti.go.jp/en/china/09060501.html?style sheet=print#figure1 [accessed December 2012].

Kwon, H. J. 2012. *SERI Economic Report.* Samsung Economic Research Institute. Seoul. 30 July. Available online at www.seriworld.org/01/wldContV.html?mn=A&mncd=0301&key=20120730000004 [accessed December 2012].

Kwong, C. C. L. 2011. "China's Banking Reform: The Remaining Agenda." *Global Economic Review.* Vol. 40, No. 2, pp. 161–78.

Lagarde, C. 2013. "Fulfilling the Asian Dream." Speech at the Boao Forum, Hainan, China. 7 April.

——2012. "New Perspectives on Asia's Role in the Global Economy." Speech at the Bank of Thailand Policy Forum, Bangkok, Thailand. 12 July.

Lall, S. and M. Albaladejo. 2004. "China's Competitive Performance: A Threat to East Asian Manufacturing Exports?" *World Development.* Vol. 39, No. 9, pp. 1441–66.

Lall, S. and H. G. Wang. 2011. "Balancing Urban Transformation and Spatial Inclusion." *China Urbanization Review.* Washington, DC: World Bank.

Lardy, N. R. 2012. *Sustaining China's Economic Growth after the Global Financial Crisis.* Washington, DC: Peterson Institute Press.

Lau, B. K. F. 2007. "The Post-ATC Scenario for Asian Exporters." Paper presented at the 85th Textile Institute World Conference held in Colombo, Sri Lanka. 1–3 March.

Lau, L. J. and J. Park. 2003. "The Sources of East Asian Economic Growth Revisited." Paper presented at Tsinghua University, Beijing. 26 March.

Lau, L., Y. Qian and G. Roland. 2000. "Reform without Losers: An Interpretation of China's Dual-Track Approach." *Journal of Political Economy.* Vol. 108, No. 1, pp. 120–43.

Lawrence, R. Z. 1996. *Regionalism, Multilateralism, and Deeper Integration.* Washington, DC: Brookings Institution.

——2008. "China and the Multilateral Trading System", in B. S. Eichengreen (ed.). *China, Asia and the New Global Economy.* Oxford: Oxford University Press, pp. 145–67.

Lawrence, R. Z., M. Drzeniek and S. Doherty. 2012. *The Global Enabling Trade Report 2012.* Geneva, Switzerland. World Economic Forum.

Lazaro, D. C. and E. M. Medulla. 2006. "Rules of Origin: Evolving Best Practives for RTAs." Manila, Philippines. The Philippines Institute for Development Studies. Discussion Paper No. 2006–01.

Lee, C. J. 2011. "Prospects for a China-Japan-Korea FTA", in *Financing for Regional Economic Development.* Published by The Korea Institute for International Economic Policy, Seoul, Korea, pp. 38–65.

Lee, E. Y. 2013. "It May be Time to Lower the FDI Sluice Gate." *China Daily on Line.* Available online at europe.chinadaily.com.cn/epaper/2013–01/11/content_16104826.htm [accessed December 2012].

Lee, G. 2007. "Long Run Equilibrium Relationship between Inward FDI and Productivity." *Journal of Economic Development.* Vol. 32, No. 1, pp. 183–92.

Lee, J. H. 2008. "Patterns and Determinants of Cross-border Financial Asset Holdings in East Asia." Manila, Philippines: Asian Development Bank. Working Paper, No. 13. February.

Lee, J. H. and I. Park. 2005. "Free Trade Areas in East Asia: Discriminatory or Nondiscriminatory?" *The World Economy.* Vol. 28, No. 1, pp. 21–48.

Lee, H. and M. G. Plummer. 2011. "Assessing the Impact of the ASEAN Economic Community." Osaka, Japan: Osaka School of International Public Policy. Discussion Paper No. 2011-E-002. 23 March.

Lee, H. H., D. Park and J. Wang. 2011. "The Role of People's Republic of China in International Fragmentation and Production Network." Manila, Philippines: Asian Development Bank. Working Paper No. 87. September.

Lee, J. W. and K. Shin. 2006. "Does Regionalism Lead to More Global Trade Integration in East Asia?" *The North American Journal of Economic and Finance.* Vol. 17, No. 2, pp. 283–301.

Lemoine, F. and D. Unal-Kesenci. 2004. "Assembly Trade and Technology Transfer: The Case of China." *World Development.* Vol. 32, No. 5, pp. 82–850.

Lewis, W. A. 1954. "Economic Development with Unlimited Supplies of Labor." *Manchester School of Economic and Social Studies.* Vol. 22, pp. 139–91.

Li, C. 2011. "China in Transition." Washington, DC: Brookings Institutions. Available online at www.brookings.edu/interviews/2011/0919_china_li.aspx [accessed December 2012].

Li, P. P. 2007. "Towards an Integrated Theory of Multinational Evolution: The Evidence of Chinese Multinationals." *Journal of International Management.* Vol. 13, No. 3, pp. 296–318.

Li, C. and J. Gibson. 2012. "Rising Regional Income Inequality in China: Fact or Artifact?" Hamilton: University of Waikato. Department of Economics. Working Paper No. 09/12. July.

Li, G. and J. Woetzel. 2011. "What China's Five Year Plan Means for Business." *McKinsey Quarterly.* July. Available online at www.mckinseyquarterly.com/What_Chinas_five-yearplan_means_for_business_2832 [accessed December 2012].

——2009. "China and Regional Integration in East Asia." Aalborg: Aalborg University. Center for Comparative Integration Studies. Working Paper No. 9.

Li, H., L. Li, B. Wu and Y. Xiong. 2012. "The End of Cheap Chinese Labor." *Journal of Economic Perspective.* Vol. 26, No. 4, pp.57–74.

Li, W. and L. Putterman. 2008. "Reforming China's SOEs: An Overview." *Comparative Economic Studies.* Vol. 50, No. 2, pp. 353–80.

Liang, H. 2005. "China's Ascent: Can the Middle Kingdom Meet its Dreams?" *Global Economic Papers,* No. 133. New York: Goldman Sachs.

Lin, J. Y. 2011. "China and the Global Economy." *China Economic Journal.* Vol. 4, No. 1, pp. 1–14.

——2011. "New Structural Economics: A Framework for Rethinking Development." *The World Bank Research Observer.* Vol. 26, No. 2, pp. 193–221.

——2010. *New Structural Economics: A Framework for Rethinking Development.* Washington, DC: World Bank. Policy Research Working Paper No. 5197. December.

——2010. "The China Miracle Demystified." Paper presented at the Econometric Society World Congress in Shanghai. 19 August.

Lin, C. H., C. M. Lee and C. H. Yang. 2011. "Does Foreign Direct Investment Really Enhance China's Regional Productivity?" *The Journal of International Trade & Economic Development.* Vol. 20, No. 6, pp. 741–68.

Lin, J. Y. and Y. Wang. 2012. "China's Integration with the World: Development as a Process of Learning and Industrial Upgrading." *China Economic Policy Review.* Vol. 1, No. 1, pp. 1–33.

Lipsey, R. E. and F. Sjoholm. 2011. "South-South FDI and Development in East Asia." *Asian Development Review.* Vol. 28, No. 2, pp. 11–31.

Lipsky, J. 2011. "Remarks by John Lipsky at the Conclusion of Article IV Mission to China." Beijing. 9 June. Available online at www.imf.org/external/np/speeches/2011/062011.htm [accessed December 2012].

Liu, X. and P. Cheng. 2011. "Is China's Indigenous Innovation Strategy Compatible with Globalization?" Honolulu, HI: East-West Center. Policy Study No. 61.

Liu, Q. and A. Siu. 2010. "Institutions, Financial Development and Corporate Investment: Evidence from an Implied Return on Capital in China." Hong Kong: Hong Kong Institute of Economic and Business Strategy. University of Hong Kong. Paper No. 1162. July.

Long, C. and X. Zhang. 2010. "Patterns of China's Industrialization: Concentration, Specialization and Clustering" (unpublished manuscript).

Lu, F. and Y. Li. 2009. "China's Factor in Recent Global Commodity Price and Shipping Freight Volatility." Beijing: Peking University. China Center for Economic Research. Working papr No. E2009007. 15 December.

Lucas, L. 2011. "China Consumer Goods: Left on the Shelf." *Financial Times*. London. 4 April, p. 13.

Lucas, R. E. 1993. "Making a Miracle." *Econometrica*. Vol. 61, No. 2, pp. 251–72.

Lundin, N. and S. S. Serger. 2007. "Globalization of R&D and China: Empirical Observations." Stockholm: Research Institute of International Economics. IFN Working Paper No. 710.

Ma, G. and Z. Haiwen. 2009. "China's Evolving External Wealth and Rising Creditor Position." Basel: Bank for International Development. BIS Working Paper 286. July.

MacFarquhar, R. 2013. "Tackling Graft Must Come Before the Chinese Dream." *Financial Times*. London. 12 April, p. 7.

MacIntyre, A., T. J. Pempel and J. Ravenhill (eds). 2008. *Crisis as Catalyst: Asia's Dynamic Political Economy*. Ithaca, NY: Cornell University Press.

Maddison, A. 2006. "Asia in the World Economy 1500–2030." *Asian Pacific Economic Literature*. Vol. 20, No. 2, pp. 1–37.

——2001. *The World Economy: A Millennial Perspective*. Paris: Organization for Economic Co-operation and Development.

——1991. *Dynamic Forces in Capitalist Development: A Long-Run Comparative View*. New York: Oxford University Press.

Magnus, G. 2012. "Will Asia Shake or Shape the World Economy?" Brussels: European Center for International Political Economy. Policy Brief 05. July.

Mai, Y. 2004. "The Monash Multi-Country Model." CoPS Working Paper No. G-150. Melbourne: MONASH University. Center of Policy Studies.

Mai, Y., P. Adams, P. Dixon and J. Menon. 2010. "The Growth Locomotive of the People's Republic of China." *Asian Development Review*. Vol. 27, No. 2, pp. 82–121.

Makin, J. H. 2011. "Can China's Currency Go Global?" *Economic Outlook*. Washington, DC: American Enterprise Institute. February.

Mallon, G. and J. Whally. 2004. "China's Post WTO Stance." Cambridge, MA: National Bureau of Economic Research. Working Paper No. 10649. August.

Marsh, P. 2013. "China Looks to Drive the Car Industry." *Financial Times*. 2 January, p. 14.

——2011. "China Noses Ahead as Top Goods Producer." *Financial Times*. 13 March, p. 9.

——2010. "US Manufacturing Crown Slips." *Financial Times*. 20 June, p. 14.

Mathews, J. A. and D. S. Cho. 2000. *Tiger Technology: The Creation of a Semi-Conductor Industry in East Asia*. Cambridge: Cambridge University Press.

Mattoo, A. and A. Subramanian. 2011. "China and the World Trading System." Washington, DC: World Bank. Policy Research Working Paper No. 5897. December.

Mattoo, A., F. Ng and A. Subramanian. 2011. "The Elephant in the "Green Room": China and the Doha Round." Washington, DC: Peterson Institute for International Economics. Policy Brief, No. BP 11–13.

McGregor, J. 2012. "China's Drive for 'Indigenous Innovation'" Washington, DC: US Chamber of Commerce.

McKay, H. and L. Song. 2010. "China as a Global Manufacturing Powerhouse." *China and the World Economy*. Vol. 18, No. 1, pp. 1–32.

McKibbin, W. J., J. W. Lee and I. Cheong. 2004. "A Dynamic Analysis of a Korea-Japan Free Trade Area: Simulations with the G-Cubed Asia-Pacific Model." *International Economic Journal*. Vol. 18, No. 1, pp. 3–32.

McKibbin, W. J. and W. T. Woo. 2003. "The Consequences of China's WTO Accession on its Neighbors." *Asian Economic Papers*. Vol. 12, No. 2, pp. 1–38.

McKinsey Global Institute (MGI). 2012. *Manufacturing the Future*. San Francisco. November.

McKinsey & Co. 2011. "2011 Annual Chinese Consumer Study: The New Frontier of Growth." Shanghai, China. October.

——2011. *Understanding China's Growing Love for Luxury*. Shanghai, China. April.

McKinsey Global Institute (MGI). 2009. *If You've Got it, Spend it: Unleashing the Chinese Consumer*. San Francisco. August.

——2005. *Addressing China's Looming Talent Shortage*. San Francisco. October.

McMahon, D., L. Wei and A. Galbraith. 2012. "Wen Appeals to Shake up Bank System." *The Wall Street Journal Asia.* 4 April, p. 1.

Menon, J. 2012. "Narrowing the Development Divide in ASEAN." Manila, Philippines: Asian Development Bank. Working Paper No. 100. July.

——2009. "Dealing with the Proliferation of Bilateral Trade Agreements." *The World Economy.* Vol. 32, No. 10, pp. 1381–1407.

Menon, R. 2012. "Regional Safety Nets to Complement Global Safety Nets." Paper presented at the opening ceremony of the AMRO, Monetary Authority of Singapore, Singapore. 31 January.

Mercereau, B. 2005. *FDI Flows to Asia: Did the Dragon Crowd out the Tigers?* Working Paper No. WP/05/189. Washington, DC: International Monetary Fund.

Mercurio, B. 2011. "Bilateral and Regional Trade Agreements in Asia: A Skeptic's View", in R. Buckley, R. Hu and D. Arner (eds). *East Asian Economic Integration: Law, Trade and Finance.* Northampton, MA, and Cheltenham: Edward Elgar, pp. 120–44.

Ming, Z. and P. J. Williamson. 2007. *Dragon at Your Door.* Boston, MA: Harvard Business School Press.

Ministry of Commerce (MOC). 2010. *Statistical Bulletin of China's Outward Foreign Direct Investment 2009.* Beijing: Government of the People's Republic of China.

Moran, T. H. 2011. "Foreign Manufacturing Multinationals and the Transformation of the Chinese Economy." Washington, DC: Peterson Institute of International Economics. Working Paper No. WP.11–11. April.

Morrison, W. M. and M. Labonte. 2011. "China's Holdings of US Securities: Implications for the US Economy." Washington, DC: Congressional Research Service. CRS Report for the Congress. 26 September.

Murphy, K., A. Shleifer and R. Vishny. 1992. "The Transition to a Market Economy." *Quarterly Journal of Economics.* Vol. 107, No. 2, pp. 889–906.

Magnus, G. 2012. "Will Asia Shake or Shape the World Economy?" Brussels: European Center for International Political Economy. Policy Brief 05. July.

Ministry of Commerce (MOC). 2011. "Ministry of Commerce." The Government of the People's Republic of China. Available online at english.mofcom.gov.cn/statistic/statistic.html [accessed December 2012].

National Bureau of Statistics (NBS). 2012. "National Economy Maintained Steady and Fast Development in 2011." Beijing. 17 January. Available online at www.stats.gov.cn/english/newsandcomingevents/t20120117_402779577.htm [accessed December 2012].

Naughton, B. 2007. *The Chinese Economy: Transition and Growth.* Cambridge, MA: MIT Press.

Needham, J. 1954. *Science and Civilization in China.* Cambridge: Cambridge University Press.

Neumann, F. and T. Arora. 2011. "Chart of the Week: Can Asia Save the World?" Hong Kong: HSBC Global Research. 26 August.

——2011. "Chart of the Week: Can Asia Save the World?" Hong Kong: HSBC Global Research. 26 August.

Ng, F. and A. J. Yeats. 2001. "Production Sharing in East Asia: Who Does What for Whom?" in L. K. Cheng (ed.). *Global Production and Trade in East Asia.* Boston, MA: Kluwer Academic, pp. 63–109.

——1999. "Production Sharing in East Asia." Washington, DC: World Bank. Policy Research Working Paper No. 2197.

Nicita, A. and M. Olarreaga. 2006. *Trade, Production and Protection, 1976–2004.* Washington, DC: World Bank.

Nicolas, F. 2009. "The Changing Economic Relations between China and Korea." *Journal of Korean Economy.* Vol. 10, No. 3, pp. 341–65.

Noble, J. and S. Rabinovitch. 2013. "Fitch Downgrades China." *Financial Times.* 10 April, p. 1.

Obashi, A. 2010a. "Stability of Production Networks in East Asia: Duration and Survival of Trade." *Japan and world Economy.* Vol. 22, No. 1, pp. 21–30.

Obashi, A. 2010b. "Stability of International Production Networks: Is East Asia Special?" *International Journal of Business and Developmental Studies.* Vol. 2, No. 1, pp. 63–94.

Okamoto, J. 2011. "Flexible Process for Integration in East Asia." *East Asia Economic Forum.* Available online at www.eastasiaforum.org/2011/01/14/flexible-processes-for-integration-in-east-asia. January 14 [accessed December 2012].

——2011. "Institutional Building for Economic Integration in Asia", in M. Fujita, I. Kuroiwa and S. Kumagai (eds). *The Economics of East Asian Integration.* Tokyo: Institute of Developing Economies, pp. 287–319.

Orefice, G. and N. Rocha. 2011. "Deep Integration and Production Networks: An Empirical Analysis." Geneva, Switzerland. World Trade Organization. Staff Working Paper No. 2011-11. July.

Organisation for Economic Co-operation and Development (OECD). 2012 "PISA 2012 Mathematics Framework." Paris. Available online at www.oecd.org/dataoecd/8/38/46961598.pdf [accessed December 2012].

——2010. *OECD Information Technology Outlook*. Paris. December.

——2010. *China in the 2010s: Rebalancing Growth and Strengthening Social Safety Nets*. Paris. March.

——2010. *Economic Survey of China 2010*. Paris.

——2010. *China in the 2010s: Rebalancing Growth and Strengthening Social Safety Nets*. Paris. March.

——2009. *State-Owned Enterprises in China*. Paris. January 26.

Orlik, T. and B. Davis. 2012. "Beijing Diversifies Away from US Dollar." *The Wall Street Journal*. 2 March, p. A1.

Orr, G. 2011. "Unleashing Innovation in China." *McKinsey Quarterly*. January. Available online at www.mckinseyquarterly.com/Unleashing_innovation_in_China_2725 [accessed December 2012].

——2013. "What's in Store for China in 2013?" San Francisco, CA: McKinsey. January.

Ozawa, T. 2009. *The Rise of Asia*. Northampton, MA, and Cheltenham: Edward Elgar.

Overholt, W. H. 2010. "China in the Financial Crisis: Rising Influence, Rising Challenges." *The Washington Quarterly*. Vol. 33, No. 1, pp. 21–34.

——2005. "China and Globalization." Testimony presented to the US–China Economic and Security Review Commission, Washington, DC, 19 May.

Panitchpakdi, S. 2011. "East Asia in the World: Prospects and Challenges." Geneva and New York. United Nations Conference on Trade and Development. 24 February.

Park, C. S. 2011. "China's Innovation Capability Is Catching Korea's." *Weekly Insight*. Seoul: Samsung Economic Research Institute, pp. 9–13. 25 July.

——2011. "China's Innovation Capability Is Catching Korea's." *Weekly Insight*. Seoul. Samsung Economic Research Institute, pp. 9–13. 25 July.

Park, D. and K. Shin. 2011. "People's Republic of China as an Engine of Growth for Developing Asia?" *Asian Economic Papers*. Vol. 10, No. 2, pp. 120–43.

——2010. "Can Trade with the People's Republic of China be an Engine of Growth for Developing Asia?" *Asian Development Review*. Vol. 27, No. 1, pp. 160–81.

Park, D. and J. S. Park. 2010. *Drivers of Developing Asia's Growth*. Working Paper Series No. 235. Manila: Asian Development Bank. November.

Park, I. 2009. "Regional Trade Agreements in East Asia: Will They Be Sustainable?" *Asian Economic Journal*. Vol. 23, No. 2, pp. 169–94.

——2006. "East Asian Regional Trade Agreements: Do they Promote Global Free Trade." *Pacific Economic Review*. Vol. 11, No. 4, pp. 547–68.

Park, S. O. and W. R. Vanhonacker. 2007. "The Challenge for Multinational Corporations in China." *MIT Sloan Management Review*. Summer 2007. Vol. 48, No. 4, pp. W8–W15.

Park, Y. C. 2008. "East Asia's Adjustments to Global Imbalances and Sub-Prime Loan Crisis." Presentation at the distinguished speaker's seminar in Asian Development Bank Institute. 13 March.

Pearson, D. 2011. "Private-Jet Firms Look to China's Affluent." *The Wall Street Journal Asia*. 27 May, p. 10.

Pei, M. 2011. "China's Cultural Devotion." *The Wall Street Journal Asia*. 9 November, p. 15.

Pelc, K. J. 2009. "The Cost of Wiggle-Room: On the Use of Flexibility in International Trade Agreements." Georgetown University, Washington, DC. Doctoral Dissertation. 7 August.

Peng, X. 2008. "Demographic Shift, Population Aging and Economic Growth in China: A Computable General Equilibrium Analysis." *Pacific Economic Review*. Vol. 13, No. 5, pp. 680–97.

Perkins, D. 1997. "Completing China's Move to the Market." *Journal of Economic Perspectives*. Vol. 8, No. 1, pp. 23–46.

Perkins, D. H. and T. G. Rawski. 2008. "Forecasting China's Economic Growth to 2025", in L. Brandt and T. G. Rawski (eds). *China's Great Economic Transformation*. Cambridge: Cambridge University Press, pp. 829–86.

Petri, P. A. 2011. "The Determinants of Bilateral FDI: Is Asia Different?" *Journal of Asian Economics*. Vol. 23, No. 1, pp. 201–9.

——2006. "Is East Asia Becoming More Interdependent?" *Journal of Asian Economics*. Vol. 17, No. 3, pp. 381–94.

Petri, P. A., M. G. Plummer and F. Zhai. 2011. "The Trans-Pacific Partnership and Asia-Pacific Integration." Honolulu, HI: East-West Center. Working Paper No. 119. 24 October.

——2010. "The Economics of the ASEAN Economic Community." 15 September. Washington, DC: ASEAN Studies Center. American University. (Unpublished manuscript). Available online at www.american.edu/sis/aseanstudiescenter/upload/Brandeis_WP13.pdf [accessed December 2012].

Pettis, M. 2011. "The Continuous Debate Over China's Economic Transition." Washington, DC: Carnegie Endowment for International Peace. 25 March.

Pomeranz, K. 2000. "Locating China in the Twenty-First-Century Knowledge-Based Economy." *Journal of Contemporary China*. Vol. 21, No. 73, pp. 113–30.

Pomfret, R. 2011. *Regionalism in East Asia: Why has it Flourished Since 2000?* Singapore: World Scientific.

——2009. "Regionalism in the Asia-Pacific Region." Adelaide: The University of Adelaide, Australia. School of Economics. Research Paper No. 2009–31. July.

Pomfret, R. and P. Sourdin. 2009. "Have Asian Trade Agreements Reduced Trade Costs?" *Journal of Asian Economics*. Vol. 20, No. 3, pp. 255–68.

Porter, M. E. 2000. "Location, Competition and Economic Development: Local Clusters in a Global Economy." *Economic Development Quarterly*. Vol. 14, No. 1, pp. 15–34.

Prasad, E. S. 2011. "Rebalancing Growth in Asia." *International Finance*. Vol. 14, No. 1, pp. 27–66.

——2011. *Rebalancing Growth in Asia*. Working Paper No. 15169. Cambridge, MA: National Bureau of Economic Research. January.

——2011. "China's Approach to Economic Development and Industrial Policy." Hearing at the US-China Economic and Security Review Commission, the Government of the United States. Washington, DC. 15 June.

——2009. "Is the Chinese Growth Miracle Built to Last?" *China Economic Review*. Vol. 20, No. 1, pp. 103–23.

Prasad, E., M. A. Kose, K. S. Rogoff and S. J. Wei. 2006. "Financial Globalization: A Reappraisal." Cambridge, MA: National Bureau of Economic Research. NBER Working Paper. 12484.

Prasad, E. S. and T. Rumbaugh. 2004. "Overview", in E. S. Prasad and T. Rumbaugh (eds). *China's Growth and Integration into the World Economy*. Washington, DC: International Monetary Fund, pp. 1–4.

PricewaterhouseCoopers (PwC). 2011. *Global Construction 2020*. London. 3 March.

Rachman, G. 2011. "When China becomes Number One." *Financial Times*. 6 June, p. 16.

Ramstetter, E. D. 2012. "Foreign Multinationals in Asia's Large Developing Economies." Japan. Kyushu University. Graduate School of Economics. Working Paper No. 2012–06. March.

Ravallion, M. 2009. "The Developing World's Bulging (but Vulnerable) Middle Class." *World Development*. Vol. 38, No. 4, pp. 445–54.

Ravallion, M. and S. Chen. 2007. "China's (Uneven) Progress Against Poverty." *Journal of Development Economics*. Vol. 82, No. 1, pp. 1–42.

Ravenhill, J. 2010. "The 'New East Asian Regionalism': A Political Domino Effect." *Review of International Political Economy*. Vol. 17, No. 2, pp. 1–31.

——2008. "The New Trade Bilateralism in East Asia", in K. E. Calder and F. Fukuyama (eds). *East Asian Multilateralism: Prospects for Regional Stability*. Baltimore, MD: Johns Hopkins University Press, pp. 78–108.

Reuters. 2007. "China's Economic Structure is Unbalanced: Wen." Available online at www.reuters.com/article/idUSPEK9902420070316. 16 March [accessed December 2012].

Robertson, P. E. and J. Y. Xu. 2010. *In China's Wake: Has Asia Gained From China's Growth?* Discussion Paper No. 10. 15 June. University of Western Australia, Adelaide.

——2006. *What's So Special about China's Exports?* Working Paper No. 11947. Cambridge, MA: National Bureau of Economic Research. January.

——2006. "Goodbye Washington Consensus, Hello Washington Confusion?" *Journal of Economic Literature*. Vol. 44, No. 4, pp. 969–83.

Ronald-Holst, D., I. Aziz and L. G. Liu. 2003. "Regionalism and Globalism: East and Southeast Asian Trade Relations in the Wake of China's WTO Accession." Tokyo, Japan. ADB Institute. Research Paper No. 20. January.

Ronald-Holst, D. and J. Weiss. 2005. "People's Republic of China and Its Neighbors: Evidence on Regional Trade and Investment Effect," *Asia-Pacific Economic Literature*. Vol. 19, No. 2, pp. 18–35.

——2011. *Outward FDI from China: Dimensions, Drivers Implications*. Washington, DC: Peterson Institute for International Economics.

Sachs, J. D. and W. T. Woo. 1997. *Understanding China's Economic Performance*. Working Paper No. 575. Cambridge, MA: Harvard Institute of Economic Research, Harvard University.

Salidjanova, N. 2011. "Going Out: An Overview of China's Outward Foreign Direct Investment." Washington, DC: US-China Economic & Security Review Commission. Research Report. 30 March.

Salike, N. 2010. "Investigation of the 'China Effect' on Crowding Out of Japanese FDI: An Industry Level Analysis." *China Economic Review*. Vol. 21, No. 3, pp. 582–97.

Samsung Economic research Institute (SARI). 2012. "Foreign Car Companies' Technology Transfer." Beijing. China. Available online at www.seriworld.org/01/wldContL.html?mn=E&natcd=KR&mncd=0305& listopt=L&sortopt=D&gubun=00&pagen=1 [accessed December 2012].

Samuelson, P. A. 2002. "Where Ricardo and Mill Rebut and Confirm Arguments of Mainstream Economists Supporting Globalization." *Journal of Economic Perspectives*. Vol. 18, No. 3, pp. 135–46.

Schott, P. K. 2008. "The Relative Sophistication of Chinese Exports." *Economic Policy*. Vol. 53, No. 1, pp. 5–49.

Searight, A. 2009. "Emerging Economic Architecture in Asia: Opening or Insulating", in M. Green and B. Gill (eds). *Asia's New Multilateralism*. New York: Columbia University Press, pp. 132–63.

Sender, H. and K. Hille. 2011. "CIC Seeks Funds out of China Reserves." *Financial Times*, 16 January, p. 13.

SERI, 2013. "China's Overseas M&As in 2012." Beijing: Samsung Economic Research Institute. 22 March.

Severino, R. C. 2011. "Politics of Association of Southeast Asian Nations Economic Cooperation." *Asian Economic Policy Review*. Vol. 6, No. 1, pp. 22–38.

Shambaugh, D. 2012. "Are China's Multinational Corporations Really Multinational?" *East Asia Forum*. Vol. 4, No. 2, pp. 7–10.

——2005. "The Rise of China and Asia's New Dynamics", in D. Shambaugh (ed.). *Power Shift: China and Asia's New Dynamics*. Berkeley, CA: University of California Press, pp. 1–18.

Shin, K. and Y. Wang. 2004. "Trade Integration and Business Cycle Co-movements: The Case of Korea with Other Asian Countries." *Japan and the World Economy*. Vol. 16, No. 2, pp. 213–30.

Shinohara, N. 2012. "Global and Regional Economic Outlook and Role of Integration in Asia." Paper presented at Chulalongkorn University, Bangkok, Thailand, on 27 March.

——2010. "Leading the Global Recovery: Policy Challenges Facing Asia." Paper presented at the Singapore National University, Singapore, 9 June.

Siow, M. W. 2010. "Chinese Domestic Debates on Soft Power and Public Diplomacy." *East-West Center Asia Pacific Bulletin*, No. 86, 7 December.

Sirkin, H. L., M. Zinser and D. Hohner. 2011. *Made in America, Again*. Boston, MA: Boston Consulting Group. August.

Solis, M. 2011. "Global Economic Crisis: Boom or Burst for East Asian Trade Integration?" *The Pacific Review*. Vol. 24, No. 3, pp. 311–36.

Song, Z., K. Storesletten and F. Zilibotti. 2011. "Growing Like China." *American Economic Review*. Vol. 101, No. 1, pp. 202–41.

Smart, A. and J. Y. Hsu. 2004. "The Chinese Diaspora, Foreign Investment and Economic Development in China." *The Review of International Affairs*. Vol. 3, No. 4, pp. 544–66.

Sternberg, J. 2011. "China's New Competitors." *The Wall Street Journal Asia*. Hong Kong. 22 September, p. 14.

Stiglitz, J. E. 2002. *Globalization and Its Discontents*. New York and London: W. W. Norton.

——1998. "More Instruments and Broader Goals: Moving Towards the Post-Washington Consensus." WIDER Annual Lectures No. 2. Helsinki, Finland. 7 January.

——1998. "Sound Finance and Sustainable Development in Asia." Keynote address to the Asian Development Forum, Manila, Philippines. 12 March.

Stimpfig, J. 2011. "The New Red Army." *Financial Times*. 2 April, p. 10.

Subramanian, A. 2011. *Eclipse: Living in the Shadow of China's Economic Dominance*. Washington, DC: Peterson Institute for International Economics.

Subramanian, A. and M. Kessler. 2012. "The Renminbi Bloc Is Here: Asia Down, Rest of the World to Go?" Washington, DC: Peterson Institute of International Economics. Working Paper No. 12–19. October.

Summers, L. H. 2010. "Parting Words." *The Wall Street Journal*. 22 November, p. 11.

——2007. "The Rise of Asia and the Global Economy." *Research Monitor*. Special Issue 4–5.

Sun, H. 2001. "Foreign Direct Investment and Regional Export Performance in China." *Journal of Regional Science*. Vol. 41, No. 2, pp. 317–36.

Sun, W., X. Yang and G. Xiao. 2011. "Understanding China's High Investment Rate and FDI Levels." *Journal of International Commerce and Economics*. Vol. 3, No. 1, pp. 157–87.

Sussangkarn, C. 2011. "Chiang Mai Initiative Multilateralization: Origin, Development and Outlook." *Asian Economic Policy Review*. Vol. 6, No. 2, pp. 203–20.

Sutherland, D. 2007. *"China's 'National Team' of Enterprise Groups: How Has It Performed?"* Discussion Paper No. 23. Nottingham: China Policy Institute, University of Nottingham.

Swartz, S. and S. Oster. 2010. "China Hunger for World's Fuel." *Wall Street Journal*. 21 July, p. 19.

Szamosszegi, A. and C. Kyle. 2011. "An Analysis of State-Owned Enterprises and State Capitalism in China." Washington, DC: Capital Trade Incorporate. 26 October.

Tambunan, T. 2005. "Is ASEAN Still Relevant in the Era of the ASEAN-China FTA?" Paper presented at the Asia-pacific Economic Association conference in Seattle, WA. 29–30 July.

Tanaka, K. 2009. "Regional Integration in Southeast Asia." *Policy Insight*, No. 90. Paris: OECD Development Centre. February.

Tang, S. and Y. Zhang. 2006. "China's Regional Strategy", in D. Shambaug (ed.). *Power Shift: China and Asia's New Dynamics*. Los Angeles, CA: University of California Press, pp. 48–68.

Teja, R. 2012. "IMF: 2012 Spillover Report." Washington, DC: International Monetary Fund. 9 July.

Thangavelu, S. 2010. "Will ASEAN Benefit From the ASEAN–China Free Trade Agreement?" *East Asian Forum*. 1 September. Available online at www.eastasiaforum.org/2010/01/27/will-asean-benefit-from-the-asean-china-fta.

Thorbecke, W. and N. Salike. 2011. "Understanding Foreign Direct Investment in East Asia." Manila, Tokyo and Japan. ADBI Working Paper Series, No. 290. June.

Tian, W. and M. Yu. 2012. "Outward Foreign Direct Investment and Productivity: Firm-Level Evidence from China." Social Science Research Network. Available online at papers.ssrn.com/sol3/papers.cfm?abstract_id=1985130& http://www.google.com/url?sa=t&rct=j&q=tian%20and%20yu%202012%20outward%20foreign%20direct%20investment%20and%20productivity&source=web&cd=2&ved=0CCcQFjAB&url=http%3A%2F%2Fpapers.ssrn.com%2Fsol3%2FDelivery.cfm%3Fabstractid%3D1985130&ei=ntuhT7LRLc7mmAWz_7n7Bw&usg=AFQjCNFCqLHpsEjpmSMBTcsFpLijSbsS7Q. 25 February [accessed December 2012].

Trilateral Joint Research (TJR). 2008. "Joint Research and Policy Recommendations on the Possible Roadmap of a Free Trade Agreement between China, Japan and Korea." Tokyo, Japan. December. Available online at www.nira.or.jp/pdf/0805report-E.pdf [accessed December 2012].

Tse, E. 2009. "China as an Oasis amid the Global Economic Crisis." New York: Booze. Available online at www.booz.com/media/uploas/China_An_Oasia.pdf.

Tuan, C., L. Ng and B. Zhao. 2009. "China's Post-Economic Reform Growth: The Role of FDI and Productivity Process." *Journal of Asian Economics*. Vol. 20, No. 2, pp. 280–93.

United Nations Conference on Trade and Development (UNCTAD). 2012. *World Investment Report*. Geneva and New York. June.

——2011. *World Investment Report*, 2011. Geneva and New York.

——2010. *World Investment Report*. Geneva and New York. July.

——2007. *Rising FDI into China: Facts behind the Numbers*. UNCTAD Investment Brief No. 2. Geneva and New York.

——2002. *World Investment Report 2002*. Geneva and New York.

United Nations Conference on Trade and Development/Japan External Trade organization (UNCTAD/JETRO). 2008. "South-South Trade in Asia." Geneva and New York.

United Nations Economic and Social Commission for Asia and Pacific (UNESCAP). 2011. *Asia-Pacific Trade and Investment Report 2011*. New York.

United States Bureau of Labor Statistics. 2011. "International Labor Comparisons." Washington, DC. 4 April.

United States Trade Representative (USTR). 2011. "Engagement with the Trans-Pacific Partnership to Increase Exports." Washington, DC. Available online at www.ustr.gov/about-us/press-office/fact-sheets/2011/february/engagement-trans-pacific-partnership-increase-export. February.

US-China Economic and Security Commission. 2011. *Report to Congress*. Washington, DC: US Government Printing Press. November.

Urata, S. and K. Kiyota. 2003. "The Impact of an East Asia FTA on Foreign Trade in East Asia" Cambridge, MA: National Bureau of Economic Research. Working Paper Series 10173.

Vermonte, P. J. 2005. "China-ASEAN Strategic Relations", in J.K. Chin and N. Thomas (eds). *China and ASEAN: Changing Political Strategic Ties*. Hong Kong: Center of Asian Studies. University of Hong Kong, pp. 85–105.

United Nations Economic and Social Commission for Asia and Pacific (UNESCAP). 2011. *Asia-Pacific Trade and Investment Report 2011*. New York.

——2011. *Fighting Irrelevance: The Role of Regional Trade Agreements in International Production Networks in Asia*. New York.

Urata, S. 2004. "The Shift from "Market-Led to Institution-Led" Regional Economic Integration in East Asia." Tokyo: The Research Institute of Economy, Trade and Industry. Discussion paper No. 04-E-12.

Verspagen, B. 1993. *Uneven Growth between Interdependent Economies*. Aldershot: Avebury.

Vincelette, G. A., A. Manoel, A. Hansson and L. Kuijs. 2011. "China: Global Crisis Avoided, Robust Economic Growth Sustained", in M.K. Nabli (ed.). *The Great Recession and the Developing Countries: Economic Impact and Growth Prospects*. Washington, DC: World Bank, pp. 110–35.

Vogel, E. F. 2011. *Deng Xiaoping and the Transformation of China*. Cambridge, MA: Harvard University Press.

Wade, R. 1990. *Governing the Market*. Princeton, NJ: Princeton University Press.

Wakasugi, R. 2007. "Vertical Intra-Industry Trade and Integration in East Asia." *Asian Economic Papers*. Vol. 6, No. 1, 26–39.

The Wall Street Journal (WSJ). 2012. "Asia Catches a China Chill." 29 May, p. 13.

——2011. "China's Self-Reforming Banks?" New York. 6 December, p. 11.

Waldmeir, P. 2012. "China Offers a Taste of R&D to Come." *Financial Times*. 13 November, p. 17.

Walter, C. and F. Howie. 2011. *The Weakness beneath China's Rise*. Singapore: John Wiley & Sons (Asia).

Wang, Z. 2010. "What Accounts for the Rising Sophistication of China's Exports?" in R. C. Feenstra and S. J. Wei (eds). *China's Growing Role in World Trade*. Chicago, IL, and London: University of Chicago Press, pp. 63–108.

Wang, J., D. Guthrie and Z. Xiao. 2012. "The Rise of SASAC: Asset Management and Ownership Concentration." *Management and Organization Review*. Vol. 8, No. 2, pp. 253–281.

Wang, Z. and S. J. Wei. 2008. "What Accounts for the Rising Sophistication of China's Exports." Cambridge, MA: National Bureau of Economic Research. Working Paper No. 13771. February.

Wang, C., Y. Wei and X. Liu. 2007. "Does China Rival its Neighboring Economies for Inward FDI?" *Transnational Corporations*. Vol. 16, No. 3, pp. 35–60.

Wang, Y. and Y. Yao. 2003. "Sources of China's Economic Growth, 1952–99: Incorporating Human Capital Formation." *China Economic Review*. Vol. 14, No. 1, pp. 32–52.

Wang, Y. 2008. "Public Diplomacy and the Rise of Chinese Soft Power." *Annals of the American Academy of Political and Social Sciences*. Vol. 616, No. 1, pp. 257–73.

——2004. "Conceptualizing Economic Security and Governance: China Confronts Globalization." *The Pacific Review*. Vol. 17, No. 4, pp. 523–45.

Wignaraja, G. 2008. "FDI and Innovation as Drivers of Export Behavior." Maastricht: UNU-MERIT. Working Paper Series 2008–61.

Williamson, J. 1990. *Latin American Adjustment: How Much Has Happened?* Washington, DC: Institute for International Economics.

Woetzel, J. R. 2008. "Reassessing China's State-Owned Enterprises." *McKinsey Quarterly*. July. Available online at www.mckinseyquarterly.com/article_print.aspx?L2=21&L3=33& ar = 2149 [accessed December 2012].

Wolf, M. 2013. "Why China's Economy Might Topple" *Financial Times.*, 2 April, p. 9.

——2012. "How to Blow Away China's Gathering Storm-Clouds" *Financial Times*. 21 March, p. 9.

——2011. "Why China Hates Loving the Dollar?" *Financial Times*. 25 January, p. 14.

Wood, A. and J. Mayer. 2011. "Has China De-Industrialized other Developing Countries?" *Review of World Economics*. Vol. 147, No. 2, pp. 325–50.

World Bank and the Development Research Center (WB/DRC). 2013. *China 2030: Building a Modern, Harmonious and Creative High-Income Society*. Washington, DC.

World Bank (WB), 2013. *Doing Business Online Database 2011*. Washington, DC.

World Bank. 2013. "East Asia and Pacific Economic Update. Washington, DC. April.

——2012. "China Quarterly Update." Beijing: World Bank Mission. April.

——2012. "East Asia and Pacific Data Monitor." Washington, DC. October.

——2011. "Country and Leading Groups." Washington, DC. Available online at data.worldbank.org/about/country-classifications/country-and-lending-groups#Low_income [accessed December 2012].

——2011. *World Development Indicators 2010*. Washington, DC.

——2011. "East Asia and Pacific Economic Update 2011." Washington, DC. March.

——2010. *China: Quarterly Update*. World Bank Office, Beijing. June.

——2010. *World Development Indicators 2010*. Washington, DC.

——2009. *From Poor Areas to Poor People: China's Evolving Poverty Reduction Agenda*. Washington, DC. March.

——2000. *East Asia: Recovery and Beyond*. Washington, DC.

World Trade Organization (WTO). 2013. "Trade to Remain Subdued in 2013." Geneva, Switzerland. Press Release No 688. 10 April.

——2012. "Trade Growth to Slow in 2012 after Strong Deceleration in 2011." Press Release. Press/658. Geneva, Switzerland. 12 April.

——2011. *International Trade Statistics 2011*. Geneva, Switzerland.

World Investment Report (WIR). 2006. Geneva and New York. United Nations Conference on Trade and Development.

——2010. *United Nations Conference on Trade and Development.* Geneva and New York.

——2012. *United Nations Conference on Trade and Development.* Geneva and New York. October.

World Trade Organization (WTO). 2012. "Trade Growth to Slow in 2012 after Strong Deceleration in 2011." Press Release. Press/658. Geneva, Switzerland. 12 April.

——2012. *International Trade Statistics 2012.* Geneva. Switzerland.

——2011. *International Trade Statistics 2011.* Geneva. Switzerland.

——2011. *Trade Patterns and Global Value Chains in East Asia.* Geneva. Switzerland. July.

——2010. *International Trade Statistics 2010.* Geneva. Switzerland. September.

——2010. *Trade Policy Review of China.* Geneva. Switzerland. April 26. (WT/TPR/S/230).

——2010. *International Trade Statistics.* Press Release PRESS/598. 26 March. Geneva, Switzerland.

Wu, Y. 2004. *China's Economic Growth: A Miracle with Chinese Characteristics.* London and New York: Routledge.

Xing, Y. 2010. "Facts about and Impact of FDI on China and the World Economy." *China: An International Journal.* Vol. 8, No. 2, pp. 309–27.

Xu, B. and J. Lu. 2009. "Foreign Direct Investment, Processing Trade and Sophistication of Chinese Exports." *China Economic Review.* Vol. 20, No. 2, pp. 425–39.

Yao, Y. 2009. *The Disinterested Government.* Research Paper No. 2009/33. Helsinki, Finland: World Institute for Development Economic Research. May.

Yamashita, N. 2010. *International Fragmentation of Production.* Cheltenham: Edward Elgar.

Yang, R., Y. Yao and Y. Zhang. 2009. "Technological Structure and Its Upgrading in China's Exports." *China Economic Journal.* Vol. 2, No. 1, pp. 55–71.

Ye, M. 2011. "The Rise of China and East Asian Regionalism", in M. Beeson and R. Stubb (eds). *The Handbook of Asian Regionalism.* London and New York: Routledge, pp. 120–45.

Yeats, A. J. 2001. "Just How Big is Global Production Sharing?", in S. W. Arndt and H. Kierzkowski (eds). *Fragmentation: New Production Pattern in the World Economy.* Oxford: Oxford University Press, pp. 63–109.

——2010. "China's Regional Policy in East Asia and its Characteristics." Nottingham: University of Nottingham. China Policy Institute. Discussion Paper No. 66. October.

Yi, K. M. 2003. "Can Vertical Specialization Explain the Growth of World Trade?" *Journal of Political Economy.* Vol. 111, No. 1, pp. 52–102.

Yiping, H. 2010. "Dissecting the Chinese Puzzle: Asymmetric Liberalization and Cost Distortion." *Asian Economic Policy Review.* Vol. 5, No. 2, pp. 281–95.

Yongding, Y. 2011. "Rebalancing the Chinese Economy." Seoul: Institute for Global Economics. Occasional Paper No. 11–03. October.

Yongjian, L. and X. Jiechang. 2012. "Serving the Nation's Future." *China Daily.* 1 June, p. 2.

Yu, K. 2009. *Democracy is a Good Thing.* Washington, DC: Brookings Institution Press.

Yuan, Z., G. Wan and N. Khor. 2011. "The Rise of the Middle Class in the People's Republic of China." Manila: Asian Development Bank. Working Paper Series No. 247. February.

Yusuf, S. and K. Nabeshima. 2010. *Changing the Industrial Geography in Asia.* Washington, DC: World Bank.

——2008. "Optimizing Urban Development", in S. Yusuf and T. Saich (eds). *China Urbanizes.* Washington, DC: World Bank, pp. 1–40.

Yuzhu, W. 2011. "China, Economic Regionalism and East Asian Integration." *Japanese Journal of Political Science.* Vol. 12, No. 2, pp. 195–211.

Zeng, D. Z. 2011. "How Do Special Economic Zones and Industrial Clusters Drive China's Rapid Development?" Washington, DC: World Bank. Policy Research Working Paper No. 5583. March.

Zhang, J. 2011. "China Backpedals." Stanford, CA: Hoover University. 12 January.

Zhang, Y. 2006. "China and East Asian Economic Integration and Cooperation." *Journal of Economic Development.* Vol. 31, No. 2, pp. 169–85.

Zhang, H. K. and S. Song. 2000. "Promoting Exports: The Role of Inward FDI in China." *China Economic Review.* Vol. 11, No. 2, pp. 385–96.

Zheng, B. 2005. "China's 'Peaceful Rise' to Great Power Status." *Foreign Affairs.* Vol. 84, No. 5, pp. 18–24.

Zheng, Y. and A. Hu. 2006. "An Empirical Analysis of Provincial Productivity in China (1979–2001)." *Journal of Chinese Economic and Business Studies.* Vol. 4, No. 3, pp. 221–39.

Zhou, X. 2009. "Some Observations and Analysis on Savings Ratio." Paper presented at the High Level Conference hosted by the Bank Negara, Kuala Lumpur, Malaysia, 10 February.

Zhou, Y. and S. Lall. 2005. "The Impact of China's FDI Surge on FDI in South-East Asia: Panel Data Analysis for 1986–2001." *Transnational Corporations*. Vol. 14, No. 1, pp. 41–65.

Zinabou, G. 2011. "East Asian Value Chain and the Global Financial Crisis." Toronto: Foreign Affairs and International Trade Office. Government of Canada. ASP No. 8.

Zinnov Management Consulting. 2011. China R&D Globalization Market. New Delhi. Available online at www.1888pressrelease.com/zinnov-globalization/r-and-d-mnc-china/china-r-d-globalization-market-at-usd-7–65-billion-growing-a-pr-309076.html. 8 June [accessed December 2012].

INDEX